Education Policy and Realist Social Theory

What contribution does realist social theory make to our understanding of education policy? Does the production line apply to children's education?

In Europe welfare state provision has been subjected to 'market forces'. Over the last two decades, the framework of economic competitiveness has become the defining aim of education, to be achieved by new managerialist techniques and mechanisms. This book thoughtfully and persuasively argues against this new vision of education.

Education Policy and Realist Social Theory is a clear and accessible introduction to the morphogenetic approach in the sociology of education, and organisation and management studies.

Robert Willmott

- establishes the theoretical framework that underpins historical and contemporary case-study research of child-centredness and new managerialism

- argues that the interplay of structure, culture and agency can be theorised via the methodological device of analytical dualism

- appraises the school effectiveness research

- provides up-to-date case-study analysis of how teaching staffs in two primary schools mediate the contradiction between child-centred philosophy and practice and new managerialism.

- and discusses the implications of the findings for primary school practice and underscores the need for a critical realist approach to theorising about education policy and practice.

This major in-depth study will be of great interest to researchers in the sociology of education, education policy, social theory, organisation and management studies, and also to professionals concerned about the deleterious impact of current education policy on children's learning and welfare.

Robert Willmott lectures in the School of Management, University of Bath. He is currently writing (with Dr Martin Thrupp) *Educational Management in Managerialist Times*, with Dr. Martin Thrupp.

Critical Realism: Interventions
Edited by Margaret Archer, Roy Bhaskar,
Andrew Collier, Tony Lawson and Alan Norrie

Critical realism is one of the most influential new developments in the philosophy of science and in the social sciences, providing a powerful alternative to positivism and post modernism. This series will explore the critical realist position in philosophy and across the social sciences.

Also published by Routledge

Routledge Studies in Critical Realism
Edited by Margaret Archer, Roy Bhaskar,
Andrew Collier, Tony Lawson and Alan Norrie

1. Marxism and Realism
A materialistic application of realism in the social science
Sean Creaven

2. Beyond Relativism
Raymond Boudon, Cognitive Rationality and Critical Realism
Cynthia Lins Hamlin

3. Education Policy and Realist Social Theory
Primary teachers, child-centred philosophy and the new managerialism
Robert Willmott

4. Hegemony
A Realist Analysis
Jonathan Joseph

Education Policy and Realist Social Theory

Primary teachers, child-centred philosophy and the new managerialism

Robert Willmott

London and New York

First published 2002
by Routledge
11 New Fetter Lane, London EC4P 4EE

Simultaneously published in the USA and Canada
by Routledge
29 West 35th Street, New York, NY 10001

Routledge is an imprint of the Taylor & Francis Group

© 2002 Robert Willmott

Typeset in Baskerville by Taylor & Francis Books Ltd
Printed and bound in Great Britain by Biddles Ltd, Guildford and King's
Lynn

British Library Cataloguing in Publication Data
A catalogue record for this book is available from the British Library

Library of Congress Cataloging-in-Publication Data
Willmott, Robert, 1972 -
Education Policy and Realist Social Theory: primary teachers, child-
centered philosophy and the new managerialism/Robert Willmott
p. cm – (Routledge Studies in Critical Realism)
Includes bibliographical references and index
1. Educational sociology – Europe. 2. Education, Elementary – Social
aspects – Europe. 3. Elementary school teachers – Europe. 4. Education,
Elementary – Europe – Philosophy. I. Title. II. Series.
LC 191.8.E85 W55 2002
306.43 – dc21

ISBN 0–415–26839–7

To my parents, Dee and Ian. Thank you

Contents

Acknowledgements

I wish to thank the following people for their kind and generous support: Maggie Archer, my brother Chris, Martin Thrupp, Glenn Rikowski, Margaret and Bob Powell, Sandra Matthews, Ann Ryan, Alan Carter, and the staff and pupils of Southside and Westside, whose contributions are invaluable yet remain anonymous.

I also wish to thank the Economic and Social Research Council (ESRC) for funding this research (Award No. R00429634324).

Finally, I wish to thank Taylor & Francis for permission to include material from articles previously published in the *British Journal of Sociology of Education*, 20 (1) (1999), 22 (2) (2001); Sage Publications for permission to include material from an article previously published in *Organization* 7 (1) (2000) and material from J. Darling (1994) *Child-centred Education and its critics*; J. Clarke, S. Gewirtz and E. McLaughlin (2000) *New Managerialism, New Welfare?*; Continuum International Publishing Group to use material from M. Bottery (2000) *Education, policy and ethics*; Falmer Press to use material from K. A. Riley (1998) *Whose School Is It Anyway?*; D. Scott (2000) *Realism and Educational Research: New Perspectives and Possibilities*; Routledge for G. Troman and P. Woods (2001) *Primary Teachers' Stress*.

Introduction

And the one thing I hate is this thing with Value for Money...

(Pat, head-teacher, Westside primary school)

This encapsulates the monumental changes that have occurred in education in England and Wales since the promulgation of the 1988 Education Reform Act. At present, all primary schools are subject to 'market forces' and the commodification of the people who work in them. Hence the head's invective against the monetary valorisation of education. In essence, the commodifying logic expunges child-centred philosophy and practice. However, the quasi-marketisation of the education system in England and Wales, undertaken by the Conservative Government during the 1980s, has not only been consolidated but also extended by New Labour. As Jenny Ozga puts it:

> In England and Wales, as elsewhere in Europe...we have seen the displacement of the old model of welfare state provision. In England and Wales, perhaps to a greater extent than elsewhere, that welfare state has been replaced by the operation of the market under the Conservative Governments of 1979–1997. The process of reformation continues in the modernizing agenda of New Labour.
>
> (Ozga 2000: 54)

This modernising agenda is pursued within the framework of economic competitiveness as the defining aim of education. The Managerialist philosophy that underpinned the 1988 Education Reform Act has now reached its zenith in national target setting, Education Action Zones and the primacy of OFSTED (Office for Standards in Education). The latter constitutes a key contradiction for primary school teachers committed to child-centred learning. Using Margaret Archer's (1995) morphogenetic approach, this book examines the backdrop to the new managerialist restructuring of education and provides an in-depth analysis of the ways in which two primary schools – one deemed 'failing' and the other 'successful' by OFSTED – mediate the objective contradiction between child-centred philosophy and the new managerialism as embodied in SATs (Standard Assessment Tasks), league tables, the National Curriculum and national target setting.

David Scott (2000) has recently underscored the increasing dominance of positivism and empiricism in the field of education. As he argues, this can, in part, be attributed to managerialist pressures and the concomitant need to produce research findings that ostensibly allow predictions to be made by school managers. Indeed, the school effectiveness research that now dominates New Labour policy-making is quintessentially positivist. The ideological import of school effectiveness research is discussed in the Preface to Part Three of the book (see also Angus 1993; Bottery 2000; Scott 2000; Thrupp 2000; Willmott 1999c). In contradistinction to the dominant positivist paradigm, this book explicitly uses realist social theory (Archer 1995). It therefore concurs with Ozga's emphasis on the importance of theorising for everyone engaged in educational work. However, as Ozga also adds, not all theories are 'of the same size, weight, complexity or quality. Theories may be quite limited in scope' (Ozga 2000: 42). The morphogenetic approach is proffered as a robust theoretical framework that captures the stratified nature of social reality, enabling the practical researcher to theorise on a multi-level basis about the conditions that promote/foster/condition change or stability. Fundamentally, theorising about educational change versus stability presupposes (implicitly or explicitly) assumptions about 'structure and agency'. Despite the current pragmatist trend whereby practical education research is carried out without reference to ontological and epistemological concerns, the morphogenetic approach is the methodological complement of transcendental realism (see Bhaskar 1989a; Scott 2000). It has its origins in the systems theory of Buckley (1967) and is offered as a workable alternative to Giddens' (1984) famous structuration theory.

Chapter 1 is critical of the organisational and educational sociology literature with respect to theorising about the interplay of structure and agency. In particular, the generic impact of structuration theory is documented and criticised. Counterposing the morphogenetic approach, it is argued that 'analytical dualism' is the methodological key for linking structure and agency, which is possible because they operate over different tracts of time, each possessing *sui generis* properties and powers. In other words, structure and agency are theorised on a sequential basis: structural conditioning → social interaction → structural elaboration or stasis. Chapter 2 argues that culture can be theorised on the same sequential basis as structure. It elaborates and defends the morphogenetic approach's distinction between the Cultural System (composed of ideas, beliefs, theories and values and the emergent logical relations that obtain between them) and the relationships between cultural agents at the socio-cultural level. A discussion of the corpus of propositions that constitutes the new managerialism is provided, and of how it contradicts the propositions that comprise child-centred philosophy. Specifically, the objective *constraining* nature of this particular contradiction is delineated and its implications for practice are examined.

Part II of the book utilises the morphogenetic approach's three-part sequential schema of Socio-Cultural Conditioning → Socio-Cultural Interaction → Socio-Cultural Elaboration or Stasis. Chapter 3 briefly traces the origins of child-centred philosophy. This provides the backdrop to the ways in which university-based philosophers of education have endeavoured to critique its central tenets, simultaneously embroiling themselves in the situational logic of a 'constraining contradiction' (see Chapter 2). The latter ascendant manoeuvring provided the ideational context of government policy-making (specifically Plowden and the increase in the number of Teacher Training Colleges). In short, a delineation of the development of child-centred philosophy and its critique by highly positioned academics is important in terms of what and who are excluded. The economic context is delineated. The relative degrees of bargaining power on the part of teachers, central government and other interest groups are analysed. However, a defence is made of the autonomous properties of the education system itself. This defence is important since it raises fundamental issues about the ontology of autonomy that have implications beyond Marxism for a wide range of reductionist 'sociologies of knowledge' that have prevailed within (and deeply flawed) the sociology of education for so long.

Chapter 4 delineates the interactional phase, focusing in particular on the Tyndale Affair and the Ruskin Speech. It underscores the importance of the changing nature of the economy in affecting the degrees of negotiating strength at the disposal of teachers and the government. Moreover, such exchange processes are ideationally embroiled. Analysis thus focuses on the use of managerialist and right-wing ideas by cultural agents. It is argued that the teaching profession did not exploit the delimited degrees of freedom at its disposal. Chapter 5 delineates the structural elaboration of the 1988 Education Reform Act in particular, the imposition of SATs (Standard Assessment Tasks) and the Dearing 'tinkerings'. The quasi-marketisation of education and its extension by New Labour, OFSTED and assessment are critically appraised. The objective contradiction between neo-liberalism and conservatism is transcendentally established. In the Preface to Part III, school effectiveness and the pragmatism of Robin Alexander are critically appraised. In particular, the ideological import of school effectiveness research is established. The extent of the decrease in teacher bargaining power is laid bare, thereby underscoring the imposition of ideas and practices ('corporate culture programmes') without their consent.

Part III provides a contemporary, case-study-based analysis of how teaching staffs in two primary schools mediate the new conditioning cycle delineated in Chapter 5. In particular, it theorises about the ways in which staff mediate the objective contradiction between child-centred philosophy and the new managerialist restructuring of their work and activities. Both chapters draw upon nine months (July 1997; September 1997 – April 1998) of participant observation and tape-recorded semi-structured interviews. Access was gained via formal letter, which set out the research objectives while at the same time offering classroom help as an assistant. Letters were sent out to six schools in a city in the south of England, of which only two were successful. Pseudonyms are used throughout in order to maintain anonymity. Chapter 6 examines the processes, mechanisms and events that followed a 'failing' OFSTED report on a Church of England primary school and the imposition of a 'trouble-shooting' head who embodied the new managerialism. The importance of contextual factors is highlighted alongside the need to specify the stringency of constraints under which agents act. Chapter 7 examines the processes, mechanisms and events that occurred and existed in a 'successful' Catholic primary school on the prosperous side of the same city. Here it is found that New Labour's imposition of national target setting is resulting, in this case, in a managerialist focus on maths, English and science at the expense of the rest of the National Curriculum. In short, it concurs with Morley and Rassool's (1999) argument that the tendency now is towards organisational isomorphism.

Both schools had distinctively differing socio-economic intakes, histories and problems. Indeed, 'Southside' was deemed 'failing' by OFSTED, despite generous degrees of funding, whilst 'Westside' was deemed 'successful', notwithstanding its OFSTED Report's request for 'better management'. Both schools were underpinned by a Christian ethos. Thus, contextual factors are crucial in explaining the extent to which schools can subvert the macro conditioning cycle of the new managerialist quasi-marketisation. However, the imposition of national targets during my time in Westside dramatically attenuated the degrees of freedom previously afforded by the school's high socio-economic intake and strong practical Catholic ethos that was supported by the majority of parents. It is a pity that I was unable to revisit Southside to examine how they dealt with the concurrent added blow of national targets (although such targets would not have been much higher than that which was demanded by the 'trouble-shooting head'). In 1997, Woods *et al.* found that a measure of deprofessionalisation had set in among their case-study primary schools, which involved

> ...the loss or distillation of skills, routinization of work, the loss of conceptual, as opposed to operational, responsibilities, the replacement of holism by compartmentalization, work and bureaucratic overload, the filling and overfilling of time and space, loss of time for reflection and for recovery from stress, the weakening of control and autonomy, and, in general, a move from professional to technician status.
>
> (1997: 84–5)

Prior to my time in Westside, local context afforded staff the ability to move back to a child-centred professionalism. However, whilst the deprofessionalisation scenario depicted by Woods *et al.* occurred at Southside, it started to reappear at Westside as a direct result of the imposition of national targets. The concluding chapter thus underscores the bleak future that children in our primary schools now face. It also recapitulates the indispensability of realist social theory for documenting and theorising about the continuing impact of new managerialism on education in England and Wales.

Part I

Establishing the theoretical framework

1 Structure, agency and educational change

Morphogenesis and the need for analytical dualism

Introduction

As indicated in the introduction, the principal aim of this book is to theorise about the interplay of child-centred philosophy, (new) managerialism and teacher mediation via the morphogenetic approach. It may therefore strike some readers as odd that my first chapter is devoted solely to thinking about social structure and human agency. Whilst structural analysis always needs to be complemented by cultural analysis, the reason for devoting this chapter to structure is two-fold. First, in order to provide a robust explanatory grip on structural (and cultural) dynamics, a particular social ontology and concomitant methodology have to be outlined and defended. The social ontology defended throughout this book is a stratified one, grounded in transcendental realism, and practically fleshed out, so to speak, by the latter's methodological complement of the morphogenetic approach. In view of the complexity of the morphogenetic approach's corpus of methodological propositions *vis-à-vis* structure, and their transposability to culture, it makes sense to spell out in some detail its explanatory methodology before linking culture in the next chapter. However, second, the morphogenetic approach is explicitly counterposed to Giddens's (1979, 1984) structuration theory in order to highlight the primacy that the former gives to ontological rigour as against structuration theory's ontological (and methodological) dilution. Many sociologists were quick to join the structurationist bandwagon (Willmott 2000b). Educational sociology has by no means been immune from this bandwagon effect. However, the reason for this is entirely laudable yet over-hasty. Its laudability derives from the need to avoid reifying social structure, treating it as a 'thing' above-and-beyond agency; its haste consists of compacting them into one indistinguishable amalgam, thereby precluding examination of their interplay over time. This chapter will proceed more slowly, arguing that a stratified approach to structure and agency does not entail reifying the two (or conceiving of them as separate).

What is transcendental realism?

At a common-sense level, it would seem that attachment to realism implies a rational grasp of the way things are, which in turn guides subsequent action. However, critical realism begins from the premise that the way things are affects us regardless of our own fallible epistemological grasp. For the lay commentator, poorly paid, recently divorced Claire, faced with the decision of whether to re-mortgage her house in order to pay for a long-awaited family holiday to Disney in Florida, would be held to exemplify realism if she opted for a weekend in Weymouth. Her reasons would conceivably make reference to the likelihood of incurring substantial debts and the impossibility of keeping up with repayments if she opted for the holiday abroad. Many would not dispute this accurate assessment. The difference, however, between Claire's assessment and any sociological assessment lies in the latter's attempt to provide an explanatory account of Claire's (objective) predicament and her (subjective) response. Here, sociology would aim to go beyond, though fundamentally not negate or disregard, actors' accounts, since social reality is not just the aggregation of agential interpretations. If that were true, then we would not be able to explain why some people are strategically manipulated into vicious cycles of debt. In brief, transcendental realism is committed to what social reality *must* be like in order to make analysis of it intelligible. In other words, it makes claims as to the necessary conditions that make it a possible object of knowledge. What is often confused is the *a priori* necessity of generalising the nature of social (or natural) reality and specific attempts to capture it theoretically (see, for example, Johnson *et al.* 1984). Transcendental social realism does not make claims as to *what* structures constitute social reality, but only that it *is* structured. Thus, for instance, any substantive disagreement about the precise role of the Secretary of State for Education and Employment, *vis-à-vis* the implementation of the 1988 Education Reform Act, *necessarily* presupposes irreducible social structures; in this case we make reference to the educational system, government machinery and so on.

The early development of transcendental realism was concerned with the natural sciences (Bhaskar 1975; Harré 1970; Harré and Madden 1975).[1] The possibility of *a priori* knowledge, namely that which can be known independently of any experience, is associated with Kant. Kant transcendentally derived such possibility; that is to say, *a priori* knowledge is knowledge of the world that must be so if the world is to be known. However, as Collier (1994: 212) points out, Kant did not think that we could know if the noumenal world in itself had these properties – he thought that our mind merely imposed this knowable form on it. Bhaskar appropriates Kant's term 'transcendental' in a slightly different sense. The difference is that, while Kant's arguments lead to a theory about the structure-imposing power of the mind *vis-à-vis* the world, Bhaskar's lead to extra-discursive conclusions, namely about what the world must be like. This is where Bhaskar parts company with Kant, since we are not dealing with unknowable things-in-themselves (we do not see the powers that are deposited within the position of Secretary of State, but we know they exist by virtue of their effects). Furthermore, Bhaskar's use of the term 'transcendental' is different, in the sense that Bhaskar posits underlying mechanisms, which are unobservable and yet causally efficacious. Such mechanisms can be posited by virtue of transcendental argumentation in conjunction with the causal criterion. Thus it could be argued that, had Kant made the distinction between transcendental arguments and transcendental idealism, 'he could have deployed a transcendental argument to establish the knowability of the transcendental subject who synthesized…the phenomenal world and thus avoided blocking off the transcendental subject and the understanding-in-itself *and* the transcendental object and the world-in-itself from the experiencing human ego' (Bhaskar 1994: 46, original emphasis).

The existence of events and the underlying mechanisms that generate them signals the *stratified* nature of reality. Part and parcel of Bhaskar's transcendental differentiation of reality into the three key strata of the real, actual and empirical is his rejection of Humean empiricism. The substantial powers at the Secretary of State's disposal (1988 Education Act) belong to the realm of the real. They are mechanisms that only exist by virtue of human agency (as impersonal social relations) but are real because of their causal efficacy. When such powers are exercised, we enter the realm of events. However, other mechanisms may (and often do) intervene to preclude simple deduction of generative structural mechanisms from such events. Indeed, events themselves may not manifest the workings of generative mechanisms, due to contingencies that suspend their powers. Moreover, agents do not always experience such events (or experience them in a manner congruent with their provenance) – to assume otherwise turns every agent into an infallible sociologist. Hence the importance of delineating the realm of the empirical. All three realms are real and must be kept distinct in order to provide satisfactory explanatory accounts of social activity. The example of the powers deposited in the position of Secretary of State should be sufficient to underscore this. For (a) such powers may remain unexercised or exercised but unperceived because counteracted by other mechanisms; or (b) may be wrongly experienced as emanating from other structural sources. To reiterate, the methodological problem that confronts any researcher is that the exercise of causal powers is not readily transparent from patterned empirical events. For example, a deputy head may confront a staff meeting whose agenda the head and senior management team had prearranged, yet at the same time s/he remains unaware of this exercise of power or that the powers of Heads of Department had been offset. Indeed, the deputy may misinterpret (or be led to misinterpret) the meeting as resulting from the machinations of governors and certain members of the management team. What complicates matters further is that Heads of Department themselves may have only a partial understanding of the situation, whose accounts cannot therefore always be held *a priori* incorrigible. Furthermore, transcendental social realism enables the social analyst to ask counterfactual questions in order to unravel the complexity of social reality. If the head had exercised powers buttressed by those of the governing body, could the head's positional powers still be exercised or exist without the existence of a governing body? Does a school remain a school without one? Though this is to jump ahead, it does provide a flavour of the explanatory power of social realism.

Essentially, Humean empiricism remains wedded to the realm of the actual, that is, at the level of observable events. Bhaskar has termed this 'actualism', which entails a denial of the real existence of underlying generative structures that account for things and/or events. The problem with Humean empiricism is its *a* causality. For Hume, the external world consists of nothing more than contingently related events. Causality is untenably implied to reside in constant conjunctions of events. There are no real or necessary connections between a child's ability to write and the handed-in piece of written work. All we can say is that event A, the child writing, was followed by event B, the handing-in of the piece of written work. In fact, to ensure Humean consistency, one cannot even talk of pupil ability, for this is unobservable. To reiterate, instead of A caused B, we have A occurred followed by B. Clearly, to say that A occurred and then B occurred does not imply that A caused B. Yet to say that A caused B is to say that the occurrence of A is a necessary and/or sufficient condition for the occurrence of B. Yet to observe regularly the teacher opening the window and Jonathan sniffing every morning at ten o'clock does not tell us whether the opening of the window is a necessary and/or sufficient condition for Jonathan's capacity to sniff. There is no necessary causal link between the two. Ultimately, empiricism cannot account for either Jonathan's sniffing or the teacher's physical ability to open windows.

In everyday life we experience mechanical causation, that is, the displacement of physical masses in time and space in terms of transitive verbs such as 'pushing' and 'pulling', which cannot be explained ostensively; rather they embody an intensional relationship between cause and effect (Bhaskar 1975: 90). This is simply a complicated way of saying that such verbs cannot specify the generative mechanisms that enable the teacher to open the window. Causality concerns not a relationship between discrete events (the teacher opens the window lock, pushes the window and it opens) but the *causal powers* or *liabilities* of objects or relations or their mechanisms (Sayer 1992: 104). The ability to open such a window exists by virtue of the body's necessary powers. Humean actualism fails to acknowledge that reality has depth, principally because of its insistence upon the criterion of observability to establish reality. Yet we cannot observe a magnetic force field, but accept its reality. We accept its reality because of its causal effects. This applies equally to social structure. Social realism insists, as a matter of intelligibility, that social structure is ontologically distinct from human agency and is knowable via the causal criterion. This distinction is not one of heuristic convenience. Social structures are held to possess *sui generis* properties and powers, that is, causal properties that are examinable independently of agency and yet necessarily depend upon agency for their existence.[2]

Transcendentally, social reality is structured and differentiated and thus provides social science with its subject matter. To explain why individuals as role incumbents perform specific tasks on a regular basis, as manifested at the level of observable events (e.g. annual public examinations), necessarily presupposes some kind of phenomenon that is extra-individual. The activities of individuals within the school setting are often structured in quite specific ways, and such activities are not about the individual *qua* individual. The very notion of role signifies that its required actions are independent of purely personal properties (though this is not to suggest passive acceptance). The 'extra-individual' is what we normally refer to as 'the social'. However, social realism differentiates the social into unintended *sui generis* emergent and aggregate properties that act back to condition subsequent activity. The activities of teachers, pupils, administrators and governors are the mediated results of *sui generis* emergent properties. Such structural emergent properties are causally efficacious (why the teacher teaches, the pupil learns, and so on) yet cannot be observed. However, not all realists subscribe to the view that mechanisms are always underlying and unobservable, since 'Clockwork, the ways of producing commodities, electing MPs etc. involve mechanisms which are no less observable than the effects they produce' (Sayer 1992: 280). Yet when MPs are elected, what exactly are we observing? We can readily observe a succession of individuals greeting election officials, who in turn direct them to booths in which slips of paper are placed into wooden boxes. These boxes are then moved to the local town hall for counting by other local government officials.

We can observe that the conditions for voting are dependent upon the observable scrutiny of voter documentation, and that the handing over of the voting slip enables the voter to mark an X in the appropriate box. The handing over of the slip enables the voter to vote, and voting would not be possible without this transaction. But the handing over of the slip is not the key generative mechanism, since the prior inspection of documentation would have been already approved. Whilst the latter is observable, the conditions for voting are not: they reside in internal social relations between positions (voter/local government official; local government official/central government official…). The electoral system cannot be seen, but proportional representation versus first-past-the-post influences how many people vote and who wins. It is granted that we may observe the mechanisms in clockwork, but is it not the case that such observed workings are the result of a stratum of combined *un*observable generative mechanisms, such as magnetic fields and the properties of the materials concerned? We can observe the teacher instructing the pupil to attend detention or read aloud, but this in itself does not explain such behaviour. Explanation of such behaviour consists of positing the unobservable reality of irreducible emergent properties (the emergent social relation between teacher and pupil). In accounting for the powers of teachers, social realists point to the internal and necessary relation between teacher and pupil (a teacher would not be a teacher without a pupil, and vice versa). As Sayer (1992) rightly argues, this internal social relation is *sui generis* because it modifies the causal powers of the individuals *qua* individuals. Sayer is either conflating a sophisticated (realist) theory and the *events* that are its subject matter, or, much more likely, neglecting the fact that unobservable social relations condition the observable mechanisms of interaction in organisations. Of course, some mechanisms are observable, but this does not make observability necessary for a generative mechanism to be at work.

The above introduction to transcendental realism may strike a positive chord with those intuitively attracted to what has been proposed or deemed not only confusingly complex but also unwarranted by those predisposed to a less ontologically driven approach to social analysis.[3] Indeed, the transcendental presumption of *sui generis* structures does not tell us what such structures consist of and how they condition agential activity. In other words, it does not provide a workable methodology that captures the processes and mechanisms of structural conditioning and subsequent structural change (morphogenesis) or stasis. So we have to infer which specific ones are at work in any given area by virtue of their effects there.

Social structure, emergence and the Cartesian legacy

An emergent stratum of social reality

As McFadden has observed, '…questions about structure and agency, particularly in education, are obviously not going away' (1995: 295). For some commentators, the 'problem of structure and agency' cannot be practically resolved (Abraham 1994: 239). It will be argued that the 'problem of structure and agency' is resolvable if one recognises that structure is *sui generis* real because it is not temporally coterminous with its creators. How, then, do we conceptualise social structure? What does not help matters is that often we are told the school is a structure, part of a system, itself a structure, which in turn belongs to society, a much bigger structure. Let's start with the school as structure.

My discussion of the unobservable nature of the relation between teacher and pupil lies at the heart of the realist conception of social structure. Structure is neither viewed as an aggregate of individuals nor as an observable regular pattern of events. Moreover, it is not held to be independent of agency; that is, it is not a 'thing' in the Lukásian sense – an immutable feature of the social world. Social realism maintains that structure is emergent from agency by virtue of its *sui generis* properties. A teacher presupposes a pupil, a head presupposes teachers, a governing body presupposes teachers, pupils, heads and administrative staff, and so on. In other words, we are talking about internal relations between roles, ontologically distinct from the individual people who fill them and whom they causally affect. The teacher–pupil relation is an irreducible emergent property because the powers deposited within the role modify the powers of the individuals as individuals. This modification arises from the combination of internally necessary social relations. A lecturer cannot self-award a first-class honours degree, just as a student cannot revoke the decision of a degree classification board. Such powers do not reside in the properties of individuals but in the social relations that presuppose such individuals for their enduring efficacy (and thus mediation).

I am not suggesting that the teacher–pupil relation exists in isolation. Schools, like all organisations, are composed of a multiplicity of role-sets and are dependent for their existence and endurance upon other organisational (structural) configurations. In other words, the school *qua* organisation is internally related to the state (Department for Education and Employment, local government…), which itself is anchored in further internal necessary relations (treasury department and so on). Of course, before the rise of the English educational system, schools were internally related to Church organisations; that is to say, they were financially dependent upon, and staffed by, the Church. We can now return to my point made earlier about the capacity of social realism to differentiate the necessary from the contingent in posing counterfactual questions. Returning to the question of whether a school requires the existence of a governing body for it to be a school, it can be argued that a school could quite effectively function without a governing body. Deem *et al.* write that:

> As organizations, governing bodies have an evanescent quality, that is best described as "now you see them, now you don't". This is partly explained by their voluntary and transitory nature, itself quite unlike the organizational character of either educational organizations or business and commercial organizations, both of which have a greater degree of permanency and taken-for-grantedness, even if their structure and processes are continually being recreated and changed.
>
> (Deem *et al.* 1995: 90)

To maintain that a governing body *per se* is an organisation is incorrect; governing bodies are part of schools as organisations. The authors draw upon Weick's (1988) concept of 'loose coupling'. For Weick, loose coupling 'carries connotations of impermanence, dissolvability, and tacitness all of which are potentially crucial properties of the "glue" that holds organizations together' (1988: 59). What would clarify the notion of 'loose coupling' and at the same time denude it of its unhelpful 'sensitizing' import is the distinction between symmetrical and asymmetrical internal social relations. The relation between teacher and pupil is symmetrically internal because each could not exist without the other. Symmetrical internal necessity does not imply symmetrical power relations, since the teacher–pupil relation exemplifies one-sided domination. In other words, structurally, teachers have the 'upper hand', though this is not to suggest that teachers exercise their powers in an untrammelled fashion, without having to mediate the effects of pupils' reflective powers. It could be asked: 'But what about the relation between parents and their pupils? Surely parents are constitutive of the school as structural entity?' This would be to confuse the fact that actors are often occupants of a number of structures and that the role of parent presupposes the role of son/daughter, not that of pupil or student. In this case, the pupil is an occupant of two distinct structures, namely the school and family. S/he might also attend various clubs, in turn embroiling him/her in causally efficacious social relations (scout–scout leader; girl guide–guide leader). However, the school would not exist without children and is thus asymmetrically related to children *qua* children. Indubitably, schools presuppose children, who in turn presuppose parents/guardians. But this is an asymmetrical relation at the biological level, not the social one: how such children are reared is contingently related to the school, and the structure for such rearing will either complement or contradict school activities (or comprise a mixture of the two).

Maintaining that people are often occupants of several social structures does not entail spatio-temporal simultaneity. In attending school, a teacher is not exercising powers as husband or wife. In explaining the exercise of marital powers, necessarily one differentiates a different spatio-temporal setting (in the marital home, and so on). The fact that children behave in qualitatively different ways at different times (why Christopher undertakes his maths examination at three o'clock, watches television at home at five o'clock and follows the instructions of his scout leader at seven o'clock) warrants the autonomy of social structure. As critics of methodological individualism rightly point out, without the autonomy of social structure, how do we account for the fact that a bank clerk does not hand over cash at a party? Such behaviour cannot be reduced to statements about individuals *per se*. It is not the characteristics of Christopher *as an individual* that accounts for his behaviour in the three structural settings delineated.[4]

However, the school is externally related to the family *qua* structure. But the familial structure can have a causal, albeit contingent, effect. The structural 'upper hand' of the teacher may be reinforced or counteracted by the familial structure. For example, most children recognise that they have objective vested interests in acceding to most parental demands, irrespective of whether they are deemed reasonable by them. One of the requests often made by parents is that their child/ren behave well in class. The mediation of this parental request to behave well in class thus buttresses the power of the teacher (and would be conceptualised as over-determining the position of the teacher because of its reinforcing effects).[5] Whilst the familial structure can be causally efficacious *vis-à-vis* the school, the school is not ontologically dependent upon it. However, any governing body is clearly not contingently related to the school in this way. The relation of the governing body to the school is internally asymmetrical. In other words, it is perfectly possible that schools could function without a governing body, but not vice versa. Yet, despite this internal asymmetry, it still remains the case that governing bodies could be further empowered via government legislation to over-ride or supplant the powers of heads and their staffs. But even if this were to happen, the specialised knowledge of the head would provide a strong deck of cards with which to circumvent, resist or partially cancel out any substantial influence of governing bodies. In this scenario, the actual outcome would have to be traced through empirically.

Governing bodies are now empowered, *inter alia*, to hire and fire staff, statutorily aided by Local Education Authority (LEA) advisors, and no head can change this. (This is not to suggest that heads cannot form a corporate body in order to effect or resist structural change, but any such attempt is not guaranteed success – the imposition of national testing arrangements bears witness to this.) Any substantive research would be concerned with what heads and their staffs do about it, not in spite of it, and thus how it conditions their behaviour. Concepts like 'loose coupling' are methodologically unspecific. We are not told *how* they are 'coupled' (or linked) and why 'loosely coupled' phenomena are ever subject to immanent dissolution. A firmer analytical grip can be maintained on schools by (a) recognising their *sui generis* reality, and (b) thinking about what precisely constitutes a school in order for it to be recognised as such. The reason that governing bodies can be so readily 'dissolved' is due to their internal asymmetry. Empirically, however, I am not convinced that they are as impermanent and transitory as Deem *et al.* would maintain. Whilst they endure, in principle they can have causal effects on the workings of a school, though staff to varying degrees necessarily mediate such effects. It can therefore be argued that Deem *et al.*'s misrepresentation of the governing body *qua* organisation stems from its asymmetrical internal relation with the school; namely, that a school does not cease to be a school once the governing body 'dissolves' (or its powers remain unexercised). The existence of equal opportunities officers in universities is a further example of an asymmetrical internal relation, for the position of equal opportunities officer necessarily presupposes a university – personnel, decision-making executive – but not vice versa. However much power is 'devolved' to that particular position, it does not alter the fact that a university does not depend upon the latter for its existence. Finally, Barber and White's (1997: 1) claim that the establishment of the School Effectiveness Division in 1994 saved LEAs from extinction shows the asymmetrical relation of dependence of LEAs upon central government.

To reiterate, that teachers have powers that are irreducible to themselves as individuals signals the stratified nature of social reality. A stratified social ontology is discernible in Pollard's (1982) approach to classroom coping strategies. Pollard extends Hargreaves' (1978) analysis, which, Pollard argues, over-accentuates macro factors and constraints on teacher action. Instead of viewing structure as above-and-beyond teachers' generic control, he sees structure as something that is processually mediated and thus considers the situationally specific perspectives, goals and interests of actors within schools. His extension of Hargreaves consists of viewing the school itself as ontologically distinct from the actors who fill its positions. Essentially, Pollard provides a more stratified approach, since Hargreaves only deals with two irreducible levels – the macro context and what teachers and pupils do – whereas Pollard more clearly distinguishes between the macro context (education system, government policy), the school (internal and necessary relations between roles) and the actors who personify such roles. Indeed, it is precisely by virtue of his adoption of a relational social ontology that Pollard can talk of the vested interests of teachers and pupils alike:

> Largely because of their differences in structural position, the power resources and interests of teachers and children are different in many ways and in a great many respects they must be seen as being in conflict. However, a problem which they share is that they both have to 'cope with' and accomplish their daily classroom lives.
>
> (Pollard 1982: 22)

Pollard highlights the non-puppet-like manner in which teachers and pupils mediate the structural context in which they work. As he rightly notes, both have objective interests in carrying out the historically specific requirements of their roles. A teacher has interests in making sure that pupils succeed in public examinations, behave well in class, complete homework, etc. Undeniably, individual properties affect the ways in which teachers personalise their roles – why some are fair-minded, funny or downright ogre-like. But role-requirements must nevertheless be met and thus have a relative independence of role-incumbents. The latter 'must' is not one of unavoidable propulsion. It signifies the fact that not to carry them out would incur a cost (initial censure and possible dismissal). In other words, stringent constraints versus degrees of freedom attach to structured positions; they are objective and have to be weighed by actors. The reasons for carrying out one's duties are objectively structured and place a premium on their execution and a price on their disavowal (Archer 1995; Buckley 1998; Porpora 1989). Yet subjective weighing of the latter is not to be taken *a priori* as always congruent, otherwise we would not witness uncomprehending debtors who continue to pay the price.[6]

So far I have discussed two irreducible levels of reality, namely individual people and the emergent social relations between them, which subsequently condition their activities. The teacher–pupil relation has been paradigmatic. However, the isolation of this internal social relation is purely artificial. The teacher–pupil relation is embedded in a wider network of relations that make up the social environment. The social environment itself has irreducible emergent properties. This is not always (if ever) made clear by the use of the portmanteau 'social structure'. The school is part of an educational *system*[7] that is irreducible to its constituent elements, and which *qua* system is causally affected by the wider polity. To treat the educational system as *sui generis*, another level of social reality, is not to imply that it exists independently of the activities of agents, and, moreover, no presumption of causal primacy is made. As Blau puts it:

> Emergent properties are essentially relationships between elements in a structure. The relationships are not contained in the elements, though they could not exist without them and define the structure...The study of social life is concerned with the relations among people and thus always with emergent properties in the broadest sense of the term. Often, however, social relations are simply treated as characteristics of individuals [the error of methodological individualism], no different from their other characteristics, for instance, when the influences of the friendships of workers and of their technical skills on their performance are examined. In these cases, the fact that a variable – such as the extent of friendships – is an emergent social property poses no special problems since it is actually ignored. In contrast, the analysis of the structure of social relations in collectivities, for example, their differentiated status structures, deals explicitly with emergent properties. A more complex illustration is the study of the interdependence between the internal structures of subgroups and the relations among them in the larger society.
>
> (Blau 1964: 3–4)

Whilst I would prefer an emphasis upon impersonal relations, rather than relationships, because of the empiricist connotations attaching to relation*ships* (Layder 1990), Blau succinctly brings home the point that social structures as human creations possess attributes that are not reducible to their individual makers. This was made clear in the example of the teacher–pupil relation, whereby individuals' powers are modified in fundamental ways. The educational system itself cannot be reduced to the school as organisation. The myriad changes brought about by the National Curriculum have to be mediated by all schools, and constitute either an operational obstruction or facilitation, depending on the congruence or incongruence of policy prescriptions with extant teaching philosophy and practices. Thus the government imposition of the National Curriculum constitutes an irreducible level that causally conditions activities in all schools. The fact that different schools respond in quite distinctive, unpredictable ways demonstrates the need to distinguish analytically between the two levels, for the macro level in no way determines in top-down fashion: macro policy has to be mediated by teaching staff. The processes of mediation are the substantive focus of current education research (Bowe and Ball with Gold 1992; Campbell and Neill 1994; Deem *et al.* 1995; Menter *et al.* 1997; Pollard *et al.* 1994; Troman and Woods 2001; Willmott 1999b; Woods *et al.* 1997). However, 'the gap between theoretical development and empirical work is especially marked in research on primary schools and their staff...in which researchers pay considerable attention to documenting changes in work practices...but give relatively little space to seeking to explain and understand these changes' (Menter *et al.* 1997: 17).

The purpose of this book is to provide an explanatory framework for understanding the ways in which (two sets of) primary school staffs mediate specific socio-cultural emergent properties. Moreover, it will theorise about the conditions that maintain for (educational) stability or change. Whilst macro policy does not determine in top-down fashion, one needs to theorise about the degrees of freedom that teachers possess *vis-à-vis* the latter. In other words, any discussion of the imposition of the National Curriculum must make reference to the (differential) degrees of bargaining power that derive from prior structured interests and their interplay over time. Initially, all schools had to confront policy prescriptions for which they were not responsible. Some schools were better placed than others to circumvent, partially accept or wholeheartedly endorse the National Curriculum. Caution thus needs to be exercised when using such metaphors as 'steering at a distance' (Ball 1994). One needs to be crystal clear about the terrain over which steering occurs. The educational terrain is hardly smooth, dry and pedestrian-free; it possesses an irreducible materiality (complex division of labour) that necessarily precludes untrammelled steering.[8] Central government certainly attempts to steer through its reforms, but as the need for the Dearing Review highlighted, bumps in the road may be unforeseen, or foreseen but inadequately acknowledged, and their potential to damage the wheels needs theorising about. Indeed, the very need to steer *at a distance* stems from the fact that complex divisions of labour require the support of spatially differentiated personnel (in this case, school and LEA staff). But even if heads and their deputies generically support quasi-marketisation of education, teachers themselves cannot be assumed *a priori* to comprise a homogeneous collection of pliable material. (The role of teaching unions *vis-à-vis* the National Curriculum will be addressed in Part II.)

The Cartesian legacy

Methodologically, the key to examining the interplay of structure and agency is analytical dualism. This methodological procedure is warranted because the two possess distinctive powers and properties. We are thus dealing with *dual* aspects of social reality. Of course, like the generic referents 'structure' and 'agency', analytical dualism is a portmanteau, since we are not just dealing with two irreducible aspects of social reality (we are talking *inter alia* about the irreducible levels of school/educational system/polity). Indeed, there is no *a priori* limit to the number of emergent social strata in society. The methodological device of 'analytical dualism' is the generic springboard from which to gain entrée to social reality because it denotes that 'structure' and 'agency' are *sui generis* levels and thus examinable dualistically (or separably) in order to examine their sequencing of mutual influence over time. However, many would be quick to pounce upon the word 'dualism', hastily bypassing the prefix 'analytical'. Yet without the latter, the morphogenetic approach simply collapses, since, essentially, we are not dealing with Cartesian dualism, that is, with disconnected entities like Descartes' mind and body.[9] Descartes' dualism of mind and body – of two completely separate entities – has profoundly influenced work on the philosophy of mind. In fact, considerable time has been expended on eschewing his absolute division between the two. Yet the concomitant problem is precisely how to avoid a complete separation of mind and body without losing their ontological distinctiveness. In other words, clearly the two interact and are mutually influential yet they are neither free-floating nor so intertwined that examination of their respective powers and properties becomes *a priori* impossible. Thus, for Shilling, the largest obstacle to the integration of macro- and micro-perspectives is the dominant conceptions of structure and agency in educational research. 'Not only are the respective conceptions of structure and agency found in macro- and micro-level work deficient in their own right, they also contribute to an *unresolved dualism which has characterised the sociology of education*' (Shilling 1992: 70, emphasis added).

The intense dissatisfaction that talk of dualism often engenders can be dispelled if one recognises that the dual aspects (mind and body) are irreducible relational entities, analytically separable because of their distinctive causal properties. An emergentist ontology argues that Cartesian dualism can be resolved by conceptualising the mind as emergent from the body – dependent upon, but irreducible to, that from which it emerged. Thus, conceptualising human agency as a causally and taxonomically irreducible mode of matter is not to posit a distinct substance 'mind', endowed with reasons for acting apart from the causal network, 'but to credit intentional embodied agency with distinct (emergent) causal powers *from the biological matter out of which agents were formed, on which they are capable of reacting back...*' (Bhaskar 1993: 51).

We are not, then, dealing with two separate substances but with irreducible strata or levels of reality. One of the enduring fallacies to bedevil social theory has been the misconstrual of structure as a level that *is* completely divorced from agency. Hence the charge of reification, for structure is then held to be above-and-beyond agency, something that unavoidably determines us, rather than something that we mould and are moulded by. The Cartesian primacy of the mind over the body understandably leads some commentators to avoid all talk of dualism. Knights (1997), for example, rightly rejects dualistic formulations that privilege structure at the expense of agency (or vice versa) and/or treat either as reified 'things'. To posit the methodological device of analytical dualism is not to privilege agency or structure. Instead, the dichotomy 'structure/agency' delineates two strata of social reality, which is warranted because of their irreducible properties and mutual influencing over time. But in rejecting (Cartesian) dualism many commentators fail to distinguish ontologically between the two, maintaining that at best we can only use the dichotomy as a heuristic device. Thus, to Knights:

> An important qualification needs to be made here, for while a concern of this paper is to eradicate dualisms, it does not imply the illegitimacy of distinctions *per se*. Clearly, communication, knowledge and language are dependent on distinctions and the classificatory schemes or typologies that are their social science counterparts. It is only when distinctions are transformed from heuristic devices into reified ontological realities that they become dualistic. What has come to be defined as the problem of dualism occurs when polarized distinctions are combined with an 'episteme of representation' wherein what is distinguished as 'this' or 'that' is reified as ontological reality rather than merely a provisional, subjectively significant, and hence contestable, ordering of

'things'. Dualistic theorizing, then, commits the fallacy of misplaced concreteness since it believes that the distinctions made as part of ordering 'reality'…are accurate or true descriptions of a reality beyond, and as if it were independent of, the theorist.

(Knights 1997: 4)

The problem with Knights' rejection of dualism is that he will only permit a heuristic distinction, disavowing an ontological status for structure. Yet to accord structure an ontological status *sui generis* is not to reify it. For, as the foregoing indicates, structural emergent properties are only causally efficacious through people, not in spite of people (the error of reification). Human agency ever remains the sole efficient cause. In his haste to avoid Cartesian dualism, Knights elides the referent. Linguistic distinctions (structure/agency) presuppose referential detachment; namely, the detachment of the act of reference from that to which it refers. 'This establishes at once its existential intransitivity and the possibility of another reference to it, *a condition of any intelligible discourse at all*. Referential detachment is implicit in *all language-use*' (Bhaskar 1994: 257, emphasis added). By existential intransitivity. Bhaskar is referring specifically to the independent existence of events, objects (natural or social), etc. The process of distinguishing between structure and agency presupposes an object (real or otherwise) to which such a distinction refers. Even to wrap such distinctions with scare quotes is to deny the possibility of (fallible) access to reality. Without the notion of reality *sans* scare quotes, social scientific theorising is unintelligible. It may be that scare quotes are used to signify social reality's contestable nature (and not its transcendental ordering). In itself this is acceptable as long as it is made clear at the outset.

Knights' emphasis upon what is 'subjectively significant' is unavoidable, since structure is not held to possess independent causal properties. Whilst race ideas may be subjectively significant for black people in terms of how they explain their lack of employment opportunities, objective economic structures are such that race ideologies may be irrelevant. Race ideas may be important for explaining who gets what in the job market and who gets laid off first during times of recession, but a clothing factory that employs only Asian people because of its geographical location would, in times of recession, collapse because of economic factors alone. Knights would be unable to account for the corrigible status of actors' accounts of social reality. Like many critics of dualism, he confuses any *sui generis* ontological status with reification.[10] This is a *non sequitur* and is avoided by adopting ontological emergence (which permits *analytical*, not philosophical, dualism). To reiterate, social reality is transcendentally differentiated and structured in order for social scientific analysis to get underway and propositions about the relative importance of sociocultural properties are indeed contestable. Necessarily, such debates make truth-claims and necessarily require phenomena to be independent of the theorist in order for them to be conceptualised. The transcendental independence of such phenomena is quite separate from the nature of their relations with the theorist (who at the same time may be causally responsible for, or irreducibly linked to, that which is being conceptualised).

Stratified social ontology: misleading metaphor?

For those, like Shilling, who wish to transcend dualism, the notion of structure and agency as referring to irreducible levels of reality is redolent of incipient reification or held to be false. Shilling maintains that

> [e]ducational research is typically constructed as addressing either large-scale structural processes...or small-scale individual interaction patterns; the assumption being that social life itself exists on different levels. As well as being a false assumption, since individuals do not occupy different 'levels' of exis-tence...splitting social life into hierarchical levels makes it difficult to conceptualise change as a dynamic process involving both structures and human agents.
>
> (Shilling 1992: 70)

   Shilling is right to insist upon the untenability of conceptualising social life in terms of *hierarchical* levels, since it necessarily implies the primacy of structure at the expense of agency (or vice versa). The Cartesian legacy must be finally laid to rest: conceptualising structure and agency as irreducible levels does not imply the causal primacy of one over the other. If the notion of stratum is taken literally, then inevitably misunderstandings arise. Human agency is not like a compact disc; that is, slotted into one 'level' of the hi-fi system, unable to affect that which controls it – simply there to be played. In a nutshell, the metaphor of ontological stratification denotes the irreducible properties of *inter alia* social structure and agency. Yet, for Bryant,

> ...most fundamentally of all, the geological metaphor of ontological depth, of the stratification of surface actualities and beneath-the-surface realities is misleading. There is but one geological stratification of Salford, the city in which I work, but there is no reason to assume that there can be but one strati-fication of social reality there. It is one thing to argue that things seen can be explained by reference to things unseen, but it is quite another to argue that all things are arrangeable in a single stratified order which has an objective exis-tence. The privileged explanatory status of the capitalist mode of production as described by Bhaskar, for example, is not an ontological discovery but a practical convention – something justified in terms of the purposes it serves.
>
> (Bryant 1995: 89)

   I find Bryant's discussion of geological stratification rather confusing. First, the geological properties of Salford do not exist in isolation from its neighbouring towns and cities. Second, such properties are not analogous to social reality in that, as Bryant points out, 'the geological composition of one geological stratum in no way governs the composition of the stratum above it' (1995: 87). Being unfamiliar with the discipline of geology, I would posit the familiar realist example of the irre-ducibility of water as a level irreducible to its constituents, for hydrogen and oxygen on their own are highly flammable. We cannot see water's constituents just as we cannot see the internal and necessary relation between teacher and pupil. Bryant has misunderstood the nature of transcendental realism (Willmott 2000b). The latter maintains that social reality is structured (or relatively ordered), which in turn provides sociology with its subject matter. It does not legislate about what ordered constituents exist: social relations are *sui generis* real and relatively enduring. It is their *sui generis* nature that enables (methodological) identification of them as a distinct level of reality. Bryant makes the untenable assumption that, because social relations are only relatively enduring, one should focus attention solely on new social phenomena. This begs the question of the nature of the structural conditions that are prior to such new phenomena. Instructively, Bryant maintains that the assumption of objective existence matters to a Marxist, 'but it would make no difference to the explanatory power of the supposed underlying reality if one were to treat it as, say, an ideal-type' (1995: 88).

Yet the issue is not one of what *matters* to social theorists, but one of what *must* be the case for social theory to be intelligible. It is odd that Bryant accepts the explanatory power of underlying relations (capital–labour), yet at the same time denies their import, suggesting that we can make whatever we want of social reality (e.g. imposing Weberian ideal-types). Finally, it is disputable that Marx would couch his uncovering of the nature of capitalist social relations in terms of 'practical convention'. Bryant has got things back to front. 'Practical convention' has to be ontologically grounded. If the discovery of the nature of capitalist social relations was not a discovery of *sui generis* generative mechanisms, then what was it? I disagree with his assertion that '[p]erhaps the most valuable contribution of scientific realism will prove to be not social ontology but to methodology' (Bryant 1995: 89). Epistemology is irreducibly dependent upon ontology and not vice versa. One cannot sensibly set about studying social life without some prior notion of what one is about to study.

Structuration theory: conflating structure and agency

Giddens writes that, in structuration theory, 'a range of dualisms or oppositions fundamental to other schools of thought are reconceptualised as dualities. In particular, the dualism of the "individual" and "society" is reconceptualised as the duality of agency and structure' (1984: 162). Indeed, a few years later he remains tenacious in arguing that '[s]tructure and action *cannot* form a dualism, save from the point of view of situated actors, because each is constituted by and in a single "realm" – human activity' (Giddens 1990: 299). Giddens is quite right to reject Cartesian dualism. However, his laudable aim to avoid the legacy bequeathed by Descartes and the concomitant need not to reify structure, regrettably results in conflation of structure and agency, thereby precluding examination of their interplay over time. Undeniably, the influence of Giddens's structuration theory has been considerable in the social sciences. In the field of organisation studies, for example, Reed notes that 'the theory of structuration is invoked and deployed by a growing number of organizational theorists' (1992: 187). Structuration theory is drawn upon by Deem *et al.* (1995) in their study of school governance, and, more recently, Elliott (1998) argues for its utility *vis-à-vis* education action research.

Apart from the influence of the Cartesian legacy on Giddens's work, he is particularly concerned to dissociate himself from naturalistic sociology, whereby social
forces are held to resemble those of the natural world. Yet, as we have seen already,
the teacher–pupil internal relation can be examined apart from agency (and therefore as a dual aspect of social reality) because the former causally conditions –
though in no way determines – the latter. Before unpacking the central propositions
of structuration theory, it is worth returning to the use of natural analogies to explicate ontological emergence in the social realm. Though Giddens is quite content to
use language as the paradigmatic analogy for social structure, he rejects any use of
natural analogies; ostensibly because social reality is so unlike natural reality,
arguably because he rejects any notion of emergence *per se*. Indeed, Giddens is
deeply resistant to the notion of emergent properties held by social realism to be
constitutive of social structure. He quotes Durkheim, who remarked that:

> The hardness of bronze lies neither in the copper, nor in the tin, nor in the lead
> which have been used to form it, which are all soft and malleable bodies. The
> hardness arises from the mixing of them. The liquidity of water, its sustaining
> and other properties are not in the two gases of which it is composed, but in
> the complex substance which they form by coming together. Let us apply this
> principle to sociology. If, as is granted to us, this synthesis *sui generis*, which
> constitutes every society, gives rise to new phenomena, different from those
> which occur in consciousness in isolation, one is forced to admit that these
> specific facts reside in the society itself that produced them and not in its parts
> – namely its members.
>
> (Giddens 1984: 171)

Giddens would baulk at the Cartesian connotations attaching to Durkheim's talk
of water as substance – and rightly so – but instead of considering the similarities
between social structure and water, Giddens swiftly dismisses the explanatory
import of the water (or bronze) analogy. He would be right to argue that structure is
not some sort of Cartesian 'substance', divorced from agency like tin is from copper.
Giddens argues that the above quotation has been particularly persuasive but is
none the less fundamentally flawed, for:

> …human actors, as recognizable 'competent agents', do not exist in separation
> from one another as copper, tin and lead do. They do not come together *ex
> nihilo* to form a new entity by their fusion or association. Durkheim here
> confuses a hypothetical conception of individuals in a state of nature…and real
> processes of social reproduction.
>
> (Giddens 1984: 171–2)

The notion of emergent properties still confuses some of those who remain
committed to Giddens' structuration theory (see, for example, Manicas 1997:
210). One of the initial problems encountered by those predisposed towards
structuration is the misplaced assumption that social reality *is* like natural reality, i.e.
self-subsistent, or, indeed, 'hard' like bronze. It does not follow that a stratified

social ontology entails that structure is somehow self-subsistent, ready and waiting 'out there'. The notion of structure as 'hard' like bronze would certainly lead one down the path of determinism. But in invoking such an analogy, Durkheim is not suggesting that people *are* tin or copper! While Giddens (presumably) would not deny that water is irreducible to its constituents of hydrogen and oxygen, he would maintain that social structure is peopled and therefore cannot be theorised about via chemical analogies. Yet the water analogy is employed simply to show the similarity between the two in terms of their causal irreducibility, which exists solely by virtue of internal necessary relations. The intention is not to anchor social structure in any form of natural analogy, since the nature of any analogy precludes exact correspondence with its referent. The manifest difference here consists of the human constitution of social structure. In other words, the dissimilarity, namely the human constitution of social structure, is emphasised at the expense of the similarity between water and social structure by Giddens.[11]

When Giddens writes that actors, as 'competent agents', cannot exist separately from one another, he is (a) eliding the distinction between actor and agent, and (b) disclaiming personal identity. The very concept of 'competent agents' only makes sense in relation to the prior existence of social structure: what people as agents can or cannot do about it. What they do within it as actors, however, denotes how they personalise their roles. The point of the use of the bronze analogy by Durkheim is to show the similarity between the latter and social structure, for social structure exists as a combination (or 'fusion') of internally necessary social relations. Such relations are ever the result of individuals, but once created they possess *sui generis* properties that act back to condition individuals' (or groups') behaviour. Individuals do not then become some non- or extra-human entity (like bronze) when they come together to create (and reproduce) irreducible structural forms! Instead, they become recognisable as agents and actors because of the modification of individuals' powers *qua* individuals.

The 'duality of structure': structure as rules and resources

> In structuration theory 'structure' is regarded as rules and resources recursively implicated in social reproduction; institutionalized features of social systems have structural properties in the sense that relationships are stabilized across time and space. 'Structure' can be conceptualized abstractly as two aspects of rules – normative elements and codes of signification. Resources are also of two kinds: authoritative resources...and allocative resources...
>
> (Giddens 1984: xxxi)

Structure is deemed 'virtual' and becomes real only when 'instantiated' by human agency. Yet when specific powers deposited in the role of teacher remain unexercised, is it tenable to conceptualise such powers as 'virtual'? Necessarily they are real, not 'virtual', and can exist unexercised for long periods of time. Moreover, to maintain that schools exist only in their instantiation immediately forfeits analysis of precisely why schools are relatively enduring. Instantiation is inherently voluntarist, for it implicitly enjoins that the school possess no prior causal determinacy. In a nutshell, 'instantiation' is empirically nonsensical. Teachers turn up for work on a regular basis primarily because they have *prior* structured interests in so doing. The school *is already there* and thus is not dependent upon agential 'instantiation'. If Giddens were to swap instantiation with mediation then I would not demur, since mediation presupposes prior structured social relations that provide agents with reasons for maintaining or changing them. Essentially, Giddens is confusing the activity-dependent nature of social relations with their *sui generis* causal properties: the two (agency and structure) presuppose each other, but not in the way Giddens proposes.

Many critics have thus accused Giddens of subjectivism (Callinicos 1985; Johnson *et al.* 1984; Turner 1986). In view of the primacy of the present tense enjoined by the concept of instantiation (that is, of structure existing as mere 'moments' of interaction), I highlighted the resonance between Giddens's approach and methodological individualism (Willmott 1999a). This is because methodological individualism also enjoins present tense analysis (Goldstein 1973). Diachronic analysis is ruled out of court because of the denial of prior *sui generis* conditioning. Yet I also highlighted the frustration endemic to Giddens's structuration theory. By no means does he place himself in the methodological individualist camp.[12] Whilst I would maintain that there is *prima facie* evidence for viewing Giddens as an 'upwards conflationist', to use Archer's terminology, whereby the individual level 'swallows up' the social, Giddens himself would maintain that efficacious 'structural properties', rather than 'structure', causally condition interaction *over time*. In fact, 'central conflation' is appropriate for two reasons. First, Giddens' dislike of naturalistic sociology has led him to squash agency and structure into one indistinguishable amalgam, which whilst insulating against reification means that analysis of their interplay is immediately forfeited. Second, Giddens' definition of structure necessarily enjoins analysis in the present tense, though not for reasons stemming from an individualist social ontology.

Giddens also maintains that structure 'is not "external" to individuals: as memory traces, and as instantiated in social practices, it is in a certain sense more "internal" than exterior to their activities in a Durkheimian sense' (1984: 25). Note the use of 'exterior' rather than 'external' and how 'internal' is not defined by Giddens. Indeed, the prefix 'more' denotes a methodological equivocality that haunts his exposition of structuration. What is interesting, however, is the reference to the past via 'memory traces'. At a basic level, continuous social activity requires that actors have a recollection of past activities. If I could not recall the location of my office or where to catch the bus for work, then (working) life would be impossible. To posit this as a necessary criterion for the reproduction of social structure is platitudinous. However, given that 'instantiation' denies pre-existence, it is clear that the criterion of 'memory traces' is doing a lot more. Yet, like instantiation, it singularly fails to explain why teachers turn up for work. To reduce the determinacy that derives from the prior materiality of structure to 'memory traces' is untenable and simply evades the issue of the nature of social structure. Teachers can remember where they teach, point to the availability of materials, regurgitate the key stages of the National Curriculum, but recall itself does not explain the latter.

The important point here is that Giddens would not countenance the social realist concept of structure (as the irreducible relations between positions in organisations and the relations between organisations). Indeed, for Giddens, social structure 'has no descriptive qualities of its own as a feature of social life…' (1989: 256). How, then, can we even make reference to such relatively enduring social phenomena as schools? Giddens would no doubt reply that we can talk of schools as sedimented over time and space because of the distinctive rules and resources that are employed by those who work within them. But this would be to miss the point, since the rule 'all pupils must complete their homework over the weekend' only makes sense within a relational context, which has relative autonomy from its makers (and reproducers). That teachers have the resources with which to enforce and/or facilitate the enactment of such a rule cannot be explained by reference to other rules and resources. The homework rule presupposes the temporal priority of the teacher–pupil relation; rules have to be relationally grounded and not vice versa. Indeed, it is only because of the *sui generis* nature of the teacher–pupil relation that the homework rule can have any causal efficacy. This is not to deny that other rules – which Giddens calls normative rules – play their part. But normative rules are not the same as those governing structural behaviour and are thus contingent.[13] To explain why Helen as a police constable follows rules specified in the Police and Criminal Evidence Act presupposes the irreducible relations of constable–sergeant, etc., and their wider (relational) anchorage (Government–Home Office). That such rules do not determine Helen's behaviour is a separate matter from their relational grounding. In examining the changes engendered by the various Education Reforms Acts, reference to rules and resources alone makes no sense. For (a) one would not be able to explain why some rules are more important than others, or why they are resisted and, moreover, (b) why there are prior per capita funding arrangements.

As Thompson (1989: 64–5) argues, Giddens' emphasis upon rules presupposes a criterion of importance that cannot be approached via rules, but rather presupposes analysis of structural relations. Without any notion of relatively enduring autonomous social relations, one cannot theorise about differential degrees of constraint. In other words, the fact that the homework rule constrains pupils' behaviour is only possible because of their relational embedding. For Giddens to reply at this juncture that such a rule also enables pupils – to succeed in exams, etc. – is not the issue, since both constraints and enablements derive from social relations and their (in)congruence with actors' needs and wishes. To reiterate, social relations are the irreducible referents of the generic term 'social structure'. In reducing such relations to rules and resources, Giddens is not only truncating structure but also removing the basis on which he can talk about power, capitalism and so on. He avoids the term *social* structure because

> [it] conforms too closely to a position…in terms of which structure appears as something 'outside', or 'external', to human action. In my usage, structure is what gives *form* and *shape* to social life, but it is not *itself* that form or shape – nor should 'give' be understood in an active sense here, because structure only exists in and through the activities of human agents.
>
> (Giddens 1989: 256)

If external is taken to mean independent in the sense of 'separate from', then Giddens is correct to avoid conceptualising structure in terms of the latter. However, it does not follow that externality entails separateness. Instead, we are talking about relative autonomy, which is warranted because of the temporal priority of social relations that causally condition activity. At the same time, the relative autonomy of structure does not nullify its dependence upon the continued activity of agency. I concur that structure gives form and shape to social life (and it is on this basis that any charge of methodological individualism fails), yet in the next breath Giddens nullifies this transcendental prerequisite at a stroke, denying pre-existence and conflating structure with the activities of human agents. This cannot prevent the question-begging issue, namely, in what ways are agents active (and can they be inactive yet still have efficacy?) and why? Giddens remains unperturbed and maintains that talk of power is permitted because '...power is an elemental characteristic of all social systems....The fact that some actors are more able...to "structure" their social environments than others is also a matter of power, *and has no direct bearing upon either the concept of "structure" or that of "system"* ' (1989: 257, emphasis added).

The powers of a governing body reside in the social relations that are a school (which are further embedded in the LEA, local government, Department for Education and Employment, etc.). Such powers are not derivable from rules and resources, though they are rule-governed and resource-implicated. Power is a relational property that cannot be reduced to 'rules and resources'. Giddens' recourse to the constraints and enablements that flow from power protect him against the charge of methodological individualism, but at the same time he removes the ontological rug from under his very feet in reducing *sui generis* relations to 'rules and resources'. It is because of his disavowal of pre-existing *sui generis* relations that critics who accuse him of subjectivism derive their strength. But without pre-existence, we cannot talk of structural constraint or enablement, for they are *relational* terms. Thompson (1989) notes that certain individuals have restricted opportunities for entry into a variety of organisations – universities and schools are cited as exemplars. He argues that such restrictions cannot be adequately conceptualised in terms of 'moral rules' or 'sanctions', since such restrictions operate independently of the rights and obligations of the agents concerned. Giddens (1989) readily concedes that there are no rules attaching to being poor, having restricted access to prestigious universities and so on. However, he maintains instead that we should analyse 'certain forms of *system reproduction*, in which complexes of "rules and resources" are implicated. For instance, Bernstein's distinction between restricted and elaborated codes...would certainly be relevant to understanding such differentials in life chances' (Giddens 1989: 257). Yet this is a restatement of the problem! Giddens is merely transposing the untenability of theorising about differential life-chances in terms of rules and resources to the systemic level, which, as we have seen, comprises emergent relational properties (between organisations).[14] His reference to Bernstein does not advance his case, precisely because Bernstein's distinction only makes sense in the context of irreducible class relations. The point is to explain theoretically why certain sections of the population are subject to a restricted code in the first place. Again, this can only be done by reference to relatively enduring *sui generis* social relations.

The Wittgensteinian inflection of structuration is undeniably attractive, since rules play a significant part in most people's lives. However, we must be careful not to elide rules and their grounding in irreducible social relations. In their *Organizational Rules* (1991), Mills and Murgatroyd are guilty of such elision. They carefully itemise different rules involved in organisational analysis but, like Giddens, disclaim pre-existence and emphasise process at the expense of product, in turn rendering the term 'organisation' vacuous (1991: 194). For, if we cannot point to a social entity that is relatively enduring, but instead can only talk of 'becoming' rather than 'being', then logically a school does not (as yet) exist. What does not help matters is that Wittgenstein himself never defined 'institution' (Bloor 1997: 27). Bloor's Wittgensteinian reduction of institution to talk and thought (1997: 32) resonates well with Giddens' equally depthless social ontology. Yet, for Giddens,

> Institutions by definition are the more enduring features of social life. In speaking of the structural properties of systems I mean their institutionalized features, giving 'solidity' across time and space. I use the concept of 'structures' to get at relations of transformation and mediation which are the 'circuit switches' underlying observed conditions of system reproduction.
>
> (Giddens 1984: 24)

This does not square with Giddens's denial of pre-existence. If institutions have 'solidity' then any attempt to re-shape them presupposes their temporal priority, and any successful change creates a new action-context that causally conditions agency (however short the temporal gap). Giddens does not define 'institution' and, moreover, will not accord it *sui generis* reality. (Note also the empiricist claim that we can *observe* the underlying conditions of system reproduction.)

Unsurprisingly, Giddens's equation of power with 'transformative capacity' further conflates the distinction between structure and agency. Teachers derive certain degrees of freedom within their work context from the social relations that comprise the education system. However, whether the exercise of their structural freedoms is successful in bringing about transformation is contingently related to their powers as agents – structural freedom is independent of agential power. If we return to the example above of the engineered staff meeting, the head may have exercised full structural powers knowledgeably, yet failed because of countervailing pressures (emanating from, say, governors and Heads of Department). Agential powers of reflection may be distorted, partially exercised or completely unexercised, thereby ensuring the status quo. To take a further example, the Education Reform Acts provide the structural potential for restructuring (transformation) yet may not be capitalised upon by agency (heads may prefer 'old-style' approaches to team-working rather than 'business-like' confrontational models). One must respect the powers and properties of structure and agency respectively and not elide them by enforcing co-variance. To accept that considerable powers may be exercised but fail is to seek answers to questions that cannot be posed by Giddens because ostensibly they re-invoke the dualist spectre. Failure to transform, say, the education system means disentangling which other factors intervened and the nature of the structural properties themselves (the system), which can be examined independently from agency.

Denying pre-existence: structure as the medium and outcome

'By the *duality of structure* I mean that social structures are both constituted *by* human agency, and yet at the same time are the very *medium* of this constitution' (Giddens 1979: 121). This more clearly establishes a denial of pre-existent social relations than 'instantiation'. To recapitulate, the notion of 'instantiation' implicitly denies pre-existent material relations because they are deemed *a priori* to have no prior efficacy. In other words, instantiation cannot be squared with the notion of social reproduction because the latter presupposes a prior, autonomous product, which must be differentially mutable in order to account for why agents are constrained to engage in replication or facilitated to pursue change. The notion of structure as medium *and* outcome explicitly removes the rug from under Giddens's reproduced 'social practices' because the two do not operate in terms of temporal simultaneity. A school has to exist before teachers can teach, however short the time gap between the construction and occupation of positions within it. So, what subsequently happens – the outcome – is temporally posterior to the construction of the school. If the school were the medium and outcome simultaneously we would not be able to explain structural change, since logically we cannot pinpoint the school at T^1 (the medium) and structural change (the outcome) at T^3.

Indubitably, the school, as structure, is ever the medium for continuous activity. Yet it cannot be the outcome at the same time, since this merely begs the question: outcome of what? A car is the (necessary) medium for driving, but the car has to be constructed before it can be driven. Moreover, it is not ever the outcome in the sense of being re-built each time it is driven. Like structure, a car cannot work unless driven by people and, in the process of driving, one is not rebuilding the car. Of course, a car remains a car when unused for years at a time, unlike structure, which is ever activity-dependent. However, the analogy is useful for accentuating the fact that *qua* product the car pre-exists any subsequent driving and can be added to or modified like social structure, in turn providing a new context for driving that is temporally posterior. It may be that Giddens' dictum is intended to show that structure is reproduced in the very process of agential activity. This is but a sociological truism and does not tell us theoretically in what ways the outcome is different and why.

To be an agent or not an agent: Giddens on agency

Quintessential to Giddens's conception of agency is the ability to 'do otherwise'. The principal reason for redefining agency in this way is his laudable yet over-hasty rejection of naturalistic sociology, whereby people are held to be like magnetic particles and structures akin to those of force fields. The education system can hardly be thought of as a magnetic field, with children and teachers conceived as iron filings pushed and shoved by some magnetic force or as part of a living system, rather like the body's lungs that provide it with its life-sustaining prerequisites. Whilst providing an important corrective to the extremes of structural determinism, the notion of 'ability to do otherwise' leads to the equally untenable extreme of voluntarism. For, in the process of redefining agency, Giddens is effectively rendering any notion of freedom redundant. If agents can ever do or act otherwise, then the positing of the stringency of constraints versus degrees of freedom makes no sense (e.g. unemployed job seekers versus headhunted graduates). The concept of agency is only meaningful in the context of (a) structural constraint or enablement and, moreover, (b) identifying the concomitant possibilities for enhancing people's freedom. Following an OFSTED (Office for Standards in Education) style inspection by LEA advisors of Southside in 1997, I asked the deputy head why she did not ask for clarification concerning inaccuracies in the advisors' report presented to the school's governing body. She replied:

> We don't actually receive the report. So you can't clarify anything....[The head] and I were given the report to read half an hour before the Governors got it...and we went through it and picked up about 6 different things I disagreed with and so did [the head]. And then we said well we want this changed and we want this changed. Then they read it to the Governors. The Governors then had to give their copies back in, so that these amendments could be made umm any that they agreed with so that we could disagree with the facts if they were wrong; *but we couldn't disagree with any judgements that were made* (emphasis added).

The reply that neither the deputy nor the head could disagree with any of the LEA advisors' judgements constitutes a stringent constraint. In order to theorise about its stringent nature, the notion of the ability to do otherwise has no explanatory purchase and necessarily undermines the materiality of social relations. Of course, the head and the deputy could walk away, but this would invoke a structured penalty. To maintain that agents can ever do otherwise entails a somewhat dubious psychological assumption, namely that agents will always be prepared to incur quite hefty costs and that structure has no determinate influence – in this case, the impediment to challenging advisors' judgements of teaching ability. In theorising about the stringency of constraints, there is no implicit determinism, for both the head and the deputy could exit the concrete situation at any point in time were they willing to pay the (career) price.

The could-do-otherwise approach means that social reality is what we make of it, not something that we confront or may be unable to change for some considerable time. That is not to say that what is socially produced can never be changed, simply that even the most stringent constraints can eventually be changed, but whilst attempts are being made to change them, they continue to exert a conditional influence upon agency. Even if the head and deputy were prepared to pay the career price, it must be remembered that in exiting one structured context they necessarily enter another one and confront its irreducible relations of constraint or enablement (another job or the Benefits Agency). In theorising about the impact of the National Curriculum, testing arrangements, etc. on child-centred practice, one is focusing on the ways in which structural and cultural properties delimit or facilitate activities for identifiable groups of specific agents (teachers, heads, pupils, government officials, etc.). Even where government officials are able to set the agenda, they are none the less constrained by prior relations and the arrangements that *they* subsequently set in place, which may have to be modified in the process.

That all teachers are required to test their pupils at Key Stage 2 cannot be theorised about adequately in terms of the ability to 'do otherwise'. Certainly some may wish to have nothing whatsoever to do with Standard Assessment Tasks and their contradictory implications for child-centred teaching, but not to carry out the statutory tasks would invoke disciplinary action and possible dismissal. It might be reasonably pointed out, however, that teachers *qua* organised collectivity could take concerted action and in fact there was a boycott of testing in 1993. But this begs the question of why the boycott was essentially an aberration and that imposition, rather than negotiation, characterised the promulgation of the various Education Reforms Acts and national testing arrangements. In fact, its failure shows the stringency of constraints: the boycott was the collective best they could do in a stringently infelicitous situation.

In essence, we should be talking in terms of degrees of freedom versus stringency of constraints, since the latter only makes sense within a prior structured or delimited context. Whilst teachers may be successful in altering or substantially revising national testing arrangements, it still remains the case that they have to teach, often using materials and curricula that are not of their making. The theoretical focus is on the room for manoeuvrability, not on how they could have 'acted otherwise', implying that the door is not only always open but exists at every wall.

The morphogenetic approach: the realist alternative

Structuration theory is ontologically 'flat', precluding the possibility of examining the interplay of agency and structure over time because of its denial of pre-existence and assumption of temporal simultaneity. This final section of the chapter will delineate the central tenets of the 'morphogenetic approach', arguing that analytical dualism is the methodological key to examining the interplay of structure and agency because the former is irreducibly emergent from the latter and causally efficacious. It can only possess causal properties and powers because structure and agency stand in temporal relations of priority and posteriority. Thus the morphogenetic approach is predicated upon an endorsement of ontological emergence and its temporal materialisation.

Origins and development

The morphogenetic approach has its origins in general systems theory. Specifically, in the growing disenchantment with the untenability of organic, mechanical and simple cybernetic systems theories that were so eagerly transposed to the social realm. The term 'morphogenesis'[15] was first coined by Buckley (1967) in order to avoid the misleading connotations that attach to such concepts as 'self-regulation', which entail an overemphasis on the internal system at the expense of situational and environmental factors. The development of morphogenesis was aimed at incorporating the often-overlooked fact that social systems are *human* constitutions; they are open and thus can never be modelled on any organic or mechanical systems analogy. As Archer puts it:

Society is not a simple cybernetic system, which presupposes a particular structure capable of carrying out goal directed, feedback regulated, error-correction. All of these are special kinds of system and society is another, which is only like itself and is itself because it is open, and is open because it is peopled, and being peopled can always be re-shaped through human innovativeness. Hence the use of the term 'morphogenesis' to describe the process of social structuring; 'morpho' indicating shape, and 'genesis' signalling that the shaping is the product of social relations.

(Archer 1995: 165–6)

The morphogenetic approach, unlike its analogical predecessors, is concerned not only with…

[t]he *causes* acting on the phenomena under study, the possible consequences of the phenomena, and the possible mutual interactions of some of these factors, but also [with]…the *total emergent processes* as a function of possible positive and/or negative *feedbacks* mediated by the *selective decisions* or 'choices' of the individuals and groups directly or indirectly involved.

(Buckley 1967: 80, original emphasis)

Agency is properly conceptualised as possessing 'degrees of freedom, selectivity…*mediating* between external influences and overt behaviour' (Buckley 1967: 95, emphasis added). That social forms are mediated by agency signals the morphogenetic approach's caesura from its reifying precursors. It is precisely the (prior) structured distribution of resources and power that enables Buckley to theorise about agency in terms of its *degrees* of freedom (simply compare Tony Blair and the *Big Issue* vendor). Social systems *qua* agential products are held to *act back* to condition agential activity differentially in the form of negative and/or positive feedback loops. These feedback loops are not reified mechanistic entities, operative above-and-beyond agency. They reside in the irreducible emergent properties (relational properties between organisations) that constitute any social system at any given time. The latter provide structured reasons that work upon the vested interests of those differently positioned, thus predisposing various agents towards maintaining a particular organisational structure or changing it.

Social and system integration: developing Lockwood's distinction

Archer (1979) utilised and extended this sequential approach to structural change via Lockwood's (1964) seminal distinction between 'social' and 'system' integration in her *Social Origins of Educational Systems*. Lockwood's principal concern was to reject the methodological individualism of conflict theory and to explain why low social integration *per se* (high level of conflict among groups of actors) is not a sufficient basis on which to account for social change: it had to be complemented by an analysis of *system* integration. The problem for Lockwood was that conflict might be both endemic and intense in a social system without causing any basic structural change. Conflict theory would have to answer that this is decided by the variable factors affecting the power balance between groups. He maintained that this was inadequate by itself and needed to be complemented by the system integration focus. In short, social integration refers to the orderly or conflictual relations between actors; system integration refers to the orderly or conflictual relations between the parts of any social system. Therefore system integration could be low, but, unless its contradictions were seized upon and amplified by sectional social groups, they could be contained and stasis would persist because of high social integration. Alternatively, low social integration could be profound without leading to any significant change unless it was linked to systemic contradictions. Thus it was the conjunction between the two states of affairs that accounted for structural morphogenesis or morphostasis.

Lockwood found it ironic that conflict theorists arrived at their respective positions through a generalisation of Marx, since it was Marx who differentiated social and system integration:

> The propensity to class antagonism (social integration aspect) is generally a function of the character of production relationships...But the dynamics of class antagonisms are clearly related to the progressively growing 'contradiction' of the economic system. One might almost say that the 'conflict' which in Marxian theory is decisive for change is not the *power* conflict arising from the relationships in the productive system, but the *system* conflict arising from 'contradictions' between 'property institutions' and the 'forces of production'.
>
> (Lockwood 1964: 250–1, original emphasis)

Indeed, the actualisation of the contradiction between the forces and relations of production is contingent and not a teleological necessity. The actualisation and amplification of the systemic contradiction (or incompatibility) is dependent upon the extent to which those with prior structured interests are able to resolve versus realise the functional incompatibility (or 'strain'). The various historical and contemporary strategies of containment need not detain us. The importance of Lockwood's distinction between system and social integration (or between the 'parts' and the 'people') lies in the increase in explanatory power gained by analysing the variable combinations between the two rather than unhelpfully reducing explanation to social integration alone – or alternatively to states of the system alone. However, Lockwood's distinction remained ontologically ungrounded and lacking in methodological specification (Archer 1995: 172). The morphogenetic approach supplies both the ontological grounding and the methodological specification of the processes involved in the variable combinations between the two irreducible aspects of lived social reality. Lockwood's ontologically ungrounded systemic 'component elements' have their referents in the irreducible relations between organisations, which themselves are emergent properties.

System and social integration: temporal priority and the possibility of analytical dualism

As Lockwood (1964: 250) rightly pointed out, system and social integration (structure/agency) are factually distinguishable because they operate over different tracts of time. Structuration theory, however, fails to acknowledge this and mistakenly construes the relation between structure and agency in terms of temporal simultaneity. Certainly, structure presupposes agency and vice versa, but they do not – or rather cannot – operate over the same tracts of time. It is because structure is temporally prior to agential activity that we can talk of it possessing *sui generis* properties that condition such activity. Indeed, the morphogenetic approach acquires its analytical bite when presented as a sequence of phases (Archer 1998: xiii). Morphogenetic processes are quintessentially sequential, dealing in endless three-part cycles of Structural Conditioning → Social Interaction → Structural Elaboration.

Structural conditioning
T^1

      Social interaction
      T^2 T^3

            Structural elaboration
                T^4

The role of teacher necessarily pre-exists its incumbent, and any subsequent role-modification provides a new action-context for its incumbent, the objective reality of which is captured by the fact that social practices are qualitatively different. As Porpora (1989: 207) rightly argues, if we want to analyse the interaction of role-incumbents, then the question is which is analytically prior, the established social relations or the rule-like routinised manner of the interaction teachers and pupils subsequently establish? As he points out, it is the powers afforded by the social relations that determine the character of subsequent interaction. Indeed, any routinised behaviour, however intimately rule-governed, presupposes a (temporally) prior *relational* context and this proposition holds good however short the time gap between the establishment (or modification) of relationally grounded rules and subsequent behaviour.

Research on the effects of the National Curriculum, quasi-marketisation, etc., is implicitly (or explicitly) theorised in sequential terms. Fitz *et al.* write:

> In implementation terms, therefore, it is not just a case of evaluating the extent to which centrally formulated policies are adopted or deflected at the periphery, rather it is the case that research has to engage as well with newly created or restructured institutions and institutional relations, the purpose of which, in part, is the efficient delivery of educational reforms.
>
> (Fitz *et al.* 1994: 61)

We are thus dealing with a 'before, during and after' analysis (that is, conditioning → interaction → elaboration or stasis). At the same time, the morphogenetic approach advances concrete theoretical propositions about the conditions that maintain for structural morphogenesis or morphostasis. Structuration theory, however, remains ever confined to the 'during' phase, unable to delineate prior social structuring and advance propositions for any later restructuring or dissolution. Fitz *et al.* also maintain that the 1988 Education Reform Act 'is as much about restructuring institutions – defining new goals, delineating fields of operation...– as it is about promulgating substantive education policies' (1994: 60). It is precisely the nature of the education system before, during and after such generic restructuring, and in particular how objective systemic contradictions or complementarities (structural and cultural) generated at the 'after' phase are contemporaneously mediated by school staffs (that is, circumvented, exploited or lived with), that is the focus of this book. The 'after' phase provides the contextual backdrop to my analysis of two junior schools. Analytical dualism is employed to examine the autonomous action-contexts that impinge on teachers, and therefore to examine what they do in it or can do about it. This is only possible because at any T^1 the school is prior to activity at T^2, whilst any morphogenesis post-dates such activity creating a new set of conditioning social relations at T^3. Any structural (or cultural) change at T^3 then constitutes a new phase of the cycle that is temporally prior to conditioned activity at T^4.

In establishing the T^1 of any sequential approach, one is not thereby embroiled in an infinite regress. In other words, the fact that the prior history of my first case-study is important in certain respects (the personality of the head, entrenched animosities, etc.) does not entail back-tracking to the establishment of the school some twenty years ago or to the relationships before the arrival of the head. Essentially, it depends on what one wants to explain and thus any T^1 will reflect the substantive preoccupations of the researcher. The time taken between interaction and any morphogenesis may consist of months, even years. In fact, the creation of a Senior Management Team in my first case-study school took place during a couple of days. As a consequence, certain members of staff thereby acquired new vested interests and powers. The establishment of the team thus constitutes a new phase in the morphogenetic cycle that is captured by the different activities of newly promoted staff. How such powers are then used, circumvented or unexercised is a matter for empirical investigation and needs theorising about.

The system–social integration distinction has explanatory utility at a number of irreducible levels. At the level of the school itself, for example, objectively we can establish any contradictions that maintain between roles and how they are dealt with by staff (unnoticed, ignored or exploited), or alternatively discover a high level of social malintegration without the latter issuing in any structural change. Malintegration at both levels may predominate, in which case any structural morphogenesis may not result because of (social) divisions precluding exploitation of the organisational fault-line. At the level of the educational system, we are dealing with contradictions or complementarities between organisations (schools, LEAs, central government bodies) and how they mould problem-free or problem-ridden situations for actors. Such contradictions may be internally necessary, thus signalling emergence at the systemic level, or external and thus contingently related.

Recently, I gave the example of the *Next Steps* initiative[16] (Willmott 2000a). Here, any substantive analysis of the development of *Next Steps* agencies requires that we focus on the structure *before* the Sir Robin Ibbs initiative (structural conditioning), the agential response (social interaction) and the subsequent outcome (structural elaboration or stasis). As Brooks and Bate (1994) found in their study, structured vested interests, ideologically backed-up, conditioned limited structural morphogenesis. Their case study demonstrates the theoretical indispensability of analytical dualism. An identification of Lockwood's 'component elements' (civil service *qua* differentiated system), irreducible to actors' understanding, provides explanatory leverage *inter alia* on those issues surrounding agential *mis*calculation. The obstructions experienced by actors may be the result of 'contradictions' (systemic incompatibilities) and are not necessarily matters of full agential 'discursive penetration'. To reduce them to agential awareness is to commit the idealist fallacy that social reality is whatever we make of it. Of course, this is not the same as saying that agents have no conception of what they are doing. As Layder (1990) rightly argues, necessarily social structures are concept-linked, but they are not concept-dependent.

Certainly, systemic incompatibilities are not constraining in abstract isolation, since their reception depends upon how they gel with human agency's extant intentions and plans. For some, they will be experienced as obstructions, creating practical exigencies; for others, they will be experienced as facilitating bonuses, unimpeding their daily behaviour. Yet how they are experienced is separate from their incompatible or complementary nature, which is ontological *sui generis* and independent of agential discursive penetration. However, Perkmann, for example, maintains that '...systemic incompatibilities can only occur if they are perceived as such at least by some actors' (1998: 495). In a later footnote, Perkmann qualifies this statement with the following: 'The argument that incompatibilities have to be perceived by actors does not necessarily imply that they cannot take actors by surprise' (1998: 505). But if incompatibilities can 'take actors by surprise' then logically they must both pre-exist actors and exist independently of them. In brief, Perkmann wishes to withdraw objective status from incompatibilities. 'I suggested that there is no "absolute" externalist outside from which society can exclusively be perceived as a "system", because this perspective can always be turned into an internalist "inside", i.e. a contingent field of action potentially liable to transformation' (1998: 503).

Marx's uncovering of the nature of capitalist social relations, specifically the contradiction between the forces and relations of production, should be sufficient to underscore the fact that systemic contradictions (or incompatibilities) are not ontologically dependent upon agential awareness. Not all recognise their incompatible nature or are misled into misrecognition via ideological manipulation, but this does not negate the objective reality of the labour–capital relation. However, whilst Perkmann maintains that 'incompatibilities are never objective', he grants that '*Reality tends to resist*, given that society consists of many entangled processes which are co-constituted with "their" respective actors and constitute "real" constraints for others' (Perkmann 1998: 503, emphasis added). If, as he rightly maintains, reality resists, then perforce we are dealing with objective material properties that are causally irreducible. Yet note the use of scare quotes around the word 'real' in the same breath. Perkmann is quite correct to point out that incompatibilities may not be recognised as such and be mistakenly identified, in turn guiding agential activity. But why only accord actors' discursive accounts objective status? Indeed, one wonders why actors in Perkmann's account have any notion of (in)compatible systemic properties if they have no objective status.

Structural conditioning: situational logic and strategic guidance[17]

The prior distribution of resources and positions provides the mediatory mechanism of the first phase of the morphogenetic sequence. Pre-structured positions supply agents with reasons for pursuing change or defending extant arrangements because of the objective vested interests deposited in them. The morphogenetic approach adds greater precision to the manner in which situations are shaped for agency. Specifically, it draws attention to the 'situational logics' of structural configurations that predispose agents towards specific courses of action. Such configurations shape action-contexts for agency, at the same time providing directional guidance. The systemic incompatibility (or strain) that causally conditioned agential activity in Brooks and Bate's case study are second-order emergent relational properties between organisations; that is, between the newly created civil service agency and Whitehall. They are 'second order' emergent properties because they are themselves (irreducibly) emergent from the structural configurations of the civil service agency and Whitehall. (This example parallels the relationship between schools and the Department for Education and Employment.) In this case study, the systemic incompatibility is an internally necessary one since the civil service agency could not exist without Whitehall and vice versa. It is conceptualised as a 'strain' because agents' situations were being moulded by operational obstructions imposed by Whitehall, which translated into practical problems that had to be dealt with 'on the ground'. The objective nature of the incompatibility is independent of the (often partial or incorrect) accounts that are given for its existence (e.g. 'Treasury mentality' or 'government hypocrisy'). The fact that agency in this instance did not respond like robotic executors of pre-programmed (Whitehall) scripts attests to its reflective powers to mediate emergent structural properties in creative and fundamentally non-deterministic ways.

The situational logic of a systemic incompatibility predisposes agency towards compromise and concession. Despite evident reluctance, the actors engaged in some form of action as a direct result of the systemic strain generated by Whitehall. Counterfactually, of course, no action (or unsubstantial restructuring) might have ensued, with agency simply circumventing the positive feedback loop set in train by the *Next Steps* initiative. Yet this might have invoked a dangerously high price. For, in deciding completely to 'drag their feet', the key agents in Brooks and Bate's case study might have misread the situation to such an extent that the systemic fault-line created by Whitehall might have been fully actualised and amplified, resulting in blanket dismissal, with the agency sold off to an independent (that is, nongovernmental) organisation. That this was not a foregone conclusion, and, as such, might have been weighed correctly by agency, attests to the *open* nature of any social system. In other words, any lack of concession or compromise does not necessarily signal end time for agency precisely because the emergent potentiality inherent in any systemic incompatibility may remain unexploited because of contingent factors that act as countervailing forces (e.g. an unforeseen but substantial increase in civil service negotiating strength, buttressed by powerful interest-groups located elsewhere). Thus we are talking about the *tendential* powers of the systemic strain (the result of internal social relations) because of their existence in an open system.

In short, the fact that the protagonists paid lip-service to the changes required by the *Next Steps* initiative does not thereby result in an expunction of the systemic strain. Whilst some agents here rightly reasoned that Whitehall would not privatise the agency, any continuing Whitehall commitment means that the systemic potentiality for actualisation may resurface, depending *inter alia* on their relative degrees of bargaining power and how it is converted into negotiating strength (Archer 1995). Furthermore, it is not being suggested that the organisation is an undifferentiated collection of agents uniformly united against the systemic tentacles of Whitehall. The systemic incompatibility (incongruence of role array) opens up possibilities for agents *within* the organisation to further their own vested interests, either by lending unequivocal support for senior management against Whitehall or by exploiting management's (potentially lethal) digging-in of heels. The fact that some may find the form of restructuring required by *Next Steps* to represent a step forward (thus entailing that prior roles were experienced as partially or wholly incongruent) lends credence to Perkmann's point that systemic incompatibilities will be experienced differently by different actors. Woods *et al.* (1997), for example, examined the ways in which three heads responded to the changes engendered by Local Management of Schools and the National Curriculum and found that only one was enthusiastic about the new managerialist role. The fact that some actors may perceive objective contradictions as complementarities does not license us to take their interpretations as incorrigible. Yet I suspect it is more the case that objective contradictions are often recognised as such, but found to be psychologically acceptable – hence the fact that some teachers welcomed the 'traditionalist' implications of the National Curriculum and testing arrangements, which contradict child-centred precepts. If sociology cannot posit objective systemic contradictions (and their complementary counterparts) and theorise about how agents should rationally act in view of them, then necessarily it loses its critical cutting edge.

The imposition (successful or otherwise) of the *Next Steps* initiative constitutes the final phase of the morphogenetic sequence, namely the use of exchange and power. Following Blau, Archer maintains thus:

> [T]he basic notion is that exchange transactions and power relations are both responsible for social elaboration. Moreover, they are inextricably linked with one another and jointly account for the emergence of reciprocity or control in the interaction between different groups...The resources which are exchanged are varied (i.e. wealth, sanctions and expertise), but these resources do not have an exact price in terms of a single medium of exchange. This is not a methodological problem, it is a matter which is undefined for the actors involved...At a formal level, institutional interaction consists in using resources to transact exchanges with others in order to attain goals, whose target may be

either social stasis or change. However, although the importance of the initial bargaining positions of the groups is indisputable...this gives no indication of even the most general conditions under which they are likely to be successful, or of the type of interaction which would be involved.

(Archer 1995: 296–7)

Here, the prior structured distribution of resources delineates the respective bargaining positions of groups (or individuals), but what then gives such groups negotiating strength requires examination of the interaction between groups, since such strength is relational. Hence, in explaining the actual outcome of the 1988 Education Reform Act, one needs to establish the initial bargaining positions of those structurally enabled to enter the exchange process, for example the teaching unions. But the actual strength of the teaching unions needs to be theorised about relationally, that is, *vis-à-vis* the polity and the relations between and amongst resource-holders. As will be discussed in Part II, whilst the initial level of resource access is important, this alone does not guarantee success, since relationships amongst the teachings unions and their relations with those with whom they are transacting (mainly local and central government) are equally important. In brief, the initial effect of prior structural differentiation is to define who can bring what (level and types of resources) to the exchange process, yet such differentiation takes place within second-order socio-cultural constraints and enablements that furnish negotiating strength. However, what then needs to be theorised about is how structural differentiation, cultural diversification (see Chapter 2) and agential re-grouping gel together. 'The generic issue now is that the structural and cultural developments may or may not gel, yet both are exerting conditional influences upon agency. Therefore, what transpires depends upon their reception by PEPs [people's emergent powers] and the negotiating strength of Corporate groups *vis-à-vis* others' (Archer 1995: 303).

Finally, the morphogenetic approach accentuates the fact that not only does structure (or culture) undergo morphogenesis, so too does agency. This is referred to as the 'double morphogenesis', for as agents attempt to promote or defend their vested interests, in the very process they undergo re-grouping. Unorganised groups, whose interests remain unarticulated, are referred to as Primary Agents, because they still exert a causal influence (the unemployed constitute part of the environment that decision-makers have to confront). When primary agents organise themselves, become aware of their structured vested interests and articulate their demands, they become corporate agents. Therefore the elaboration of groups in the process of working for change versus stability also results in unintended emergent and aggregate consequences. A classic example of this is the development and concomitant bureaucratisation of trades unions, whereby organisational structures endowed specific groups with vested interests that were not always compatible with the generic interests of union members. Nevertheless, the elaboration of emergent powers (from primary to corporate status) enhanced their initial bargaining power and the success of subsequent negotiating strength remains an issue for empirical investigation.

Concluding remarks

This chapter has maintained the need for analytical dualism in examining educational change. It has shown how this methodological device is workable because of the *sui generis* nature of structural forms and their temporal materialisation. Put simply, analytical dualism is predicated upon two propositions, namely that (a) structure necessarily pre-dates the action(s) that result in its reproduction or transformation; and (b) structural elaboration necessarily post-dates the action(s) that created it. This is the temporal mainstay of the morphogenetic approach, whose analytical teeth are the three-part sequential cycles of structural conditioning → social interaction → structural elaboration. The mutual influencing of structure and agency over time is precluded by Giddens' structuration theory, since the 'duality of structure' insists upon their temporal simultaneity. Whilst an emphasis upon 'duality', rather than 'dualism', is commendable, structuration theory is too hasty in its aim to avoid reification of social structure and the putative reification that attaches to an analytically dualistic analysis of social reality. To employ the methodological device of analytical dualism is not to reify social structure. Instead, it is to honour the relative autonomy of structural properties that causally condition agency, which again is only possible because structure and agency stand in temporal relations of priority and posteriority. The cyclical sequencing procedure of the morphogenetic approach will be fleshed out in Part II. However, as mentioned at the beginning of this chapter, structural analysis must be complemented by culture, and how their respective morphogenetic/static dynamics gel with agency. The next chapter will argue that parallel propositions can be made for culture.

2 Culture, organisation theory and the new managerialism

Introduction: the 'sticky problem of culture'

People often talk about the culture of their particular organisation in terms of 'the way things are done around here'. In requesting an itemisation of such 'things', one would anticipate a heterogeneous list of factors, ranging from the extent and depth of emotional attachments among staff, to generic work practices and the shared values that underpin them. In fact, some might go as far as to suggest that their culture is unique – not to be found in other organisations. Such heterogeneity is equally evident in organisation theory. The problem with such a heterogeneous conception of culture is that we gain limited explanatory purchase on, *inter alia*, the reasons why people share (or do not share) values and beliefs, whether such 'sharing' is imposed, and how values and beliefs change and their interplay with social structure. In fact, on the whole, distinct irreducible levels are so tightly compacted that any workable entrée into organisational reality is precluded. This chapter will argue that (a) a substantial increase in explanatory power is gained by a focus on the propositional components of culture, i.e. beliefs, theories, arguments, values, which (b) possess irreducible properties and powers among their relations that predispose their upholders to respond in specifically conditioned ways.

For Hays (1994), theorising about culture *per se* and its relationship *vis-à-vis* structure and agency is a 'sticky problem'. Superficially, the notion of stickiness is attractive, for it refers not only to culture's contested nature but also to its tendency to remain ontologically elusive. In other words, upon picking up culture, it becomes like a sweet that has fallen on to a child's hands: each time an attempt is made to put it back into the mouth, the sweet gets stuck on its fingers. It is the sticky residue that the child wants to avoid once the sweet is finally placed into the mouth. I want to argue that culture, like the child's sweet, is a human product, but, *qua* product, is irreducible to its human makers. One of the principal differences here, of course, is that the child's sweet is sucked and digested. Culture, however, is never digested in this manner: this is an ontological impossibility. It is ready-made for us at birth, constraining/enabling our actions in distinctive ways. Hays argues that

> ...social structure consists of *two* central interconnected elements: systems of social relations and systems of meaning. Systems of social relations consist of patterns of roles, relationships, and forms of domination according to which

one might place any given person at a point on a complex grid that specifies a set of categories running from class, gender, race, education, and religion...Systems of meaning are what is often known as culture, including not only the beliefs and values of social groups, but also their language, forms of knowledge, and common sense, as well as the material products, interactional practices, rituals and ways of life established by these. While not reducible to systems of social relations, culture matches the other central structure of social life in its power, its patterning, its durability, and its collective and transcendent nature. If one wants to understand the resilient patterns that shape the behaviour of any individual or group, *both* the cultural and relational milieu must be taken into account.

(Hays 1994: 65–6, original emphasis)

Hays's discussion of structure and culture resonates well with the approach adopted in this book. She rightly underscores their respective durability and irreducible causal efficacy. However, despite the need to distinguish analytically between structure and culture because of this, she contends that culture is part of social structure. This is a recipe for confusion. In realist fashion, she conceptualises structure in terms of social relations yet, at the same time, introduces cultural factors as part of this definition. Whilst class is a structural (relational) concept, race ideas are cultural phenomena and are thus contingently related.[18] As I argued in Chapter 1, a school is such by virtue of the various sets of internal necessary social relations between teacher–pupil, head–teacher, and so on. At the concrete level, race ideas may be causally influential (e.g. why children of Afro-Caribbean origin are systematically discriminated against), but such ideas are not a necessary condition for a school *qua* school. Equally, schools do not presuppose that boys and girls be treated differently or be held to possess differential levels of 'intelligence' and subsequently taught on that basis. The fact that pupils and teachers alike discriminate in varying and subtle ways enjoins that we both accord culture *sui generis* reality and distinguish its structured properties from those of social structure (*qua* irreducible relations between and within organisations).

Hays maintains that culture is systemic, possessing an 'inner logic' of its own (1994: 68), which 'not only constrain[s] us to think and behave in certain ways, [it] simultaneously provide[s] us with a range of ways to think and behave at the same time...make human thought and action possible' (1994: 69). She concludes thus:

With all of this in mind, the relevant questions we face as researchers include, first, the specification of the characteristics of both cultural and relational structures – their logic, systematicity, the ways and the contexts in which they operate, and the relative resilience of their layers of patterning. Second, we might turn our attention to the question of under what cultural and relational conditions, and through what cultural and relational processes, structurally transformative agency occurs...Finally, we confront the long and important project of determining the ongoing interconnections between systems of meaning and systems of social relations. *This project includes the recognition that these systems are empirically connected but analytically distinct, with an underlying logic of their own.*

(Hays 1994: 71, emphasis added)

Hays's final comment is crucial, since it underscores the methodological propriety of employing analytical dualism. Whilst it might be conceded by some that structure, culture and agency do constitute distinctive strata of reality, any disengagement of their emergent powers and properties in order to examine their relative interplay over time would result in an unfortunate submission to the tyranny of abstraction, inflicting unwarranted violence on everyday *lived* organisational reality. Indeed, analytical dualism – the morphogenetic approach's methodological springboard – would be taken as *prima facie* evidence for an overly 'objectivist' approach: a focus on culture *qua* disconnected object precisely because of its dualist methodological charter. Thus, to Martin,

> …cultures do not exist only in the realm of ideas and values; they constitute a specific material condition of existence that some consider oppressive and exploitative. It is misleading to portray cultures as arcane, ungrounded worlds of ideas and values, disconnected from the practicalities of earning a paycheck…

(Martin 1992: 42)

In a similar vein, Dahlström maintains that one cannot separate culture from the social as an independent system, since 'ideas and beliefs are parts of material existence and of people's everyday life…Culture is a driving force behind social life' (1982: 143). Finally, Meek (1988) argues that culture is something an organisation 'is', not something an organisation 'has' (see also Bate 1994; Meyerson and Martin 1987). Yet to elide the material, ideational and agential aspects of lived organisational reality is to relinquish analysis of their relative interplay – precisely *how* culture is a 'driving force' behind social life. The very notion that culture has 'driving force' enjoins that it is analytically separable from agency in order to examine its causal powers. As Brown (1995) rightly notes, the notion of organisation *qua* culture necessarily foregoes a causal analysis of those properties that are contingent to its structural configuration.[19] The laudable yet misplaced fear of reification has led many to assume that the only alternative is elision. However, practical consistency does not always follow. Meek concludes that

> …it seems necessary for the purposes of the interpretation of actors' behaviour that a conceptual distinction be made between 'culture' and 'structure'. It must be kept in mind, though, that both culture and structure are abstractions, and have use only in relation to the interpretation of observed concrete behaviour.

(Meek 1988: 470)

Logically, Meek cannot simultaneously maintain that an organisation *is* a culture and insist upon the (practical) necessity of a conceptual distinction between structure and culture. That Meek recognises that, in practical analysis, structure and culture have distinctive properties and causal effects, should in turn regulate the guiding social ontology. The morphogenetic approach concurs that culture and structure ultimately derive from concrete behaviour. But it insists upon the transcendental claim that such abstractions refer to *real*, relatively enduring phenomena that are ontologically distinct from the human agency that created them. As Hays intimates, they are ontologically distinct because they possess *sui generis* causal powers ('an underlying logic of their own', as she puts it), whose interplay is teased out sequentially via the methodological device of analytical dualism. What often complicates matters is the fact that the adjective *abstract* is taken to entail vagueness or incomprehensibility. In social science, however, an abstract concept (such as power or gender) isolates in thought a one-sided or partial aspect of an object. What we abstract from are the other aspects that constitute *concrete* objects. Let's take the example of using a word-processor within the home environment. In order to explain such concrete activity, we would use abstract concepts. Thus, in the process, we would not need to consider the eye-colour of the person using the computer, his/her nationality, whether s/he had reached a high degree of typing proficiency, etc. (I am, of course, artificially bracketing power relations within the familial structure and their wider relational anchorage.)

It should be clear, then, that we use abstractions to aid explanation of concrete objects and activities (such as schools, educational systems). As a concrete entity, the school combines influences and properties from a wide range of sources, each of which might be isolated in thought in order to arrive at an explanatory account of their combined effect (Sayer 1992: 87). Such sources would include personality, attitude, physique, etc. We abstract the impersonal social relations that comprise such concrete entities as schools because, among other things, whilst personality affects the ways in which individuals personalise their work-related tasks (why some heads are funny or ogre-like), this in itself does not explain why it is that teachers put up with ogre-like head-teachers. Again, we abstract the pre-existing social relations that account for a head's capacity not simply to behave in an ogre-like fashion but why s/he can get away with it. Moreover, abstractions are not heuristic devices; that is, devices that simply order our observations of organisational life. Clearly, abstractions are different from the objects to which they refer (this applies equally to observations and concrete objects) but, as Sayer rightly points out, this does not mean that they cannot refer to real objects and the constituents that make them what they are.

Note that our ogre-like head does not have to justify such behaviour via simultaneous attempts at ideological manipulation. The fact that s/he may use ideas to buttress ogre-like behaviour ('We're all managers now and if you want to survive in the education market place you will do as I say!') does not mean that the structural powers at his/her disposal are dependent upon such ideas for their efficacy. What is of interest here is how such ideas embroil their takers in logical relations *vis-à-vis* other (necessary or contingent) ideas that predispose towards specific courses of action, and how they gel with extant structural arrangements. However, this is to jump ahead. Culture and agency are not 'ungrounded worlds', as Martin would put it: they are intertwined in organisational life but can be analysed dualistically because of their irreducible causal properties (and their sequencing of mutual influence over time). The aim of the morphogenetic approach is to theorise what Dahlström termed culture's 'driving force'. One of the key propositions of the morphogenetic approach that insulates against charges of reification is that its 'driving force' is only operative *through* human agency, and is never hydraulic in fashion but ever conditioning. Without human agency constituting the sole efficient cause, we end up in Martin's reified world. However, the morphogenetic approach is not concerned simply with upholding the truism that ideas are causally influential *vis-à-vis* structure and vice versa. Its rigour inheres in its ability to specify the conditions that maintain for cultural (and structural) stability or change – in the conjunction between culture and socio-cultural interaction and how such interaction is itself rooted in the structural domain.

Theorising culture from the morphogenetic approach

As Hays has already argued, culture pre-exists its users and modifiers, constraining what can or cannot be said in a particular language, for example. Transcendentally, therefore, it is the pre-existence, autonomy and relative durability of culture that establishes its ontological warrant as an irreducible entity that predates socio-cultural interaction, whilst any cultural morphogenesis post-dates such activity. As with structure, this provides the temporal basis for distinguishing analytically between the 'parts' and the 'people'. Culture (and structure) and agency are intertwined in reality; the morphogenetic approach simply disengages those properties that provide explanatory leverage on such lived reality because of their *sui generis* nature. In other words, disengaging the properties and powers of structure and culture does not entail a concomitant proscription of methodological attention to real actors and their interpretations. Those who wish to misconstrue the morphogenetic approach as unavoidably 'objectivist' tend to focus on the first part of the morphogenetic cycle, namely the identification of cultural (and structural) properties independently of agency. Yet the whole point of this is to examine how the cultural context is shaped for actors in order to gain explanatory insight upon what they subsequently do in it or what they can do about it.

The so-called interpretivist (or 'subjectivist') paradigm thus constitutes an instance of those who want to have their ontological cake and epistemologically eat it. Put simply, such an approach collapses irreducible socio-cultural properties into actors' accounts. At its extreme, such an approach reduces social reality to language (e.g. Boden 1994). As Reed argues, such reductionism 'provides a classic restatement of a single-level social ontology that conflates "agency" and "structure" in such a way that they are analytically rendered down to localized social practices bereft of any institutional underpinnings or contextualization' (Reed 1997: 25). Organisations are held to be mere 'objectifications', having their locus of existence only in the minds of actors. In short, the interpretivist paradigm is another variant along the central conflationist (structurationist) line. It denies the pre-existence of causally efficacious socio-cultural forms, thereby removing the very basis of its epistemological claims. For actors' interpretations are interpretations of something independent. Without the transcendental reality of irreducible structural and cultural properties, the interpretivist paradigm cannot account for *mis*interpretation and, moreover, how and why it is possible that actors are manipulated, misdirected or deceived. Many capacities for manipulation derive not from capricious inter-subjective machinations, but from irreducible social relations that have relative autonomy from the actors whose activity they condition. The ineluctable end-result of interpretivism is hyper-voluntarism, since the primacy of epistemology means that reality is whatever we make of it. This is not simply assertoric, because inter-pretations and meanings must be anchored ontologically. In reducing organisational reality to subjective meanings, interpretivism commits the epistemic fallacy, namely the fallacy that statements about being can be reduced to our statements of knowl-edge about being.

Culture: establishing its 'World Three' status

The morphogenetic approach holds culture-systems to be more or less co-terminous with Popper's (1979) 'World Three'. In brief, Popper distinguishes 'Three Worlds': 'World One' refers to *physical* states and processes; 'World Two' refers to *mental* states and processes; 'World Three' refers to the *products* of human minds. Such products range from sculptures, paintings and ancient plays, to highly complex scientific theories. All 'World Three' products *qua* products possess the dispositional capacity to be understood (and used). Whether the instructional programme to construct an Airfix kit is successfully implemented is a matter of contingency. Put simply, we are dealing with objective cultural phenomena that are independent of cultural actors, yet that retain the dispositional capacity to be understood or used (hence the existence of literary criticism, which presupposes such prior objective material as Shakespeare's plays). Only 'strong' social construc-tionists would disclaim the objective dispositional nature of 'World Three' phenomena.[20] Anybody who has watched an episode of the 'Antiques Roadshow' on TV should recognise the 'strong' social constructionist absurdity that we can make whatever we want of historical artefacts. The fact that we get things wrong or tentatively proffer dates and uses of artefacts simply demonstrates the objective nature of Popper's 'World Three'. In other words, such human products *constrain* any human understanding of them. What makes the archaeological task no easy ride in comparison with that of the natural scientist, of course, is the fact that specific *meanings* are attached to artefacts, how they were arranged and so on. The wooden table at one level, then, has intrinsic properties such as hardness, but *how* the table was arranged at a particular time could entail considerable symbolic importance (e.g. sacrificial slaughter). Thus, without much or any context, it may indeed turn out that we can never arrive at an adequate understanding of partic-ular 'World Three' entities.

However, Popper is more concerned with *objective knowledge*, viz. hypotheses, theo-ries, arguments, unsolved problems. The morphogenetic approach distinguishes the Cultural System (CS), as that inherited sub-set of (cultural) items to which the law of contradiction can be applied at any given time. These items are therefore propo-sitions, because only those statements that make a claim to truth or falsity can be deemed to be in contradiction with or to be consistent with one another. It is at this juncture that Hays' talk of logic is salient, for it will be argued that specific 'situational logics' predispose cultural agents towards distinct courses of action by virtue of the logical relations that obtain between propositions. Drawing upon Mannheim, Hays argues that

> ...ideas exist as part of powerful and ordered cultural systems...Systems of meaning...shape not only what particular ideas we use, *but also the logic we use when stringing those ideas together.* To put it another way, culture influences not only what we think about, but *how* we think about it.
>
> (Hays 1994: 68, emphasis added)

It is by virtue of the logical relations that obtain between CS properties that we can say that culture influences (constrains or enables) agential activity, but only as and when such properties have their takers. This will be fleshed out later. For the moment, however, the morphogenetic approach concurs with Mannheim that

> ...the universality of mathematics and logic was such that neither could be explained by reference to anything about the specific cultures in which they were adopted...However, [the morphogenetic approach] restores certain logic principles to where Mannheim left them, thus retaining their serviceability in the attribution of properties like 'contradiction', 'consistency' and 'independence' to CS items located anywhere in time or space.
>
> (Archer 1988: 113)

The Cultural System is objective and has autonomous relations among its components (theories, beliefs, values, arguments; or more strictly between propositional formulations of them). Its objective nature[21] is due to the fact that its components are 'totally independent of anybody's claim to know; it is also independent of anybody's belief, or disposition to assent; or to assert or to act. Knowledge in the objective sense is *knowledge without a knower*: it is *knowledge without a knowing subject*' (Popper 1979: 109, original emphasis). Thus any contradictions or complementarities between its components are not dependent upon us. The Cultural System would not, of course, exist without its human makers. However, this does not nullify its autonomy, even though we constantly act upon it and are acted upon by it: 'it is autonomous in spite of the fact that it is our product and that it has a strong feed-back effect upon us; that is, upon us *qua* inmates of the second and even of the first world' (Popper 1979: 112).

The Cultural System is referred to metaphorically as 'the Library' because of the indubitable fact that vast tracts of it are written down in books, journals, pamphlets, statutes and so on. Importantly, this is not to suggest that organisational actors have to pop out every five minutes in order to be able to act at all. On the contrary, it simply affirms the impossibility of the human mind(s) to store everything that has been said, debated, theorised, mooted, conjectured, discovered, etc.[22] Athey, in her *Extending Thought in Young Children*, underscores the reality of 'World Three':

The central feature of the curriculum is knowledge. *This exists objectively in ency-clopaedias and so on* [CS level], *and it remains external to the knower* until constructed psychologically in the individual [S-C level]. External knowledge, once vali-dated for 'truth', 'worthwhileness', 'relevance', 'usefulness' and 'generalizability', must be discovered, assimilated and mastered by the learner. If knowledge is to be successfully assimilated it must fit in with the learner's 'lived experience'...

(Athey 1990: 43, emphasis added)

Athey's key point is that bibliothèque knowledge cannot be simply delivered by teachers like letters in the mail. Such knowledge has to be 'delivered' (I prefer 'taught') in such a way that is congruent with the cognitive processes of the child *qua* child. Athey also recognises that bibliothèque knowledge is independent of its truth or falsity.[23] Ineluctably, some 'World Three' properties have to reside in our heads, since otherwise social life would be impossible, namely language (yet even here we do not store the totality, or we would never consult a dictionary). Everyday recourse to government-supplied statistics, curriculum documentation and orders, appraisal reports, newspapers, employment law texts and various types of *aide-mémoire* establishes the objective nature of the CS at any given time. Even those (propositional) properties that have their locus of existence in the human mind are nevertheless irreducible and may stand in a contradictory or complementary rela-tionship to other CS denizens independently of the actor's awareness.[24]

Furthermore, it is not being argued that knowledge *in toto* is co-terminous with the CS. 'Know-how' is central to much of what takes place in organisations, from making a cup of coffee to using a word-processor. In view of the focus on proposi-tional knowledge, educationists would be rightly concerned that I am thereby ignoring those practical know-how processes that underpin successful teaching, such as knowing when a child is capable of being extended or needs remedial attention. I do not wish to downplay or deny the importance of such processes: the issue here is at which level of social reality one focuses one's analytical attention and the reasons for so doing. Teachers could not effectively teach without intuitive knowledge or know-how, yet, at the same time, such *practical teaching is ideationally grounded (or specifi-cally underpinned by philosophical assumptions)*. In terms of this book, therefore, the substantive focus is on the structural–ideational context in which such practices take place, since the structurally conditioned use of ideas *vis-à-vis* the imposition of the National Curriculum is undeniable (e.g., proponents of child-centred learning are 'loony left' ideologues). And the very use of ideas itself conditions activity. As will be addressed in Part II, the actual processes by which teachers assess pupils' needs are currently contradicted by the structural constraints embodied in the National Curriculum, which are ideationally backed-up. Indeed, they have logical implica-tions for practice, of which actors may be aware, partially aware or unaware. And such lack of awareness may be the result of strategic manipulation (by central government, teaching groups, head-teachers).

Athey argues that experience of teaching is a necessary but insufficient condition for professional advancement, since there is 'a great deal of difference between "know-how" and consciousness of "know-why" [knowledge of the Cultural System irreducible to, but dialectically grounded, in practice]' (1990: 31). Following Volpe (1981), she argues that an ideal teacher is one who

> combines practical 'know-how' with the conceptual understanding that can only come from study and reflection. There are indications that, in spite of the politically-motivated, anti-theoretical *Zeitgeist* of the present time, many teachers of young children wish to evolve from intuitive knowledge towards a more articulate system of professional understandings.
>
> (Athey 1990: 31)

For Bruce, teaching, to some extent, 'has to be an act of intuition embedded in educational principles [CS properties]. The teacher has to have confidence in offering and organising the prepared lesson. It is an act of intuition because there is not much tangible feedback from these internal processes, especially with children of three to five' (1997: 50). Such intuition is conceptually underpinned, which is subject to immanent revision or modification. Bruce acknowledges the one-hundred-year difficulty of articulating the conceptual framework of know-how practices and argues that '[t]hose who can speak and write effectively and clearly about their work, as well as put it into practice, are more likely to be listened to' (1997: 66). Indeed, research suggests that teachers rely almost exclusively on practical classroom experience as the main source of their professional knowledge and give little credence to formal educational theory (Blenkin *et al.* 1997: 220). (The lack of effective articulation will be discussed in Part II.) In sum, the focus on the conceptual underpinning of teaching practice is equally as important as the practice itself and their mutual intertwinement. Again, the reason for focusing on its conceptual (CS) foundations stems from the government-led attack on them, which culminated in the various Education Acts and testing arrangements. Finally, Athey notes that, recently,

> [s]everal books have been published with seductive titles that promise information on 'concepts', 'schemas', 'cognition', 'action', 'perception' and 'representation'. Interesting though these books are, they are of doubtful use to teachers of young children because *the emphasis has shifted from the human, biological and psychological aspects of the above concepts towards the logical*. They may lead to advances in information technology that may, at some point, help in the study of human cognition but this stage has not yet been reached.
>
> (Athey 1990: 45, emphasis added)

As the foregoing indicates, I am concerned with the logical properties of the Cultural System. Fundamentally, the morphogenetic approach does not ignore or deny the psychological and quasi-propositional aspects of concrete educational (social) life, for this is an S-C affair. In fact, a focus on the logical properties of the CS would, for some, arouse immediate suspicion that important facets of social life are being truncated at a stroke. First, as Archer (1988) points out, by no means is the logical exhaustive of the meaningful: the reason for abstracting the relational generative properties of the CS is due to the undeniable significance of claims to truth. Second, commentators might wonder about the importance of personality in accounting for the variable responses to the imposition of national testing arrangements. The morphogenetic approach does not wish or aim to nullify any stratum of reality. As will be discussed in Part III, the personality of the 'trouble-shooting' is indispensable in explaining the tempo and extent of her drive. However, this begs the (referential) question of precisely what she could have a drive about. The fact that she enthusiastically endorsed elements of the New Managerialism directs substantive analysis to the temporal priority of the latter's constituents. In abstracting the *sui generis* causal properties of the Cultural System, it is not my intention nor wish to play down the importance of the factors that constitute good teaching practice. In fact, it is precisely the New Managerialist discourse that *does* play down the importance of quasi-propositional and embodied knowledge, since the latter is not readily (or possibly ever) 'translatable' into performance indicators and associated proxies. As we shall see in the Preface to Part III, Professor Robin Alexander's disparaging remarks about so-called 'Primaryspeak' underscore his managerialist co-option, since Primaryspeak is held to be tacit and therefore not 'proper' knowledge that can aid 'good' teaching practice and hence is devalued.

However, the use of ideas in power play is not without its costs or benefits. As Popper argued, 'World Three' has a strong feedback effect upon us. Already we can discern similarities between structure and culture, since structure acts back to condition its makers. The morphogenetic approach provides the methodological specification of the feedback mechanisms in the form of costs–benefits that result from the use of ideas that shape action-contexts for their users because of their embroilment in specific logical relations. In establishing the parallel with Lockwood (see Chapter 1), the Cultural System (CS) is analysed in terms of its *logical consistency*; that is, the degree of consistency between the component parts of culture. What agency does with such cultural emergent properties (or 'World Three' entities) is conceptualised in terms of *causal consensus*; that is, the degree of cultural uniformity produced by the imposition of ideas by one set of people on another via legitimation, manipulation, persuasion, argument, etc. Thus the issue of power becomes marked, though such uniformity is not *ever* implicated in the exercise of power. Cultural uniformity does not necessarily require the exercise of power in the sense of getting people to comply with your wants (cf. Giddens 1979). For example, the government may exercise considerable powers in attempting to eradicate 'institutional racism' within Britain's police forces, but it cannot be assumed that success will follow. On the other hand, Her Majesty's Constabularies may provide adequate learning sessions about the origins and immorality of race ideology, at the end of which police officers are persuaded of its inherent perniciousness and reorient their behaviour accordingly. Such learning processes that promote cultural uniformity could only be termed compliance by rendering the term vacuous (to accept the force of the anti-racist argument is not compliance).

However, in parallel with Lockwood, we can talk about the variable degrees of 'Cultural System integration' and 'Socio-Cultural integration', for the two are not co-variant. In short, the former refers to the emergent relations between the components of culture (the degree of *logical* consistency, which exists independently of human awareness); the latter refers to relationships between people (the extent of *causal* cohesion). Cultural morphogenesis is thus theorised on the same sequential basis as structure: Cultural Conditioning → Socio-Cultural Interaction → Cultural Elaboration.

Cultural conditioning
T^1

                   Socio-cultural interaction
                  T^2 T^3

                                   Cultural elaboration
                                       T^4

The methodological employment of the invariant rules of logic (laws of identity and non-contradiction) to distinguish the non-coextensive levels of reality does not entail that actors are mere clones of Mr Spock. To insist that actors ever live logically would be grossly to distort social (and personal) reality and, indeed, to rob us of that which makes us human, rather than robot-like, beings. The fact that there is an objective contradiction between child-centred philosophy and the implications for its enactment as embodied in SATs may not be recognised by actors, or recognised but ignored and so on. As Buckley argues, 'the human personality can harbor fairly great incompatibilities in ideas, beliefs, attitudes, ideologies, while operating quite effectively' (1967: 16). Therefore, those critics who arraign the morphogenetic approach on the charge of an incipient cognitivism and/or rationalism (see Nellhaus 1998; Shilling 1997) confuse the objective contradictions and complementarities that obtain amongst CS components at any given time with what *people* do with them.

The use of culture is particularly evident in the organisation theory literature, which is currently being raided by education sociologists and education management texts. Jang and Chung's (1997) case study of a corporate renewal initiative in Korea, for example, exemplifies the reality of a generic *lack* of awareness of systemic contradiction: here between Confucianism and Western discourses (Taylorism, managerialism). Jang and Chung interviewed approximately seventy of Samsung's middle managers in order to ascertain the extent of awareness of the contradiction between New Management principles and Confucianism:

> In these interviews, we found that most of the managers are not conscious of whether the stated principles of New Management are contradictory. After the contradictions were pointed out, however, most seemed to agree reluctantly with the argument...In conclusion, Korean workers are not conscious of this contradiction in everyday life, which may produce a considerable amount of confusion for westerners.

(Jang and Chung 1997: 66)

The assumption of 'Western' confusion is attributable to the untenable proposition that East Asian 'logic' asserts that a thing can be both X and non-X (Jang and Chung 1997: 59). Yet how can I be in the process of writing this book and simultaneously not be writing this book? Jang and Chung maintain that Koreans do not take seriously 'the Western-style logic of syllogism (e.g., the rule of contradiction), *at least when they consider management discourses and practices.* Furthermore, Koreans feel comfortable in the coexistence of A and non-A in the same place' (1997: 61, emphasis added). If there is not a universal law of contradiction, how could Jang and Chung conceivably engage in any form of conversation with their interviewees? How, indeed, could they point out the (logical) contradiction between Confucianism and Western management discourse, which their seventy or so interviewees 'reluctantly' understood? Further, 'feeling comfortable' is an S-C phenomenon, independent of the logical properties of the CS. It is instructive that the authors note that the rule of contradiction is not contravened with impunity beyond management practices. Unfortunately they elevate the generic lack of agential awareness of contradiction to a fundamentally (alien) logic axiom that somehow guides organisational activity. They seem to be confusing the subsequent toleration of contradiction with the impossibility of its simultaneous invocation and revocation. In fact, the contradiction in this example is one of contingency (i.e. New Management does not presuppose Confucianism), and may therefore go some way to explaining why it left actors unruffled. Whereas a *necessary* contradiction, to be discussed, entails that its upholders engage in some form of cultural repair work, as and when they recognise, or are made to recognise, the dependency of their ideas on their ideational antithesis.

Nevertheless, Jang and Chung's case study testifies to the salience of ideational aspects of organisational behaviour. What would have been of interest here is if some of Samsung's more ambitious younger members had been aware of the contradiction and whether the systemic fault-line was then exploited and amplified in order to advance their own vested interests. Confucianism provided ideological legitimation for older members of the organisation to remain within the upper echelons of the hierarchy; Western-style management discourse, on the other hand, viewed this as a potential obstacle to profitability and entrepreneurship. In this case study it simply would not have been in the younger members' interests to exploit the fault-line because structurally the cards were stacked against them. However, any downturn in the Korean economy and/or internal restructuring would provide, *ceteris paribus*, the younger members with objective reasons for so doing. In the latter scenario, the hierarchy's defence of its vested interests may result in ideational change in the form of, say, some redefinition to legitimate their vested interests that are structurally rendered vulnerable. In Jang and Chung's case study we witness S-C orderliness and CS disorderliness. CS disorderliness may remain unexploited because of structural factors. Indeed, as will be discussed, whilst cultural morphogenesis may be at the mercy of the conjunction between the two levels, the CS itself nevertheless has properties and powers irreducible to, and independent of, social structure.

Unsticking the glue

It should be clear from the foregoing that the Cultural System is not a tightly-knit web of logical complementarities that provides an inherently 'stabilizing force' (Schein 1992b) enabling any dysfunctional organisation to get back on track. Not only did Buckley acknowledge that actors can harbour contradictions in their daily lives, he also argued that 'so can and do socio-cultural systems embrace wide diversities and incompatibilities while remaining amazingly persistent over long periods' (1967: 16). A major flaw that characterises a significant number of approaches to culture, particularly within organisation theory, is the *a priori* assumption that, on the contrary, culture is that which we all share or hold in common, thereby ensuring social cohesion and solidarity. Anthony exemplifies this position: 'The development of culture is a process natural to and inseparable from the development of communities, in which people come *to share values and beliefs...Communities are cultures*' (Anthony 1994: 50, emphasis added). To Hampden-Turner, the investigation of 'corporate cultures' involves looking at how people behave and discovering the glue that holds together the corporation: 'culture gives continuity and identity to the group...The values within a culture are harmonious' (1990: 21). And to Schein, culture is simply stability and normality, and cannot exist unless there is a group that 'owns' it: culture is held to be embedded in groups – it cannot be determined unless there is a definable set of people with a shared history (1992a: 241; see also Schein 1992b, 1996).

Notwithstanding the conflation of the CS/S-C distinction, the generic *a priori* assumption is empirically (and ontologically) refutable. In fact, Schein, like Parsons, readily accepts the reality of the systemic incompatibility and S-C disorderliness, but swiftly denies any theoretical significance deriving from the latter, assuming that a cognitive drive for order and consistency in the brain will ensure that human groups will gradually learn sets of compatible ideas. However, in *Organizational Culture and Leadership* he documents high levels of confrontation and fighting within and between groups:

> To reach a decision and to get 'buy in', you must convince others of the validity of your idea and be able to defend it against every conceivable argument. This causes the high levels of confrontation and fighting that I observed in groups, but once an idea has stood up to this level of debate and survived, it can then be moved forward and implemented because everyone is now convinced that it is the right thing to do.
>
> (Schein 1992b: 34)

This merely begs the question of the socio-cultural conditions that facilitate the success of one person's (or group's) idea over another's. In the first case-study school, by no means did all staff welcome the changes initiated by the so-called 'trouble-shooting' head. Thus, *contra* Schein, the fact that certain ideas were implemented does not necessarily mean that their implementers were convinced of their efficacy or rightness. Indeed, the majority of organisation/business studies texts on organisational culture are concerned more with the need to impose management precepts on subordinates in order to achieve collective compliance and not with its causal properties and how they gel with agency. In other words, that teachers carried out SATs does not mean they welcomed such ideas and procedures, but generally did so for structural reasons.

If culture is shared, its components consistently interwoven, then how does Schein account for high levels of protracted ideational debate? Logically, Schein's approach precludes cultural morphogenesis (Collins 1998). Such inconsistency derives from culture's anthropological heritage, specifically the empirical findings that document a high degree of S-C orderliness over long periods of time. The generic assumption was transmuted into an unalterable axiom that later reached its zenith in the Parsonian central-value system. In fact, the CS itself was never viewed as conditioning the S-C level as a result of its own *internal* dynamics. In sum, Schein should not confuse a counter-factual (utopian) conception of culture with its current systemic configuration, which *is* characterised by logical consistency and contradiction. Furthermore, referring to subcultures does not solve the problem of heterogeneity or contradiction: organisational ideologies can be divided into fundamental and operative groups (Alvesson 1993: 63). The use of the prefix 'sub' denotes Schein's unremitting *a prioristic* need to render culture an integrative force within organisations, untenably playing down the role of contradiction. Many of the school improvement and management texts in education enthusiastically endorse the Scheinian approach. Roger Smith's *Successful School Management* (1995) talks only of shared values and cohesive social practices. In *Strategic Planning for School Improvement*, Philip Mann writes that school cultures '...are the sum of the *shared beliefs and values*, in short the character and personality (*sic*) of the school. Techniques and developments *need* to be employed that can be used to develop a shared culture within a school' (1996: 173, emphasis added). He then quotes West-Burnham, who asserts that '[c]ulture only has meaning when it is given expression, when it is expressed in tangible forms. The critical difference about culture is that it is those abstractions which are shared, those which are widely held and dominant' (1996: 173). Instructively, Mann adds that '[w]ithout this understanding [i.e., West-Burnham's], *school improvement can be hindered*'.

Yet, if culture consists of shared values and beliefs, why the *need* to develop techniques to ensure this state of affairs? And why talk of their dominance? To assert dominance is to imply the existence of alternatives within the Cultural System, which may indeed be contradictory. Mann's comment about school improvement is evidence of the ideological nature of the imposition of CS properties, in particular managerialist values that emphasise group solidarity and cohesion in order to effect organisational change (be it 'down-sizing' or national testing arrangements). The purpose of this chapter (and Part II of the book) is to argue that notions of organisation culture have no explanatory purchase but themselves constitute the object of theoretical study. Such conceptions talk of 'the power of culture', yet (a) do not theorise about its properties and arguably (b) are mere slogans that practitioners and managers (both inside and outside education) can adopt in their attempts to effect change: at present they are synonymous with business values.[25] This book is about providing explanatory leverage upon the use of specific ideas, how they causally condition their takers and their relationship *vis-à-vis* structure. The irony of a morphogenetic analysis of the interplay of child-centred philosophy and the 'new managerialism' is that the latter's use of the notion of culture is deemed not only inadequate but also subject to immanent (ideological) critique. To recapitulate, (a) the notion that culture only exists when people own it is to conflate its objective nature with its subjective reception (and genesis) and, moreover, (b) to posit consistency as its hallmark is empirically untenable. As Blenkin *et al.* note:

> Words and terms used in defining culture – 'standard practices', 'shared expectations', 'core values', 'regularities', etc. – seem to imply that cultures are heterogeneous entities...This is clearly not true of cultures in general or of school cultures in particular. Admittedly, the nature of schooling is such that teachers do, to a significant extent, share a common occupational culture...But...there are considerable variations both between and within schools in the uniformity of their cultures. *Rather than homogeneous entities, schools are sites where a number of different cultures intersect and interact...*
>
> (1997: 219, emphasis added)

The morphogenetic approach posits the CS/S-C distinction in order to explain what people do with the culture they inherit: how they can or cannot change it because of the conjunction between the structural realm, the irreducible powers of the CS and people's powers of reflection. In other words, it sedulously maintains the distinction between social practices and social structure/cultural practices and cultural structure (i.e., between 'the parts' and 'the people') and the need to examine the interplay *in and between* them over time. In turn, this avoids Hays' methodologically unhelpful (though ontologically correct) comment that '[c]ulture is, in fact, both external and internal, objective and subjective, material and ideal' (1994: 70). Of course, the CS is not ontologically conjoined with the S-C level: to maintain that culture is objective and subjective is simply to recognise that people make it, accept or reject parts of it, change it but are not *ever* the bearers of it. Menter *et al.* write:

> We believe that a significant element of the marketization project lies in its consequences for the work cultures of educational organizations. Thus the fact that we found considerable constraints on the operation of a primary school market in County Town led us to consider the work that the market was doing in reshaping those cultures, particularly the traditional cultures of autonomy in primary schoolwork, and amateurism in its management.
>
> (1997: 15)

Confusion is easily dispelled and analytical leverage gained if attention is focused on the CS/S-C distinction. First, the effects of the market are separate from their ideational origins, legitimation or critique. The reasons for welcoming, tolerating or actively circumventing such effects are almost invariably cultural. Second, that teachers were (or were not) traditionally autonomous is a structural, rather than cultural, phenomenon. The structural conditions for such autonomy were culturally backed up, but this is not an ontological prerequisite. Indeed, the current generic lack of autonomy is quintessentially culturally embodied (in managerialist and anti-progressivist or anti-child-centred discourses), but it does not follow that such structurally induced lack of autonomy requires cultural (ideological) legitimation.[26] Clegg and Billington (1997) argue that culture can be almost entirely divorced from structure, but not from values and ultimately not from behaviour. Whilst they rightly recognise the *sui generis* nature of each and equate culture with values, I would question their subsequent conflation of the CS/S-C levels. They cite Stoll and Fink (1996) who, in their view, correctly distinguish between structure and culture because structures can be changed without a corresponding change in culture (i.e., concurrent structural morphogenesis and cultural morphostasis). They conclude that, structurally,

> ...most schools have staff meetings or senior staff meetings. These are not in themselves particularly indicative of a school's culture. The way people behave within those meetings, what is acceptable or unacceptable, the allocation and the location of powers, and the attitude to conflict and disagreement would be much better indicators of what the culture of the school is like. To begin really to describe a desirable culture we need to look at fundamental values and how they may be manifested; this may have some implications for structures, but would have much more fundamental implications for the nature and quality of the relationships within the school.
>
> (Clegg and Billington 1997: 39)

This resonates well with the morphogenetic approach. A focus on values and particularly on that which is deemed to be acceptable/unacceptable within the school setting attests to the undeniable importance of claims to truth or falsity. Conflict and disagreement quintessentially involve propositions ('that children do not learn in that manner', 'that the head is wrong to treat certain staff like production-line workers', 'that base-line assessments are of no help to us as early years practitioners') and how power is used in the process. That the authors refer to the manifestation of values entails an endorsement of the CS/S-C distinction, whereby values may remain unnoticed or unexplored. Furthermore, they rightly note that CS properties may have implications for structure. Indeed they do, and the next section will theorise about the causal properties of the Cultural System (which exist whether or not actors activate them) and how they mesh with structure and agency.

Cultural conditioning: situational logic and strategic guidance[27]

Our methodological interest here is with those contradictions or complementarities, which, for whatever reasons, people uphold. And as Schein (1992b: 148) rightly noted, not all systemic items are relevant to any given issue the organisation may be facing (and the substantive concerns of the researcher). Explaining the action-context shaped by upholding an incompatible learning proposition does not, for example, entail reference to sexist ideology, since the latter is logically unrelated to it, although it may be contingently linked. Morphogenetic analysis proceeds sequentially, first by examining the relational properties of the systemic items of interest; second, by explaining the consequences for people of holding specific theories or beliefs; and third, by delineating any cultural morphogenesis (which may parallel structural morphogenesis). Thus, like structure, culture has emergent relational properties (of logical contradiction or complementarity) that *act back* to condition their makers. But they only do so when invoked by actors. Morphogenetic analysis of the Samsung case study would primarily focus on the agential invocation of systemic items that mould action-contexts for their invokers. However, in this case, middle managers were unaware of a specific CS contradiction (between Confucianism and Western management discourse), yet even a general awareness, as discussed, may nevertheless have not 'moved' agents for reasons residing in the structural realm.

When agents are 'moved' because of the relational properties between specific CS items, the morphogenetic approach provides explanatory leverage on the mechanisms of constraint or facilitation that condition cultural action and morphogenesis. To reiterate, none of this occurs within a structural vacuum. Necessarily, recourse will be made to the structural realm (initial relative distribution of power; availability of resources...), yet cultural dynamics are not only irreducible to the latter: they may be out of synchrony with the latter, thereby confronting actors with a *third-order* emergent property of constraint or enablement that derives from their incongruence or congruence. However, in maintaining the parallel with Lockwood, an example of cultural 'strain' will now be elucidated.

The situational logic of a 'constraining contradiction'

The necessary yet contradictory (or incompatible) dependence of relations of production on the forces of production, for example, predisposes agential concession or compromise in order to prevent actualisation and amplification of the systemic fault-line. Clearly, the very nature of this internally necessary relation threatens its durability. The structural contradiction between the forces and relations of production represents an obstruction for certain institutional operations and these translate into problem-ridden situations for those involved. The problem here is not so much resolved as contained via various well-known safety nets (unemployment benefit; bonuses; trade-union recognition; personnel managers...).[28] Similarly, this incompatibility has its counterpart in the cultural realm, theorised as a 'constraining contradiction'. A contradiction between A and B is an irreducible property of the CS and only exerts a conditional influence upon agency (the S-C level) if any actor(s) wish to uphold it. In brief, those who uphold A also unavoidably invoke B and with it the logical contradiction. This *necessary* connection is due to the dependence of A on B: without B it cannot work and is only operable in terms of it. At the same time, B constitutes a threat to A because it simultaneously conflicts with it.[29]

The systemic constraint or 'strain' derives from the necessary dependence of A upon B, for agency cannot simply repudiate B yet if B is fully actualised then it threatens to render A untenable. Therefore, the situational logic dictates that, for those who wish non-dogmatically to uphold A, then, since direct resolution is logically impossible, *corrective* repairs must be undertaken. Importantly, contradictions mould problem-ridden situations for actors that they are enjoined to confront *if and when* they realise, or are made to acknowledge, that the proposition(s) they endorse is enmeshed in some inconsistency (Archer 1988: xx). Subsequently, cultural agents have the option of engaging in some form of syncretism, abandoning the cultural project or entering the mire of irrational dogmatism. Archer gives the two examples of the development of Christian beliefs and the advancement of scientific theories:

> Both are cases of birth into a hostile ideational environment, with which they had to cope if they were to survive but which constituted an unending threat to their survival. To claim that both surface(d) in inhospitable surroundings is not like saying they had the misfortune of bad 'home backgrounds'…for without their respective environments we cannot conceive of them at all. Thus Christianity had to tangle with Antiquity because it emerged enmeshed in it, just as scientific propositions have to tackle observational data because the (f)act of stating a hypothesis entangles it in them. The key feature shared by these disparate instances of constraining contradictions is that both are concerned with the relationships between *ideas* (with a belief in relation to other beliefs, with a theory in relation to other theories)…
>
> (Archer 1988: 149–50, original emphasis)

Briefly, the situational logic generated by the 'constraining contradiction' generically results in the sinking of differences to achieve unification. Such ideational syncretism can follow three paths (and not in any necessary order):

(1)   A ← B, that is, correcting B so that it becomes consistent with A;

(2)   A ←→ B, that is, correcting both A and B so they become mutually consistent;

(3)   A → B, that is, correcting A so that it becomes consistent with B.

Clearly, for proponents of A, path (1) is the preferred option. Any corrective repairs in order to 'stick' (or be accepted) at the Socio-Cultural level must gel with the extant distribution of structured vested interests. I will crudely sketch out the determinate effects of a constraining contradiction by reference to child-centred philosophy and its more recent critics.[30] A fuller examination will be provided in Part II.

In brief, child-centred philosophy has its origins in Rousseau. The ideas contained within *Emile* (1762) have been developed notably by Pestallozi (1894), Dewey (1897, 1900) and Kilpatrick (1916, 1918). At the core of their respective contributions to systematisation is the view that education should reflect the nature of the child; that childhood is not a defective version of adulthood and that what is to be learned should be determined by an understanding of the child's intrinsic nature at each stage of his or her development.

In underscoring the 'World Three' nature of child-centred philosophy, Darling notes that in Britain the influence of these thinkers 'beyond the world of ideas was for a long time very limited' (Darling 1994: 2). Initially, constraining (or competitive) contradictions may be concealed by a variety of Socio-Cultural 'containment strategies' and the temporal extent of their success is a matter of socio-cultural contingency (see Archer 1988, Chapter 7). Thus, for example, when *Emile* was published it was burnt on the streets of Paris. However, the influence of child-centred philosophy can be traced to its official recognition in the Hadow Report (1931) on Primary Education. Yet it was not until the establishment of the Teachers' Training Colleges, legitimated and buttressed by the Plowden Report (1967), that the requisite fertile soil for its practical implementation was provided. It was recognised that a class is not a homogeneous entity of Durkheim's indeterminate material but rather a heterogeneous collection of individuals who are not all the same and who therefore work at different learning speeds that require careful monitoring.

Unlike the pre-war conditions that acted as negative (morphostatic) feedback loops precluding practical fruition of child-centred philosophy, the post-war period of full employment, *inter alia*, provided the socio-cultural context that was required. The Plowden Report (1967) underscored the benefits to be had from the study of the ways in which children grow, and endorsed an approach to primary education that focuses on children *qua* children rather than on some long-distance end product (Darling 1994).

> ...activity and experience, both physical and mental, are often the best means of gaining knowledge and acquiring facts. This is more generally recognised today but still needs to be said. We would certainly not wish to undervalue knowledge and facts [CS level], but facts are best retained when they are used and understood, when right attitudes to learning are created, when children learn to learn. Instruction in many primary schools continues to bewilder children because it outruns their experience.
>
> (CACE 1967: 195)

Furthermore, the Plowden Report expressed palpable dissatisfaction with a subject-based curriculum: '...knowledge does not fall into neatly separate compartments...[and] children's learning does not fit into subject categories' (CACE 1967: 203). For reasons of brevity, the socio-economic conditions that have subsequently shaped the counter-reaction will not be dissected. Suffice it to say, *pro tem.*, that child-centred philosophy now has its antithesis embodied in the National Curriculum, SATs examinations and league tables. However, the critique by university-based philosophers of education is exemplary of the syncretic repair work engendered by the unleashing of a constraining contradiction undertaken by Peters (1958, 1963, 1964, 1967, 1969), Hirst and Peters (1970), Hirst (1974), Dearden (1968, 1969, 1976) and all three together (1975), during the 1960s and 1970s. The salient point here is that the latter are constrained to deal with child-centred philosophy in order to advance their defence of, *inter alia*, a subject-based curriculum, not because they wish to juxtapose what they believe to be an irrefutable critique, but because in the very process of providing their critique they ineluctably invoke child-centred philosophy, which simultaneously threatens to undermine it. Darling (1994) has nicely documented the various illogical ruses developed by Peters *et al.* However, each author could not function without the metaphysical claims *vis-à-vis* children. Indeed, Peters (logically) could not escape enmeshment in child-centred philosophy: 'It was understandable about forty years ago that reformers should proclaim that "education is growth" or that children should be encouraged to learn from experience; *for there was a great deal wrong, both morally and psychologically*' (1969: 1, emphasis added).

We should thus not be at all surprised that Peters and his colleagues swiftly proceed to relegate this acknowledged importance to the historical dustbin – a mere fad that has since been supplanted. The logic of the constraining contradiction enjoins that proponents of anti-child-centred thinking must not invoke its hostile ideational environment *in its entirety* yet cannot avoid invoking some aspects of it – hence the acknowledgement of the psychological and moral merits of child-centred philosophy and its simultaneous relegation to that of historical fad. Of course, the indubitable importance of the psychological aspects of child development cannot be acknowledged and simultaneously dismissed as something of mere historical interest. Any test or public examination, for example, presupposes the very cognitive basis on which people learn.

During a tape-recorded interview, the 'trouble-shooting' head maintained that there 'doesn't have to be' a contradiction between child-centred learning and the secreted reductionist philosophy of SATs. On five separate occasions the head postponed the tape-recorded interview, despite a firm promise well before the first date was arranged. The head was defensive and reluctant to address many of the issues on which I wanted to focus during the interview. I tried almost in vain to return to the contradiction, eventually being dealt what she considered a resounding blow that would complete that part of the interview. Her 'blow' consisted of an attempted A (SATs) ← B (child-centred learning) syncretic manoeuvre: she asserted quite simply that 'You need to *redefine* what you mean by child-centred learning...' (emphasis added). Regrettably this was said near the end of the 50-minute interview and consequently I was unable to pursue the matter any further. Nevertheless, it was when she was forced to recognise the *necessary* contradiction that she was conditioned to engage in corrective repair. Of course, here the head followed the preferred path (1). I had hoped to force her down path (3), where correction of A takes place in order to make it consistent with B. That there is a *necessary* contradiction is due to the inescapable fact that examinations presuppose the cognitive nature of their subjects, in this case children. Yet the technicist-cum-managerialist underpinning of SATs denies this necessary presupposition yet cannot operate without it.[31]. Hence the emphasis upon its *secreted* reductionism, because implicitly it cannot avoid making assumptions about the cognitive processes by which children are able to undertake such examinations (and do so successfully), yet wants to eschew any discussion about child cognition. Indeed, the later systematisation of child-centred philosophy was precisely to unmask this implicit presupposition and ultimately to negate it. As already discussed, such negation provided the hostile ideational environment for Peters *et al.* However, if SATs had been explicitly grounded in anti-child-centred propositions about the cognitive development of children, then we would be dealing with a *competitive* contradiction between the avowed philosophical underpinning of the tests and child-centred assessment approaches. This is not made clear by the interview excerpt with the head. In fact, what should have been made clear to the head during interview is that SATs disclaim the very basis on which they make sense; that is, they deny the tenability of offering *any* substantive propositions about the cognitive processes by which children learn. SATs are the product of the New Managerialism, whereby the means are separated from the ends. To reiterate, the philosophy of SATs attempts to deny the 'means' of its approach yet necessarily cannot avoid it.[32]

In both schools, the majority of staff was aware of the contradiction between the child-centred philosophy that underpinned their daily work (any theory–practice inconsistency is not at issue here) and the thrust of the secreted SATs philosophy. SATs philosophy, *inter alia*, is part and parcel of the 'performance indicator' disease that since the mid-1980s has infected almost every nook and cranny of the public sector. The problem with SATs is its reductionism, by-passing the cognitive processes by which children learn and develop. Thus, to Cutler and Waine, '[t]he intangible character of outcomes means that measures are always dependent upon constructs, which attempt to generate proxies or substitutes for the outcome. The central difficulty, therefore, lies in the fact that the proxy can be criticised for failing to capture the character of the outcome' (1994: 35). As they rightly point out, how do we measure whether 'quality of life' has been improved and, if knowledge has been developed, how do we determine whether we are adjusting to the goals of school pupils and discover whether our curriculum is appropriate? As Ball (1990) argues, the parameters of OFSTED (whose essential remit is to assess the 'effectiveness' of schools in improving SATs scores) operate judgementally within the input–output logic of the commodity form and displace and *exclude* other criteria of judgement. For these teachers, the government imposition of the National Curriculum and yearly SATs constitutes a stringent obstruction to what they hold primary teaching to be about. Certainly, they accept the need for a structured framework, but one within which child-centred philosophy can be enacted, not stultified, subject of course to the contextual limits provided by the number of children and limited resources. Yet for the deputy head in the second school, the National Curriculum and SATs, despite some minor limitations, were welcomed. This underscores the fact that socio-cultural properties are not constraining or enabling in abstract isolation. Whether they are constraining depends on their incongruence with the aspirations and wishes of the actors concerned. Thus, structural or cultural constraints are relational terms *vis-à-vis* actors. As Blenkin *et al.* succinctly put it, '[w]hat is a frustrating constraint for one teacher is a golden opportunity for another' (1997: 226).

For most staff, then, the philosophical–practical implications of SATs constitute a fundamentally unwelcome third-order emergent property, exacerbated by the systemically incongruent second-order emergent property between central government and the school (restructuring and overloading of teachers' roles via imposition of the National Curriculum, per capita funding arrangements, League Tables, etc.). If we want to theorise about how different teachers deal with objective (un)activated cultural systemic properties, then we have to adhere to a working distinction between the causal and the logical. If the 'trouble-shooting' head in the first school had confronted a staff meeting in which a member of the Senior Management

Team pushed for a more child-centred approach in developing the School's OFSTED-imposed Action Plan, then without the acknowledgement of autonomous logical relations impinging upon agency, we would forfeit an explanatory account of the subsequent use of power to deflect such an initiative.

The situational logic of a 'competitive contradiction'

In direct contrast to the 'constraining contradiction', the invocation of A does not invoke some B and is therefore not a matter of systemic constraint. The existence of opposing groups or individuals championing different ideas is an essential precondition of a competitive contradiction. Its accentuation is an S-C affair and basically its logic is one that predisposes *elimination* as opposed to the syncretic *correction* enjoined by the constraining contradiction. As Archer puts it, '[b]ecause partisans of A and B are unconstrained by any dependence between these items, there is nothing which restrains their combativeness for they have everything to gain from inflicting maximum damage on one another's ideas in the course of competition' (1988: 240). Exemplars of competitive contradictions are, of course, ideologies and their use in concealing vested sectional interests.

The recent literature on the changing nature of personnel management is an interesting example of the way in which ideational contradiction has resulted in a structurally conditioned stalemate, currently embodied in that ideational mélange called 'human resource management'. As Legge has rightly argued, '[b]oth the activity and personnel specialists are driven by contradictions that promote ambiguity of action. The chief contradictions are those embedded in capitalism' (1995: 10). The role of personnel manager exemplifies the situational logic of concession generated by the existence of the structural (necessary) incompatibility; in this case, the generic incompatibility (or contradiction) between the forces and relations of production. Historically, in providing a legitimatory gloss on their role, personnel managers have invoked 'collectivist' ideas, reflecting their 'caring' or paternalist approach. They were endowed with the capacity to override the sectional interests of individual employers. This structured capacity derived from the successive legislative enactments prior to the Second World War that were designed to protect employees. Of course, the issue is not one of benign protection but rather one of mediating the inherent contradiction of capitalism, ensuring unimpeded extraction of surplus value by obscuring the commodity status of labour. The ideas used to buttress and legitimate the role of these 'caring' mediators whilst contradicting individualist market ideas did not depend upon the latter for their agential invocation, in contrast to the constraining contradiction. In other words, collectivist ideas do not automatically summon up individualist ones, which in turn unavoidably threaten to engulf them.

Structurally, those within organisations who abhorred the paternalism of personnel managers were unable to banish them. Contracts *had* to be negotiated (or 'seen' to be negotiated, thereby ensuring a role for the personnel manager, however attenuated or inflated). Personnel managers had structured vested interests in supporting trade-union *de jure* rights and obligations, at the same time remaining committed to the goals and aims of capitalist organisations. Thus, '[a]ny mediatory role, as with the proverbial Janus, runs the risk of giving an impression of two-facedness, with attendant loss of credibility' (Legge 1995: 19). But prior to the inauguration of the Thatcher years, one side of the face could be accentuated at the expense of the other since, structurally, the conditions were especially conducive – relative full employment being one of the obvious key factors. However, the Thatcher years of recession – of the 'enterprise culture' – and the substantial truncation of employment legislation have combined to force personnel managers to show the other cheek, so to speak. In fact, both cheeks are often shown, leading commentators (Legge 1989, 1995; Blyton and Turnbull 1992) to underscore its contradictory nature, as reflected in the generic inconsistency between so-called 'hard' and 'soft' versions of human resource management.

Here, the contradictory items cannot be eliminated because otherwise, as Guest has noted, personnel managers would effectively render themselves redundant. As he puts it, 'if HRM is to be taken seriously, personnel managers must give it away' (1987: 51) since it contradicts the latter's traditional collectivist underpinning. It is precisely because they cannot be eliminated, due to the extant structural context that gives the 'upper hand' to senior management, that the (logically) inconsistent approach of 'human resource management' has been constructed. Critics such as Legge (1995) and Blyton and Morris (1992) remain sceptical about HRM's survival given its mutually inconsistent premises (which centre round the three related issues of individualism versus cooperation; commitment versus flexibility; and a 'strong culture' versus adaptability). However, at the S-C level the contradictory mélange of HRM sticks at present because other actors (viz., middle managers), whilst structurally predisposed towards elimination, currently need to buttress their own precarious positions and thus join in the unholy alliance in maintaining the essential rhetoric of HRM.

Finally, any package that is bundled together for purposes of structural change (or *ex post facto* ideological legitimation) does not perforce entail logical coherence. Grace notes that '[t]he New Right populist project appropriated very effectively and very skilfully the rhetoric of democratic accountability in schooling and sought to integrate this with the discipline of market accountability – *despite the many contradictions which result from this conjunction*' (1995: 25, emphasis added). The issue then becomes one of who recognises the contradiction (i.e., the extent of cultural discursive penetration) and what they subsequently do (or can do) about it. Democratic accountability does not presuppose market accountability in order for it to work *qua* corpus of propositions, and thus we are dealing (at the CS level) with two contradictory items, which, when perceived by actors, may be accorded social salience by opposing groups in order to advance their divergent interests (at the S-C level). As and when opposing groups accentuate such systemic contradiction, the situational logic of the competitive contradiction comes into play, i.e. elimination. Indeed, one of the containment strategies attempted by the Tory Government during competition (between 'traditionalist' and 'progressive' teaching methods) was dismissal-by-devaluation, as Archer puts it. Yet the latter are not internally homogeneous: at the CS level progressive theories are not tightly woven logical complementarities (simply compare Piaget and Vygotsky). However, the S-C import of such heterogeneity will be addressed in Part II.

Culture and managerialism

Clegg and Billington write that managerialism has some claims on being aware of
the importance of the nature of 'organisational culture':

> As the proponents of managerialism are confronted by the limitations of their
> incantations they seek new avenues to explore. Culture is seen as such a new
> avenue. Organizational culture is, ironically, a feature of organizations that
> may have been instrumental in exposing the limitations of managerialism. The
> story could be told about how the theories of managerialism were entirely
> correct, but the culture of the organization prevented the ideas from taking
> hold: in effect people were not ready for the initiatives...The Chief Inspector's
> frustration about the apparent unwillingness of teachers to engage in a debate
> about teaching strategies was attributed to the particular culture of the primary
> school...What we are again presented with is the desire to manipulate the
> culture to achieve particular ends and, for some, these ends would not be desir-
> able.
>
> (Clegg and Billington 1997: 36–7)

Where they write that culture has been instrumental in exposing the limitations
of managerialism, they are talking about the existence of CS items that generally
have informed practices in primary (and other) schools and that contradict managerialist propositions. Parts II and III of this book will explore the genesis and impact
of the new managerialism and how two sets of primary school staff mediate it.
Precisely how they mediate is necessarily complex and requires recourse to anterior
socio-cultural conditioning (Part II). It is not specific items of the Cultural System
alone that frustrate Chris Woodhead (at one time the Government's Chief
Inspector of Schools), but rather the Socio-Cultural (S-C) use of CS properties in
circumventing the imposition of contradictory CS items and concomitant structural
arrangements. The manipulation of culture is better theorised about in terms of
attempts at the S-C level (involving use of structural power) to impose structural
change via CS properties that themselves possess dynamics with which agency is
conditioned to deal (i.e., objective contradictions and the situational logics they
entail). The usefulness of the CS/S-C distinction is indicated by its ability to
pinpoint objective contradictions and/or complementarities that may remain unnoticed, or noticed but unexploited, because of factors residing in the structural realm.
Even here, such structural factors may be unperceived or partially understood and
the task of the morphogenetic researcher is to identify reasons, where possible, for
partial discursive penetration (of either or both realms): namely, how the properties
and dynamics of structure and culture mesh with the irreducible reflective powers
of agency.

Again, such objective socio-cultural properties are not readily transparent to
actors. In some, especially post-modernist, quarters, the morphogenetic approach's
identification of objective emergent cultural properties and the logical relations
among them independently of human agency would be deemed untenable in its
putative 'privileging' of the researcher over the subject(s) whom s/he is studying. Yet

such 'privileging' is part and parcel of the nature of critical social analysis. To return to the earlier example of the precarious economic position of black workers, it may be that in times of recession, race ideologies are not causally influential. If critical sociology cannot make claims as to this objective state of affairs independently of such workers' beliefs or theories, then its status as critical interrogator is erased at a stroke. There is a difference between objectivity *per se* and our *fallible* claims to know it. Furthermore, epistemic fallibility does not mean that *all* truth-claims are ever subject to falsification (see Norris 1996). Grace writes that

> ...[t]here will be major dilemmas for those headteachers whose conceptions of educational leadership have involved giving priority to moral and spiritual values or to professional, cultural and human values. Faced with the calculus of market imperatives in contemporary English schooling such values may be easily marginalised. On the other hand, some headteachers *will see no necessary opposition* between these values and the new trading conditions for schools.
>
> (Grace 1995: 43)

But objectively there is a contradiction between the values of the market and the professional values of primary school teaching. That specific heads may not perceive it is an S-C affair – i.e., primarily a psychological one – and is independent of the CS. Conceivably, it may be that certain heads, supportive of the new managerialism in education, are aware of the contradiction but would deny its existence or salience because of the S-C counter-reaction that would emanate from staff.

New managerialism

Yet what is (new) 'managerialism'? In fact, we have not been told about the more precise constituent propositions of 'child-centred philosophy'. The nature and genesis of child-centred philosophy will be addressed in Part II. Now, many approaches to managerialism tend to conflate the CS/S-C distinction. In some ways, this is unavoidable since much social scientific (and everyday) discourse uses portmanteau concepts (like the generic term 'social structure') as a convenient form of shorthand. Indeed, as with the catch-all 'child-centred philosophy' there is a world (in the Popperian sense) of difference between the corpus of ideas that constitute managerialism and how they are used, modified or unexploited *in practice*. That is to say, we must stick to the CS/S-C distinction in theorising about the impact of (new) managerialism on education. Put another way, we need to distinguish analytically between structural emergent properties, cultural emergent properties and agential practices: the former are temporally prior to the practices that embody them and any subsequent change constitutes a new conditioning context that post-dates such practices.

Everyday talk of management tends to conjure up the image of suited wo/men in plush offices earning above-average salaries, making high-level decisions and possessing near-untrammelled power over their subordinates. Alternatively, talk of *the* management is taken to be synonymous with bosses in general. Consequently, any reference to ideas, their material grounding and their use in power play is played down or unexplored. However, more sociologically minded approaches to management theorise about the explicit (or secreted) propositions that underlie managers' practices and their structurally conditioned attempts to impose and/or enforce them. Exworthy and Halford (1999) note that, traditionally, the public sector has been characterised by Taylorist management, in other words that it is bureaucratic, inflexible and mainly concerned with control and cost cutting. By contrast,

> [t]he *new* managerialism emphasized innovation, creativity and empowerment. The new managers are policy 'entrepreneurs', highly motivated, resourceful, and able to shift the frame of reference beyond the established norms and procedures. In addition, the new managers enable staff to make their own contributions and, in doing so, to generate greater identification with, and commitment to, the corporate success of the organization.
>
> (Exworthy and Halford 1999: 6)

Drawing upon Pollitt (1990), Flynn argues that the new managerialism embodies a number of different assumptions and values, which are assumed to be unproblematic and include 'the idea of progress through greater economic productivity, technological innovation, worker compliance and managers' freedom to manage. It is a diffuse ideology which privileges commercial models of organization and management practice and insists that these can (and must) be transplanted to public sector services' (1999: 27). The *idea* of progress through worker compliance, technological innovation and so on is ontologically distinct from its ideological nature, however, which is an S-C affair, since *qua* CS denizens, such ideas remain simply ideas, until activated by actors in pursuit of their sectional interests. Flynn rightly differentiates managerialism *qua* assumptions and values from managerialism *qua* practice. Indeed, following procedures, establishing commitment and worker compliance are S-C phenomena. Morphogenetic analysis is interested in the propositional use of managerialist ideas that underpin public sector restructuring and/or *ex post facto* legitimation of structural change. This is because we can then identify the conditions that maintain for change or stability and the situational logics into which actors become embroiled. However, it is not being suggested that the efficacy of managerialist ideas is dependent upon their propositional manifestation. The changes brought about by the 'trouble-shooting' head in Southside were underpinned by managerialist ideas, yet such ideas were never publicly defended *qua* propositions. This does not vitiate the analytical bite of the morphogenetic approach. Instead, it begs the analytical question of why actors did not request (propositional) defence or clarification of the changes enacted by the head, in turn focusing attention on the structural realm and the extent of agential discursive penetration.

Equally, Ball (1994) distinguishes between management as theory (CS) and management as practice (S-C). Furthermore, he argues that it is not a unitary whole.

> There are at least two, perhaps three, discourses of management in play here within the reform process in the UK. They have different effects. One is what might be called 'professional management'. This is articulated around a development planning perspective and relates particularly to the production of school management plans...it is a 'clean' (context-free) management insofar as it treats the school in isolation and concentrates upon the business of *education* rather than education as *business*...It divorces management practices from values and from politics...It is technically oriented, rational and apolitical...The second discourse I would term 'financial management'. It begins from a concern with balancing the books, with maximizing the budget, and with doing educationally what can be afforded. This is for many practitioners the unacceptable face of management...There is a close relationship between the discourse of financial management and the third discourse, which I call 'entrepreneurial management'. Here the market is to the fore; image, hype and PR, and competition, diversification and income generation are prominent in the managers' lexicon.
>
> (Ball 1994: 67–8)

At the S-C level, Ball points out that these discourses are not mutually exclusive. At the CS level, however, '[t]here are contradictions...between versions 1 and 2, and in ethos and method between versions 1 and 3' (1994: 69). What is of interest here is whether (a) heads use a mélange of contradictory CS items, and, if they do, (b) whether other actors perceive the contradiction and consequently amplify it. Even at the classroom level, it is widely recognised that teachers proffer inconsistent premises for their behaviour, and even when consistency characterises their approach, their actual practice belies it. However, Ball maintains that schools differ in terms of the extent to which any of these discourses become 'dominant and pervasive. The possibilities here are very much related to a school's history and market position' (1994: 71). Whilst discourses may be dominant, one must remember that because people uphold specific CS items at the expense of others (crudely, child-centred versus traditional), other S-C factors may preclude their practical realisation. Ball's point about the efficacy of S-C action in upholding CS items and concomitant practices against S-C encroachment or domination being related to the school's history and market position is an important factor *vis-à-vis* my two case-study schools, as will be discussed.

Let us now examine more closely the nature of the new managerialism. Given that one significant dimension of the reconstruction of the welfare state has been the process of managerialisation, it is hardly surprising that public sector management was one of the significant growth areas of employment and education during the 1980s and 1990s. A variety of studies has discussed the emergence or rise of what is commonly known as the New Public Management (NPM) (e.g., Butcher 1995; Dunleavy and Hood 1994; Ferlie *et al.* 1996; Hood 1991). This book represents both a theoretical and substantive contribution to such literature. Clarke *et al.* (2000) note that the NPM is usually taken to refer to some combination of processes and values that was developed in the 1980s as a distinctively different approach to the coordination of publicly provided services. Although there are variations, typical characteristics ascribed to the NPM include:

- Attention to outputs and performance rather than inputs;
- Organisations being viewed as chains of low-trust relationships, linked by contracts or contractual type processes. The separation of purchaser and provider or client and contractor roles within formerly integrated processes or organisations;
- Breaking down large-scale organisations and using competition to enable 'exit' or 'choice' by service users;
- Decentralisation of budgetary and personal authority to line managers. (Taken from Clarke *et al.* 2000: 6).

However, Clarke *et al.* (2000) note that such views of the NPM have some limitations. Among these is

> ...a tendency to a rather over-unified or over-coherent view of the NPM as a form of co-ordination. For example, Ferlie and his colleagues have suggested that a singular view of the NPM disguises the existence of four overlapping, but separate, models of the NPM. They distinguish between the 'Efficiency Drive', 'Downsizing and Decentralization', 'In Search of Excellence' and 'Public Service Orientation' models...There are other difficulties, too. The NPM is too often treated as a coherent whole of global significance and force despite the fact that comparative studies have tended to show wide national divergences in reform programmes, albeit often utilizing the language – or discourse – of New Public Management as a means of legitimation and institutionalisation...
>
> (Clarke *et al.* 2000: 7)

However, Clarke *et al.* rightly imply that confusion surrounding the status of NPM is immediately dispelled if we resist conflating or eliding the CS and S-C levels. As they point out, many examinations of the NPM conflate the politics and practice of public service reform, treating the NPM as though it has been installed as the only mode of coordination. Such examinations also conflate the descriptive and normative aspects. Instead, Clarke *et al.* suggest that the impact of NPM *qua* ideas has been 'more uneven, contested and complex than can be accounted for in a view of a simple shift from public administration to New Public Management or from hierarchies to markets or networks [at the S-C level]' (2000: 7). Furthermore, they argue that accounts of the New Public Management tend to focus on management *qua* activity and occupational group, in turn occluding the more complex social, political and economic organisational changes. Indeed, when talking about managerialism, we are talking about more than just 'the work of managers', for managers can and do work in a variety of ways, depending upon what they are asked to do, which necessarily includes the value and political framework within which they manage (Bottery 2000: 62).

Thus, Clarke *et al.* rightly argue that a more productive starting-point is to recognise, at the outset, that management is not a neutral, technical activity; any such invocation of neutrality lies at the core of managerialism. However, for our purposes, what is particularly fruitful theoretically is their distinction between managerialisation and managerialism, which maps neatly onto the CS/S-C distinction. Indeed, their reservations about the use of the term NPM stem from the generic conflation of the CS and S-C levels. The utility of retaining NPM *qua* shorthand derives precisely from adhering to the CS/S-C distinction. As they put it, 'we have tended, on the whole, to explore processes of *managerialisation* and the cluster of beliefs and orientations best described as *managerialism*' (2000: 8, original emphasis). They go on to write that managerialism

> ...defines a set of expectations, values and beliefs. It is a normative system [CS] concerning what counts as valuable knowledge, who knows it, and who is empowered to act in what ways as a consequence [S-C]. Indeed, a central issue in the managerialisation of public services has been the concerted effort to displace or subordinate the claims of professionalism. It can no longer be assumed that 'professionals know best'; rather we are invited to accept that managers 'do the right thing'...we see managerialism both as a 'general ideology'...that legitimises and seeks to extend the 'right to manage' and as composed of overlapping, and sometimes competing, discourses that present distinctive versions of 'how to manage'. Its natural home has been the corporate capitalist organization that provides the reference point for claims about 'behaving in a businesslike way'.
>
> (Clarke *et al.* 2000: 9)

Clarke *et al.* are quite right not to assume that managerialism is composed of a web of congruent ideational items. As we have already seen, 'human resource management' is a mixture of contradictory ideas ('soft' versus 'hard'). Now, with the latter, the contradiction is competitive, not constraining, in nature. I want to reiterate the constraining contradiction that is the (new) managerialism in education. Crucial to my argument here is the fact that the latter expunges, in Taylorist fashion, humanity.

Taylorism: the Revised Code of 1862 and payment by results...déja vu

It was mentioned earlier that, traditionally, Taylorist management has characterised the public sector, which was contrasted with the new managerialism. It must be emphasised here that the new managerialism does not dispense with Taylorism. On the contrary, in education especially, managerialist restructuring is quintessentially Taylorist: the 'new' inflection must not detract us from this. The system of payment by results that was introduced in 1862 represents a chilling precursor. Essentially, it consisted of a payment to inspected elementary schools for each child, one-third of which was for attendance; the remainder was a payment that was reduced by one-third in each of the three areas of reading, writing and arithmetic if the child failed to satisfy the inspector. The children had to be presented for an examination in set 'standards', and the regulations also provided for further grant reductions if the buildings were inadequate, or there were insufficient pupil teachers (Silver 1994: 32). At the same time – and in a manner congruent with OFSTED philosophy – each school's religious and moral tone were to be taken into account by the inspectors. Silver quotes Fitch, who wrote in 1901 that payment by results is 'a business-like and sensible plan for apportioning the public grant among school managers, and…a satisfactory assurance to the taxpayer that he was receiving a good educational equivalent for his outlay' (Silver 1994: 32). This quotation could readily have been taken from comments made during the past decade. Indeed, as with the Education Reform Act, there was strong opposition to the system of inspection, which proved equally ineffectual. Matthew Arnold, one of the inspectors, rejected the payment-by-results system on the grounds that it would result in a mechanistic preparation of children for examination.

The crucial question is whether such mechanistic preparation was an unintended consequence or a necessary constituent of the philosophy underpinning the payment-by-results system. In fact, the mechanistic ways in which children were taught as a result of the payment-by-results system were inextricably underpinned by managerialism. As Fitch makes quite clear, the focus was on examination results, which were held to be attainable independently of any reference to, or consideration of, children. The impetus was on what should be achieved in relation to a specific amount of cash spent; as if a cash-value could be readily placed on a child's achievement of a specified number of examination passes. The payment-by-results system thus predates Ball's argument about the commodification of education brought about by the 1988 Education Act, since here the system likewise excluded the human element; namely that children were (and are) part of the examination process. The fact that a retired Inspector of Schools for the London County Council, G A Christian, wrote in 1922 of the reactionary influence of the 1862 Revised Code, which resulted in 'at best a pernicious influence on education', is attributable to the technicist or technocratic philosophy of the Revised Code. A recent former Head of the Education and Equal Opportunities Department at the National Union of Teachers (NUT), Professor Michael Barber, maintains that a technocratic approach to the school curriculum involves a narrow view of learning. *Vis-à-vis* the technocratic nature of the pre-Dearing national curriculum, Barber writes:

There are many recent examples of technocratic influence on the curriculum. The GCSE [General Certificate of Secondary Education] general and subject criteria are strongly influenced by this approach. However, the best example is the pre-Dearing National Curriculum which set down in great detail, through Programmes of Study, Attainment Targets and Statements of Attainment, what both the content and proposed outcomes of the curriculum at every level should be. The most enduring image of the pre-Dearing National Curriculum

> – a primary teacher ticking boxes – is a testament to technocracy gone wild...*It seems likely that, as long as we have a national curriculum, an element of the technocratic approach will be with us. It has, however, been subjected to some important criticisms. One is that it purports to be value-free. In other words, it is an approach to planning a curriculum, but it assumes agreement about the goals of the curriculum.*
>
> (Barber 1996: 13, emphasis added)

First, it is a *non sequitur* to assume that an element of the technocratic approach is an ineluctable accompaniment of any (national) curriculum. Indeed, as will be discussed in Chapter 5, the initial Task Group on Assessment and Testing's (TGAT) proposals submitted to the Secretary of State for Education were designed specifically to avoid any narrow technicist approach to the curriculum. Second, and more important, the 1988 Act, as with the Revised Code of 1862, did not purport to be value-free: it was value-free in that, *inter alia*, values about children, more specifically about the 'good life', could not be entertained because of its managerialist underpinning. The criteria of managerialism are palpable in the Revised Code: efficiency, productivity and cost-effectiveness ('value for money' in OFSTED terminology).

We will return to the theme of accountability in Part II. What needs to be emphasised here is that the technicist core remains firmly in place; the 'newness' of current managerialist approaches stems from its additional accentuation of 'entrepreneurship', the 'right to manage' and the maximisation of group commitment to 'total quality'. As we have seen, Ball distinguishes between the business of education (essentially an intra-school affair) and education as business. The latter is technicist in orientation and underpins the SATs-cum-League-Table philosophy. Clearly, the payment-by-results system is managerialist in Ball's latter sense of education as business. The precursory effects of the National Curriculum and testing arrangements are reflected in Silver's reference to an interview with a teacher conducted by the Cross Commission in 1887 on the working of the elementary education Acts. The teacher commented that the payment-by-results system had 'a very harassing effect upon the teachers' and that the teaching of children was 'very much pleasanter' prior to the Code. At the same time, the Code encouraged such fraudulent activities as fixing attendance figures. Contemporaneously, rumours of SATs cheating in my case-study area abounded in 1997 and, indeed, were to be found throughout England and Wales. The 'trouble-shooting' head in my first school was especially keen to develop a variety of figures, ranging from truancy and graffiti levels to the number of parents who attended Parents' Evenings.

The progenitor of Taylorism is Frederick W Taylor. Taylor was the founder of 'scientific management'. He is well known for his book *Principles of Scientific Management* (1911). He began his working life as an apprentice and proceeded to become chief engineer of a large steel company. He was a member and later president of the American Society of Mechanical Engineers. Taylor assumed *a priori* that people are intrinsically lazy and will thus attempt to get away with doing the minimum amount of work. Taylor was opposed to any form of group activity, maintaining that group involvement resulted in a decline in productivity. The reasoning behind this stemmed from his belief that self-interest was an overriding human characteristic.

For Taylor, work tasks should be well planned in advance and the worker should be given written instructions. He operated bonus schemes and was not in favour of trades unions, mainly because he believed that the principles of scientific management would considerably attenuate conflict between employees and management. Moreover, he advocated authoritarian methods of management. As Clegg and Dunkerley note, Taylorism offered the most thorough de-humanisation of work ever seen under capitalism:

> ...Taylor presents the individual in the same way as he would an item of machinery. The worker thereby is perceived as a means of production. In just the same way that management's task is to maximize output from capital equipment, under the principles of scientific management it is also part of the managerial task to maximize the output of the human component. Pursuing this analogy, in the same way that there is no psychological involvement with capital equipment, under the principles of scientific management, similarly there is none with human assets; as machines are fuelled by coal, gas or petrol, so humans are regarded as being fuelled by money...
>
> (1980: 96)

This applies with equal force to the current examination and league table regime, which focuses solely on the 'output', negating the 'input'; that is, the children and their intrinsic cognitive and emotional capacities. Moreover, the imposition of competition via league tables enjoins that children's different and distinctive cognitive capacities are ignored at a stroke, since the pressure to reach high scores ultimately means that any actual understanding (or lack of) be at best played down. The salient point here is that the 1862 Code was underpinned by the same managerialist considerations that currently underpin the National Curriculum and testing arrangements, whereby children *qua* children are negated (yet transcendentally cannot be). The payment-by-results system, like the LMS and league table structures, necessarily excludes reference to the human (child) element as part of their ideational underpinning: the rationale focuses on matters pecuniary, namely the (impossible) requirement that ever-improving results be obtained at the cheapest possible cost.[33] Hence the contradiction between child-centred philosophy (or, indeed, any reference to children *per se*) and the managerialist accountability regime because of the Taylorist negation of the human and the concomitant reduction of learning to ostensibly valid measurable outcomes, which are the result of the drive for cost effectiveness and efficiency.

(New) managerialism and necessary contradiction

For Bottery, managerialism

> ...does not only feed back into the workings of the state to influence the actions and thought of policy-makers: it also has wider, more pervasive and therefore probably more damaging effects on society at large. In particular, in the pursuit of management objectives, it reduces first-order social and moral values to

second-order values. By doing so, managerialism not only achieves a hegemony within organizations; it also parasitizes and weakens those values upon which the wider society – *but also its own existence – depend*...Now it is accepted that wherever managerial and non-managerial relationships and values exist side by side, there will always be a tension between them. Yet wherever managerial values achieve hegemony, these wider values are cheapened and debased...

(Bottery 2000: 68, emphasis added)

It is precisely the *necessary dependence* of managerialism upon such 'first-order' values that I am arguing for in this book: managerialism denies that which it depends upon in order to work *qua* normative system. The point here is that any action in invoking managerialism also ineluctably invokes its antithesis. Such first-order values include autonomy, criticality, care, tolerance, equality, respect and trust. As Bottery notes, the key words in the managerial mantra are economy (curbing the amount being spent), efficiency (getting the most out for the money being spent) and effectiveness (achieving as near as possible the aims designated at the beginning of the process). The quantifiable has taken precedence over the qualitative. Thus, such values as care have tended to be sidelined in the pursuit of monetary considerations.

Yet, perhaps even more importantly, where care is espoused, it tends to be regarded as a value-added component to a service, rather than as an integral and primary feature of any human relationship. In other words, because it is assigned this second-order status, it is conditional upon managerial calculation rather than being an unconditional ethic, and this leads to all human relationships being treated as means to ends rather than as ends in themselves.

(Bottery 2000: 70)

As we shall see in Chapter 6, the trouble-shooting head set up a self-esteem programme in order to improve SATs scores, whereby the children were treated as means to managerial ends. What is of interest here is whether teachers are aware of the contradiction and what they can or cannot do about it. For me, the purpose of the qualitative research in the two primary schools was, in part, to ascertain the level of discursive penetration of the necessary contradiction. Now, at the S-C level we have seen that the situational logic of a constraining contradiction conditions ideational unification (attempt to sink differences). The situational logic only comes into play when people wish to maintain it or are forced to maintain it. All primary teachers in England and Wales are structurally conditioned to maintain the contradiction, more specifically to engage in managerialisation. In other words, those committed to caring for children *qua* children are conditioned to uphold A ← B (where A = managerialism; B = child-centredness) at the practical, everyday level. We are not just talking about the ideational here: teaching practice has to be accordingly reoriented. The extent of such reorientation depends upon a host of factors, particularly the extent of attachment to B.

We have seen that attempts to sink differences may follow three paths. The preferred option is to rework or revise the antithetical element (that is, B). But the important point to note here is that child-centred teachers do not want to uphold A at the outset. In other words, such teachers are being forced to sink that which they do not want to sink *in the practice of teaching*. Managerialisation here, then, is about an enforced union of A ← B, which, again, cannot logically and practically be enforced, since, whether actors recognise it or not, A cannot function with B, even though B ever threatens to engulf A. Moreover, children *qua* flesh-and-blood cognitive, emotional reality necessarily set limits on managerialisation. Thus, at the ideational level managerialism, as Bottery notes, cannot work without the values it expunges; at the practical level, its structured manifestation (LMS, SATs, league tables) cannot eschew the reality of children and teachers. Both in theory and in practice human beings cannot be expunged. Bottery rightly argues that managerialism in education is anti-humanitarian:

> Just as in much modern business, where targets are set beyond the reachable, so they are increasingly set in education, and (of course) by those who do not have to reach them. Stress is then caused, not only by the pressure this puts on the teacher to try to achieve them; it also causes untold stress in that they have to reach these targets with children who have no hope of attaining them, and for whom they are equally stressful and anti-educational.
>
> (Bottery 2000: 78)

Of course, anti-humanitarianism both in theory presupposes some notion of humanity and in practice deals with real human beings. Managerialism erases such values as caring since it is value-less; yet, of course, in the very process of attempting to be value-less it is ineluctably value-laden. It is not at all surprising that advocates of managerialism in education are ineluctably constrained by such ('practical') values as caring. I am arguing that this is the result of a necessary contradictory relation: child-centredness *per se* does not presuppose managerialism, yet managerialism (and managerialisation) in education cannot eschew child-centredness (however crudely defined). The former is necessarily dependent upon the latter – it cannot work without it. Thus, as we shall see in Chapter 6, although the head actively championed the argument that 'we're not social workers!', contradictorily early morning meetings ever kept an eye on children whose home backgrounds were causing concern. In fact, her self-esteem programme, regrettably, resonated with Bottery's point that caring has become conditional upon managerial calculation. Indeed, here the head justified the self-esteem programme solely in terms of achieving higher SATs scores.

New Labour, New Managerialism: 'modernising' managerialism in education

It was during my time in Westside that the Labour Government introduced national target setting. Briefly, I want to conclude my discussion of new managerialism by highlighting the fact that New Labour has *intensified* managerialisation in education. As Clarke *et al.* put it, New Labour has 'proved to be just as enthusiastic about the reconstruction of welfare as a major political task, seeing it as a means through which a distinctively "modern" British people might be constructed' (2000: 1). In essence, New Labour in education, as in other spheres, has adopted most of the premises of neo-liberalism, many of its objectives, and nearly all of its methods of delivering them. As Fergusson succinctly puts it:

> Competition, choice, and performance indicators remain the unchallenged totems of policy, not in overt policy statements but simply by being left untouched by New Labour reforms. Structurally, little that is fundamental is changing in the ways in which schools and colleges are run. Markets and managerialism hold sway. Structures and methods remain largely unaltered. Only the rhetoric of what schools and colleges can and should produce changes. The commitments to excellence and diversity are softened in favour of raising standards for all. The projects of the New Right and of New Labour begin to look ideologically consonant. The point of difference is not whether schools should be better, but which ones should be made better first. And what counts as 'better' remains largely locked inside the black box of the National Curriculum, testing, and how to teach more effectively.
>
> (Fergusson 2000: 203)

Indeed, the emphasis on performance has not supplanted the competitive model of separate self-managing schools with devolved budgets. However, there is an important difference between the New Right model and New Labour's modernisation strategy. As Fergusson notes, the New Right model was outcomes-focused and precisely how those outcomes were achieved and who benefited was of little concern. The skill of individual teachers in improving pupils' achievements was implicitly viewed as a kind of enterprise, underpinned by mechanisms of promotion and demotion. In contrast:

> New Labour's version is *much more interventionist,* and *considerably more managerialist.* Outcomes remain the focus, but they are now constituted as targets and benchmarks, rather than just comparisons with other institutions. And once criterion referencing has eclipsed norm referencing in this way, externally determined performance indicators are necessary...the imposition of numeracy and literacy hours is an attempt by government to shape the processes that improve performance.
>
> (Fergusson 2000: 208, emphasis added)

Indeed, the modernising process by the state takes the pursuit of improved performance much further than the marketised version. Finally, 'The discursive power of targets, improvement and performance is great, and even where it is not embraced positively, it provokes defensive adaptation that is in itself tacit acknowledgement of a new regime of truth' (Fergusson 2000: 209). We need to be careful here not to elide structure and culture, since the ideas of targets, improvement and performance would not have been entertained by the majority of teachers in both schools: the 1988 Education Reform Act and subsequent legislation are structural changes that are ideational in origin and secretion. What I am arguing in this chapter is that discursive (ideational) formations do possess emergent relational powers and properties, which predispose towards specific courses of action. At the same time, in order to account for their un/realisation one must ever pay attention to the structural realm and agential discursive penetration.

Concluding remarks

The purpose of this chapter has been to argue that cultural analysis would benefit from a focus on that sub-set of cultural items to which the law of non-contradiction can be applied, thereby paralleling Lockwood's seminal distinction between 'the parts' and 'the people' (between social and system integration). At the same time, it has elucidated the nature of the 'New Managerialism' (or New Public Management), arguing that many approaches tend to conflate the CS/S-C levels. This chapter has thus been explicit in its rejection of current portmanteau conceptions of culture, which at best conflate the logical and the causal (CS/S-C), encompassing a disparate collection of organisational phenomena. However, not only has it been argued that culture be rid of its catch-all status, it has been further argued that the Cultural System has emergent relational properties (of logical contradiction or complementarity) that causally condition specific courses of action for those who uphold its item(s). Such an approach is grounded in a stratified ontology, which in turn enables identification of the causal mechanisms and processes involved. The methodological means for this is analytical dualism, which is workable because of the *sui generis* nature of culture (like structure) whose mode of being is temporally prior to agential activity, whilst any modification post-dates such activity. Whilst there is nothing intrinsically wrong with portmanteau terminology, it must be remembered that such terms unhelpfully compact distinct strata.

Cultural dynamics are theorised about on the same sequential basis as structure, i.e. Cultural Conditioning → Socio-Cultural Interaction → Cultural Elaboration. Cultural morphogenesis may get underway without paralleling structural morphogenesis. Whilst each penetrates the other, each is none the less ontologically distinct, possessing *sui generis* properties and powers. Thus, modifications of child-centred philosophy (cultural morphogenesis) did not parallel structural morphogenesis (restructing of state educational system to accommodate new practices and methods). Finally, however, such cultural morphogenesis leads to the reshaping of agency in the process (the 'double morphogenesis', as discussed in Chapter 1). Very briefly, the development and systematisation of child-centred philosophy led to re-grouping and the establishment of new groups (the Froebel Institute, for example). The morphogenetic umbrella will now be opened to capture the interplay of structure, culture and agency at their sequential intersection in the following chapters.

Part II

Child-centred philosophy, new managerialism and the English education system

A morphogenetic account

3 Socio-cultural conditioning

Plowden, the philosophers and teacher training

Introduction

Archer's elaborated morphogenetic sequence finished in 1975. Her *Social Origins of Educational Systems* was published four years later and concluded thus:

> [I]n England when the 1944 Act signalled an unprecedented degree of unification and systematization, this did not imply supremacy for the process of political manipulation. On the contrary the post-war period was one of the richest for internal initiation, with the teachers gaining mastery over curricular development...Certainly it is true that...their respective centres [England and France] would like to gain more control, particularly over higher education at the moment...What is much more important to emphasize is that they cannot achieve such control at will: the acquired rights of the profession and of external interest groups are defended and retained. Furthermore, we must resist the temptation to endow the most recent events with a greater significance than their predecessors. It is certainly the case in England *at the present time that the centre seems poised to intervene more roughly at both secondary and higher levels, but this is better interpreted as one of the periodic re-orderings conducted by the central authorities than as a dramatic change in the nature of educational control.*
>
> (Archer 1979: 787–8, emphasis added)

The task of the following three chapters is to explain and delineate how, just over a decade later, England and Wales witnessed not simply a 'periodic re-ordering' but a complete reversal of curricular fortunes, embodied in the imposition of the 1988 Education Act (and subsequent modifications). The 1988 Reform Act constitutes the start of a new morphogenetic sequence that provides the contextual backdrop to my two case-study schools. The 1988 Act endowed the Secretary of State with over three hundred new powers, prescribed what was to be taught and enjoined examinations at the ages of 7, 11, 14 and 16. In fact, notwithstanding its inherent contradictions, the Act was designed to subject the education system to the logic of 'the market'; that is, through open enrolment, local management of schools (LMS) and pupil-based funding formulae. The centrally imposed National Curriculum and its associated testing requirements were thus part of the quasi-marketisation of the education system – to provide parents with published information (league tables) on which to make 'informed' decisions about the 'efficiency' of schools.

However, the 'battle ground of ideas' (Riley 1998) that was part and parcel of the lead up to the Act not only involved 'Right versus Left' socio-cultural machinations but also embodied the (equally) crude polarisation between child-centred philosophy (or progressivism) and traditional teaching methods. As Riley puts it:

> The battle for ideas was played out at many levels: in the Black Papers and the many articles and books which challenged, or supported that analysis; in the 'Think Tanks' and Policy Forums...It was played out in the classrooms of William Tyndale Junior School, Islington and in the rooms of London County Hall...
>
> (Riley 1998: 19)

The above quotation neatly heads in the direction of a morphogenetic account, specifically the adoption of the CS/S-C distinction (that is, between knowledge without and with a knowing subject). In other words, Riley distinguishes between the CS (articles, books, 'Think Tank' pamphlets...) and what people do with them at the S-C level: such CS properties may remain unexploited, even unnoticed, for extended periods of time, and only 'awoken' during specific structurally conditioned struggles. Equally, of course, even when animated by actors, such ideas may not move them to act, for various reasons. However, Riley helpfully accentuates the need for a stratified analysis, since the school is irreducible to the educational system of which it is a constituent part, which itself is irreducible to the polity. At the same time, ideas about how children learn, their nature and their needs and the contingent relationship between them and other ideas are irreducible not only to each other but also to the school, education system and polity.

However, before entering the Plowden Era, a defence of the autonomy of the education system is mounted because of the resurgence of interest in a Marxist educational sociology, which disavows the morphogenetic analysis undertaken in this book.

A critical commentary on Marxism and the sociology of education

A defence of the autonomous properties of the education system is important since it raises issues about the ontology of autonomy that have implications beyond Marxism for a wide range of reductionist 'sociologies of knowledge' that have deeply flawed the sociology of education for so long.

This section takes as given the continuing relevance of radical political economy. The explanatory utility of the distinction between use-value and exchange-value and of the concepts of capital accumulation, labour-power and uneven development is indubitable. This section has two modest aims. First, to reaffirm the autonomy of the education system. Marxist educational sociology has tended to play down or expunge the irreducible autonomous properties of the education system. A typical (yet ambiguous) example delineated below is that of Dale, who tends towards an

Althusserian 'determination-in-the-last-instance' approach. Second, it takes issue with the recent adoption by Rikowski (1996, 1997) of the universal internal relations ontology of Bertell Ollman. The universal internal relations ontology asserts that all social relations form an internally related totality; it precludes the possibility (and reality) of external social relations. Any adequate Marxist sociology of education must eschew this path, since one of the consequences of this is to withdraw autonomy from the education system. The rejection of the universal internal relations ontology enjoins that we respect the autonomy of the education system and pay due attention to the open nature of any social system. In brief, we must not reduce concrete social reality to the 'Capital Relation'.

Prior to Rikowski's incipient attempt to develop the rudimentary building blocks of 'labour-power theory', the primacy accorded to *capitalist* social relations (be it theoretically or practically) as subsuming the education system (and the state in general) is readily discernible in the Marxist literature. Thus, to Dale, for example:

> While very many social forces affect education in very important ways, the major motor of educational change in capitalist societies is the changing nature of the capitalist state. Thus, while I would, for instance, agree very largely with Margaret Archer's (1979) view of the influence of the organized teaching profession on educational change since the war and especially over the last 20 years, neither the profession's rise to the peak of its influence, nor its recent fall from that peak can be explained by examination of its composition, its policies, its leadership, its size, its level of expertise or anything else internal to it. All these factors are necessary to explain the *form* that the rise and fall took, but cannot explain *why* it took place. To do that, we have to examine the changing demands on the State in carrying out its basic functions...
>
> (Dale 1989: 45)

Dale's criticism resonates well with Broadfoot's comment that Archer's 'elaborate model of educational systems might be criticised by neo-Marxists for its failure to address the characteristics of the over-arching capitalist order' (Broadfoot 1996: 109). There is a tension here. For, on the one hand, Dale acknowledges the *sui generis* autonomy of the structure of the teaching profession (particularly its nature as a corporate group), yet, on the other hand, wants to subsume this under the 'major motor of the capitalist state'. He accepts the reality of other (that is, non-capitalist) social factors that account for the nature of the education system at any given point in time, but assumes *a priori* that capitalist factors are invariably more important. But the relative importance of non-capitalist factors is an *a posteriori* matter. In fact, one of Archer's key arguments was that, at the beginning of the 1980s, 'the single most neglected question in the vast literature on education [prior to the 1980s] concerns the educational system itself...The defining characteristics of a *state* system are in it having both *political* and *systemic* aspects' (cited in Broadfoot 1996: 102). The education system possesses emergent *sui generis* properties, of which the centralised or decentralised configuration conditions agential activity in distinctive ways. Whatever the functional needs of capital (perceived or otherwise), there is no *tabula rasa* on to which economic or cultural needs can be readily imprinted, modified or expunged at will.

Crucially, *any* state education system *qua* system possesses *sui generis* properties that are irreducible to the nature of the economic system (capitalist, state socialist, market socialist or post-capitalist) in which it is embedded. Dale's implicit reductionism of the *sui generis* properties of the state education system to capitalism implies considerable degrees of freedom on the part of those fulfilling the needs of capital, yet historically this is not the case. In fact, Archer does not artificially isolate the education system from the wider influences of the polity. She maintains that any macro-sociology of education involves recourse to the complex social interaction that results in particular forms of education and the complex types of social *and* educational structures that shape the context in which such interaction and change occur.

> It is a complicated task because it involves separating out the factors which impinge upon education and those which may be ignored at any given time because they do not impinge upon it. It also follows that the factors which are included are themselves treated as unproblematic – for instance, in incorporating the educational consequences of economic organization we do not try to explain the nature of the economy, but treat it as given.
>
> (Archer 1979: 4)

Archer is thus not denying the (obvious) importance of the economy and its organisational implications for education. Instead, she is simply highlighting the methodological implications of one's substantive focus. When incorporating the impact of the economic recession during the 1970s (see Chapter 4), one does not need to spell out in detail its temporal dynamics, since this would be to detract from the substantive explanans in hand. But, of course, methodologically to take the economy as given is to accord autonomy to the education system as a prior ontological commitment. Such a commitment is a transcendental realist one, since any system (educational, civil service…) *has* to possess autonomous relations among its parts in order for it to be identified as such. However, Dale maintains that the largest category of staff in the education state apparatus is teachers, and that therefore

> …no account of how education state apparatuses operate and what they can achieve is complete without *some* reference to the teaching profession. I do not want to go into this in any great detail, but I do want to suggest that teachers are not merely 'state functionaries' *but do have some degree of autonomy*, and that this autonomy will not necessarily be used to further the proclaimed ends of the state apparatus. Rather than those who work there fitting themselves to the requirements of the institutions, there are a number of very important ways in which the institution has to take account of the interests of the employees and fit itself to them. It is here, for instance, that we may begin to look for the sources of the alleged inertia of education systems and schools; that is to say that what appears as inertia is not some immutable characteristic of bureaucracies, but is due to various groups within them having more immediate interests than the pursuit of the organization's goals.
>
> (Dale 1989: 57, emphasis added)

That 'some' autonomy is granted *vis-à-vis* the teaching profession evinces Dale's ontological equivocality about the relative causal efficacy of the profession *qua* corporate group *vis-à-vis* the polity and the basis for such efficacy. However, such equivocality is more apparent than real. The underlying prioritisation of the capitalist nature of the educational system(s) logically enjoins that Dale eschew any detailed analysis of the profession: he is not so readily inclined to put all his ontological cards on the table, so to speak. Yet his concession that teachers have *some* autonomy immediately throws up the question of the degrees of freedom versus stringency of constraints; namely, that 'some autonomy' entails that capitalist needs cannot be deemed *a priori* of more importance. The fact that teachers have interests begs the question of their *structural* provenance; here Dale only accords the system itself at best a pale materiality. He writes above that any inertia is not due to the nature of the education system *per se* but rather to the immediate interests of various groups. This elision of vested interest groups and their structural embedding means that Dale would be unable to explain why concerted efforts by either the government or teaching groups (or both) does not necessarily result in structural change because of the nature of the system itself.

The nature of assessment, whilst a key concern of this book, is useful in highlighting the materiality of the education system; namely, its independent properties *vis-à-vis* capitalist economic dynamics. For, as Broadfoot (1996) rightly points out, the education system is now inconceivable without some form of external assessment. Indeed, assessment has been central to the creation of educational systems *per se*. Whatever the imperfections of past and current assessment procedures and their intended/unintended inegalitarian consequences, it remains that the assessment rationale is constitutive of educational systems, in turn conditioning what central government and teachers can do within in them and/or about them. Dale (1989: 55) notes that the government is unable to institute effective day-to-day control over every aspect of an apparatus's activities but does not adequately specify the ontological basis for this. I would want to add that this is the case for *any* government. That is, capitalist and non-capitalist polities alike confront similar systemic properties that condition their activity. Any educational system objectively provides teachers with vested interests because of the irreducible materiality of the system itself and the associated division of knowledge and expertise. It is the latter expertise, *inter alia*, that needs theorising about in terms of the degrees of objective bargaining power that teachers bring to the negotiating table and their subsequent negotiating strength that can then be analysed in conjunction with other factors. In other words, teachers' relative bargaining power derives from the skills and knowledge afforded by the education system rather than simply from the social relations of production. Therefore, I am not denying that capitalist societies condition activity in distinctive ways from their 'state socialist' counterparts. The point is that both have to contend with common features that are independent of their economic–systemic anchorage. Hence the metaphor of 'steering at a distance' discussed in Chapter 1, whereby the educational division of labour precludes untrammelled top-down central control. In a similar vein, Sayer notes that whether formal ownership yields actual control over property and activities depends upon the material and informational qualities of their objects.

Thus the token character of 'social ownership' derives not merely from contingent forms of organization but from the fact that millions of people cannot hope to control and co-ordinate the products of property that is diverse, often dependent on arcane specialisms and information, and highly dispersed.

(Sayer 1995: 3)

In a nutshell, the educational systemic division of labour and the associated division of knowledge and expertise do not comprise a pliable bundle with which any state can do as it pleases. If the process of meeting capitalist needs were simply a one-way untrammelled process of clarification and subsequent imposition, then one wonders why in the eighteenth and nineteenth centuries the development of the capitalist economy could be impeded by Anglican instruction and that entrepreneurial groups were compelled to become 'self-taught scientists, to experiment with industrial applications on a trial and error basis [and] to develop in-service training for mechanics, operators and accountants...' (Archer 1979: 113).

Indeed, without a detailed examination of the organisation, values and related negotiating strength of the teaching profession, one would be unable to provide an adequate account of the Plowden Report; that is, of how groups exploited anterior socio-cultural conditioning (Hadow Report, nature of the economy and so on). Equally, for example, the 1993 teacher boycott of tests cannot be explained away as a sort of capitalist hiccup. Yet, for Dale, in the final analysis, one must focus attention on the 'major motor of change' (the needs of the *capitalist* state). What he omits, of course, is that any state within an advanced economy will have needs that may not be met by the education system for the very reasons discussed above. The problem with the *a priori* importance accorded to the needs or functions of the capitalist state is that we miss many important things.

Rikowski: the withdrawal of autonomy

However, Whitty (1985) refers to Dale (1982), who wrote that we should be aware of trying to relate everything that goes on in schools back to the functions of the state on behalf of capital. In turn, one can argue that Dale does not allow a reduction of the concrete social reality – specifically the autonomous properties of the education system – to that isolated in abstract thought, namely the capital relation. But for such Marxists as Rikowski (1996, 1997) and Sharp (1986) the opposite maintains. We should thus not be surprised that Rikowski takes to task so-called 'relative autonomy' Marxists such as Fritzell (1987). For, as Fritzell puts it, 'In the structural context, autonomy may be seen to refer to a type of relationship in which significant properties or internal relations of one system cannot be empirically derived from corresponding features within another system...' (1987: 25). In other words, he is talking about ontological emergence and the irreducibility of social structure (see Chapter 1). To recapitulate, the internal and necessary relation between lecturer and student is an irreducible emergent property since the powers of the individual as individual are modified. Even though this emergent property depends for its existence upon continued state funding, the powers of the relation between lecturer and student are not reducible to the Department for Education and Employment and/or Local Education Authority. Following Gordon (1989), Rikowski believes that he has defeated the 'relative autonomy' theorists:

> Firstly, [Gordon] argues that it lacks meaning. How much strength are we to give to the notion of 'relative' in 'relative autonomy'? Just like arguments about angels on pinheads, it implies that there is an answer to a question that defies answers...Secondly, whilst she sees that relative autonomy theory is appealing for those who wish to escape vulgar Marxism...[she] also notes that the determinism lurking within it in its insistence on 'determination in the last instance' (of educational forms and practices by the economy) through the workings of the capitalist state...Thirdly, Gordon notes that the work of Apple (1985) and other supporters of relative autonomy theory is schizoid as it tends to oscillate violently between an 'all-powerful' state as a juggernaut pushing through education measures of the New Right which are purportedly in the interests of capital, and the ability of students and teachers to 'resist' the seemingly irresistible through a variety of counter-hegemonic cultural forms and practices.
>
> (Rikowski 1997: 559)

Rikowski argues that 'A dualistic structure–agency dilemma runs through the relative autonomy discourse which is indeterminate' (Rikowski 1997: 559). He concludes that Gordon's alternative ends up as a variant along the same relative autonomy theme:

> She attempts to construct a theory of the 'limits' and 'capacity' of the state and apply this to education. 'Limits' suggests that the state is unable to do certain things regarding education, thus it becomes 'relatively autonomous' once more and Gordon's critique falls back upon itself.
>
> (Rikowski 1997: 559)

First, there is nothing dilemmatic about the structure–agency distinction, since it delineates two irreducible strata of social reality. Rikowski is correct to point out that to posit the (transcendental) reality of the autonomy of structural forms does not tell us the extent of such autonomy (or degree, as Dale rightly notes). What is sometimes missing from the equation, then, is a specification of the degrees of freedom versus stringency of constraints. The 'schizoid' tendency of relative autonomy theorists as described by Gordon is precisely that specification; in this instance recognition of the (now) substantially increased degrees of freedom at the state's disposal to impose policy underpinned by New Right philosophy. What needs to be emphasised here is that even the most stringent constraints do not determine agency in puppet-like fashion, since they have to be mediated. Thus agency can exit at any point in time, but, as I argued in Chapter 1, to do so would incur a structured penalty.

Second, we need to bear in mind that Rikowski (1996, 1997) wishes to *dissolve* the structure–agency dualism, not because of the usual (though misplaced) assumption that the dualism is a Cartesian rather than an analytical one. Rather, it is because of the all-powerful omnipresence of the 'Capital Relation', whose immanent 'transcendence' is left to the sociological imagination. Indeed, whilst undoubtedly Rikowski would deny the charges of reification and determinism, we are left with a residual sense of agency responding to, rather than shaping, the 'logical' outcome of the unfolding of the Capital Relation. However, he writes that, whilst the notion of the education system *qua* autonomous entity is the antidote for 'simple economic reductionism', he follows Sharp, arguing that we should not view the relations between capital, the state and education as a set of relations between institutions or systems – 'Capital is a social relation' (1997: 560). Indeed it is, but so, too, are the lecturer–student relation, head-teacher–teacher relation, husband–wife relation and so on. Rikowski, like Sharp, is making redundant any adequate sociology of education. We are denied the capacity to assess the extent to which policy can be imposed and how policy intentions match their implementation. In fact, they are committing the fallacy that the material character of what is organised by the state has no effect. Ultimately, one would expect empirical reality to lead Rikowski to reassess his prior ontological commitments. However, his conflation of a multiplicity of *sui generis* strata leads him to recommend the '*destruction* of the project of "Marxist educational theory" in its entirety. Whoever treads this path ends up as a Labour-power Theorist rather than a Marxist Educational Theorist' (1997: 568). So, education is out of the equation altogether now. But clearly a focus on labour-power is somewhat unhelpfully narrow. But such is the logic of his approach, since '...a focus on the social production of labour-power necessitates a theoretical perspective where *process* and *processes* replace systems and institutions at the heart of analysis. The social production of labour-power cuts across and through institutions' (1997: 568–9).

Rikowski wants to expunge ontologically institutions and systems yet, naturally, cannot avoid using such terms. A focus on process and processes will not do. The processes involved in deciding whether to market a school aggressively take place within a 'product' namely the school. The concept of school necessarily entails reference to *sui generis* social relations (paradigmatically the teacher–pupil social relation). However, Rikowski maintains that...

> [o]nly a philosophy of internal relations allows' us to think in these terms [process rather than product]. Flat, static thinking through such concepts as 'institution' and 'system' makes analysis of the social production of labour-power as process and as trajectory impossible...Through utilising a philosophy of internal relations following Ollman (1993), the attention shifts away from 'systems' and 'institutions' (the usual fare of much sociology of education and Marxist educational theory).
>
> (1997: 569)

The next section critically dissects the Ollman social ontology adopted by Rikowski, extending its logic to argue that not only does it disavow a disaggregative analysis (Sayer 1995), but also precludes any adequate explanatory methodology.

Ollman, internal relations and the omnipresent capital relation

Class, capital and the division of labour

In the context of the division of labour in both capitalist and non-capitalist advanced economies, Sayer (1995) has convincingly argued that the generic flaw in Marxist analysis of capitalism is its inability to appreciate the materiality, complexity and intractability of an advanced division of labour, whose properties and powers are independent of the mode of production. I would argue that this criticism applies equally to the recent (and past) treatment of the education system. As Sayer rightly points out, if we have too few abstractions over too narrow a range of angles, then material aspects of social reality are lost at a stroke. Possibly in Dale's case – and certainly in Rikowski's – we end up missing the materiality of the education system itself and the differing degrees of freedom it affords the teaching profession (or fragmented groups thereof).

Whitty (1985) refers to the work of Holloway and Picciotto (1977) as illustrative of the limitations of neo-Marxist accounts of shifts in education policy. He notes that for Holloway and Picciotto, like Rikowski and others, the central dynamic of the whole social formation is provided by the 'capital relation', which enters into all features of social life under capitalism. Although Whitty notes that Holloway and Picciotto introduced many caveats into their argument, in turn distinguishing it from a 'logic-of-capital' thesis, their approach still eluded an adequate understanding of the complex relative interplay of economic, political and ideological practice. Whilst Whitty acknowledges the importance of economic needs on education policy, he does not elevate it to an ontological proposition that engulfs social reality *in toto*. On the contrary, what cannot be assumed is that economic pressures

> ...will always generate policy initiatives whose character can be derived directly from them, nor indeed is it necessarily the case that they will bring about *outcomes* that are incontrovertibly functional for capital. Much of the progress of the Great Debate in England...has to be understood in terms of the peculiar political, professional and cultural character of the English educational system and the existence within it of elements to which capitalism is 'relatively indifferent' or 'had great difficulty in changing'...
>
> (Whitty 1985: 85)

Holloway and Picciotto's privileging of the 'capital relation' is not uncommon in current neo-Marxist theorising, both within and outside the sociology of education. The assumption is that the effects of capitalism's central processes are so far-reaching that everything in such a society is to some extent capitalist. Indeed, we are now used to such terms as 'cultural capital', 'human capital', and so on.[34] Any advanced division of labour possesses an irreducible materiality that is more funda-mental than particular modes of coordination. As Sayer (1995) argues, it is not only capitalism that generates macro-economic problems but also market socialism. This should alert us to the fact that the social relations of production do not assume causal primacy or, indeed, constitute the key abstraction for Marxist theory, espe-cially in the sociology of education.

In addition to our routine attachment to such over-extended concepts as 'cultural capital', there is a pervasive tendency both in Marxism and mainstream sociology to subsume the effects of division of labour under class. Put simply, class is conflated or confused with division of labour, thereby obscuring the different sources of power at different corporate groups' and individuals' disposal. The teaching profession's varying degrees of negotiating strength are not derivable directly from the social relations of production. Equally, technical divisions of labour objectively create scope for conflicts and inequalities within and between firms and these objective power-bases can (and did) exist in state socialist society. The salient point here is that the materiality of an advanced division of labour greatly attenuates the causal primacy accorded to private ownership by Marxism, *inter alia*, because of the consid-erable variety of power-bases it creates (which may or may not be strategically exploited) and the associated dispersal of knowledge. As Sayer (1995: 51) argues, such multiple sources of power cannot be subsumed under one single heading (i.e., class), yet this is precisely what much Marxism or 'class theory' tries to do. He suggests that those who resist the idea of treating professional employees and employee cleaners as in the same class probably do so because they cannot drop the habit of using an *overburdened* concept of class that attempts to cover all differences in power, income and life-chances. (This is one habit of which I am culpable.)

Bertell Ollman and universal internal relations: the repudiation of disaggregative analysis

The common Marxist emphasis on the totalising nature of the Capital Relation has its origins in the universal internal relations ontology, which can be traced back to the work of such prominent Marxist thinkers as Bertell Ollman and Marx himself. Rikowski's recent contributions attempt to supersede the historical problems that have bedevilled 'Marxist educational theory', such as the well-known 'correspondence theory' and 'resistance theory'. However, whilst applauding his engagement with such past problematics, his unfinished programme is fatally flawed because of his adoption of the Ollman internal relations approach. One can glean Rikowski's programme from Ollman's account of his dialectical approach:

> My account of the dialectic stresses its roots in the philosophy of internal rela-tions which holds that the irreducible unit of reality is the relation and not the thing. The relations that people ordinarily assume to exist between things are viewed here as existing within (as a necessary part of) each thing in turn, now conceived of as a Relation (likewise, the changes which any 'thing' undergoes). This peculiar notion of relation is the key to understanding the entire dialectic,

and is used to unlock the otherwise mysterious notions of totality, abstraction, identity, law and contradiction. In the interests of clarity, these notions are examined in Hegel as well as Marx and contrasted with their equivalents in Aristotelian logic and its watered-down version – common sense.

(1990: 74–5)

For Ollman, all 'Relations' are aspects of the whole. Crucially, he writes thus:

> The twin pillars of Marx's ontology are his conception of reality as a totality composed of internally related parts, and his conception of these parts as expandable relations, such that each one in its fullness can represent the totality. Few people would deny that everything in the world is related as causes, conditions or results; and many insist that the world is unintelligible except in terms of such relations. Marx goes a step further in conceptually interiorizing this interdependence within each thing, so that the conditions of its existence are taken to be part of what it is. *Capital, for example, is not simply the physical means of production, but includes potentially the whole pattern of social relations which enables these means to function as they do.*

(1990: 100, emphasis added)

Contrary to Ollman, common sense would immediately question the bizarre notion that *everything* is part of an internally related whole – a totality. The totalising reductionism is transparent: capital is the whole pattern of social relations. Of course there are causes, conditions and results in the world, but not all conditions are internally related. Water is composed of the internal and necessary relation between two molecules of hydrogen and one of oxygen. Yet water is not internally related to human beings (despite our asymmetrical internal dependence upon it). In other words, water provides one of the conditions for human existence, but water can exist without us although we cannot exist without it. To extend the internal necessity that characterises the capital–labour relation as applying to *all* social relations and objects is at best an extremely unhelpful *non sequitur*. At worst, it makes any form of critical social theory pointless. But if everything is internally related, how is it possible to step back? I would suggest that the internal relations ontology precludes critical standpoints.

Nevertheless, Rikowski quotes Holloway, who maintains that 'If all aspects of society are to be understood as forms of social relations, then clearly they all form part of an internally-related whole...' (Holloway 1995: 166). He maintains, again following Holloway, that the state, money, capital and so on are *apparently* separate: 'they are forms of social relations, the interconnections between which should be understood *not as external (causal relations, for example)*, but as internal, as processes of transformation or metamorphosis' (Holloway 1995: 165, emphasis added). An unfortunate repudiation of explanatory power *per se* is the (heavy) price paid by adopting Ollman's universal internal relations ontology. The complete lack of explanatory purchase on concrete educational systems and their interplay with the polity is readily gleaned from the above restriction of causality to the state and capital respectively in the above reference to Holloway and Rikowski's own (unfinished) exposition of 'labour-power theory'. Surely if they are interconnected, as Holloway maintains, then they must possess some modicum of autonomy in order to be so identified? And if they possess autonomy, then perforce they have properties independent of, and irreducible to, each other. But to recognise their irreducibility (which is not to deny any form of necessary interdependency) would be to accept that they have independent (autonomous) structural identities, which the universal internal-relations ontology disclaims.

A universal internal-relations ontology would disclaim the tenability of the asymmetrical relations between schools and their governing bodies discussed in Chapter 1, since the former can exist without the latter. Inconsistently, Rikowski (1996: 445), following Hatcher, argues that it is possible to envisage gender equality in capitalist societies. This belies the internal-relations ontology, since gender is not ontologically dependent upon capitalism for its existence and vice versa. As Sayer puts it:

> The ontology of universal internal relations leads one to assume that objects or processes cannot be the same under different circumstances. It simply excludes the possibility [and empirical reality] that particular processes that exist in capitalism could also exist in a society with non-capitalist social relations of production, for it assumes that they must be different, and not just superficially but fundamentally.
>
> (1995: 29)

In fairness, Sayer points out that, with respect to the relationships between class, division of labour, money, commodities and property relations, Marx tended to assume ubiquitous internal relations in Hegelian fashion. However, the denial of external social relations means that Ollman *et al.* cannot conceive of the asymmetrical relation between money and capitalism, namely that the former can exist without the latter but not vice versa. In fact, Sayer argues that it would be maintained that if the social relations of production were different, then everything would be different (!). Yet, *pace* Sayer, the very identification of that which is different is impossible. The universal internal relations ontology cannot explain (or identify) enduring causal entities at all, since any change enjoins that some form or entity possess causal powers proper to itself, that is, an independent *sui generis* identity in order for the identification of change to be possible. Transcendentally, therefore, the universal internal relations ontology is false. How, indeed, could Marx identify the transition from feudalism to capitalism if the latter did not possess an independent structural identity? In sum, the internal-relations ontology disallows a disaggregative approach, whereby we can consider whether particular elements of political–economic systems can exist in combination with one set of other elements or whether they can also co-exist with other sets.

The Plowden Era – the beginning is the end

For some, the choice of the Plowden years as the starting point of my morphogenetic conditioning cycle would be deemed unhelpful given the rich systematisation and cultural work carried out prior to it. This is undeniably true. However, no definitive account of child-centred philosophy and practice can be given because of the obvious constraints of any research project and, indeed, the fact that child-centred philosophy itself does not constitute an easily identifiable, homogeneous corpus of tightly woven logical complementarities. In his introduction to his historical account of the progressive schools (c. 1881–1967), Stewart notes that the term 'progressive' may be applied to a range of schools 'which themselves span wide differences in theory and practice...' (1968: xvi). He concluded that such schools were numerically small, aimed at reforming educational practice. 'We have emphasized more than once that *no corporate movement was shaped in radical education*, and we have said that the strength of this group of schools has been their individual identity...' (1968: 345, emphasis added). The international movement of child-centred philosophy developed during the inter-war years, under the auspices of the New Education Fellowship (NEF). Of the NEF, Stewart remarks that 'It represents a remarkable achievement of voluntary effort based on principles that cannot be too precisely stated if schisms are not to appear' (1968: 240). Equally, Selleck has criticised the NEF for lacking rigour and exuding 'vague principles' (1972: 46). Finally, Punch argues that progressive philosophy 'never approximated to a readily identifiable doctrine but was more a philosophical flag of convenience that tenuously united a diverse group of thinkers and practitioners' (1973: 4).

That there were doctrinal differences is not disputed here. However, there is an underlying philosophical thread that facilitated the uniting of this diverse group of thinkers and practitioners that is almost invariably traced back to Rousseau. What must not be confused is the concomitant complementarity embodied in developmental psychology. For at the level of child psychology we encounter CS disorderliness; most notably between Vygotsky and Piaget. Here one can identify other important contemporary 'schools of thought', such as information processing (IP), the structuralists, the metacognitive influence and the nativists. Indeed, we can even differentiate between fundamentalist Piagetians, neo-Piagetians and post-Piagetians (see Sutherland 1992). The nativists, for example, represent a radical biological approach whose implications for teaching are deterministic, leaving little teacher control over the learning process. Sutherland's (1992) text on cognitive development itself documents the thrust and counter-thrust at the S-C level between the Vygotskyans and the Piagetians; that is, the S-C unfolding of a competitive contradiction.

However, the focus is on child-centred philosophy and not on its concomitant complementarity, though the S-C schisms generated by CS contradiction at this level are clearly important in terms of accounting for structural (educational) stasis. As Stewart rightly noted, CS disorderliness ultimately precluded the development of a united corporate group. When we look at the teaching profession as a whole today, we can see that structural cleavages (objective division of labour between primary and secondary–secondary and higher education) and the associated status hierarchy further militate against corporate agency. To reiterate, the Vygotskyans and Piagetians *both* operate within child-centred philosophy: necessarily their propositions presuppose the metaphysical assumption that children *qua* children are different from adults and thus have distinctive needs and processes of development. Hence the concomitant, rather than contingent, nature of the systemic complementarity. Both accept that teachers must start with the child and his or her extant needs. Whether the contradictions between Vygotskyans and Piagetians are more apparent than real (i.e., mere family squabbles) is a crucial area of enquiry – especially the issue of innate stage development – it is not the concern of this book. The salient point to be stressed is that both follow the child-centred (or progressive) view that children are not 'defective adults', passive receptors of knowledge dished out at the front of the classroom by an authoritarian teacher. This is an appropriate point at which to discuss the provenance of child-centred philosophy and its celebration in the Plowden Report (1967).

Jean-Jacques Rousseau: contra traditionalism

Many of the progressive schools discussed in Stewart's book were set up as a result of a radical dissatisfaction with traditional practice. (And, as will become clear, the progressive–traditional dichotomy is abused and used as part of various S-C strategies in the pursuit of vested structural and ideal interests.) The traditional versus progressive dichotomy is not a convenient rhetorical or heuristic device. Instead, it refers to specific CS (incompatible) properties, almost invariably written down in books, pamphlets, school prospectuses and international journals. Darling draws attention to the indubitable importance of CS inheritance as embodied in the latter.

> We have noted that today's primary schooling can be traced to yesterday's books, with training colleges performing the intermediary role of fostering child-centred ideas in student teachers…two writers can be identified as intellectual giants by any standards – Rousseau and Dewey. What is significant…is that both were philosophers as well as advocates of child-centred education, a fusion of thought that showed no signs of internal tension [CS level].
>
> (Darling 1994: 52)

What is often unexamined in the literature is the concurrent critique of child-centred philosophy undertaken by the university and college philosophers of education. In discussing the teachers between 1964 and 1975, Archer, for example, does not address the latter.[35] Instead, she describes the period as witnessing the 'high water mark of professional normative consensus with the publication of the Plowden Report…In many ways it was the pinnacle of the liberal NUT influence over professional values…' (Archer 1979: 560). She also refers to organisational and ideological factors as the key factors in accounting for the dissolution of professional consensus by the 1970s, *inter alia* the failure of the unions to deliver satisfactory pay settlements, which resulted in a more militant posture and the failure of the Educational Priority Areas. This chapter therefore aims to fill an important lacuna. The education philosophers' critique is important for the basic reason that trainee teachers were (and are) confronted with structurally skewed CS properties. In other words, lecturers and staff predisposed towards the philosophers' critique (or subject to their S-C machinations) are structurally positioned (or coerced) to delimit who has access to tracts of the CS. Any arts or social science graduate should recall that each course reading list necessarily comprises a fraction of the relevant CS items and that its compiler will be predisposed towards certain texts, unwittingly or not. The implications for classroom practice and corporate union activity should be obvious. Teachers who have been subject to a staple diet of anti-child-centred precepts are necessarily at a corporate disadvantage if they find that the National Curriculum directives that are underpinned by the latter do not square with the reality of children's needs, intuition and, indeed, experience itself. Such corporate and/or individual disadvantage stems from the structurally enforced debarment from access to the systematised (child-centred) conspectus from which to choose items at the S-C level (i.e., classroom practice). And, as we saw in the previous chapter, lack of effective systematization at the early-years level has exacerbated the lack of corporate agential activity.

I mentioned above that a definitive account of child-centred philosophy and practice cannot be given and that the latter does not constitute a nicely woven web of logical complementarities. This is not to say that child-centred philosophy cannot be referentially fleshed out. On the contrary, there is a generic philosophical core, whose propositions have been added to, partially replaced (consistently or otherwise) or sympathetically critiqued. Punch's comment above (1973: 4) conveys the impression that the referents of child-centred philosophy, because vaguely espoused by the international movement, do not in fact exist. This is untrue: Punch is confusing the S-C level with the CS level, which played down the nature of the richly systematized nature of the CS. Child-centred philosophy resulted from dissatisfaction with traditional practice. The traditionalist paradigm emphasised mastery of factual knowledge. Pedagogically, the teacher instructs the class, and not individual pupils. Pupil motivation is held to be dependent solely upon compliance and competition. As Darling rightly notes, it is precisely the variety of critical reactions to this that makes any definitive account impossible. Equally, one could not provide a definitive, once-and-for-all account of Marxism. However, it would be absurd to say that one cannot provide a generic framework for Marxist (and child-centred) thought.

Essentially, exponents of child-centred philosophy focus on children's growth and development. As Darling summarises:

> Children's development is seen as a gradual and 'natural' progression, which is best aided by adults who have an appreciation of and a respect for the ways of children...Childhood, it is insisted, is not a defective version of adulthood...progressives emphasise that it is the nature of the child to be active. Traditionalists are seen as being either unaware of this central characteristic, or as seeing it as something regrettable...The findings of educational psychology [show] that children are intellectually curious, keen to find things out, and actively engaged in making sense of the world...Child-centred education is not just a respecter of childhood, but a respecter of individual children and their differences.
>
> (Darling 1994: 3)

One of the principal precursors of the above is, of course, Rousseau. For Rousseau, individual children vary, implying that education thus needs to be individualised. Each child is held to be innately predisposed towards activity. Like Piaget, he saw children growing through a series of developmental stages, and that consequently appropriate techniques must be developed for each stage. More importantly, he emphasised the intrinsic differences in powers of thought between children and adults. Indeed, he wrote that the child 'should remain in complete ignorance of those ideas which are beyond his grasp...I cannot too strongly urge the tutor to adapt his instances to the capacity of his scholar' (Rousseau 1911: 141–4). More recent child-centred approaches have subsequently focused on the notion of 'readiness'; that is, delaying the teaching of knowledge and skills until the child is ready. In *Emile*, Rousseau is critical of the (traditional) approach that pays no attention to what a child is capable of learning at different stages of development. Such capability is held to be constitutive of the intrinsic nature of the child *qua* child. Thus the notion of readiness is a cognitive one, grounded in the bio-psychological emergent (and emerging) powers of the child. The traditional approach (along with technocratic/managerialist approaches) disavows any need to unpack this (and in the case of the latter, attempt to erase it).

Critics of child-centred philosophy wrongly maintain that an emphasis on the child's readiness entails an overly voluntarist hue, namely that the child decides what s/he wants to do, irrespective of the teacher. Undeniably, A S Neill's (in)famous Summerhill reflected this (see Stewart 1968 for an excellent account). However, the key principle to be drawn from Rousseau's *Emile* is that 'discovery learning' is not left to the child. On the contrary, in *Emile* we find that the tutor engineers learning experiences. The whole point of the notion of 'readiness' is that one cannot force a child to learn something that cannot be learned because of its intrinsic make-up, just as you cannot drive to work on a frosty morning if the car's windscreen has not been cleared of ice. Like the car, the child has to be ready. Where the analogy breaks down, of course, is that a child may perform well in tests, despite not being ready, since a concomitant lack of understanding is not easily discernible, whereas you simply cannot see to drive the car. Finally, then, Rousseau emphasised the importance of understanding and how easy it is for teachers to be misled into thinking a child has understood something.

As we saw in Chapter 2, Rousseau's ideas have been subsequently developed; such ideational development underpinned the Hadow and Plowden Reports. The generic nature of the Plowden Report is discussed in Chapter 2 and need only detain us briefly. The 'constraining contradiction' that Peters *et al.* unleashed will not be addressed. In sum, the unfolding dynamic of the constraining contradiction is less important than the success of Peters *et al.* in dominating at the S-C level. The S-C success of Peters *et al.* is a significant yet often-neglected factor that further weakened resistance to the post-Plowden political and populist critiques of child-centred philosophy. However, we have already seen that Plowden was not an anarchist's charter, as some on both sides of the Tyndale affair later interpreted it (see Chapter 4). On the contrary, to reiterate, the tutor subtly and painstakingly *plans* and *monitors* learning situations congruent with the child's extant ability.

Plowden argued that there had been too much class instruction and that a greater *balance* needed to be fostered between class teaching, individualised learning and group work. As Riley sums up:

> Both critics of the day and recent critics have tended to present an *over-simplified* view of the arguments presented in the Plowden Report. In the 1990s, there have been calls to suggest that 'Plowdenism' retains a stranglehold on our education system, generating relativist views about pupil performance, rather than belief in absolute standards of achievement to be expected from all pupils...Critics of progressive education have implied wrongly that Plowden advocated one approach to teaching and learning. *The issue...is not what Plowden advocated but how people have chosen to interpret it.*
>
> (Riley 1998: 15–16, emphasis added)

I would argue instead that the issue is precisely the philosophical nature of Plowden, its cogency and implications for practice; the analytical focus is on how and in what ways critics at the S-C level selectively extract components as part of the competitive process. Equally, at the S-C level attention to its advocates has shown how they failed to develop and sustain any substantial progressive momentum, misreading and ignoring the potential and direction of the critics (as will be discussed in Chapter 4).

Plowden, the reality of teaching practice and the philosophers

Lowe (1997) has documented several factors that co-determined the Plowden Report. First, the 1964 Education Act enabled some local authorities to abandon transfer at 11-plus by introducing middle schools. This freed schools from the hated intelligence tests. Second, the establishment of the Schools Council led to the widespread dissemination of new approaches to primary school teaching. Third, there was a speedy expansion of teacher training colleges. According to Lowe, this had several results.

> First, the introduction of three- and then four-year courses of teacher training and of the B.Ed degree gave an academic respectability to initial teacher training which it had previously lacked, and meant that the new entrants to primary school teaching might have been expected to have greater self-confidence in terms of curriculum definition and teaching method. *The growing army of college tutors fed these students on a diet of Piagetian psychology and background work in the educational disciplines, all intended to enhance professional self-awareness and autonomy.*
>
> (Lowe 1997: 49, emphasis added)

I wish to return to this in a moment. Fourth, one also needs to supplement Lowe's list of factors by reference to the widespread economic prosperity that Britain enjoyed at this time. Unemployment was negligible and consequently parents had no reason to assume that their children would not be able to find employment. At the same time, a number of local authorities disseminated new approaches to pedagogy, notably Oxfordshire, Leicestershire, the West Riding of Yorkshire, Bristol and London. The Nuffield Foundation provided an important focus for primary school curriculum reform. For instance, in 1964 it sponsored a major project on the teaching of mathematics, which widely disseminated the theoretical work of Z P Dienes. However, a rosy picture of Plowden and the extent of progressivism during the following years is often painted. Dearden, for example, comments that

> ...[c]lassrooms became much more colourful places as more time was found for creative work. Topic work flourished...The contribution of educational publishers to making possible some of these changes deserves note. Teacher–pupil relationships became more relaxed and friendly, though not merely permissive...Plowden's ideal may have proved practical for a few...But something of the spirit of Plowden has found a permanent place.
>
> (cited in Lowe 1997: 51)

Yet surely the issue is precisely the extent of practical fruition rather than any nebulous 'Plowden spirit'? Lowe raises serious doubts as to how far the 'Plowden spirit' was borne out in the teaching strategies adopted in the majority of classrooms in the 1970s and 1980s. In 1972, for example, a report by HMI (Her Majesty's Inspectorate) commented favourably on work being carried out in a large sample of open-plan schools, but these schools were a minority. However, Lowe argues that 'What can be seen in retrospect as a more significant and more pervasive set of influences was the growing backlash which identified progressivism and child-centred approaches in the primary schools with falling standards. This first emerged in the 1969 *Black Papers*' (Lowe 1997). The backlash to which Lowe refers will be discussed in Chapter 4. What is required here is an account of the influence of the education philosophers. For his reference above to the teaching of Piagetian psychology does not acknowledge the education philosophers' simultaneous negation of it and their impact on teacher training college curricula.

At the beginning of the Plowden decade, philosophers of education became critical of the development of progressive educational theory. Prior to this, the philosophy of education had no prominent status. The development of philosophy of education by Peters *et al.* was greatly influenced by the work of A J Ayer, particularly his *Language, Truth and Logic* (1936). In brief, Ayer's philosophy was verificationist. In other words, for a statement to be meaningful it must be possible in principle to verify it or at least to establish its probability by gathering evidence through sense experience. Consequently, 'good', 'wrong' and 'beautiful' were designated pseudo-concepts. Indeed, such metaphysical issues as the existence of God or the nature of the good life were deemed meaningless. As Darling notes,

> The force of [Ayer's] polemic dealt heavy blows to philosophy of education and political philosophy. Traditionally, enquirers in these fields have sought to justify forms of human relationships, institutions and transactions, and have tried to demonstrate that some forms are more desirable than others. The message from *Language, Truth and Logic* is twofold: (i) this is not a proper kind of

activity for philosophers; and (ii) any conclusions reached about the nature of a good society or a good education are strictly meaningless.

(1994: 54–5)

In essence, verificationism is a species of the epistemic fallacy, namely the fallacy that statements about being can be reduced to our statements of knowledge about being. What exists is reduced to sense-data experience. Transcendentally, the objects of such experience exist independently. Upon upholding the distinction between ontology and epistemology, the verificationist immediately recoils, since the very notion of independent *sui generis* phenomena would be taken to be meaningless. For the verificationist, the meaning of a proposition consists in the method of its verification; that is, in whatever observations or experiences show. In essence, the verifiability principle is the basis of an attack on theology and metaphysics. At best, then, the propositions of metaphysics, like those of aesthetics or ethics, are only permissible as expressions of emotional attitudes, rather than *de facto* statements. The untenability of this position need not detain us, although Peters *et al.*, as will be discussed shortly, have consistently adhered to its central tenets. The influence of verificationism, particularly the attribution of ontological status via the senses, has been profound. In Chapter 1 the empiricist influence embodied in methodological individualism was noted, which gained its strength from the fact that *sui generis* emergent properties are unobservable. The empiricist doctrine enjoins that, because value-judgements cannot be verified via the senses (smelled, tasted and seen...), then any such judgements are meaningless.

Fundamentally, there is at best something rather odd in the idea of anyone writing about education in a way that eschews all value-judgements (Darling 1994). I would simply maintain that this is a (logical) consequence of a sustained commitment to Ayer's 'philosophy'. Indeed, for Peters, 'Many philosophers who have been brought up in the "revolution" [reference to Ayer]...are...rather aghast when they encounter what is often called "philosophy of education" with its rather woolly chatter about "growth", "wholeness", "maturity", "discipline", "experience", "creativeness", "needs", "interests" and "freedom" ' (Peters 1964: 141–2). Furthermore, Peters denigrates an historical approach to philosophy, asserting that modern philosophers are

> ...aghast when they learn that students very often are brought up on an antiquated diet of Plato, Rousseau, and Froebel – perhaps with a dash of Dewey to provide a final obfuscation of issues. It is as if a course on educational psychology consisted mainly of snippets from Aristotle, Locke, James Mill, Herbart and Thorndike.
>
> (Peters 1964: 142)

Darling (1994) argues that any contemporary study of philosophy presupposes knowledge of its past – sociology does not owe a fleeting gratitude to Marx, Durkheim and Weber! Whilst the above is not at all surprising, it is a consistent result of the situational logic in which Peters has embroiled himself. Undeniably, his own work secretes a series of contradictory (i.e., ethical–aesthetic) positions, but the key point for our purposes is the generic anti-metaphysical thrust of his writings (and those of his acolytes), which permeated teacher training colleges and post-graduate courses throughout England and Wales. Criticism of progressive educational theory also permeates the writings of Hirst and Dearden (previously referred to in Chapter 2). Most of the child-centred critique is to be found in *The Philosophy of Primary Education* (1968) by Dearden, *Perspectives on Plowden* (1969), edited by Peters, and *A Critique of Current Educational Aims* (1975), edited by Dearden, Hirst and Peters. In the introduction to *A Critique of Educational Aims*, it is stated by the editors that 'The authors in this collection are usually critical of attempts to charac-terise education in terms of "growth" or the satisfaction of "needs" ' (1975: ix). The actual critique of needs and growth need not detain us. The critique itself, to reit-erate, is an empiricist (or logical positivist) one. Thus, for example, given that a need is not a property that can be reduced to empirical methods (since it is prior and may not manifest itself empirically), then one should not be at all surprised that the concept is disparaged as 'woolly' or 'vacuous'. Indeed, such concepts as need, growth and creativity are dismissed at a stroke yet at the same time accorded a superficial plausibility. As I argued in Chapter 2, the situational logic of a constraining contradiction entails that they cannot repudiate such concepts alto-gether since their critique is only operable in terms of their metaphysical anchorage.[3] However, what is important is the power of Peters *et al.* to dominate at the S-C level.

Barrow and Woods' book, referred to in Note 36, is not an aberration. Indeed, the Inspectorate in the mid-1970s adopted Hirst's thinking. Hirst's work on forms of knowledge was used to sustain a subject-divided curriculum. In the early 1980s, Scotland's educational establishment began to waver in its commitment to child-centred philosophy for the first time since 1965. In *Primary Education in the Eighties* the Committee on Primary Education noted that the Memorandum's use of the 'growth' and 'needs' concepts had been 'rigorously examined' by Dearden. The key question, however, centres on the factors that co-determined the S-C dominance of the child-centred critique during the 1960s, 1970s and 1980s. A useful starting point is Peters *et al.*'s style of writing, which exuded academic rigour and repute in the eyes of the education world. As Darling puts it:

> Unlike Rousseau, Peters wrote in a cultural atmosphere where the highest acco-lades had long been reserved for scientific forms of study. The prevailing view was that any enquiry which is to establish sound answers must be: (i) detached, impersonal, unemotional; (ii) precise, methodical, orderly; and (iii) small-scale, piecemeal, cautious. These are today the hallmarks of rationality, and they are not to be found in Rousseau, whose style is by these standards dubiously intu-itive. The new philosophy of education, by contrast, was produced by professional academics. In their writing, Peters and Dearden proceed cautiously, and generate conclusions which verge on the conventional.
>
> (1994: 88)

Moreover, practically every philosopher of education in the country appeared to share the putative intellectual dubiety of child-centred philosophy. The reason for this is attributable to the position that Peters occupied in philosophy of education and the concurrent developments in teacher training. One of the recommendations of the 1963 Robbins Report was that training colleges be renamed 'colleges of education' and that they should prepare students for the new B.Ed degree. This resulted in a 'search for academic and theoretical substance' (Browne, cited in Darling 1994: 91). Such new colleges now had to establish their academic credibility and thus their courses had to be seen to be of the 'right kind'. Students would therefore have to study education with the kind of rigour that would bestow academic status.

In 1964, the then Department of Education and Science (DES) suggested that a conference be held to discuss the nature of educational studies. One of the key speakers was Professor Peters, whose seminal paper identified 'the foundation disciplines of philosophy, psychology and sociology'. The academic world allowed Peters to define the parameters of educational studies because (a) he had impressive academic credentials, and (b) teachers in the London Institute of Education have almost invariably exercised an extraordinary influence. As Darling notes,

> Much as Susan Isaacs revitalized the study of child development in this country when she went to London…so Peters brought a new standing to the philosophy of education by bringing with him credentials from a different, but related field…He had more than won his spurs in a 'hard' discipline and his move was instrumental in helping philosophy of education to lose some of its 'marshmallow image'…*In philosophy of education Peters rapidly took up a position of absolute dominance*; as one of his colleagues put it, Peters 'not only redefined British philosophy of education *but set its programme for some twenty years*' …
>
> (1994: 91–2, emphasis added)

In 1966, Peters founded the Philosophy of Education Society of Great Britain, of which he was chair. He also became editor of the *Journal of Philosophy of Education*. From such a position, buttressed by the government and his band of acolytes, he was able to exercise considerable cultural power in excluding articles that did not fit with what he and his colleagues believed to constitute 'good' education philosophy. This is an interesting S-C strategy of containment and one that did not rest solely upon control of the defining journal in the field. In his edited collection *The Concept of Education*, published at the same time as the Plowden Report, all articles contained therein were mutually consistent. And Peters was the series editor of Routledge and Kegan Paul's 'Students' Library of Education'.

Furthermore, at the DES-sponsored conference held in 1964, Peters informed delegates that the ideal of one philosophy of education specialist on every staff was being met by the training afforded by the London Institute's MA – a training that eschewed (unsurprisingly) the history of philosophical ideas. In 1983 Peters acknowledged that a significant percentage of British philosophers of education graduated from the London Institute's philosophy of education department. In all probability, then, those armed with an MA from the Institute went on to teach a philosophy of education that explicitly rejected the metaphysics of child-centred theory and practice. A 1982 *Times Education Supplement* survey of the twenty most frequently prescribed textbooks in pre-service training showed that three were philosophy books: Dearden's *Problems in Primary Education* (1976); Hirst's *Knowledge and the Curriculum* (1974); and Hirst and Peters' *The Logic of Education* (1970). The TES survey noted that the reason why Peters did not feature more prominently was that his votes were distributed over a number of titles. The survey also highlighted the absence of Plato and Rousseau. As a result, colleges of education were 'often effectively transmitting two contradictory messages. Since the war they had been committed to the principles of Froebel and Hadow...Yet the view implicit (and sometimes explicit) in the books used on philosophy of education courses was that child-centred education was incoherent, confused, and intellectually unrespectable' (Darling 1994: 95). Child-centred thinking – particularly with respect to the early-years work on child development – is not renowned for its intellectual rigour (though I would venture that this is occasionally more an S-C manoeuvre designed to denigrate). Thus, those working in the colleges of education would not have had the 'cultural capital', or, indeed, the academic power, to mount a stringent riposte. Since philosophy of education was seen as playing a central and rigorous part in establishing the academic credibility of the new colleges, for child-centred practitioners 'to dismiss the philosophers' contribution would have been to risk sawing off the branch of the tree of knowledge on which they were perched' (Darling 1994: 96).

The foregoing shows that the Plowden decade could hardly be described as one in which child-centred philosophy became widely entrenched at the S-C level. With the benefit of hindsight, my heading on p. 90 'Plowden – the beginning is the end' is clearly appropriate. For, even before its publication, influential educationists worked against its metaphysical underpinning – which, of course, dated back to Rousseau and Plato. I have emphasised the role of the education philosophers because, whilst it is now recognised that socio-culturally child-centred practice was not as widespread as the Golden Age of Plowden often suggests, there were important factors working against Plowden at the outset. It was precisely those institutions that were indispensable, if Plowden were to gain an adequate foothold, in which the child-centred critique was imposed. The education philosophers derived their cultural power from, *inter alia*, the structural conjunction between the buoyant economy and the development of the teacher training colleges. Those staff committed to child-centred education were not structurally predisposed to counter the philosophers' critique. However, this is not to suggest that the stringent constraints that staff confronted were such that no attempt could be made to override them, since, firstly, at the level of the school the scope for autonomous action on the part of teachers was widening. At the beginning of the decade, the government had 'little, if any, direct hold over the patterns of curriculum and development' (Kogan 1971: 20). Second, at the same time, the teaching profession continued to be successful in inserting itself on various decision-making agencies by virtue of its recognised expertise.

Indeed, the National Union of Teachers was represented on 125 official educational bodies and advisory committees. In 1964 it had thirty-seven MPs in the House of Commons. The main advancement in insertion came with the establishment of the Schools Council for Curriculum and Examinations (1965). The teaching profession was successful in insisting that this body should rest with teachers' control. However, the college tutors could not rely upon the teaching profession for corporate support. Objectively it could be argued that the profession was in a position to mount a potentially successful campaign *contra* the burgeoning influence of Peters *et al.*, yet did not exploit its freedom. Such freedom, of course, was not untrammelled. The state delimited its degrees of freedom via financial dependency, legal control and etatist values (Archer 1979) in order to keep the lid on internal innovation. However, expertise remained an important bargaining chip and, as already noted, the profession as a whole had its fingers in the parliamentary and local government pie. But internal schism, exemplified by an increase in militancy, and the lack of success in the union's ability to deliver pay increases and the turn away from children following the failure of the Educational Priority Areas, were contingent factors that inhibited any attempt to stem the Peters tide. Towards the end of the 1960s, internal criticism mounted of the way in which the union executives were more concerned with maintaining respectability than with militancy (in order, of course, to maintain their influence *vis-à-vis* the polity). What I am arguing, then, is that the bargaining chip afforded by expertise was undermined by internal schism. At the same time, the lack of pervasive impact of child-centred theory on practice received little, if any, attention. This, coupled with the Peters phenomenon, hardly constituted an auspicious set of conditioning circumstances *vis-à-vis* a generic implementation of Plowden.

Concluding remarks

From the foregoing, one can argue that structurally matters were auspicious for any concerted push towards an overall implementation of Plowden: the development of teacher training colleges, the generous degrees of curricular freedom accorded to teachers, the establishment of middle schools (1964 Education Act), the Plowden Report, the Schools Council and the buoyant nature of the economy. However, such felicitous structural arrangements were only partially exploited by exponents of Plowden. Moreover, such partial exploitation was overshadowed by, *inter alia*, the dominance of the education philosophers and their role in shaping curricular developments in teacher training colleges and internal schisms within the NUT. In the case of the teacher training colleges, we can point to structural morphogenesis that, once stabilised, was not accompanied by cultural morphogenesis and the expected S-C hegemony of child-centred theory. In other words, CS disorderliness (Peters versus child-centred philosophy) was not paralleled by S-C disorderliness (accentuation of incompatible elements) for the reasons delineated above. Peters *et al.* derived their power to impose cultural uniformity by virtue of factors residing purely in the structural realm. Nevertheless, other sites did witness both structural and cultural morphogenesis that gelled, which in turn provided the impetus towards a consolidation of child-centred philosophy and practice. Yet such sites were in the minority. Finally, that the teachers *qua* corporate body did not fully exploit the structural situation to any child-centred advantage enjoins that, *pace* Dale, we respect the nature and organisation of it at the same time analysing factors both within and outside the education system that gel or do not gel with its unified or diverse aims and interests. Of course, what makes analysis more difficult, but still necessary, is that such interests may be misunderstood, negated or altogether unrecognised. In sum, the argument of this chapter, with the benefit of hindsight, is that the Plowden Report was more or less moribund from the minute it hit the presses. As will be seen from the next chapter, before the onset of the economic recession there was an opportunity, albeit limited and diminishing, to fight the anti-progressivist critique and extend progressive practices. The question to be addressed next is precisely how and why the precarious position of child-centred practice was subject to a particularly vociferous string of S-C campaigns to turn back the 'Plowden Years'.

4 Socio-cultural interaction

Tyndale, Ruskin and the 'Black Paper' years

Introduction

disprove

So far reference has been made almost exclusively to the 1988 Education Reform Act and its general negation of child-centred philosophy. Whilst in the next chapter it will be made clear that the legislative impetus towards quasi-marketisation of the education system began in 1980, the Act itself may reasonably be taken as the structural elaboration of a new morphogenetic conditioning cycle. We saw in the previous chapter that child-centred practice did not reach the mythical heights often depicted during the 1960s and 1970s. The structured potentiality for a pervasive change in teaching practices remained unexploited. The purpose of this chapter is briefly to sketch out the concatenation of factors that facilitated the swift destruction of this potentiality during the 1980s. Structurally, the education system did not undergo any notable morphogenesis. The Labour Government's circular on comprehensive reorganisation, 10/65, was simply a request to local authorities – there was no statutory obligation until 1976. Here the teachers' unions, the Local Authorities, the Labour Party and the then Department for Education and Science (DES) did not individually (or collectively) provide a coherent strategy. Indeed, the tendency to portray the 1965 circular, like the Plowden Report, as a decisive turning point masks the extent of continuity. As Ball puts it, 'In contrast to the comprehensive movement the Conservatives have successfully managed to integrate and maintain and manage a high degree of contradiction and incoherence within their critical educational discourse' (1990: 31).

Ball's comment upon the Conservatives' successful ability to play down CS divisions in order to maintain a united (S-C) front is paralleled by the international progressive movement of the late nineteenth and early twentieth centuries discussed in Chapter 3. The salient point here is that the Conservatives, like the progressives, recognised their objective common ground. This is in stark contrast to the teachers. Minority dissension fuelled internecine conflict, particularly over the role of education in maintaining the capitalist status quo, which should have been quickly nipped in the bud. The lack of concerted corporate activity was typified by the Tyndale affair. The chance provided by Tyndale to spell out, defend and maintain the nature of progressive theory and practice was lost: the NUT's (National Union of Teachers) stance was reactionary and there were divisions within and between teaching unions. In a nutshell, there was no proactive attempt both prior to and after the Tyndale affair to mount an articulate defence of the Plowden philosophy. In fairness, however, the economic recession (1973–5) exacerbated by the oil crisis, and the sustained attacks played by the media during and after the Tyndale affair, were factors beyond the control of teachers. But, bearing this in mind, it still remains that delimited opportunities were not exploited. If anything, the Tyndale affair highlighted the misunderstood nature of child-centred or progressive philosophy, particularly the elision of the abstract and the concrete (children *qua* children and the structural context within which they are taught). Nevertheless, the OPEC oil crisis exposed for many the under-lying weaknesses of Keynesian social democracy. These years provided the fertile soil for the widespread dissemination of right-wing ideas. As Chitty notes, the post-war welfare consensus 'relied on an increasing prosperity for any success it might have had in creating a semblance of social unity; and when that prosperity disintegrated, so, too, did the consensus...[T]he Keynesian approach...simply could not cope with the economic shocks and adjustment problems of the 1970s' (Chitty 1994: 12). The inability to cope with the economic crisis and the concomi-tant need to tighten the budgetary belt furnished the ideational backdrop to the new managerialism of the 1990s, with its emphasis on 'value for money' (that is, more for less).[37] It does not provide the ingredient 'new', since this denotes the entrepreneurial aspect of 1980s managerialism that has its origins in the Hayekian inflection of 'Thatcherism'.

That the teachers did not fight the right-wing onslaught during the late 1960s and 1970s simply attests to its failure to exercise agency at various levels. To reit-erate, there were factors that by no means facilitated corporate collective action but, at the same time, the structural conditions (curriculum autonomy, parliamen-tary representation, 'liberal' union leadership, higher education expansion...) could have been exploited in the battle against the anti-progressive critique. The extreme views and activities of the key players in the Tyndale affair were not symptomatic of the majority of teachers. Here, the NUT simply engaged in a process of muted distancing. However, notwithstanding the dominance of the education philosophers in higher education that undermined Piagetian psychology, and the generic lack of progressive practice, exponents of child-centred practice came under attack from such Black Paper authors as Rhodes Boyson and the right-wing-dominated media. Moreover, they had to contend with the concurrent ramifications of James Callaghan's 1976 Ruskin Speech. In essence, the Ruskin speech was the turning point for teacher autonomy: at the S-C level it widened and legitimated a fundamental questioning of the power of teachers to determine curriculum, assessment and pedagogy.[38] The Tyndale affair was a potential (yet missed) opportunity for the teaching profession to address the widely propagated *extreme* nature of the Tyndale protagonists and to point to the improvements brought about by progressive practice, whilst at the same time extracting and accentuating the policy inconsistencies that constituted the (CS) corpus of the 'New Right'. Ruskin ultimately destroyed the teachers' already-precarious potential to rebut the anti-progressive onslaught.

Tyndale, the media and progressivism

'Head who thought writing was obsolete' (*Daily Mail*, 1975). 'Who can mediate in the class war?' (*Guardian*, 1975). 'Trotskyist Teachers' Warning to Parents' (*Evening News*, 1975). Such were the populist headlines during the Tyndale affair. If an effective riposte to the media onslaught were to be provided, then clearly corporate agential activity would be no easy ride. But, at the same time, circumstances were not such that the Orwellian spectre can be invoked to show that matters were a foregone conclusion. As already mentioned, the NUT stance was essentially reactive. There was a failure to take advantage of, *inter alia*, the 1972 HMI Report that commented favourably on the work being carried out in a large sample of open-plan schools, despite their minority status, and the 1975 Bullock Report, which failed to substantiate media claims that standards were falling in primary schools. However, the purpose of this chapter is not to detail the variety of 'what ifs' and the structural-cum-cultural potentialities they embodied. The importance of the Tyndale affair lies in its role as the catalyst for the Ruskin speech. Specifically, the media-led frenzy coincided with both the appointment of James Callaghan as Prime Minister following the resignation of Harold Wilson in March 1976 and the pressing problem of inflation (then running at 21 per cent). The economic crisis stringently shaped the Labour Government's agenda, whereby such issues as progressivism would have been at best played down or more likely dismissed. Such contingencies as the role of the Downing Street Policy Unit and Callaghan's personality further reduced the negotiating strength of the teachers.

The William Tyndale junior and infants schools were located in the St Mary's Ward of inner-city Islington. They were also based near the then home of most national newspapers, Fleet Street. The saga began in the spring of 1973 with the resignation of the incumbent head-teacher of the junior school. Terry Ellis took up the post in January 1974. Within two terms, the school had hit crisis point. How was this possible within such a short period of time? One needs to examine the crucial role played by a recent appointee, Brian Haddow, a part-time teacher, Mrs Walker, and Terry Ellis. Brian Haddow took up his post in January 1974 and the acting head, Mrs Chowles, returned to her post of deputy. Supported by Brian Haddow, the head initiated a series of debates about teaching methods and the function of schools in society. Divergent views were expressed about whether the role of education was to provide working-class children with generic life-skills, or whether it was merely a means for ensuring that children conformed to the status quo. The left-wing connotations were deliberate. There were heated disagreements about how the school should be run and also the decision-making mechanisms in place for staff as a group. Mr Ellis wanted to widen school democracy and suggested that the position of head-teacher should be abolished and decision-making handed over to staff. Whilst majority decision-making mechanisms were not established, teachers who opposed Mr Ellis were marginalised. In fact, Mr Ellis informed the deputy that her role was no longer of any significance and ostracised Mrs Walker.

In the second half of the first term, Mr Haddow, following Mr Ellis's approval, introduced a twenty activities options scheme for his class. The scheme was meant to promote freedom of choice and individualised learning, in turn promoting self-motivated active learners. But, as Riley notes, 'the options scheme, as many of the other changes at Tyndale, was poorly planned and badly executed. Neither parents, nor other teachers in the school had been informed, or involved in the reorganization (despite the commitment to democracy)' (1998: 24). However, there were some notable successes, epitomised by the winning of an ILEA (Inner London Education Authority) prize for excellence. Indeed, reading levels improved substantially. However, schisms deepened. The issue of democracy hit the agenda once more, and some teachers wanted to open the staff room to children in order to remove barriers. There were thus two camps – those who wanted to promote freedom and choice and expression and those who wanted to promote basic skills and discipline. There was also a third, minority group of staff that simply withdrew altogether. Notwithstanding the deep chasm that was by now firmly entrenched at Tyndale, all teachers were united in the need to develop a new reading scheme. However, as already noted, the new scheme was inadequately planned and beyond the experience of a number of staff.

> Criticisms began to erupt from a range of sources during that summer term. Critics included Miss Hart (head-teacher of the infant school) who was concerned about the breakdown of behaviour of children in the junior school. Mr Ellis rejected Miss Hart's criticism on the grounds that '*she had sold out to the middle classes*'…The district inspector received further complaints about the school and discussed these with Mr Ellis but the situation continued to deteriorate…
>
> (Riley 1998: 28, emphasis added)

In May 1974 Mrs Walker called a Parents' Evening and produced a paper: 'Commentary on William Tyndale School'. She also produced another paper: 'A Criticism of the "Free Choice" method of education based on total children's rights at William Tyndale Junior School'. This paper was subsequently identified as part of the Black Paperite tradition. Importantly, she met up with Rhodes Boyson MP. Rhodes Boyson viewed the Tyndale affair as a direct result of the activities of a left-wing clique within the NUT – 'head-bangers concerned with ending the system…' (cited in Riley 1998: 29). Whilst Mrs Walker's involvement led some at Tyndale to talk of a right-wing conspiracy, equally, on the other side of the divide, Mr Ellis and his colleagues viewed education as a means to tackling social disadvantage. The Auld Inquiry (set up to investigate the Tyndale affair) concluded that Mr Ellis and Mr Haddow encouraged staff to adopt progressive teaching methods. For Rhodes Boyson, however, speaking in 1989, progressive education was anathema:

> Often you can define something most clearly by defining the opposite. The opposite of progressive education is structured education where the teacher is a teacher and he comes into the classroom and he says 'sit down' and the pupils all sit down facing the right way, and he says, 'we are doing this and you are going to learn something'…The opposite is the idea like a bud of a flower,

almost 'Rousseauesque' that all you need to do is free people and they will then become the learners themselves. The child is desperate for knowledge and development, and thus you do not have a structure for learning. Each child does what it wants to do, possibly playing table tennis with another in the corridor to disrupt everyone else in the school...

(cited in Riley 1998: 31)

This extract is from a BBC interview, and its central criticism was widely espoused by Boyson and his Black Paper colleagues during the period. The crude structured-versus-unstructured dichotomy certainly had populist appeal, but failed to acknowledge one of Rousseau's key points, namely the subtle *structuring* of learning experiences by the teacher. Here the power of media lies in its role of information provider, a role that is quintessentially non-neutral. Those parents who, for whatever reasons, do not possess knowledge of germane components of the CS register rely upon the media as the only source of reliable information. The political hue of the medium means that selectivity will take a particular form. Necessarily the nature of the medium entails that not everything can be reported. Moreover, the political dimension enjoins a specific form of filtering of the fraction of information to be provided.[39]

However, the ambiguous, almost non-existent nature of school governance *per se* became an important focus during (and, indeed, after) the affair. Pursuant to the 1944 Education Act, local authorities were obliged to appoint school managers, although there was no requirement to appoint managers for individual schools. As Tomlinson (1993) notes, by the mid-1960s only 21 out of 78 county boroughs had established governing bodies for each school. It was Tyndale that led to a fundamental questioning of the nature and extent of school governance. Two governors tried unsuccessfully to clarify their role and powers with the ILEA in July 1974. It was made clear, however, by an ILEA politician that, whilst it was acceptable for governors to ask the head for information, they could not tell the head what to do. In the event, then, the ILEA provided insufficient guidance. Nevertheless, the school's managers continued to campaign for ILEA intervention. Informally, they used the Labour Party in order to bring their concerns to the attention of County Hall. Again, the ILEA failed to act. On this occasion, a petition was organised. In response, the staff at Tyndale appealed to the ILEA for help against the managers. Matters escalated and the teachers refused to allow managers to visit the school during school hours. Physical debarment led some managers to involve the national press. The chair of the managers described the teachers' ban in the following terms:

The whole concept of the managerial system is under attack. The authority must decide the relationship of managers *vis-à-vis* the school. It is extremely shortsighted of teachers not to allow managers in on the education of children. You cannot sweep things under the carpet.

(cited in Riley 1998)

When staff refused a suggestion by the ILEA that the infant and junior schools be inspected, an inspection was ordered. In response to this order, the staff went on strike and opened an alternative school in a neighbouring building, where they continued to teach for two weeks with twenty-four pupils. The Inspectorate produced an interim report and the chair of the governors passed it on to the press ('Rebel School is Slammed, School of Shame' was one of the headlines). The following week the teachers returned to Tyndale, cooperated in the inspection and agreed to give evidence at the public inquiry.

At the heart of the Tyndale affair was the extent and nature of progressivism. Riley notes that the analysis of progressivism resonates well with Sharp and Green's (1975) critique. In brief, both emphasised its (ostensible) voluntarism and individualism, which thus constituted a new form of (state capitalist) social control. Riley argues that the Tyndale staff 'failed to reconcile their aspirations with the practical realities of planning, progression and challenge and to accept that boundaries need to be set...' (1998: 33). I would argue that it is not about the unavoidability of reconciling progressivism with planning, progression and challenge, since the latter are constitutive of it. Indeed, as we saw in the previous chapter, Plowden was emphatic about the need for careful monitoring and record keeping. As Peter Wilby noted, schools such as Prior Weston primary school in London were exemplars of progressive teaching at the time because they recognised that 'informal teaching requires hard work, careful preparation, skill, patience and good record-keeping' (Riley 1998: 41).

At the S-C level, progressivism was identified with left-wing and/or extreme radicalism. As Jones puts it:

> Despite its diverseness, it can still be termed a modernizing tendency of a broadly left-wing kind. In the 1920s – its classical period – it had been critical of 'industrial society' and social authoritarianism. As taken up in the 1960s by promoters of reform, it added to these commitments a concern to eradicate educational disadvantage.
>
> (Jones 1991: 89)

Yet the reason for its critical stance *vis-à-vis* 'industrial society' stems not from industrialism *per se* but from its disrespect for the nature of children *qua* children. In other words, in order for children to become equipped for their lives as adults, the industrialist logic should be kept at bay *until* that time. Progressivism abstracts from concrete social reality the cognitive capacities and stages of children *qua* children. That such abstract needs are, at the concrete level, contradicted, denigrated or denied must not be confused. However, such confusion, as discussed in Chapter 3, led to a shift of focus from children to the nature of 'social class' inequality. In their misguided quest to improve the lot of their working-class children, the radicals at Tyndale lost metaphysical sight of the young pupils in their charge. The fact that children need structured routines that underpin staged autonomous development is contingently related to any external (in)congruent influences.

In October 1975 Robin Auld QC was appointed to conduct a public inquiry into the teaching, organisation and management of William Tyndale junior and infant schools. At the same time no one anticipated the duration and widespread publicity.

The inquiry opened on 27 October 1975 and continued until 10 February 1976, with almost daily press coverage. Evidence was heard from one hundred and seven witnesses, and six hundred documents were submitted in written evidence. Eleven barristers in all represented the various parties at the inquiry. The teachers were criticised for their lack of planning and unresponsiveness to parents. Equally, the local authority was criticised for having no policies on attainment standards and for failing to intervene at an earlier stage. Despite criticism of the governors, it was the local authority that took the brunt, particularly over its not having established a framework of governance that could deal with such events as Tyndale. As Riley rightly argues, the two-year power struggle at Tyndale brought into sharp relief the question of school governance:

> It created demands for a clearer settlement between local authorities, teachers, school governors and parents. It raised issues about teacher professionalism, the autonomy of head-teachers, the authority of governors and the rights of parents…Tyndale also demonstrated conflicting definitions of progressive education and differing interpretations of the needs and aspirations of working-class children.
>
> (Riley 1998: 50)

Again, the fact that Tyndale teachers were dealing with *working-class* children evinces the complex nature of concrete social reality through which progressivism must navigate. Furthermore, the critical role of the media must not be underestimated. The *Daily Mail*, for instance, changed the wording of a quotation from William Blake that Mr Haddow had written on the blackboard. Instead of 'The tigers of wrath are wiser than the horses of instruction', Mrs Chowles and Mrs Walker maintained that Mr Haddow had written 'The tigers of destruction are stronger than the horses of instruction'. Yet the quotation metamorphosed further in the *Daily Mail* as 'The smile on the face of the tiger is revolution'. Clearly, the quotation was 'reworked' in order to fan the flames of suspicion; namely that Mr Haddow was attempting to indoctrinate children in his charge. Part and parcel of any S-C strategy embroiled in the throes of a competitive contradiction (right versus left…) is to attempt to naturalise one's propositional corpus. Consequently, Mr Haddow and Mr Ellis's ideas were seen as (malignly) ideological, whereas the views of the Black Paper authors were presented as an objective, natural view of the world.

One of the key weaknesses identified by Auld centred on the lack of criteria against which to judge the 'effectiveness' of a school following disagreement between heads and the local inspectorate. (Without lapsing into teleology here, one can start to pinpoint the origins of the OFSTED inspection regime.) In essence, Tyndale was taken up by the right-wing press as a 'loony-left' manifestation of a pervasive educational phenomenon, despite the fact that Tyndale practices were at odds with the majority of successful progressive developments in London and elsewhere.[40] For critics it exemplified the need not only for a clearer articulation of the teacher–parent–local authority relationship but also for a concomitant change in the nature of political control.

The effects of Tyndale: Callaghan's Ruskin speech and the failure of agency

The extent and nature of press coverage of the Tyndale affair meant that the Labour Government could not escape it. During the affair, Callaghan was Foreign Secretary, and upon becoming Prime Minister the affair hit the headlines again following the publication of the findings of the Auld Inquiry. In July 1976, the *Sunday Telegraph*'s headlines were 'Save Our Children'; *The Sunday Times*'s 'How to Control the Teachers'; the *Evening Standard* referred to the teaching staff as 'The Classroom Despots'. When questioned in 1996, Callaghan said that 'I was deter-mined that the Tories were not going to line us up with Tyndale...and every idiotic teacher who was sympathetic to the Labour Party' (taken from Riley 1998: 58). Moreover, he commented that:

> I was concerned with what was being said to me in the constituency about literacy and numeracy, not exactly in those terms but people were talking to me about those things. Some parents were expressing disquiet as to whether their children were being taught or not, *because of the child-centred approach*...There was a feeling of dissatisfaction. The 1944 Settlement seemed to be getting frayed at the edges, *particularly by the activity of the unions*...The Tyndale school was rattling on, getting a lot of publicity and that wasn't doing the teaching profession any good....The Government could not escape its responsibility. *I was also talking to the CBI about those battles and they were complaining about the quality of the school*...I spoke with Bernard Donoughue as I was looking for themes which I could take up as Prime Minister...
>
> (Riley 1998: 59, emphasis added)

The issue of 'the child-centred approach' caused the Labour Party leadership much embarrassment (Chitty 1994). Such embarrassment stemmed from the associa-tion of the party in the eyes of the public (whipped up by a predominantly Tory press) with putative progressive education, in particular the antipathy towards hierarchy and inequality. But, as I have argued, the issue of inequality was (unhelpfully) conjoined with the Rousseauesque underpinning of the progressive philosophy. The first three Black Papers were published in 1969 and 1970, and basically recommended formal teaching in primary schools and emphasised the high standards held to be co-termi-nous with grammar-school education. Chitty notes that it was only in the last two Black Papers, published in 1975 and 1977 (Cox and Boyson 1975, 1977), that support was given to the introduction of educational vouchers and increasing the scope for parental choice of schools. 'By the mid-1970s, the politics of *reaction* had been replaced by the politics of *reconstruction*' (Chitty 1994: 14). Chitty maintains that Rhodes Boyson's triumphalism was not unfounded. In May 1976, at a meeting of the National Council for Education Standards, Boyson was quoted as saying that: 'The forces of the Right in education are on the offensive. The blood is flowing from the other side now' (Chitty 1994: 15). Chitty points to the remarkable extent of right-wing success in seeing the legislative realisation of its ideas. Part of the success is attributable to the changing patterns of decision-making since the mid-1970s.

The nature of decision-making will be discussed in a moment. Clearly, the role of Callaghan himself was equally as important as the position he held and the powers it afforded, as well as the jockeying for favour by right- and left-wing pressure groups. There was a corporate (teacher) failure to pinpoint and consolidate the propositional nature of child-centred philosophy, which is contingently related to the nature of structured inequalities (even though the latter may affect the practical realisation of the former). Silver (1994) has emphasised the lethargy of progressive educators and their lack of discursive penetration in dismissing the Black Paperites and the media-fuelled momentum during and after Tyndale. As he rightly notes, 'progressive' education is shorthand for a range of positions and that homogeneity has never characterised the progressive movement of the twentieth century. In the 1960s and 1970s, progressive educators were involved in, *inter alia*, curriculum reform, the development of new pedagogies, the exposure of educational and social inequalities, the explanation of disadvantage and underachievement. Nevertheless, from the 1960s,...

> [t]he progressive movement gradually lost its sources of energy, failing to see through its inertia the strength of emergent conservative values and policies. In Britain as in many other countries progressive educators failed to see not only the seriousness of the challenge of traditionalist views, but also the changing economic circumstances that would make them more assertive and acceptable.
>
> (Silver 1994: 154)

The response to the Black Papers was a mélange of derision, silence and an expectation that the threat would quickly dissipate. Silver concludes that progressive education had become self-assured to the extent that it no longer felt the need seriously to defend extant positions and practices. That there was a failure of agency is undeniable. I would only add that practically-minded progressive educators were essentially a minority phenomenon. However, Silver's point about agential failure to act indicates the extent to which a degree of freedom existed but remained unexploited. Such delimited freedom, of course, was audaciously transformed into stringent constraint within a relatively short period.[41]

Donoughue and the Downing Street Policy Unit

The Downing Street Policy Unit was a creation of Harold Wilson in 1974, shortly after the Conservative electoral defeat. It was headed by Dr Bernard Donoughue and, in the first five years of its existence, was described by Hennessy as 'a prime-ministerial cabinet in all but name' (cited in Chitty 1994: 15). Donoughue was acutely aware of the potential role of the Unit in influencing the Prime Minister. It was Donoughue who argued that the Labour Government had to respond to the Conservative charge of declining educational standards. By the mid-1970s, the government was looking perilously vulnerable on this issue, and there was scant evidence of a genuine concern to mitigate public disquiet. The resignation of

Harold Wilson provided Donoughue with the opportunity to make education a major issue of concern. Consequently he sent Callaghan an extensive memorandum in April 1976 suggesting that he raise publicly the issue of declining educational standards. This resonated with Callaghan's own concerns and prejudices about child-centred education. As Chitty notes, essentially the Policy Unit wanted to use the Prime Minister as a lever in forcing the DES to adopt a more interventionist stance in policy-making.

According to Donoughue, the teachers' unions had made no effort to stem the influence of militants and progressives, thereby downgrading any concern with developing children's skills and aptitudes. Donoughue also maintained that young people were not being trained in job-seeking skills. This is congruent with Callaghan's interview excerpt quoted on p. 110. Furthermore, however, Donoughue's proposed solution was for (central) government to make teachers more accountable to politicians, employers and parents. Yet, note Donoughue's elision of militancy and progressivism. To reiterate, militancy in this context is associated with the political left and therefore is not *necessarily* tied to progressivism (in the abstract). Indeed, whilst advocates of progressivism would campaign for structures and curricula that focus on the child *qua* child, it does not enjoin that unequal employment structures be abolished or remedied, etc., as a necessary concomitant. Both progressive practitioners and the teaching unions did not unpack this elision. Callaghan took it at face value, embraced Donoughue's analysis of the problems facing education, and welcomed the idea of making an important speech at the earliest opportunity.

The replacement of Sir William Pile by James Hamilton as Permanent Secretary at the DES in June 1976 signalled the growing importance of the role of the Policy Unit. It was the Unit that was responsible for drafting the questions to be asked of Fred Mulley by Callaghan at an important Downing Street interview, and for coordinating the various drafts of the speech on educational standards that was to be delivered by Callaghan at Ruskin College, Oxford, in October that year. The 1977 Green Paper was a direct result of Ruskin, though its final contents did not match the degree of challenge that Donoughue had wanted. During 1976–7, the DES produced a 63-page confidential document known as the Yellow Book. It was commissioned by Callaghan and reported on the education system. The Yellow Book was against the notion of inspection and, overall, was positive, suggesting that some issues needed addressing and clarifying, particularly in relation to the Schools Council and issues *vis-à-vis* preparation for work. Certain sections of the document were leaked to *The Guardian* and *The Times*. Donoughue was especially keen that Callaghan's speech emphasise the need to improve standards and the issue of teacher accountability. As Chitty points out, the Ruskin speech was indeed an important development,

> both for what it chose to highlight and expand upon and on account of its peculiar origins…it seems clear that the early months of the 1976–9 Callaghan administration can be recognized as the first occasion when a body of influential advisers operating *outside* the normal policy-making networks played a

major role in determining the future direction of government education policy. By the spring of 1976 Donoughue was anxious to circumvent the teachers' unions, the local authorities and, above all, the civil servants of the DES. Callaghan's new concern with value for money and his fear of the populist appeal of the opposition campaign on standards meant that he was not prepared to rely solely on the DES for strategic advice.

(Chitty 1994: 19)

Under the new Permanent Secretary at the DES, James Hamilton, civil servants developed a new interest in policy, efficiency and the need to make effective use of limited resources (as a result of the deepening economic crisis). At the same time, it was widely accepted by both civil servants and politicians that there had to be greater control of education, especially the secondary curriculum, in order to improve standards, and that teachers had their role to play in improving relations between education and industry. Crucially, after 1976, partnership was replaced by *accountability* as the dominant metaphor *vis-à-vis* the distribution of power in the education system (Chitty 1994: 19). The role of the Policy Unit played an even bigger role in the development of education policy following the election success of the Conservatives in 1979, and is therefore crucial in accounting for, but not determining, the 1988 Reform Act. The role of personality cannot be subsumed under some all-embracing logic of capital, since, counterfactually, Callaghan's personal predilection and prejudices might have been diametrically opposed to the views of Donoughue and Hamilton. Indeed, that Kenneth Baker's equally highly personalistic imprint on the 1988 Education Reform Act was (contradictorily) supportive of 'New Right' philosophy does not lend credence to any logic-of-capital teleology. The contingent nature of the complementarity of viewpoints cannot be accommodated by the over-arching emphasis accorded to the 'Capital Relation'. However, we shall return to the role of the Policy Unit and the use of 'New Right' ideas in the next chapter. In brief, Ruskin was a defining moment, since 'it raised issues of accountability and control and echoed some of the concerns of the Black Papers...it represented for Labour a shift to the Right in thinking about education' (Riley 1998: 66).

The economic factor

Callaghan's concern with 'value for money' is inextricably bound up with the economic crisis; a crisis that was exacerbated by Britain's weak underlying industrial base, which, in turn, necessitated fiscal belt-tightening. Yet, to reiterate, the consequences of the crisis were not inevitable. There was no capitalist-determined cure-all. The reasons for the crisis and, in particular, the reality of Britain's precarious situation *vis-à-vis* the rest of the world were incorrectly diagnosed, thereby fuelling and buttressing the anti-progressive onslaught. However, a flavour of the extent of the changes in policy-making is readily gleaned by the strategies delineated in a section from the 1977 Green Paper for improving school-to-work relations. 'School and working life' emphasised

...[a] basic understanding of the economy and the activities, especially manufacturing industry, which are necessary for the creation of Britain's national
wealth. It is an important task of secondary schools to develop this understanding, and opportunities for its development should be offered to pupils of
all abilities. These opportunities are needed not only by young people who have
careers in industry later but perhaps even more by those who may work elsewhere, so that the role of industry becomes soundly appreciated by society in
general.

(Secretary of State for Education and Science 1977)

The 1977 Green Paper was part of the flurry of documents produced during the
so-called 'Great Debate' unleashed by Ruskin. Yet the idealist fallacy underpinning
the need for a greater understanding of industry is hardly new. During the 1880s or
the 1920s, the economy was crucial in the focusing of attention on the purpose,
content and outcomes of the education system (Silver 1994). In his Ruskin speech,
Callaghan emphasised that schools should play a more conspicuous and integral
part in preparing pupils for working life as a key to economic development. The
idealist fallacy lies in the widely endorsed notion that a swift dose of technological-
cum-scientific understanding, mixed with some time spent gaining work experience,
would regenerate Britain's declining economy, as if knowledge of the intricacies of
corporate banking endows one with a steady flow of cash! While it might be
possible to make a case that formal education systems can help set the scene for
technological innovation and economic development, 'in reality the transformations
which have revolutionised world and national economies have taken place *outside*
formal education systems...school systems may reflect economic and technological
change but are unlikely to play much part in generating it' (Lowe 1997: 25).

What did not help the progressive cause was its alleged anti-industrialist bias (see,
for example, Mathieson and Bernbaum 1988). But, as already discussed, this
approach, grounded in a historiographical tradition of blaming 'English culture'
and the educational system for Britain's economic decline, is an elision. As Ahier
rightly notes, the most effective development of progressivism took the form of a
child-centredness 'which was built on notions of the nature of childhood and its
stages' (1991: 131). Culture-as-the-cause advocates generally adduce (school) history
textbooks as exemplary of the 'British disease'. Yet for young children in particular
it was thought that, because such children cannot grasp the abstractions of money,
markets, capital, investment and profit, the development of capitalism had to be
'dumbed down' for them (Ahier 1991). It has been argued that, against a background of political attempts to make British industrialists more accountable to the
state and their employees, the industrialists turned such demands on to the teachers
(Beck 1983). However, as Ahier rightly argues, notwithstanding the plausibility (or
otherwise) of Beck's argument, the very notions of a national economy and a
'national culture' are somewhat questionable, both in those accounts that blamed
the schools and culture for the economic decline and those which blamed the industrialists themselves. As he puts it:

At a time when the economy seems to open, so easily influenced by the strength or weakness of the American dollar, so penetrated by manufacturing imports, and so dependent on decisions by multi-national companies based both in the UK and elsewhere, the appeal of a thesis which keeps explanations of economic failure and future success within national boundaries is reassuring to many. Plus, when the explanation requires a revised national culture, enshrined, perhaps, in a national curriculum and prompted by the spread of enterprise initiatives, then it is truly comforting.

(Ahier 1991: 134)

The continuing onslaught: Bennett on 'ineffective progressive methods'

However, given that the economy was in dire straits, the concurrent 'evidence' of ineffective progressive teaching methods was a veritable godsend for critics of progressivism and the Right in general to posit a causal link. (In reality, of course, we are dealing with a correlation, which does not pretend to any necessary causal relationship.) In 1976, at the time of Tyndale and Ruskin, Neville Bennett and colleagues published what was, according to Silver (1994), probably the most talked-about educational book of the decade in Britain. *Teaching Styles and Pupil Progress* focused on the 'effectiveness' of different teaching approaches. The overriding message of the book, gladly disseminated by a sympathetic media, was that progressive methods simply did not work. Bennett was well aware that his findings would be disturbing to many parents and teachers. The findings documented that, in reading, the pupils of 'formal' and 'mixed' teachers progressed more than those of 'informal' teachers, with some four to five months' difference in attainment. In mathematics, 'formally' taught pupils were superior *vis-à-vis* 'informal' and 'mixed' styles of teaching. It was reported that 'the teaching approaches advocated by the Plowden Report, and many of the educational advisory staff and college lecturers, often result in poorer academic progress, particularly among high ability children' (cited in Silver 1994: 90).

However, a project carried out by researchers at Leicester University contested *Teaching Styles and Pupil Progress.* It pointed to the classroom management problems that resulted from Plowden recommendations in classes of thirty or more. Moreover, the research was unequivocal in its view that progressive teaching hardly existed in practice. A few years later, a re-examination of Bennett *et al.*'s data found significant methodological weaknesses. Nevertheless, the importance of *Teaching Styles and Pupil Progress* lies in the media-directed attack on progressivism and its pressing for the superiority of formal teaching methods at the primary level. And, as should be clear from the foregoing, they were not short on ammunition. Following Tyndale, Auld, Ruskin, *The Yellow Book* and Bennett, the anti-progressivist offensive continued unabated. In March 1977 a BBC 'Panorama' programme attacked the Faraday comprehensive school in West London. The programme conveyed the impression that schools *in general* were undisciplined, poorly organised, thereby contributing to Britain's dire economic situation. More important, however, is that by the time of this programme, parental choice, a National Curriculum, testing at ages seven, eleven and fourteen, the publication of test results and an emphasis on the core curriculum were being articulated as key components in educational policy.

Indeed, as Lowe (1997) notes, this was the juncture at which 'New Right' thinking began to permeate the Conservative Party as a whole. Boyson used the Conservative Political Centre as a base from which to publish such pamphlets as *Parental Choice*, which was aimed at grassroots Tory supporters. The Centre for Policy Studies, set up in 1974 by Keith Joseph and Margaret Thatcher, promptly became a key focus for these ideas. By 1975 the Conservative Research Department's journal began to echo the ideas of the Black Papers, and in the same year the so-called pressure group FEVER began to lobby actively for the use of vouchers in education, drawing its inspiration from ideas first voiced by Milton Friedman in 1955. Consequently, 'Thatcher's assumption of the leadership of the party in the same year meant that any future Conservative administration would have the question of educational reform at the heart of its agenda and would be sympathetic to this lobbying' (Lowe 1997: 156). In a nutshell, New Right concerns were reflected on a daily basis. The 1977 Taylor Report called for closer parental involvement in the running of schools (although it was not until the 1980 Education Act that LEAs were required to make such provisions). Furthermore, the focus of the British research community had shifted somewhat by the end of the decade, too. As Silver notes, economic stringency, inflation and poor industrial performance were central to the emergence of accountability and standards as central themes of policy discourse, and to an accelerating search for a common curriculum. 'By 1979...a research emphasis on "the assessment of performance" and testing was strong, including controversy over the nature and role of evaluation...These preoccupations were to be important in the new policy climate created by the Conservative government in the 1980s' (Silver 1994: 91). Such preoccupations are part of the focus of the next chapter. Indeed, the education research community now finds itself divided and subject to internecine debate. Specifically, there is a significant proportion of university academics and researchers who have provided, and continue to provide, the impetus for an international school effectiveness movement, whose ideological import is indisputable (Willmott 1999c). Such research is intimately allied to past Conservative and present Labour policy, particularly its links with OFSTED.

However, in 1978 an NFER (National Foundation for Educational Research) study *Sources of Difference in School Achievement* undertaken by Alan Brimer and colleagues highlighted the methodological problems of measuring effectiveness and the failure of large-scale surveys to indicate whether children benefit from school. The study also looked at the relative importance of home and school and the differential impact of schools. Silver is surprised by the study's lack of impact. But agential failure has been the hallmark of the teachers' unions and the Labour Party itself. The importance of Ruskin and the Great Debate lies in the change of political context, namely one that increasingly demanded restrictions on teacher autonomy. As Bates puts it:

The Great Debate reflected a trend towards defining and limiting the bound-aries of teacher autonomy. The very initiation of a public debate on education, involving the unprecedented consultation of industrial organizations and parents as well as educational organizations, served as an explicit reminder to the teaching profession…that the curriculum was not solely their responsibility to determine.

(1984: 199)

It would be tempting to suggest that the death of child-centred philosophy and its minority practising status was complete by the end of 1976. (Its death is metaphorical, of course, since its CS status precludes ontological erasure.) But despite the call for circumscribing teacher autonomy, a core national curriculum – which would be more attuned to the world of work – and making teachers account-able to parents and the state (for which read: more for less in climate of economic stringency), the child-centred approach was not denied any role. Undeniably there were strong voices in the Conservative Party and especially in its affiliated think tanks that wanted a 'return' to 'traditional methods'. But, as Chitty points out, while the National Curriculum has its roots in the Great Debate of 1976–7, 'its *raison d'être* has changed dramatically in the hands of the policy-makers of 1987–8' (1990: 12). As we shall see in the next chapter, it was during these years and after that manage-rial considerations took centre stage. Indeed, it was at the final stages of the genesis of the Act that child-centred practical underpinnings were erased following, *inter alia*, the direct intervention of the Prime Minister. The so-called 'New Right' corpus of propositions about society and, in particular, the state's role *vis-à-vis* the educa-tion system will be discussed in the next chapter. Successive Secretaries of State for Education during the 1980s explicitly drew upon such contradictory CS properties (of which the potential S-C import will also be addressed).

Concluding remarks

The interactional phase delineated above indicates the overall morphostatic nature of the educational system following the publication of Plowden and the generous degrees of curricular freedom bestowed upon the teachers. Equally, there was no concurrent corporate regrouping. Instead, this period witnessed schism and dissen-sion, including a manifest failure practically to develop Plowden and to maintain its impetus. During the 1960s and 1970s the debate on the school curriculum was conducted largely among teachers, local authority advisors, teacher-trainers and Her Majesty's Inspectors (Lowe 1997). Such debate was not translated into widespread progressive practice and, moreover, it was subject to acerbic attack by right-wing think tanks and pressure groups. In terms of the eventual expunging of child-centred considerations from the testing and curricular arrangements of the 1988 Education Reform Act, one must be careful to avoid the illegitimate imputation of any *post hoc* teleology. Whilst the growing interventionism of government was the result of economic trends that were endemic and retrospectively ineluctable, the actual outcome of the National Curriculum was not. But, of course, such an outcome could not be envisioned without the CS components bequeathed by the expanding corpus of right-wing, anti-progressivist pamphlets, books and related media that found a ready and willing audience in the Conservative Party, particularly its leader and successive Secretaries of State for Education.

The cultural morphogenesis exemplified by the Black Papers and the numerous CS items disseminated by cognate groups was not paralleled by the progressivists (notwithstanding some important work in modern languages, mathematics and science). To be fair, much of the morphogenetic cultural embroidery had already been carried out, yet it was not defended in the light of the right-wing onslaught, for reasons already discussed. What did not help matters was the dominance of the education philosophers discussed in Chapter 3, and undoubtedly the economic situation that was exploited fully by the right-wing press, the Conservative Party and the Prime Minister of the Labour Party. Indeed, during the Tyndale affair, successful child-centred programmes were being successfully installed in London itself. Its unexploited success was symptomatic of a divided, yet still potentially relatively powerful, teaching profession that grossly underestimated the turning tide. The bargaining power of the teachers was diminishing almost on daily basis whilst the profession's alleged deficiencies were unremittingly trumpeted. Objectively, their professional knowledge – backed by Plowden, the development of teacher training colleges and University education departments, and so on – was not exploited as the key (or rather the only) component of relative negotiating strength.

The portentous origins of the 'managerial state' (Clarke and Newman 1997) were clear enough: the need for improved 'quality' (often entailing better exam results at reduced price) brought about by stringent *management* of cannot-be-trusted teachers. In other words, it was not simply pedagogy that was at stake but the teacher autonomy *per se* and the nature of their work, which any potential Conservative Government would insist upon curtailing in the British context. The overly managerialist restructuring of teachers' work was not a foregone conclusion at the beginning of the Thatcher years. Of course, part of the staging was provided during this period following the discussion about accountability, value-for-money and school governance that the 'Great Debate' unleashed. In fact, testing at the ages of 7, 11, 14 and 16 was not the brainchild of the 1980s. To reiterate, a managerialist approach to testing was not the overriding or, indeed, subsidiary concern. The question to be addressed now is how the tide completely engulfed the teaching profession during the 1980s, following the electoral success of the Conservatives in 1979, which culminated in the 1988 Act and its subsequent legislative consolidators. For reasons of expository convenience, a more detailed examination of the 'New Right' corpus is provided in Chapter 5. However, mention has already been made of Hayek, who is one of the key ideational players *vis-à-vis* the 1988 Act. These ideas are part and parcel of the interactional phase, but since they were put into practice during the late 1980s and early 1990s, it is more helpful to elaborate them in the next chapter.

5 Socio-cultural elaboration

The 1988 Education Reform Act and the new managerialism

Introduction

The purpose of this chapter is to delineate the final phase of the morphogenetic sequence, which in turn provides the temporal starting-point of a new conditioning sequence. The three-part sequential schema adopted for this part of the book is necessarily generic because of its broad sweep. Fundamentally, it should be clear that the phases of Conditioning → Interaction → Outcome have not been arbitrarily plucked out of the historical time-scale. The explanatory power of the morphogenetic approach lies in the link between substantive research and the *temporal multi-sequential nature of social reality*: what is to be explained is necessarily anchored in *sui generis* strata and their temporal materialisation. In other words, a broad-brush analysis of the type I have provided dictates a broad sequencing procedure. Thus, at almost innumerable points in each chapter could a morphogenetic sequence begin: again, where it begins depends on what one wants to explain. The establishment of the Senior Management Team in my first case-study mentioned in Chapter 1 constitutes the start of a new conditioning sequence, which is the end-product of a temporal sequence of social interaction. The point is that, whilst this sequence lends itself to detailed empirical enquiry, it is part of a wider (macro) morphogenetic sequence. Any study that detailed the minutiae involved in the establishment of the management team without recourse to the wider sequence would be somewhat vitiated. However, the multi-sequential nature of social reality enjoins that we respect the fact that at any given point in time there are cycles within cycles, operating at different (irreducible) levels of social reality. The number of cycles at any one level cannot be determined *a priori*, but established *a posteriori*.

Within any school one can conceive of cycles in terms of various specific committees alongside the Senior Management Team and their associated roles and deposited powers, which are analytically distinct from their concrete operation. A significant number of teachers will therefore also be members or heads of committees, equal opportunities officers, parent–school coordinators, and so on, whereby role-associated powers shape activities often unrelated to classroom practice. This applies equally at the level of the DfEE, which itself provides the conditioning cyclical background to schools and LEAs. It is because the DfEE constrains and/or facilitates activities at the school (and LEA) level that one can talk of second-order (systemic) emergence. (Here, of course, the LEA itself may overdetermine school activities.) In essence, at whichever level(s) one is theorising about, the temporal unfolding of morphogenetic/static dynamics cannot be avoided. Unlike structuration theory, the temporal priority of structural (and cultural) conditioning is a transcendental prerequisite for any substantive research however short or long the time-scale adopted.[42]

The 1988 Education Reform Act (ERA) removed restrictions that previously prevented parents opting to send children to schools of their choice. It gave schools substantially increased control over their budgets. Funding was allocated according to numbers on the roll (per capita funding). Formal examinations at the ages of 7, 11, 14 and 16 were imposed. Central control was increased over the content of schooling. A National Curriculum imposed three core subjects and six or seven foundation subjects, which were to be taught to all children from the ages of five to sixteen. The Secretary of State determined the programmes of study. Teachers' hours were specified for the first time. The 1987 TGAT (Task Group on Assessment and Testing) Report augured well for teachers committed to child-centred practices. However, such recommendations contradicted the managerialist quasi-marketisation of the education system, envisaged in particular by Thatcher, and were soon discarded. Increased competition via the publication of League Tables was later promoted. In fact, under the current 'New' Labour administration, league tables remain firmly on the educational agenda, alongside the recent imposition of national target setting. Part of the managerialist consolidation of ERA is the Education (Schools) Act 1992, which established arrangements for independent inspections (on a four-yearly basis) by registered inspectors to be trained by, and responsible to, OFSTED. The OFSTED rationale is managerialist and reinforced by the School Effectiveness Movement, which is dominated almost exclusively by international academics upon whom past Conservative and current Labour ministers rely for advice. The tight link with national and international universities means that OFSTED and the ERA constitute a particularly stringent obstruction for child-centred primary school teachers.

Such structural elaboration is necessarily intertwined with, and underpinned by, ideas. The elaborated corpus of ideas used both to construct and legitimate the ERA is characterised by logical contradiction, specifically between neo-liberalism and conservatism. The transcendental realist argument for the objectivity of the latter and concomitant practical untenability of the Act is provided. It is argued that the so-called paradoxical elements of the Act are the result of an immanent contradiction. The precise playing-out of how corporate agents dealt with the contradiction is delineated. Here, it is maintained that corporate agency is necessarily enjoined to commit theory/practice inconsistency. A lengthy analysis of the contradictory CS items that underpinned the ERA and subsequent legislation is provided, since the contradiction is almost invariably not recognised by neo-liberals and, moreover, accounts for the (contradictory) nature of the restructuring of the education system in England and Wales; that is, for example, the desire to devolve autonomy to individual schools versus the concurrent imposition of a national curriculum and inspectorate. Equally, when it is recognised by critics, it is played down or dismissed as ultimately reconcilable. Crucially, therefore, the decentralisation versus centralisation paradox is an objective S-C contradiction derived from the untenability of neo-liberalism. Furthermore, since the explanatory critique offered here enjoins the identification of unwanted constraints, it is especially relevant in the present context of a Labour administration, since the latter has not only consolidated the Conservative bequest but also extended it (viz. Education Action Zones and national target setting). The economistic, technicist driven nature of the ERA meant, though by no means determined, that congruent ideational items be used to justify a managerialist approach to assessment and accountability. Indeed, the then Secretary of State warmly welcomed the TGAT proposals, which emphasised formative assessment at the expense of short, sharp standardised tests. The managerialist usurpation of assessment and co-option of leading academics was not a foregone conclusion. Whilst it was not a foregone conclusion, however, the market rationale of the reforms made it unlikely that such proposals would be adopted because of their cost.

To recapitulate, this chapter will (a) scrutinise the neo-liberal inflection that provided the basis for the quasi-marketisation of the education system, which was concomitantly restructured along managerialist lines; (b) delineate the lead-up to the ERA. The ERA and the subsequent legislative consolidation provide the backdrop to the two case-study schools analysed in Part III. I should like to reiterate that it is simply for expository convenience that I have postponed discussion of the generic tenets of the 'New Right' (CS) corpus until now. This is because analysis of the contradictions of the 1988 Education Reform Act (ERA) is thereby facilitated. (In fact, the burgeoning 'New Right' corpus has already been spelled out, specifically the attack upon progressivism and the illegitimate elision of it with left-wing ideology.)

New Right philosophy and systemic contradiction

Back to the Downing Street Policy Unit

In the previous chapter the burgeoning powerful role of the Policy Unit in the development of education policy was discussed. The power of the Unit increased considerably during the mid- to late 1980s.[43] Indeed, by 1983 the Prime Minister of the day, Margaret Thatcher, relied increasingly for advice, encouragement and a steady supply of radical ideas on a growing number of young right-wing analysts who came to occupy key positions in the Unit. During the early years of her tenure at 10 Downing Street, Thatcher strengthened her own personal resources, whilst at the same time weakening those of her Cabinet colleagues for the performance of their collective deliberations. In fact, Thatcher got rid of the Central Policy Review Staff (CPRS), a creation of Edward Heath, which had provided policy advice for the Cabinet as a whole and had been an important feature of collective government (Chitty 1994). In a nutshell, Thatcher welcomed the Policy Unit into what Hennessy has dubbed 'a shadow Whitehall', with each of its young members covering a variety of subject areas (cited in Chitty 1994: 20). The Unit challenged extant Conservative orthodoxies and, following Professor Brian Griffiths's appointment to oversee its daily running in October 1985, it became particularly influential *vis-à-vis* education policy.

Under the direction of Professor Griffiths, the Unit was part of the Prime Minister's own Downing Street machinery. Consequently, any advice was not subject to censure or rebuttal by the Cabinet. According to an ex-member of the Unit, David Willetts, members were 'always on the lookout for new policy ideas, the fresh angle, the new policy proposal worth putting before the Prime Minister', and its main task was to undertake 'the politically impossible' (Chitty 1994: 21). Rosenhead neatly sums up thus:

> The Policy Unit supplies the Prime Minister with a radically new policy consistent with her principles and instincts. She then announces this policy in a glare of publicity, thereby establishing a political *fait accompli*. The debate having thus been finessed and forestalled, the relevant Department is left with the job of trying to make the innovation work.
>
> (cited in Chitty 1994: 21)

However, it is salutary to remind ourselves that education policy especially was not the result of the Policy Unit. Indeed, after 1985, the Unit was essentially a channel for a number of influential right-wing pressure groups, notably the Centre for Policy Studies and Margaret Thatcher herself. By 1987, such groups had provided a set of policy prescriptions designed specifically to establish marketisation of the education system (and indeed the public sector as a whole). Alongside the Centre for Policy Studies, which was founded in 1974, was the Institute of Economic Affairs, which established its own Education Unit whose director was Stuart Sexton, and the Hillgate Group, which comprised Caroline Cox, Jessica Douglas-Home, John Marks, Lawrence Nocross and Roger Scruton. Of course, one cannot pinpoint with accuracy which group was responsible for specific elements of education policy. However, as Chitty notes, when Kenneth Baker was offered the education portfolio in May 1986, he was well aware that the CPS, the IEA and the Hillgate Group were the policy-makers as far as Margaret Thatcher was concerned. Furthermore, the three groups are influential exemplars of an array of like-minded study groups and organisations. Nevertheless, given the ease of access to Brian Griffiths and thus Downing Street, Roger Scruton *et al.* were ideally placed to influence the policy-making process. During 1986–7, a number of educational planning meetings were held in Downing Street. For the Hillgate Group, the main objective was to restructure the education system such that all schools would be owned by individual trusts, their survival in the education market place contingent upon their ability to satisfy their customers. Yet all right-wing groups by no means shared the Hillgate's key objective.

> The one issue on which the various groups failed to reach agreement concerned the desirability or otherwise of a centrally imposed National Curriculum. This source of conflict could be said to reflect a major paradox within Thatcherism itself. For, as has often been pointed out…what makes New Right philosophy special is a unique combination of a traditional *liberal* defence of the free economy with a traditional *conservative* defence of state authority. This combination of potentially opposing doctrines means that the New Right

can appear by turns libertarian and authoritarian, populist and élitist. For neo-liberals the emphasis is always on freedom of choice, the individual, the market, minimal government and *laissez-faire*; while neo-conservatism priori-tizes notions of social authoritarianism, the disciplined society, the nation and strong government...Keith Joseph, Stuart Sexton and Alfred Sherman could be said to be leading figures on the neo-liberal wing of the movement; while the leading exponent of neo-conservatism is probably Roger Scruton...

(Chitty 1994: 23)

It was the Hillgate Group that pushed for the introduction of a detailed national curriculum for all pupils. The group envisaged that such a curriculum would encompass such concerns as respect for the family, the church, private property and so on. At the same time it would underscore the need for the virtue of free enter-prise and the pursuit of profit. In direct contrast, Stuart Sexton categorically opposed the idea of an imposed curriculum. However, Kenneth Baker and key DES advisors were able to enlist the support of the neo-liberal camp for central control of the curriculum. Chitty (1994) maintains that a national curriculum is not incompatible with the furtherance of the quasi-marketisation of the education system, since *inter alia* it would provide evidence to parents of the desirability or otherwise of individual schools via a national programme of testing. 'In other words, additional consumer information provided by the test results would actually *help* a market system to operate more effectively' (Chitty 1994: 24). Equally, Whitty maintains that the neo-liberal and neo-conservative positions 'may ultimately be reconcilable' (1991: 105). In brief, the contradiction centres on the fact that the 1988 Act gave 'market forces' a leading role within areas of policy that had hitherto been subject to detailed regulation and planning by central and local government, yet introduced curricular prescription into an area where there had been generous degrees of autonomy.

Contradiction: apparent or real? Hayek, social ontology and the nature of 'the market'

Chitty is right that a national curriculum is not incompatible with the furtherance of the marketisation of the education system, since it would provide evidence to parents of the relative performance of schools. However, what is missing from Chitty's analysis is that the neo-liberal ideas, upon which such marketisation is based, preclude any form of national curriculum since this necessitates state involvement. In other words, we need to differentiate different levels of analysis: the fact that the provision of evidence may help parents become better 'consumers' is anterior to the inconsistent enactment of the latter. As Ball notes, the neo-liberal and neo-Conservative elements of the New Right 'display a number of *vital* contra-dictions' (1990: 41, emphasis added). I want to argue that Ball is quite right not to lose sight of the objective contradictory mélange that is the 'New Right' philosophy; that is, between the neo-liberal and neo-conservative constituents.[44] To recapitulate, central to the morphogenetic approach is the identification of objective socio-cultural contradictions and complementarities, which both shape action-contexts and at the same time may remain unnoticed or noticed yet stringently obstruct (and vice versa). The origins of the neo-liberal conspectus can been traced back to the collapse of Keynesian social democracy, particularly the oil crisis, as discussed in the previous chapter. The temporal coincidence of such neo-liberal ideas as the need for the state to withdraw from, rather than continue to inhibit, the spontaneous workings of 'the (capitalist) market' and the oil crisis provided the necessary (but insufficient) conditions for the imposition of the managerialist (or business) model on to the public sector as a whole. The Black Paperites contributed to the anti-statist thrust of the neo-liberal critique of the state. In particular, their elision of left-wing ideology with progressivism and imputation of deeply entrenched vested interests of progressivist teachers in an unwieldy, bureaucratic education system resonated well.

In contrast, the neo-conservative strand of 'New Right' philosophy underscores the need for 'strong' state involvement. As Gamble notes, the conservative element is characterised by its emphasis upon the *conditions* that are required for the establishment and maintenance of social order, namely:

> the need for authority, hierarchy and balance. Conservatives have generally been fierce critics of liberal doctrines of individualism which justify the removal of all restraints...Both [the neo-liberals and Conservatives], however, regard the trends established by the growth of public sectors and the kind of government intervention practised since the 1940s as pernicious. Both focus on the rise of a 'new class' of public sector professional employees who come to staff the agencies of the public sector and who have a vested interest in its continued growth.
>
> (Gamble 1988: 54–5)

Clearly, then, in order to provide the conditions that are necessary for the maintenance of 'authority, hierarchy and balance', irreducible social structures are unavoidable. However, it is important to mention that at the S-C level neo-conservatives, whilst (unavoidably) responsible for the creation of social structures/systems (e.g. civil service), may at the same time subscribe to voluntarism, or more specifically, the fallacy of composition. This is the assumption that what is possible for an individual must *ipso facto* be possible for all individuals at the same time. An example of this is the view that *all* children have the opportunity to attend university and subsequently to enter one of the professions. The fact that all children have differential opportunities is thereby repudiated, for there is no notion of the *structuring* of life-chances, namely that the education system requires successes *and* failures.

The complex reasons for the incorporation of monetarist nostrums, the repudiation of any state involvement and the glorification of the ostensibly superior regulatory efficacy of 'the market' have already been touched upon in the previous chapter. However, Jonathan (1997) has convincingly argued that the populist appeal of the 'New Right' agenda for restructuring – or the quasi-marketisation of – the public sector needs to be traced back further than the oil crisis. It stems more from the liberal promises of equality following the 1944 Butler Act. She argues that New Right attacks on education tapped a reservoir of popular unease. Such unease was not unsurprising since, 'despite reformist measures over three decades, the post-war education project of individual emancipation for each and simultaneous social progress for all had failed to deliver to many what they had hoped for from it' (Jonathan 1997: 57). Indeed, it was the failure of Keynesian social democracy that resonated well with 'liberal' thinking that dates back further than the oil crisis. One of the key arguments of this chapter is that the New Right panacea was both misconceived and contradictory. Such contradiction and misconception will be teased out via an analysis of the ontological underpinning of the neo-liberal project whose aim is to inject the competitive nature of 'the market' into a stifling, inefficient and expensive public sector.

I have deliberately placed scare quotes around the word liberal in the preceding paragraph, since neo-liberalism, whilst anchored in eighteenth- and nineteenth-century premises about the danger of well-intentioned paternalism leading to authoritarian coercion, fails to engage with unresolved questions about the interdependence of agency in the social world. Thus, to Jonathan,

> ...nineteenth-century liberal niceties about the relation of the individual to the social are conspicuous by their absence in the pronouncements not only of politicians of New Right persuasion...but also in some philosophical writing and in the exhortations of 'opinion-formers' in right-wing 'think-tanks'. The claim that neo-liberalism represents the eclipse of politics by economics may seem superficially surprising when apologists are typically keen to adopt the mantle and invoke the authority of the early liberals, *but that invocation is seriously misleading.*
>
> (1997: 48–9, emphasis added)

Part of the S-C process of systematisation of the 'New Right' philosophy places a premium on a (potentially rewarding) search for congruent CS items; hence the selective use of CS items from Mill, Hume, Smith *et al.* during the 1980s by such organisations as the Centre for Policy Studies, the Adam Smith Institute and the Institute for Economic Affairs. As we saw in the previous chapter, the Centre for Policy Studies was founded by Margaret Thatcher and Keith Joseph and quickly became a focus for the ideas of such right-wing thinkers as Milton Friedman and F A Hayek. The underlying theme for the ideas systematised by the sections of the New Right was the alleged superiority of market mechanisms and the need for sound money. Such cultural embroidery was carried out against the backdrop of the Black Papers, of which the last was published in 1977.

> [Henceforth] the discursive cudgels of the conservative educational offensive were taken up by a variety of related and overlapping New Right agencies and groups...What makes them markedly different from the rather informally produced *Black Papers* is the degree and sophistication of their organisation and strategies for dissemination...By the 1980s...neo-liberal texts, particularly the work of Hayek, and monetarist theories like those of Friedman, are paraded as a basis for social and economic policy making...
>
> (Ball 1990: 34–5)

However, as Gamble (1988) notes, the call for the restoration of sound money has been the New Right's centrepiece and is the issue on which the New Right first made a major impact. Despite continuing disagreement about the nature of the economy, the widening of divisions between competing macro-economic perspectives and the undermining of the theoretical underpinnings of monetarism, it was the marked deterioration in economic performance in the 1970s that accounts for its ascendancy. Monetarists argue, *inter alia*, that the control of inflation should be prioritised, irrespective of any increase in unemployment. New Right economics decries state intervention because it is held that administrative and bureaucratic structures are inherently inferior to markets as a means of allocating resources. With regard to public expenditure and taxation, New Right economists assert that market solutions would in every case be superior to the established public provision. At the same time, there evolved the contribution of 'public choice theory', which argued against the notion that public bodies were disinterested and enlightened, while private individuals and companies were self-interested and avaricious. The argument here is that the pursuit of self-interest by private bodies is licensed by the existence of a competitive framework of rules that does not exist in the public sector. Consequently, many in the New Right concluded that 'markets were much superior to democracy in representing and aggregating individual choices. It was only a short step to arguing that democracy needed to be hedged around with restrictions to ensure that it did not permit encroachments upon the private sphere' (Gamble 1988: 52).

The 'moral argument' proffered by New Right thinkers will not be addressed here (see Gamble 1988 and Jonathan 1997). I want now to focus on the social ontology that underpins the 1988 Education Reform Act. We have briefly looked at the need for 'sound money' embodied in the monetarist doctrine, whereby taxes and public expenditure should be as low as possible and its institutions be subject to the competitive ethic of the market. New Right thinkers and politicians alike readily adopt the rhetoric of the so-called *free* market and how its wealth-generating, dynamic properties should be transposed to the public sector. In brief, the argument that an objective contradiction underpins the 1988 Act (as well as all public sector policies that have introduced quasi-market principles) is a transcendental one. It will be argued that those critical commentators who argue for the apparent reconcilability of the neo-liberal and neo-conservative elements (at the CS level) are confusing an S-C necessity brought about by an immanent contradiction.

Hayek's catallaxy: the denial of social structure

The key thinker used by the neo-liberals in their unrelenting drive towards quasi-marketisation of the public sector is Hayek. As already mentioned, neo-liberalism – and the 'New Right' generically – is also employed as a portmanteau, which embraces Friedman's economic liberalism, Nozick's libertarianism (the advocacy of the minimal state) and Hayek's Austrian economics. In Chapter 3, I discussed the nature of the materiality of the division of labour, whose materiality is autonomous of capitalist social relations. Hayek lends support to the *sui generis* properties of the division of labour. He distinguishes between 'catallaxy' and 'economy'. His conception of economy is a restricted one, referring to clusters of economic activities that are organised for a specific purpose and have a unitary hierarchy of ends, in which knowledge of how to achieve ends is shared. A catallaxy, on the other hand, has no unitary hierarchy of ends, but a mass of innumerable economies without a specific purpose. As Hayek has famously pointed out, it is the product of *spontaneous* growth as opposed to design. One of Hayek's central arguments, *contra* state socialism, is that the catallaxy eludes regulation by central control. This is because of the extraordinary division of knowledge immanent to any advanced industrial economy. Thus *the* fundamental economic problem is not calculational but epistemological, namely how to coordinate the actions of innumerable agents without the possibility of any adequate centralised knowledge of their needs and resources. Consequently, competition operates as a discovery procedure and the main role of markets is in generating information, through the price mechanism, as to how economic agents who are ignorant of each other may best attain their equally unknown purposes (Sayer 1995).

The salient point, then, is that the complex and evolutionary nature of the catallaxy makes its qualities unknowable to any single mind or organisation. Hayek correctly takes to task the socialist vision of a collectively controlled and planned advanced economy – a 'fatal conceit', which he terms 'constructivism'. As Sayer points out, many Marxist positions have failed to acknowledge the fundamental difference between running a technical division of labour for producing a particular type of commodity and coordinating a social division of labour involving millions of different commodities, thousands of enterprises and billions of customers. This is not to license chaos, for although catallaxies are unplanned they are ordered. Yet, for Marx, the only good order 'must be the product of conscious collective purpose, a Hegelian legacy of humanity rising to consciousness and control over itself...Marx is resistant not only to actions having bad unintended consequences, but to unintended consequences *per se*' (Sayer 1995: 76). However, Hayek adopts the extreme counter-position to Marx. In brief, he reasons that because unintended consequences of actions are central to the functioning of catallaxies, one must not intervene. This is simply a *non sequitur* and, *inter alia*, excuses problems that can – and should – be confronted and removed (ecological problems, poverty...). More crucially, Hayek denies that catallaxies possess emergent properties.

> Absent from Hayek's image of capitalism as an unimaginably complex mass of individuals responding to one another through markets is any notion of major social structures...while modern societies and advanced economies are indeed catallaxies, they are *also* systems with grand structures...his celebration of the miracle of the market simply ignores the temporal and spatial upheavals associated with the creative destruction of capitalism. Hayek's exaggeration of 'order' is the complement of Marxism's exaggeration of 'anarchy'.
>
> (Sayer 1995: 77–8, original emphasis)

It is thus not surprising that the ontological erasure of relatively enduring social structures leads to an emphasis on 'the market' as a sphere of freedom. Yet a market encompasses not simply commodity exchanges and associated transfers of money, but also enduring organised practices that facilitate such exchanges on a regular basis. It is worth briefly discussing the different types of market and the multiple meanings of 'market'.

The nature of 'the market'

Essentially, makers differ according to the way in which transactions are organised, particularly with regard to pricing. 'Spot markets' are those in which prices are flexible and relationships between actors ephemeral. Spot markets approximate economic models. Yet most real markets do not fit this type of market. Instead, fixed prices provide a stable environment for calculating costs and organising production and distribution. Economic models tend to assume the universality of 'arm's length contracting', whereby little information other than price is provided and buyer–supplier relationships are minimal. 'Relational contracting', by contrast, involves the sharing of information, the careful building of trust and collaboration between buyer and seller, before and after the transaction. However, neo-liberals wrongly contend that markets work best 'on the spot', at arm's length, and thus discourage information sharing. Hayek *et al.* overestimate the sufficiency of price as the source of information for buyers and sellers in markets. Prior to commodity exchange, non-price information normally has to be exchanged and is usually provided at no extra cost to the buyer.

The New Right is well known for its trumpeting of the 'free' market, in which all that exists (or, rather, matters) are spontaneous exchanges between individuals who have something to sell. The role of the state is thus held to distort this smooth-running, spontaneous gathering of free individuals. 'Yet far from being an unnecessary interference, *the state is a normal feature of real markets, as a precondition of their existence.* Markets depend on the state for regulation, protection of property rights, and the currency' (Sayer 1995: 87, emphasis added). We will return to the latter shortly. Clearly, markets are not 'free', since their regulation does not benefit all. There are enduring *structured* power imbalances. However, Sayer points out that the conceptual slides endemic to employment of 'the market' are a feature of both lay and academic uses and are found in right/left-wing, liberal and economic theory. The Right proffers idealised models of markets as descriptions of *de facto* markets; the Left avoids any rigorous scrutiny of their properties. Sayer argues that concepts of markets different according to (a) their level of abstraction; (b) their inclusiveness; (c) whether they are couched within a 'market optic' or a 'production optic'; (d) whether they refer to real or imaginary markets.

Real markets may be conceptualised at different levels of abstraction. One can talk about the local fruit-and-vegetable market concretely (who the sellers and buyers are, what is sold, etc.) or more abstractly, namely in terms of the exchange of commodities and property rights for money or as a mode of coordination of the division of labour. At the same time, concepts of markets also differ in inclusiveness. Markets may be defined narrowly in terms of routinised buying and selling, or inclusively to cover production and consumption of exchanged goods and the particular property relations involved. Restricted concepts exclude major contextual influences that explain behaviour. As Sayer puts it, 'The dynamism of capitalist economies is not simply a consequence of markets in the restricted sense, but of capital, obliged to accumulate in order to survive, and liberated from the ties which bind petty commodity producers' (1995: 99). What is included on the Left is determined by a 'production optic', in which markets are marginalised. For the Right, what is included is determined by a 'market optic', whereby production is conflated with exchange. For our purposes, we are concerned with the 'market optic' of the Right. The market optic ignores production and its social relations. Indeed, in mainstream economics, the whole economy becomes *the* market (in the singular) and almost invariably counterposed to the state. The salient point here is that *markets are not an alternative to production, firms or hierarchies* (Sayer 1995: 101). Instead, they are a mode of coordination of the division of labour.

Furthermore, one can distinguish between literal concepts referring to real markets from those referring to imaginary and also from those that use market metaphors that have limited similarity with real markets. As Sayer argues, it is not the level of abstraction used in metaphorical approaches, but their quality, that is important. Indeed, what are often lost are the social relations that underpin real markets. Thus the notion of latent markets

> ...which only need freeing figures strongly in neo-liberal rhetoric, and contrasts strikingly with the view...that markets are social constructions whose birth is difficult and requires considerable regulation and involvement by the state and other institutions to achieve...The liberal underestimation or denial of this institutional support is partly derived from the elision of the difference between potential or imaginary and the actual in its concept of 'the market'.
>
> (Sayer 1995: 104)

The rest is supplied by the ontological effacement of *sui generis* organisations and the relations between them.

The transcendental argument

Transcendentally, the neo-liberal social ontology cannot be sustained: market exchange requires state involvement. By corollary, the existence of schooling is equally necessary. Given that the market is not 'free' and necessarily subject to some form of institutional regulation, then

> ...deregulated governance of education loses its justification, and the [neo-liberal] project loses its rationale even on its own terms...If this line of reasoning can be sustained when elaborated, it would provide a transcendental argument against the existence of principles of free-market exchange into the governance and distribution of education...Furthermore, if neo-liberal principles can be shown to be incompatible with the governance of that social

practice without whose alignment no vision for the ordering of society can be realised, then the vision itself is called into question, not only on grounds of equity...but on grounds of coherence.

(Jonathan 1997: 25–6)

There are two distinct issues here. First, there is the transcendental argument that markets – or Hayek's catallaxy – are regulated by institutions that are irreducible to individuals. Second, Jonathan's argument is that the very institutions that underpin market relationships themselves require an educated workforce, in turn negating the neo-liberal project of subjecting the education system to market disciplinary mechanisms. Put simply, the rationale of the neo-liberal marketisation of the education system would ultimately preclude the possibility of market activity. However, what is important for our purposes is that the neo-conservative element of the New Right corpus contradicts the Hayekian contention that 'free' markets do not require regulation. Moreover, neo-liberals themselves could not avoid the fact that the education system is state-run and did not appear out of thin air. The argument for reconcilability is centred on the short-term need for the state to establish the conditions for a market-based education system. Yet the fact that the state *has* to regulate belies the neo-liberals' atomistic social ontology that is central to the argument for state non-intervention. Following Gamble, Whitty maintains that

> ...the paradox of at one and the same time building a strong state through increased expenditure on the military and the apparatuses of law and order, while at the same time using state power to roll back state intervention from whole areas of social activity, does have a degree of consistency. This is because the state needs to protect the market from vested interests and restrictive practices and prevent the conditions in which it can flourish being subverted either from without or within...On this basis, the government's curriculum policies may not necessarily be as much at variance with its policies on the structure of the education system as is sometimes suggested, even at the level of principle. The contrast between apparent centralization in one sphere and apparent decentralization in other may not be the paradox it at first appears.

(Whitty 1991: 108)

Here, Whitty is providing a transcendental argument against neo-liberalism. He is confusing the ineluctable need for state intervention (which will always be necessary) at the S-C level with propositions about the nature of the social at the CS level. In fact, equivocality characterises the above: there *may* not be contrariety between policies and the structure of the education system and the centralisation–decentralisation issue *may* not be the paradox it at first appears. The fact that the neo-liberal elements of the ERA deny the need for state intervention has serious implications for heads and their staff in terms of what is to be taught, how it is to be taught and under what conditions of service (*inter alia* demanding more for less as schools become subject to the discipline of quasi-market mechanisms). Yet, as Whitty maintains, 'It has also been pointed out that, provided the discourse of the New Right as political rhetoric strikes a chord and can command assent, *its internal inconsistencies and its eclectic philosophical roots are something of an irrelevance...'* (1991: 107).

That the New Right mélange may strike a chord among the electorate is an S-C affair, whose potential S-C import should be dissected given that it was unexploited by the teachers' unions. The unions generically were more concerned with pay rather than matters curricular and organisational. The protracted teachers' strike of 1984–7 helped to divert attention away from the glaring objective CS incompatibilities that were feeding into Conservative social policy and, moreover, to attenuate union bargaining strength. In fact, even up to the 1993 Dearing Review of the National Curriculum, union division again precluded exploitation of the CS level, irrespective of the concomitant issue of success. The union action, according to Warnock, 'will go down in educational history as one of the most disastrous times in the relationship between the teaching profession and the public' (1989: 107). As Pietrasik (1987: 188) notes, the reasons for the failure of the teaching unions centre on governmental strength of purpose and disunity. Crucially, however, the devolution of control to individual schools contradicted the neo-liberal corpus, since such devolution was done at the behest of central government. Any notion that such centralised control was to be ephemeral, a necessary prelude to complete deregulation, is simply to conceal the contradiction: the need for state control ever remains whilst we have an education system. The transcendental impossibility of deregulation of the education system is readily gleaned from the reduction of LEA involvement and powers. The Hayekian approach disclaims the need for any form of planning, partly because of its state socialist connotations. Consequently, LEA plans for limiting the number of children per school were dismissed out of hand and instead replaced by LMS (Local Management of Schools) funding arrangements, whereby schools were funded on a per capita basis and empowered to recruit as many pupils as practicable via open enrolment. Yet, as has often been pointed out, such LEA planning structures *worked* and generally were efficient.

Indeed, markets can never be a complete alternative to planning and hierarchy. *Contra* the down-sizing, hierarchy-flattening nostrums of the new managerialism,

> ...bureaucratic control, in Weber's non-pejorative sense, is the norm for organizations of any scale, whether operating in markets or outside. It is by no means associated with public ownership; private organizations need a significant degree of bureaucratization if they are to cope with large throughputs of information and materials. Though bureaucracy has well known deficiencies, especially with respect to flexibility and motivation, *it is efficient,* and even the most post-Fordist of firms *need significant degrees of hierarchization and routinization of activities in order to function.*
>
> (Sayer 1995: 106, emphasis added)

There is a world of difference between planning a division of labour within an organisation or enterprise and the central planning of the *whole* social division of labour, as in state socialism. The Hillgate Group's idea of providing vouchers for parents would itself, if implemented on a wide scale, have required significant planning.[45] Moreover, such planning would have been expensive and not as efficient as the LEA system. That state socialist planning failed does not negate the need for planning *per se*. At the end of the day, the neo-liberal diagnosis of the relatively poor economic performance of Britain and the concurrent oil crisis of the 1970s was fundamentally flawed. So-called 'public choice theory' is (truistically) right in maintaining that bureaucratic structures endow their incumbents with objective vested interests, in turn accounting for structural morphogenesis/stasis at a number of levels. Where things go drastically wrong is the insistence that such structures *per se* can be ontologically erased, subjecting *individuals* solely to discipline of the market. This is simply to adopt the methodological individualist conflation of the *sui generis* nature of social relations and the individuals who occupy roles within them. The point is that the vested interests of bureaucrats, teachers, and NHS workers derive from irreducible social relations. Consequently, the denial of *sui generis* social reality ineluctably degenerates into voluntarism. It is precisely because of the teachers-can-do-whatever-we-tell-them corollary of the New Right project that, *pace* Whitty, its CS contradictions and S-C import be unpacked.[46] To reiterate, the structured nature of social inequality necessarily delimits the extent to which heads and their staff can raise 'standards' (for this read: examination results). Yet, at the same time, the ERA is underpinned (contradictorily) by a depthless social ontology that promotes an intra-school 'optic', namely on how 'better management' of staff and limited resources *will* raise standards.

For Sayer, commodified education permits those with sufficient money to buy it without any justification to others who have equal need but from whom resources may be diverted. And whilst there may be dangers of paternalism in state provision, 'right-wing claims that markets encourage self-reliance instead of dependence tend to ignore inequalities in the resources needed to be self-reliant or overlook the question of whether those inequalities are deserved and justifiable...' (Sayer 1995: 121). Whilst this is true, the transcendental argument is prior to such issues. Finally, whatever the extent of inefficiency or abused state-funded resources, the New Right has created a situation in which it is wrongly assumed that a dose of less money, market discipline and New Managerialist nostrums will improve the education of the nation. The events that led to the ERA – particularly the resultant managerialist usurpation of assessment – will now be delineated.

This section has provided the transcendental grounds for the untenability of the neo-liberal rationale for the quasi-marketisation of the education system. In so doing it has elaborated the variety of definitions of 'the market' and how the 'market optic' of the neo-liberals denies the irreducibility of social structure. In turn, this accounts for the oft-noted paradox of concurrent centralisation and de-centralisation of the education system, since markets are regulated.

Keith Joseph, Kenneth Baker and the ERA

The reason for drawing attention to Joseph and Baker in this section is to under-score the non-teleological nature of the genesis of the ERA and briefly to show how the attempted enactment of marketisation of education results in theory–practice inconsistency. The final outcome was a result of a complex interplay of contradictory ideas, compromise, and personality of the incumbent Secretary of State and cannot be reduced to any logic of capital dynamic unleashed at the time of the Great Debate. As Ball puts it, 'Clearly it is a mistake to dwell overmuch on the significance of personality differences…but the style, the political standing and the personal concerns of the incumbent have been of increasing importance in understanding changes in the way policy is made and implemented' (1990: 179). Both Joseph and Baker were committed advocates of the neo-liberal project. They found LEAs and trades unions abhorrent, with the latter in particular held to impede the spontaneous nature of the market. However, Joseph was more consistent than Baker in adhering to neo-liberalist tenets.

The move towards accountability and competition is evidenced by the promulgation of the 1980 Education Act, which required schools to publish their examination results and to hold compulsory Open Evenings. Here we can pinpoint, non-teleologically, the start of the legislative impetus that led to the ERA. For in enjoining schools to publish their exam results, parents – now 'consumers' – have information with which to chose where to send their child/ren. Indeed, the principle of a Hayekian market rests upon diversity. In one sense, then, one can comprehend the ERA, the (failed) development of CTCs (City Technology Colleges) and 'Opting Out' arrangements as a logical outcome of the commitment to providing more 'choice' and diversity. However, this is to negate the neo-liberal argument against state intervention. In consistency, Keith Joseph saw the fundamental problem with the education system as residing in the fact that it is a state system and a compulsory one at that. This of course begs the question of what is to be its non-state replacement? Consistent neo-liberals maintain that the curriculum should be left to market forces. This begs the question of (a) how is the economy to remain competitive without the services provided by the state; (b) how parents can find out what should be taught, where it should be taught, how it should be taught, and (c) reconcile different (i.e., unequally structured) interests? But, again, we return to the transcendental argument against marketisation of the curriculum, since Hayek's catallaxy enjoins some form of state provision. Given that Hayek's market is quintessentially one in which there is *financial exchange*, this cannot be transposed to the education system. Here, consumer choice does not impact directly upon the income or well-being of the producers. Joseph was well aware of this, which is why he wanted to introduce the equivalent idea of bankruptcy into the education system (namely the threat and actuality of closure).

In Hayekian fashion, Joseph was dismissive of LEAs and the teaching unions. Thus in 1983 he abolished the Schools' Council precisely because the teaching unions dominated it. The School Curriculum Development Committee (SCDC) and Secondary Examinations Council (SEC) replaced it. Whilst the teachers' unions were outraged, there was no national forum in which the professional voice in the curriculum debate could be heard. Alan Evans, the then Head of

Education at the NUT, sounded out colleagues in other unions and among the LEAs on the possibility of the establishment of their own curriculum council. He was unable to generate sufficient enthusiasm. Given the exploitation of this vacuum by central government, 'the foresight of Evans's proposal is apparent, but at the time the prevailing view was that sooner or later the *status quo ante* would be restored. With hindsight, of course, it is clear that this was not remotely possible' (Barber 1996: 26). Indeed, objectively the teaching unions' bargaining strength was somewhat circumscribed; it was not a question of a missed opportunity but of making the best of an unpropitious situation. They found themselves in conflict with the government over curriculum, appraisal, pay, conditions of service and the decision-making process. The former was never high on the agenda. The teachers' strike of 1984–7 simply confirmed Joseph's prejudices and reduced popular support. During the period 1981–6 he emphasised standards and quality, rather than entitlement, at the same time focusing on assessment, rather than content. In his January 1984 speech at the North of England Conference and in the DES White Paper of 1985, *Better Schools*, he pointed to the twin aims of raising standards and securing the best possible return from resource investment.

Keith Joseph consistently eschewed a legislative National Curriculum. However, we can expect at least some degree of theory/practice inconsistency (at the S-C level). Joseph was not averse to indirect forms of intervention – for example, approval of use of GCSE criteria – and was intent upon using Attainment Targets in the primary area.[47] Indeed, for the Hillgate Group, testing, attainment targets and the publication of results are viewed as an effective form of accountability. Yet, as Ball rightly points out, testing, 'despite its role as a basis for market comparisons and consumer choice, does not sit easily with the strict neo-liberals' (1990: 52). This was recognised by Sexton and Boyson, yet is played down. In fact, Joseph's introduction of the GCSE (General Certificate of Secondary Education) was decried by the neo-liberals since it accorded too much control to teachers via the process of continuous assessment (a matter which was resolved to their satisfaction under John Major's premiership). Such contradiction was not prised apart by the teaching unions and amplified in their transactions with central government. At the time of the 1985 White Paper, the NUT's response was simply one of concern.

However, the 1986 Education Act continued to accord curriculum responsibility to the head-teacher. In essence, the Act changed and enhanced the role and constitution of school governors. The head was required to seek approval from the governing body on curriculum policy. For the DES, this was a successful part of their fast growing influence over the policy-making process. The resolute personality of Joseph combined with his antagonism *vis-à-vis* the Schools Council enhanced the power of the DES officials. With the swift demise of the Schools Council, competition now operated between the DES and HMI, including such right-wing think tanks as the Centre for Policy Studies. Yet the philosophy of the think tanks tended to complement the bureaucratic-cum-assessment-driven approach of DES officials. The DES imposed a highly restricted brief on the SCDC. Despite its official independent status, the SCDC started from a low level of resourcing and expectations; it also had its freedom restricted by DES officials. By 1984 both the DES and HMI had succeeded in clearing the ground for control over education policy by marginalising or muting LEAs and the teaching unions. It was Joseph's personal and political exasperation with the teachers and their local authorities that buttressed the position of DES officials. However, when Kenneth Baker took office in 1987, it was decided that education would be made into a major issue for the 1987 General Election.

The principal ideological difference between Joseph and Baker centred on the issue of a *nationally* prescribed curriculum: Joseph was set against a common, standard National Curriculum. Indeed, it was on this issue that Joseph, in the House of Lords, opposed Baker. Ironically, Joseph's period in office witnessed a move away from formal examinations (via the use of coursework – in some cases there were no formal examinations). A number of educationally progressive programmes were set up, since Joseph maintained that the best way to motivate was not via a one-off examination. However, Joseph's approach to curriculum change was predicated upon exhortation rather than legislation and was not shared by his Cabinet colleagues or, indeed, by Margaret Thatcher. A further difference between the two was that Baker provided the political will to carry through a fundamental reform of the education system. Whereas 'Keith Joseph's ideology of reform remained embedded in the last vestiges of partnership...The dramatic shift came when Kenneth Baker replaced Keith Joseph' (Ball 1990: 177–8). As Ball points out, it was Baker 'who left behind the doubts, worries and hesitations and to push on towards a large-scale, radical and reforming Education Act' (1990: 181). Indeed, Baker was a key figure in the process. He set the membership of the working parties, commented directly on interim and final reports, received the Consultation Report from the National Curriculum Council (NCC), and approved Statutory Orders (specifying attainment targets and programmes of study). Whilst civil servants oversaw much detail, Baker was almost invariably involved in the scrutiny and re-working of earlier reports.

The TGAT Report and the ERA

Baker set up the Task Group on Assessment and Testing (TGAT). The TGAT report was educationalist, rather than managerialist, in its substance. The Group was accorded a high degree of independence and was not subject to interference by either DES officials or Baker himself. However, later curriculum working groups were subject to 'guidance' from DES officials. The TGAT report emphasised the central place of teacher assessments. It recommended a system of terminal and summative assessments at the end of each Key Stage to ensure comparability and reliability of teacher assessments. Within a criterion-referenced framework, it proposed a ten-level system to encourage progression, with the average pupil expected to change levels every two years. The reason for a criterion-referenced framework was to provide written statements for achievement. The report was fundamentally opposed to assessments unconnected to curricula. It suggested that only at the end of Key Stage 3 should results be published, without adjustment for socio-economic intake.

For primary school teachers, then, publication of 'raw' results was not on the table, thereby permitting teachers to focus on the processual nature of teaching, rather than a focus solely on its 'product' (examinations), in order to provide as far as possible high scores for league tables. However, it became clear that Margaret Thatcher did not share the educationalist underpinning of the report. On 10 March 1988, a letter (dated 21 January) from her office to a Private Secretary at the DES was leaked. The letter first underscored the disturbingly complex and elaborate system proposed by TGAT that would entail setting up two new powerful bodies, namely the Schools Examination Council and the National Curriculum Council. Second, the letter indicated Thatcher's concerns: (a) that the purpose of assessment is diagnostic and formative rather than summative; (b) the role envisaged for the LEAs in the implementation of the system; and (c) the lack of attention to the overall costs. The issue of increased expenditure took up the remainder of the letter. The assessment context for my two case-study schools was altered radically following the ERA.

Before scrutinising the TGAT report, and delineating the managerialist usurpation of assessment, it is worth recapitulating the main characteristics of the 1988 ERA. Whilst the 1988 Act constitutes the main break with the past (thereby providing the start of a new conditioning sequence), the 1992, 1993 and 1994 Acts consolidate and extend its managerialist-cum-competitive nature. In essence, the ERA established, without any substantive consultation with the teaching profession and LEAs, the conditions for a competitive market in publicly funded school provision in order to enable parents (*qua* consumers) to make informed choices. The Act removed restrictions that prevented parents opting to send their children to schools of their choice. It gave schools substantially increased control over how they used their budgets. Funding was allocated according to numbers on the roll (per capita funding), which was intended as a market mechanism to reflect the success of particular schools. Indeed, the market attraction of schools was to be judged via examination results at ages 7, 11, 14 and 16. Schools were required to publish an information booklet for prospective parents and an annual report to be presented at a public meeting.

At the same time, central control was increased over the content of schooling. The National Curriculum imposed three core subjects and six or seven foundation subjects, which were to be taught to all children from the age of five to sixteen. The Secretary of State, using detailed attainment targets that would underpin the publication of results, determined the programmes of study. Also, teachers' hours were specified for the first time (Baker abolished the Burnham Committee in 1987) and schemes for teacher appraisal were to be required. Performance-related pay was also envisioned. Employers and local business interests were to play a leading part on school governing bodies. Schools were empowered to spend money in a competitive market place rather than enjoined to spend it on services provided by LEAs. Finally, a majority of parents could vote to 'opt out' of LEA control, funded instead by central government as GM (Grant Maintained) schools.

The quasi-marketisation of the education system necessarily involves winners and losers. The fact that losses are ineluctable stems, *inter alia*, from inadequate funding. Yet, as we have seen, the neo-liberal project wrongly assumes that decreased funding, dispersed via the market, will improve standards, despite a few casualties here and there. This ignores both the socio-economic intake of children and the transcendental need for adequate state provision of educational services. Sinclair *et al.* (1995) rightly point out that a central purpose of the 1988 Act is to reduce state spending. (The issue of whether the neo-liberal project is simply an ideological ruse, dressed up in liberal philosophical garb, is not important here.) Given that the government's objective is to reduce spending without lowering standards, the issue of pay and performance arises. Not surprisingly, this has been the key concern of the teaching unions post-ERA. In view of the inability of the unions to insert themselves on to key committees and bodies both prior and subsequent to the ERA, it is not surprising that assessment and curriculum issues were accorded little significance. Sinclair *et al.* write that

> League tables of examination results, truancy rates and other performance indicators add a further dimension of market competition among schools [in addition to LMS]. Schools are under pressure to provide evidence of high standards of quality to the parents of both existing and potential pupils. The combination of budgetary and competitive changes places an imperative on management to extract higher levels of teacher performance at lower cost...School managers are required to maintain quality while increasing both the volume and the intensity of the teachers' workload and this involves the mobilization of human resource management (HRM) techniques.
>
> (1995: 251)

The immediate question here is, what about the children? Where do the children fit into the competitive system that intensifies teachers' workload and continually expects unremitting quality improvement across the board? More specifically, are the processes involved in learning eclipsed by the unremitting need for teachers to be ahead of their competitors in the education market place?

The managerialist usurpation of assessment

The argument of this section is to maintain that the managerialist thrust of the ERA and subsequent legislation is precisely to eclipse or rather expunge the reality of children and their distinctive processes of cognitive and emotional development. The conflation of children and examination results is directly attributable to the managerialist nature of the ERA and its market-driven assessment arrangements. The current nature of the education system is underpinned by economic rationalism, whereby education is commodified and education policy is the means by which it can be more efficiently regulated and distributed. Indeed, the logic of the commodification of education is that we lose sight of the intrinsic 'use-value' of knowledge and concomitantly the children who are taught to understand it. Whitty *et al.* draw upon the notion of the 'evaluative state', where,

> [instead of] *a priori* evaluation, we have *a posteriori* evaluation. What matters is not the process by which goals might be achieved, but the output...this shift of emphasis from process to product, from input to output, indicates a significant new development in the relationship between the state and education system.

First, it replaces the predominant concerns of quality of provision and equity of access and opportunity. Second, by focusing on output, it redefines the purpose of education in terms of the economy rather than individual demand.

(Whitty *et al.*: 1998: 37)

The reason for the conflation of children and examination results (cognitive development underpinned by process and the end product) stems from the (attempted) appropriation of managerialist principles and practices. When all that matters is a few quantifiable proxies (viz., examination results), whether they have improved and how much they cost, then necessarily children do not enter into the equation. As Fergusson (1994) has argued, managerialism in education is flawed because teachers' knowledge, skills and values are rooted in teaching and learning. Their motivation is inextricably bound up with this and therefore league tables are of little (educational) value. Thus, to Gunter, 'Children's work is determined by efficiency rather than welfare, and they are tested according to a timetable rather than readiness and capability' (1997: 15). As we saw in Chapter 3, notions of readiness are quintessential to child-centred approaches. *Yet the overriding logic of a competitive system, of which one central mechanism is examination results, negates this.* However, I now want to return to the TGAT report and the years that led to the 1993 Dearing Review.

Criterion referencing, accountability and Dearing

The TGAT report recommended a criterion-referenced, rather than norm-referenced system. Its appeal is, on the one hand, to the bureaucratic and, on the other, to the pedagogic (Butterfield 1995). Norm-referencing is the determination of assessment by the attainment of an individual in comparison to others. A familiar example is the 11-plus examination used at one time for selection to grammar, technical and secondary modern schools. Criterion-referencing replaces the notion of ability with a notion of achievements (in the plural), which can be individually represented and enable progress to be documented. Psychologists concerned with techniques of arriving at better (more valid and reliable) tests initially developed the term educational measurements. Here we find technical debates about what precisely are a criterion and the nature of mastery. Nedelsky (1954) developed a method known as the Minimum Pass Level method, applied to multiple-choice tests. This method is concerned more with establishing the difficulty of an item than with ensuring its validity in terms of any particular criteria. Glaser (1963) developed 'criterion-referenced measures', whereby the latter depend upon an absolute standard of quality, while norm-referenced measures depend upon a relative standard. However, as Butterfield points out, his exemplification of the difference does not resolve the difficulty of separating criteria from distributive judgements.

The scores obtained from an achievement test provide primarily two kinds of information. One is the degree to which the student has attained criterion performance; for example, whether he can satisfactorily prepare an experimental report, or solve certain kinds of word problems in arithmetic. The second type of information that an achievement test score provides is the relative ordering of individuals with respect to their test performance; for example, whether Student A can solve his problems more quickly than Student B.

(cited in Butterfield 1995: 119–20)

The definition of a satisfactory achievement is likely to be derived from knowledge of performance of that age group; i.e. from the normal distribution of results. However, Hambleton *et al.* (1978) argued that domain of behaviours was meant, not a minimum proficiency level. In other words, in Glaser's example of 'satisfactorily preparing experimental reports', the criterion is not to be as 'satisfactorily' but the domain 'prepare an experimental report'. Yet, as Butterfield points out, the National Curriculum sidesteps this debate by using both definitions: Attainment Targets constitute domains (e.g., speaking and listening), whereas the Statements of Attainment constitute the minimum proficiency definition.

The domain–proficiency duality helps to explain the contradictions and tensions that teachers are experiencing in their attempts to assess pupils against National Curriculum levels. One of the problems with the minimum proficiency model is that it draws upon the notion of mastery, which itself might be seen as a state or judged along a continuum. The state model distinguishes only between mastery and non-mastery, and teaching is usually structured so that the great majority of pupils achieve mastery of each stage. The continuum model suggests that there may be stages or degrees of mastery. The National Curriculum is not clear about whether it is underpinned by a state or a continuum approach. Whilst the term is used in training manuals, it is not defined. The key point is that the continuum model involves a greater degree of input of teacher judgement, yet such judgement is precisely what the National Curriculum has been designed to nullify. However, evidence for the success of the more rigid application of mastery learning is questionable (see Slavin 1987).

Notwithstanding this the model chosen by the government rests on the assumption that it is possible to define levels of achievement and to assess these levels nationally. Butterfield suggests that this might have appeared to open up large questions about the relationship of levels and ages and about the advisability of teaching and assessing all pupils of a similar age together. Indeed, 'Work on graded assessments in the UK focused on the need to consider *stages* rather than ages of learning, *as a logical concomitant of criterion-referencing*' (Butterfield 1995: 127, emphasis added). In an early critique of the National Curriculum, Murphy wrote: 'There is little justification for prescribing attainment targets in related to fixed ages. Optimum attainment levels should be recorded and rewarded regardless of age when they are reached by individual pupils' (cited in Butterfield 1995). (The Dearing Review in its discussion of the ten-point scale did not question the appropriateness of an age approach.) Whilst the TGAT report seemed to augur well, ambiguities and contradictions were clearly apparent. In fact, Scott (1994) argues that criterion-referenced systems conflate logical hierarchies of skills and content with developmental approaches to learning employed by pupils.

Furthermore, the TGAT proposals supported conflicting notions of accountability. Scott distinguishes between contextualised and decontextualised approaches to assessment. The contextualised model centres on the timing of the assessments, their relationship to the specifics of the course and the conditions under which they are taken. The focus is solely on the teaching and learning of pupils and their past achievements – comparisons with other schools and pupils cannot be drawn. This clearly belies the market mechanism of competition and re-establishes professional autonomy. The contextualised model is thus concerned with *internal* accountability, directly to the pupils, which is tempered by professional integrity. The decontextualised model prioritises *external* accountability. As Scott puts it:

> here a high emphasis is placed on comparability, so that variables peculiar to specific pupils, teaching situations or schools are not given the same priority as they are in the first model...[It is] *competitive* – a teacher's work is judged in relation to the achievements of his or her peers. This model also strongly emphasizes external accountability. Indeed, in line with Kogan's (1986) free-market consumerist model of accountability, failure in the context of the public market place leads to loss of income for the school and of employment for teachers. Aspects of both models featured in the initial TGAT report, *though subsequent arrangements made for assessment...are more in line with our second model.*
>
> (Scott 1994: 51, emphasis added)

Indeed, the shift towards external accountability was speedy. Its starting-point has already been discussed, namely the Prime Minister's personal intervention. However, the key point here is that, despite its flaws, criterion-referencing would have been welcomed by the majority of teachers, particularly at the primary level given its individual-level diagnostic rationale. Yet the legal requirement of reporting the overall performance of schools and LEAs is antithetic. The managerialist need for quantifiable data that permit comparison of schools as part of the competitive process necessarily negates such issues as cognitive development, the impact of socio-economic background on pupil intake and, indeed, non-quantifiable phenomena. As I argued in Chapter 2, we are dealing with a constraining contradiction (albeit one that remained fundamentally unexploited by corporate agency). For managerialism negates 'the input'; that is, children. Logically, it cannot avoid any treatment of the input and arguably the managerialist usurpation of assessment in turn *secretes* a factory model of children, whose cognitive capacities are fleetingly acknowledged or reduced to one-way dependence upon society. The fact that the latter is secreted must not lead one to assume this is what was meant all along: the constraining nature of the contradiction stems from managerialism's erasure of humanity *per se*. Thus its secreted factory model would be of no interest or, rather, recognised as logically possible. The fact that schools are working with a model that links progression firmly to fixed curriculum objectives and marginalises alternative notions of progress or development should not be taken to be an implicit acknowledgement of the cognitive nature of children *qua* children. However, we need to complete the story that led to the Dearing Review.

The purpose of SATs was to ensure reliability and comparability; these should work at the class level and not the individual level. If there was any divergence, the teacher assessment was to be adjusted. In 1989, SEAC made recommendations to the Secretary of State. These recommendations formed part of the final Standing Orders published in July 1990. The Orders signalled a radical change of direction. In essence, SATs were to be the main method of assessment, with teacher assessments being marginalised. However, the then Secretary of State, John MacGregor, argued in favour of a number of the TGAT principles, viz. that assessment should be connected to curricula and that parity of importance be granted to teacher assessment. In 1990 Kenneth Clarke took over from MacGregor. In a nutshell, Clarke was determined to reassert central control and wanted to circumscribe the power of the individual teacher. He inherited a number of problems. SATs were too long-winded, difficult to manage and required considerable input by teachers. Moreover, doubts about their reliability and validity were expressed (see Butterfield 1995; Davis 1998). Consequently, at Key Stage 3, for example, shorter tests were requested; the Mathematics Development Agency devised three one-hour tests. Ineluctably, the ability to make diagnostic and formative judgements was eliminated at a stroke. There was also a considerable emphasis on the publishing of league tables. However, the irremediable unmanageability of the National Curriculum led to the Dearing Review (1993).

Dearing recommended that national tests and teacher assessments should be shown separately in all forms of reporting. He proposed that the prescribed curricular arrangements (as expressed in the Public Orders) should be cut back. In turn, the time released would permit teaching of non-statutory SCAA material. It was suggested that the ten-level system should be re-evaluated. As already mentioned, this re-evaluation did not consider the appropriateness of an age-related structure. The overriding concern was to simplify within a managerialist framework. Indeed, Dearing still maintained the need for publication of summative data about pupils and schools. Though sympathetic, he was not convinced about the need to re-work the raw test scores to allow for socio-economic factors. The conflict between the two models of accountability remained, weighted more firmly on the 'decontextualised' model. The market mechanism of examination failure for some (resulting in possible closure) underscores the managerialist underpinning of the curriculum: any conceivable reference to the differential needs of children would enjoin the closing down of a system that links income to examination performance.

This section has delineated the speedy ascendancy of economic rationalism. Despite the ambiguities and contradictions of the TGAT proposals and the conflicting notions of accountability contained therein, the legal requirement that schools provide quantifiable data to ensure comparison and the decontextualised model of assessment that Dearing kept intact combined to ensure that the central government remained firmly in the managerialist driving seat. At the same time, the creation of its overseer, OFSTED, and the considerable influence of the School Effectiveness Movement contingently overdetermined the managerialist usurpation of primary (and secondary) education. The next section dissects the Taylorist nature of quasi-marketisation, and the Preface to Part III addresses the contingent compatibility of the School Effectiveness Movement, which continues to inform and strengthen the managerialisation of education.

Taylorism and organisational culture

In Chapter 2, reference was made to the scientific management of F W Taylor. The managerialist restructuring of the public sector has spawned a huge literature on the extent to which Taylorism is characteristic of the latter and related issues of TQM (total quality management) and organisational culture generically. Ackroyd and Bolton's (1999) study of the mechanisms of work intensification in the provision of gynaecological services in an NHS hospital concluded that such mechanisms are not Taylorist. The authors accept that some deskilling has occurred, alongside grade dilution and the employment of increasing numbers of nurses on non-standard contracts and the use of bank and nursing agencies. Furthermore, they note that those managerialist nostrums such as management by objectives (MBO), performance management (PM) and total quality management (TQM) have obvious points of continuity with Taylorism.

> Not least of these is that they all feature concern for specific measures of performance and output. It would be strange indeed if new managerial regimes in the NHS had escaped all influence from management ideas like these…Performance management and performance-related pay, for example, do seem to be applied to the work of senior managers…But, there is, equally, little evidence that such ideas are being used to set quantitative measures of efficiency and performance for the likes of individual nurses and social workers…Meeting targets is not usually the responsibility of individual nurses and this is certainly the case in [our] hospital…
>
> (Ackroyd and Bolton 1999: 373–4)

Their argument against Taylorist restructuring of nurses' work is that (a) NHS managers do not directly control the work of nurses and, moreover, (b) managers have not *redesigned* nurses' work in order to improve efficiency. The key criterion is job redesign. As they point out, NHS managers do not have the requisite knowledge. In contrast, the ERA and subsequent legislation is Taylorist. The National Curriculum *prescribes* what is to be taught. Primary teachers are now required to set aside two hours per day for mathematics and English (so-called 'Numeracy and Literacy Hours'). Subjects have been *externally imposed with the avowed intention of expunging professional judgement*. Moreover, the publication of league tables diverts attention away from the less able, and focuses attention on exam success at the expense of understanding. The eventual emphasis on external assessment at the expense of teacher assessment further underscores the Taylorist underpinning of the reforms. Equally, the recent Labour imposition of national target setting and the creation of Education Action Zones represents its educational zenith.

As Fergusson (1994) notes, many of the key features of managerialism in schools cluster around the head-teacher. The head-teacher is ceasing to be a senior peer embedded within a professional group. The head is now responsible for pursuing centrally-determined objectives and methods, ensuring the compliance of staff. In contrast to the NHS managers, heads do have significant knowledge of what their staff does (or should do). For Fergusson, school managers 'can bring about a more thorough-going and far-reaching overhaul of the methods and purposes of service delivery than an army of policy-makers and inspectors...They are in this sense a *sine qua non* of systemic reform...' (1994: 95). The weak management lines between heads and classroom teachers that existed prior to ERA have been strengthened by the introduction of appraisal systems. Changed procedures of promotion and the incentive allowance scheme have vested governing bodies with sole responsibility. And HMI has effectively been supplanted by OFSTED. Heads' principal source of power derives from the devolution of financial control. Although responsibility for the internal allocation lies formally with governors, heads have used their knowledge and position to usurp the powers that derive from this. Thus, to Fergusson,

> Heads have acquired both power and responsibility to oversee the content of teachers' work, to scrutinize its outcomes as measured by tests, truancy rates and leavers' destinations, to appraise performance, and to account for all these to governors, as well as exerting a powerful influence over promotion...
>
> (1994: 97)

It is thus not surprising that heads exploit the budgetary powers afforded to them to justify autocratic behaviour. The Audit Commission (1993) found evidence of important budgetary information being withheld from governors, and improper use of funds. In my first case-study school, ostensibly democratically-run staff meetings were subject to prior agenda fixing, as will be seen.

Managerialism and organisational culture

The irony of the new managerialism centres on the employment of 'cultural' techniques designed to improve efficiency and effectiveness, whereby employees are 'empowered'. Such cultural techniques have their origins in the early 1980s, during which the 'culture' of corporations emerged as a central theme in the field of management and organisation studies. The so-called gurus of 'excellence' (notably, Peters and Waterman's *In Search of Excellence*) promoted the project of strengthening corporate culture. It was argued that improvements in productivity and quality derived from corporate cultures that systematically recognise and reward individuals for identifying their sense of purpose with that of the organisation's values. *Qua* ideational corpus, corporate culture's key characteristic is to promote employee commitment to a monolithic structure of feeling and thought in the name of empowerment or expanded autonomy. The successful imposition of 'corporate culturism', as Hugh Willmott (1993) puts it, is an S-C affair, whose outcome cannot be decided *a priori*.

The origins of 'corporate culturism' need not detain us (see Harvey 1989). Programmes of corporate culturism (human resource management and TQM) seek to promote a corporate ethos that demands loyalty from employees as it excludes, silences or punishes those who question its creed (Willmott 1993: 519). The so-called 'strength' of culture is tied to the extent to which contradictory or 'rival' values are absent (at the S-C level). Each employee is encouraged to become embroiled in a process 'that structures work situations by means of intensive training, planning, continuous learning, and the use of various human resource management techniques' (Hydebrand, cited in Willmott 1993: 523). In so far as employees are drawn to the allure of what Hydebrand calls 'technocratic informalism', they come to *discipline themselves* with feelings of anxiety, shame and guilt that are aroused when they sense themselves to fall short of the sacred values of the organisation (523). Textbooks on how-to-do intensive training, planning and continuous improvement are easy to find in the veritable growth industry of education management.[48] Such texts emphasise the teacher *qua* manager and at the same time neutralise the processes of management – they are held to be apolitical and thus the stress is placed on consensus-building. Hence consensus-building is often the result of the use of power to impose S-C uniformity, and my task has been to assess the extent to which S-C uniformity has prevailed in two schools.

Thus 'culture' here is about the imposition of values. In our phraseology, it is concerned with both the CS and S-C levels: how managers/corporate leaders must impose a set of compatible ideas, which in turn must be enthusiastically imbibed by employees. There is no room for dissent at the S-C level, despite the existence of (potentially) numerous fault-lines at the CS level. The overriding aim of any corporate culture programme is to erase critical reflection; i.e., as a prelude to any agential surveying of the CS for incompatible items. Of course, the intrinsic human capacity to reflect can never be erased – this is a transcendental impossibility. Thus, 'under the guise of giving more autonomy to the individual than in organisations governed by bureaucratic rules, corporate culture threatens to promote a new, hypermodern neo-authoritarianism which, potentially, is more insidious and sinister than its bureaucratic predecessor' (Willmott 1993: 541). Indeed, what's 'new' about the current corpus of propositions and practices that comprise managerialism is the shift from bureaucratic rationality to market rationality, which demanded 'a metamorphosis in prevailing organizational subjectivities or identities. The characteristic forms of motivation and action associated with "organization man" or the "bureaucratic personality" was to be replaced by those definitive of the "enterprising or calculating self". The "culture of the customer" emerged as a "total ideology"...' (Reed 1995: 44). Hence the expectation that LMS and per capita funding arrangements, underpinned by the competitive mechanism of examination league tables, would result in the adoption of entrepreneurial values and practices. This has certainly been borne out.[49]

As Reed notes, on the surface TQM may be seen as a mundane procedural mechanism directed to the technical requirements for operational efficiency and effectiveness within work organisations.

> But this surface reality occludes an underlying logic and strategy of control deployed in the service of values and interests held by those occupying positions of governance within corporate hierarchies...In its most conceptually pristine or ideal typical form, it offers an effective organizational integration of core values and control technologies through which ideological homogenization and behaviour conformity can be jointly secured...*However, the actual*

*implementation of TQM-type principles and methods is likely to be much more partial and
contested than the ideal type would indicate.*

(1995: 47, emphasis added)

The extent and nature of contestation is a matter for empirical investigation at
the interface between the structural and cultural realms. That contestation is likely
is, of course, attributable to the dehumanising thrust of the new managerialism and
its form contingent upon the values and practices that it attempts to displace.
Children and their developmental needs, along with teachers and their needs as
professional human beings, have no place. Thus we should not be surprised that the
National Curriculum has no educational aims but plenty of managerial ones.
Hence both Baker and Clarke's disregard for matters theoretical and the incredible
speed with which Baker pushed through the reforms. As Butterfield rightly points
out, no curriculum is genuinely atheoretical. Hence the constraining contradiction
delineated in Chapter 2. Managerialism cannot conceive of *any* theory that underpins children's learning, since it denies the existence of children *per se*, but
transcendentally cannot operate (in the context of education) without them. To do
so would belie the technicist-cum-commodifying nature of its rationale.[50]

Concluding remarks

This chapter has delineated the final sequence of the generic morphogenetic cycle,
of which the end product is Structural Elaboration in the form of the 1988
Education Reform Act and its subsequent legislative consolidation, and Cultural
Elaboration in the form of systematised new managerialism and contradictory
mixture of neo-liberalism and conservatism. The details of the Act and subsequent
legislation have been documented. In brief, the mixture of economic rationalism,
new managerialism and pragmatism has resulted in the negation of the differing
rates of cognitive development of children. Furthermore, the neo-liberal-cum-
conservative ideational mix that underpinned the legislation has been scrutinised.
The contradiction between neo-liberalism and conservatism is objective and the
untenability of the 'market optic' of neo-liberalism has been transcendentally established. This explains the practical problems experienced by legislators, viz.
centralisation in one sphere versus de-centralisation in another. Crucially, the immanent contradiction cannot be reconciled. Such contradiction was not accentuated at
the S-C level and amplified by the teaching unions. Instead, the manoeuvring of
the unions has been essentially defensive, focusing on traditional matters of pay and
conditions. Successive Secretaries of State rode roughshod over the unions, creating
an unmanageable, near-crisis situation, whose urgent reappraisal came about in
1993. Yet, as we have seen, the Dearing Review remained within the managerialist
mould and did not question the fundamentally anti-educational nature of the
National Curriculum, especially the inequitable nature of the market mechanisms.
Indeed, the arbitrary nature of the levels of the curriculum and the decontextualised nature of examinations (and issues of reliability and validity) equally
remained out of reach.

One of the key contradictions that is the focus of the book is encapsulated in the following: 'If a school is about to be "OFSTEDed" and rings you up for a consultancy to prepare the staff, it is a foolish consultant who refuses a day's training on efficiency and effectiveness and tries to persuade the school that what they really need is a day on the theory of how children learn' (Gunter 1997: 12). That is, the managerialist quasi-marketisation of the education system represents a stringent obstruction to the enactment of child-centred philosophy. Now, the overriding concern for heads is to manage their limited budgets and their staffs so that they do not become losers in the battle that is now education. The neo-liberal input of the 1988 ERA has engendered a situation in which teachers are implicitly held to be the cause of 'failing' schools, rather than inadequate funding, work-overload and the reality of 'school mix' (Thrupp 1999). Indeed, the lack of discursive penetration on the part of New Labour has exacerbated the latter, since now primary teachers are stringently conditioned to meet imposed national targets, of which one response is discussed in Chapter 7. The charge here rests on the fact that a purportedly pro-egalitarian government has uncritically endorsed and consolidated legislation that is (contradictorily) grounded in neo-liberalism and conservatism. In turn, the role of OFSTED under the direction of Chris Woodhead was strengthened. The important role of the School Effectiveness Movement will now be documented and criticised for its methodological individualism, which (contingently) complements and buttresses the neo-liberal restructuring of education. The managerial co-option of leading UK academics will also be highlighted, underscoring the ways in which their critiques of 'Primaryspeak' and progressivism complement the neo-liberal education project. Whilst not publicly aligned with OFSTED and School Effectiveness, Robin Alexander's co-authorship with Woodhead of *Curriculum Organisation and Classroom Practice in Primary Schools* is instructive.

In sum, then, the picture looks somewhat bleak. The substantive question to be answered now is how two schools, one deemed 'failing' by OFSTED and the other deemed as giving 'value for money', mediate the contradictions and pressures embodied in the new conditioning cycles.

Part III

At the managerial chalk face

Southside and Westside

Preface to Part III

OFSTED, School effectiveness and managerialism

Part and parcel of the new managerialist restructuring of the education system (which incorporates and expands upon the core principles of Taylorism) is the inspection system managed by OFSTED. Quintessentially, effectiveness and efficiency underpin the OFSTED rationale – technical matters about how best to improve 'standards'. The Education (Schools) Act 1992 established the arrangements for independent inspections (on a four-yearly basis) by registered inspectors to be trained by, and responsible to, OFSTED. Teams of inspectors, which include lay inspectors, are designed to provide 'regular and rigorous inspection under the watchful eye of the new and powerful Chief Inspector for Schools'. The arrangements for the conduct of inspections are detailed in the *Handbook for the Inspection of Schools*. The 'Framework' contained therein and the 1992 Act have established a public set of criteria about effectiveness. Whilst I accept Butterfield's point that the criteria go beyond the issue of 'standards', the Framework embodied in the Handbook is underpinned by the achievement of 'procedural objectivity' (Eisner 1991), which is designed to eliminate the scope for personal judgement. Indeed, the managerialist rationale means not simply that we cannot measure, for example, whether 'quality of life' has improved, but that any consideration of 'quality of life' *per se* is disavowed. Such issues are consistently played down by OFSTED (despite nebulous references to pupils' spiritual development and school ethos). In short, why-questions are consistently eschewed. As discussed in Chapter 2, *qua* performance indicators, SATs grossly distort reality because of their reductionism, by-passing the cognitive processes by which children learn. To recapitulate Ball's (1990) point, the parameters of OFSTED operate within the input–output logic of the commodity form and thus displace and exclude other criteria of judgement.

OFSTED's rationale and policy prescriptions are intimately connected with, and derived from, a large and particularly influential section of the academic research community in England and Wales. In fact, this research community forms part of an international School Effectiveness Movement (SEM). Research on 'school effectiveness' has become a major international industry. School effectiveness research has now had a major impact on policy-making at the national, local and school level. The DES

established a School Effectiveness Division in 1994 which has become increasingly influential in the years since then. It has sought explicitly to learn from
the research...and to apply its lessons to policy on, for example, failing
schools...The revival of local educational authorities in recent years has been
built around the same body of research. Indeed, it would be only a slight exag-
geration to say that it saved them from extinction.

(Barber and White 1997: 1)

The quasi-marketisation of education and the concomitant idealised drive for
efficiency have been aided by the factorial prescriptions designed to ameliorate
'average' or 'failing' schools, which have emanated from the school effectiveness
research. Many critics (Angus 1993; Ball 1990, 1995; Chitty 1997; Elliott 1996;
Hamilton 1998) have convincingly demonstrated that such research is being used to
lend spurious support to neo-liberal policy because of its promotion of an approach
in which it is assumed that 'educational problems' can be fixed by technical means
and that inequality is an intra-school affair – to be managed within the classroom.

Bottery argues that SEM has fitted the following four government demands: the
introduction of markets and competition; the centralisation of policy at the same
time as the decentralisation of responsibility for implementation; the development
of performance management techniques; the continued standardisation and
deskilling of workforces.

- In terms of markets and competition, SEM has provided policy-makers with
  the kind of data from which league tables can be compiled, and by which
  parents can be urged to compare one school with another;
- In terms of centralisation/decentralisation, it has provided policy-makers with
  the key factors...ostensibly existent in successful schools, which they can then
  demand be transported and implemented by a vigorous managerialism into
  those schools apparently less successful or failing;
- In terms of performance management, by describing context-free factors, SEM
  has provided the kinds of objective output criteria required by policy-makers,
  and against which teachers' performance may be monitored and appraised;
- In terms of standardisation and deskilling of work, the movement has, through
  the production of these key factors, provided policy-makers with the arguments
  to suggest that teachers' work is essentially concerned with the implementation
  of such context-free factors, thereby implying that teachers' work (and training)
  should be standardised to achieve these factors (taken from Bottery 2000:
  106–7).

Bottery then rightly argues that, precisely because the educational process occurs
in personal encounters between pupil and teacher, policy and management cannot
be nearly as directive. Indeed, following Silcock, he argues that, once teachers have
done their best to facilitate learning, they can never guarantee it.

However, the focus on the classroom/school level re-directs attention away from
the wider socio-economic context. Thus critics have arraigned school effectiveness

researchers on the charge of ideological commitment. This has prompted indignation. Thus, to Mortimore and Sammons, for example, 'How can anyone who understands research methodology...make such an unfair accusation? We reject – utterly and completely – this accusation and challenge its makers to provide evidence for the statement or to withdraw it' (1997: 185). Recently, I have taken up the gauntlet (Willmott 1999c), upholding the charge of ideological commitment. Specifically, I focused on the ontological secretions of the school effectiveness movement's methodology. The positivist methodology employed by school effectiveness researchers secretes an atomised social ontology. My argument is that it is in social practice that the ontological presuppositions of positivism become ideological. It is not the 'theoretical' presuppositions *per se* that are ideological, but the social uses to which they are knowingly or unknowingly put. In brief, there is a contingent compatibility between the neo-liberal (Hayekian) inflection of the New Right corpus and the secreted social ontology of positivist research methodology.

The OFSTED framework implicitly disavows the stratified nature of social reality. Its focus thus remains at the level of observable events and cannot theorise about the generative mechanisms that underlie them. Essentially, relatively enduring socio-cultural emergent properties are erased by positivism. For Hamilton, school effectiveness research is bundled within an overall national efficiency package.

> It comes bundled with master's degrees in business administration (MBAs)...the centralization of teacher training...and the segregated, management training of promoted teachers...All of these innovations have been part of a new right-inspired and centrally funded exercise to transfer – by fiat – drive systems from one sector of the economy to another.
>
> (Hamilton 1998: 18)

Hamilton also points to the ecological fallacy intrinsic to the aggregate measures undertaken by effectiveness research (whereby aggregate measures are invalidly extrapolated to the performance of individuals) and the privileging of the productivity of schools over the performance of individuals, in turn creating tensions at the school level. However, more important is his recognition of OFSTED's model of causality (which is embedded in positivism). The overriding concern of the school effectiveness research is on that which can be observed and measured. This is basic to any positivist research methodology (see Chapter 1 for a discussion of positivism).

That the OFSTED framework implicitly denies the *sui generis* reality of enduring socio-cultural emergent properties is not therefore surprising, given that necessity is disavowed by positivism. In other words, the internal and necessary *sui generis* social relations that are constitutive of a school and its systemic anchorage do not exist and thus cannot have causal efficacy. We can thus account for the arguments of Chris Woodhead that there are no limits to improvement, since the notion that the (dehumanised) child who, being nothing, can be filled up with anything – without limits – necessarily results from a secreted atomised social ontology and the new managerialism. However, to return now to the OFSTED model. *Key Characteristics of Effective Schools* (Sammons *et al.* 1995) is a review of the school effectiveness research commissioned in 1994 by OFSTED. The authors are based at the International School Effectiveness and Improvement Centre of the London University Institute of Education. Their task was to summarise current knowledge about school effectiveness and to provide OFSTED with an analysis of the key determinants of school effectiveness in secondary and primary schools. Hamilton suggests that the reviewers were reluctant to focus unilaterally on causality and, moreover, that they and OFSTED did not share the same view of causality. One can discern a straightforward, linear model of causality underpinning the OFSTED model. As Hamilton puts it:

> In linear systems, a straightforward cause leads to a straightforward effect. In non-linear systems the outcome is so sensitive to initial conditions that a minuscule change in the situation at the beginning of the process may result in a large difference at the end. OFSTED assumes that…outcomes can be linked directly and unambiguously to inputs. OFSTED believes, in effect, that it is possible to predict the final resting-place of a set of billiard balls on the basis of the prior cue stroke.
>
> (Hamilton 1998: 15)

Hamilton points out that the Institute's reviewers shared a more elaborate view of causality. They openly acknowledge such problems of interpretation and prediction, but disregard their own caveats. 'Key determinants' are replaced by 'key factors', and the preamble to the table of eleven factors denotes them as 'correlates of effectiveness'. The focus on correlates exemplifies the positivist anchorage. Consequently, Hamilton argues that social engineering assumptions are smuggled back into the analysis. As Bottery (2000) rightly argues, it is suggested that such factors can and should, via a battery of managerial techniques, be engineered into other school contexts. 'The model is appealing to policy-makers in its apparent simplicity and linearity, and with the necessary external direction…' (Bottery 2000: 113–14). In fairness, however, he notes that, while it is likely that no SEM researcher would agree with the latter, 'there must be a strong suspicion that some policy-makers have taken the model to mean nothing more than taking a set of factors from "good schools", the planting of them in other less-good schools, and thus obtaining a rise in pupil achievement' (Bottery 2000: 114). (As we shall see in Chapter 6, the trouble-shooting head-teacher held the list of factors to be the incontrovertible way to 'improve'.)

I would want to add that the use of mathematical modelling by school effectiveness researchers again points up its positivist nature. Part and parcel of the process of factor-extraction is the extensive use of sophisticated statistical techniques. Mathematics is quintessentially an acausal language. As Sayer puts it, mathematics 'lacks the categories of "producing", "generating" or "forcing" which we take to indicate causality. Mathematics functions such as $y = f(x)$ say nothing about what makes y or x…' (1992: 179). At best, mathematics records the effects of underlying generative mechanisms and inherently cannot provide an explanation of them.

Such effects are extracted at the level of observable events; hence the use of mathematical modelling, since the identification of internal or external relations is impossible. The inability of mathematics to distinguish necessary from external or contingent relations invites the positing of spurious correlations. This is not to suggest that mathematics *per se* presupposes an actualist social ontology, but rather a positivist methodology of which mathematical modelling is an integral yet contingent part. One can easily quantify such phenomena as levels of truancy, examination results differentiated according to sex, and so on. But this is only part of the story: causal mechanisms (in the form of irreducible structural and cultural properties) need to be brought in to explain the latter (Hamilton 1990: 15).

Hamilton argues that the tacit OFSTED assumption seems to be that causal factors are independent, universal and additive; i.e. they do not interfere with each other and are uninfluenced by their contexts. The OFSTED reviewers, in return, 'fully acknowledge that these conditions rarely apply in the multivariate world of education. Yet, as before, they appear disinclined to confront OFSTED's innocent assumptions…The[ir] aspiration to simplify – in the interests of packaging and marketing – becomes self-defeating' (Hamilton 1990: 15). Hence the privileged explanatory role accorded to school ethos in the effectiveness/OFSTED literature, since the issue of overcoming socio-economic disadvantage is effectively neutralised. Indeed, school 'climate' or 'ethos' is frequently used to explain away processes that might alternatively be seen as the result of what Thrupp (1999) calls 'school mix' (i.e., the social class composition of pupil intake). Whilst socio-economic factors have now been belatedly acknowledged, commitment to the positivist paradigm has led to mere statistical incorporation of the latter. The reality of structured inequality is transformed into a statistical variable that more complex mathematical models somehow 'take into account'. This explains the repeated denial that school effectiveness research is ideological. Yet, to reiterate, structured inequalities presuppose a relational (or 'depth') social ontology, which positivism disavows. The quasi-umbilical link with OFSTED remains, as does the charge of ideological commitment.

Nevertheless, Goldstein and Woodhouse's (2000) recent contribution represents one of a small number of attempts by SEM researchers to deny the charge of ideological commitment and/or New Right association, whilst at the same time recognising the limitations of some research within the field itself. Such engagement with critics of school effectiveness is long overdue and welcome. Goldstein and Woodhouse are cognisant of the quasi-umbilical relationship with past and present UK governments. In fact, they recommend that school effectiveness research should rename itself as Educational Effectiveness precisely in order to separate SE research from government influence. Furthermore, Teddlie *et al.* (2000: 105–15) present growing reservations within the SE community about the use of multi-level modelling because of, *inter alia*, its excessive scientism, which accompanies discussion of the modelling now required. In short, they argue that ultimately the high hopes held for multi-level modelling have not been realised. This is a welcome move away from Mortimore and Sammons's riposte to SE critics that '…the use of MLM [multi-level modelling] has enabled us to tease out the impact of a school on pupils with quite different educational backgrounds and to make the case on their behalf' (1997: 185). Indeed, they concluded then that 'More complex models are needed to reflect the complexity of the educational processes...In general, we seek to use a range of quantitative and qualitative methods...' (1997: 186–7).

What is conspicuously absent here is any discussion of the inherent lack of explanatory power of modelling to account for the complexity of educational processes and outcomes. There is no serious attempt to assess the extent to which statistical modelling adequately represents the complexity of social reality. School effectiveness researchers who adopt statistical methods do not ask what real objects and processes must be like for mathematical representations of them to be adequate. The emphasis upon data, how data are used, how much data should be used, how reliable and so on, detracts from any exploration of social ontology and explanatory methodology. In other words, when problems are acknowledged, there is no exploration of the conceptual and metaphysical problems implicit in the use of statistics.

For Goldstein and Woodhouse, the issue is not about statistical modelling *per se* but about how well it is used by SE researchers:

> Statistical modelling, of course, is only as good as the data which it attempts to model. It is also often the case that such models oversimplify reality to the point of distorting it and producing misleading inferences. To point to specific inadequacies, however, or to list inappropriate uses of such models does not invalidate them per se.
>
> (Goldstein and Woodhouse 2000: 359)

This exemplifies my point about the primacy accorded to data, rather than social ontology and explanatory methodology. The authors are concerned about 'the failure of the "qualitative" critics properly to understand the nature of quantitative techniques', which, they argue, 'is quite serious since these critics do have valid points whose force is often dissipated through lack of proper understandings of the nature and substance of quantitative models' (Goldstein and Woodhouse 2000: 359). The crucial issue here centres on the explanatory utility of statistical modelling. The issue again for critics like myself is that the use of modelling as an aid to causal explanation is problematic since its language is acausal and astructural. It is unable, among other things, to distinguish causal from accidental relations. Indeed, the concept of variable, for example, is indifferent *vis-à-vis* causal explanation: variables can only register change, not its cause. The minute we start to ignore causal properties and powers, it is easy to see why New Labour educational policymaking can so readily argue for 'zero tolerance', since prior conditioning by structural and cultural properties is erased at a stroke (or held in abeyance). The Education Secretary's recent slogan 'standards, not structures' is palpable here.

For Sayer:

> The blindness of mathematics to internal relations and emergence encourages...the belief that complex actions can be treated as reducible to some simple combination of simple behaviours which in turn are regular responses to set stimuli, as if each stimulus and action had the same meaning regardless of context.
>
> (Sayer 1992: 200)

His argument is that individualistic theories that portray society as a structureless aggregate of externally related individuals resonates more easily with the use of quantitative methods. Thus Goldstein and Woodhouse are correct to argue that statistical models 'certainly have no inbuilt requirement for any particular managerial structure' (Goldstein and Woodhouse 2000: 355), but they cannot see that they resonate strongly with the neo-liberal restructuring of education. The relationship is one of contingent compatibility, not necessary concomitance, between statistical methods and the new managerialist/neo-liberal restructuring of education in England and Wales.

To be fair, Goldstein and Woodhouse are aware of the ideological usurpation of SE research by past Conservative and New Labour administrations. However, they do not accept the charge of New Right association. Whilst their recognition of the role played by SER in New Labour education policy is welcome, it is important to reiterate the charge of right-wing ideological commitment. For New Labour's modernisation project, the growing emphasis upon 'what works' and statistical modelling all share the same social ontological bed; namely, an ontology that denies the irreducibility of society to individuals. What Goldstein and Woodhouse have yet to acknowledge is that statistical modelling's implicit social ontology renders it susceptible to right-wing appropriation.

As I have argued, the charge of ideological commitment derives from the concealment of the transcendental necessity of *sui generis* structures that delimit agential action. In other words, the implicit denial of structural properties enables SER proponents and New Labour to assume that all schools can perform well independently of contextual constraints, in turn creating the work overload and stress reported among the teaching profession. As Scott puts it, 'What is at issue in short is that a method from within a positivist/empiricist framework…cannot help but provide support for an agenda which emphasizes control, prediction and the rejection of a holistic view of education' (2000: 70). Statistical methods and the generic positivism of SER lend themselves to individualistic social philosophies and policies. Indeed, as Thrupp (forthcoming) rightly argues, critics of SER are not concerned with the technical issues in statistical modelling: the issue is whether modelling is able to capture the school processes it is expected to measure. The fact that they lack explanatory power and cannot measure such processes should encourage SER statisticians and users of such statistics to reassess their role as educational researchers and reflect upon the untrammelled ease with which New Right policies appropriate their findings.

As we have seen, Goldstein and Woodhouse are concerned about the failure of some critics properly to understand the nature of quantitative techniques. They argue that the power of multi-level modelling can only be realised once we have 'quality' data. But we are not told which data and why. The debate is (again) played out at the level of methodology. SE researchers need to move beyond the level of methodology and engage with the priority of ontology. Thrupp (forthcoming) notes that 'SER's generally offhand approach to its critics may be especially unfortunate if proponents and critics of SER are often talking past each other as a result of different epistemological commitments as Willmott (1999) has argued'. This is indubitable. However, the principal argument of my article (Willmott 1999c) concerned ontology, namely the secreted social ontology of positivist/statistical methods and its contingent congruence with neo-liberalism.

For Goldstein and Woodhouse, however,

> Perhaps the most extreme criticism of the use of [mathematical] models comes from Willmott, who mounts a general attack on 'positivism'. The difficulty with this critique is that it is very difficult to recognize any real researchers as practising positivists – at least according to Willmott's definition. For example, he asserts that positivism is unable to take account of subtle variations of social relationships within institutions over time, yet there are many studies which do model changing relationships of various kinds over time – the main problem being with the availability of the data rather than with the technical procedures required to do the modelling.
>
> (2000: 359)

The last comment is instructive, since the authors remain firmly wedded to mathematical modelling. They do not acknowledge that, precisely because they remain wedded to mathematical modelling, they are positivists: mathematical modelling *cannot* take account of subtle variations of social relationships over time. Let us be clear what we mean by positivism. Positivism is a theory of the nature and limits of knowledge. As Bhaskar puts it:

> Particular knowledge is of events sensed in perception; general knowledge is of the patterns such events show in space and over time, which, if it is to be possible, must be constant...Sense-perception exhausts the possible objects of knowledge...Positivism is a theory of knowledge. But any theory of knowledge presupposes an ontology...Thus the Humean theory, which forms the lynchpin of the positivist system, presupposes an ontology of closed systems and atomistic events...Moreover any theory of knowledge presupposes a sociology in the sense that it must be assumed, implicitly if not explicitly, that the nature of human beings and the institutions they reproduce or transform is such that such knowledge could be produced. Thus the Humean theory presupposes a conception of people as passive sensors of given facts and recorders of their given constant conjunctions, which has the corollary that knowledge can always be analysed in a purely individualistic way.
>
> (1989b: 49–50)

Bhaskar then argues that it is in the inconsistent system so resulting that positivism's tremendous versatility and flexibility as an ideology lies. It functions as an ideology for social practices other than science 'by encouraging, by injunction or resonance, certain substantive conceptions of the nature of nature, society, persons and their interconnections' (Bhaskar 1989b: 50).

Indeed, as we shall see in a moment, Goldstein and Woodhouse want to incorporate – inconsistently – the fact that schools function within a social and political system and, at the same time, retain the primacy of statistical modelling. Ultimately, then, this means that they cannot avoid the denial of social reality *qua* structured and open system that is intrinsic to mathematical modelling. In brief, there are two conditions that must be met for a closed system. First, there is the intrinsic condition for closure; that is, there must be no change or qualitative variation in the object possessing causal powers if mechanisms are to operate consistently. Second, the relationship between the causal mechanism and those of its external conditions must be constant if the outcome is to be regular (the extrinsic condition for closure). As Sayer (1992) points out, the intrinsic condition for closure is ignored even if the extrinsic one is acknowledged. Moreover,

> The presence of uninterpreted constants, parameters or coefficients in many models bears witness to the inadequacy of their attempts to produce a correspondence between mathematical and causal order. If they cannot be interpreted as 'standing for' a particular process or characteristic they may more justifiably be described as 'fudge factors' in that their only function is to conceal the inadequacies of the model by providing a means of fitting it to any data set. (With enough parameters, any model can be fitted to any data.)...Modellers may not be aware of it, but the inclusion of parameters whose values vary from case to case provides a retrospective but uninterpretable way of allowing for the non-satisfaction of the intrinsic and extrinsic conditions for closure and the mis-specification of causal structure.
>
> (Sayer 1992: 184–5)

The transcendentally false assumption that social reality is a closed system is congruent with the OFSTED inspection regime, which is underpinned by SER. To reiterate, OFSTED assumes that learning outcomes can be linked directly and unambiguously to inputs (viz. teaching). Indeed, the tacit OFSTED assumption is that causal factors are independent, universal and additive; that is, they do not interfere with each other and are uninfluenced by their contexts. The ideological import is palpable: teachers are blamed for pupil 'failure' (for this read: poor examination results). Furthermore, OFSTED's focus on key determinants (later reworked as key 'factors') that constitute 'effective' schools are culled at the level of observable events and, in positivist fashion, there is no attempt to differentiate between contingency and necessity. That there may be a contingent relation between successful learning and strong leadership cannot be entertained. Here, we return to the perennial problem of spurious correlations that haunts the use of statistics because of its inability to distinguish accidental from necessary relations. Thus, for Hopkins, 'The so-called "effectiveness correlates" however sophisticatedly defined are no substitute for models or theories of how schools function. Without this knowledge it is difficult to see how the [SE] field can progress' (1996: 30).

Again, the main problem is that statistical modelling cannot deal with components that are not qualitatively invariant (children, teachers...) or where they interact causally with one another, or where emergent powers arise or are dissolved through combinations and separations. As Sayer succinctly puts it, 'Attempting to explain the effects of an object which has emergent powers in terms of the relative contribution of its constituents is like attributing a certain percentage of behaviour of water to hydrogen effects and the rest to oxygen effects!' (1992: 181). Thus we would not explain why students attend lectures in terms of attributing a certain percentage to lecturer effects and the rest to student effects. Instead, we employ such explanatory concepts as social structure – in this case the irreducible emergent structural property of lecturer/student and its wider structural embedding (university, polity, economy and the necessary irreducible relations between them). We can count how many students turn up to lectures, but this does not tell us why they do. SER may tell us how many students from working-class backgrounds gain A*–C GCSE passes but it does not tell us how and why. It may also tell us that certain schools achieve better results for their working-class students, thereby indicating their 'value-addedness'. But it does not tell us why. This explains why such results become so easily appropriated by New Right government(s), since it is a short step to argue that *all* schools can achieve high levels of attainment, irrespective of social background. Without adequate explanation (or even attempts at explanation), SE data are ever open to political manipulation. One would reasonably expect exploration of the material limits to current imposed crude indicators of effectiveness. Statistical techniques do not exist in abstract isolation: the socio-political context must always be taken into account, theoretically and ethically – not as a mere afterthought exemplified by the belated recognition of the importance of social class.

Ironically, as Goldstein and Woodhouse call for more sophisticated models and 'data', Sayer (1992) argues that the value of statistics is depreciated as our knowledge of causal mechanisms becomes more complete. However, he does argue that the usefulness of statistical methods depends crucially upon the type of objects to which they are applied and the type of research design in which they are employed. In a nutshell, evaluation of the possibilities for statistical analysis requires a non-statistical examination of the objects of interest: this is conspicuously absent in the SE research concerned with mathematical modelling. A common criticism of statistical analyses of relationships among variables is that they tend to abstract from qualitative change in their key objects and from changes in context; often the two are linked and internally related (Sayer 1992: 198). Sayer gives the example of industrial change, where students have for many years abstracted from the continually changing interdependence between the qualitative nature of particular industries and the competitive environment in which they operate, as if the variables were only externally related and as if the economic environment were just a passive backcloth to the action. This has also characterised SE and SI (School Improvement) research. As Goldstein and Woodhouse note:

> Schools function within a social and political system which has its own structures and processes, whether these be one of inter-school competition or those determined by externally imposed constraints of curriculum or resource. Despite the recognition of this by many within SE and SI...there seems little in the research itself that seriously attempts to address this problem. While SE research has gone some way towards modelling within-school complexities, it has made almost no attempt to contextualise schools within the wider environment. To do so, of course, would involve political as well as social and cultural considerations and it is doubtful whether this would be welcome to government.
>
> (Goldstein and Woodhouse 2000: 356)

Here, we have, on the one hand, a welcome discussion of the importance of the structures and processes that shape what goes on in schools and the recognition of the likely disapprobation of government of research that incorporates the latter, yet, on the other hand, the need for contextualisation is reductively couched in terms of modelling. There is a crucial recognition of the need to contextualise the environment in which schools function, yet immediately we are returned to the familiar territory of mathematical modelling. There is no discussion of the materiality of political and social systems, and of the internal necessary relation between schools, the state and economy, and how the latter cannot sensibly be statistically represented. SE researchers cannot have their ontological cake and statistically eat it! Coe and FitzGibbon (1998) are quite right that there are factors beyond the control of the school, which account for variation between schools. Here, statistically minded SE researchers should take on board the fact that mathematical models assume a closed system, as we have seen. People and their social environments are not externally related and susceptible to treatment as 'variables'.

As I have already argued, Goldstein and Woodhouse are quite right to insist that statistical methods have no in-built requirement for a particular managerial structure. However, such methods do not exist in abstract isolation. As Thrupp (forthcoming) rightly notes, the in-house concerns of SER proponents do not run as deep as their critics because they see the problem mostly as a matter of encouraging a more satisfactory use of their findings by politicians rather than acknowledging the current managerialist climate. Goldstein and Woodhouse argue that much of what we know about the effects of class is derived from careful statistical modelling. Yet the crucial point is that 'careful statistical modelling' can never explain what is registered statistically. One must be careful not to elide explanation and effects. Indeed, it must be remembered that managerialist structures have been imposed and underpinned by the quantitative data supplied by SE researchers. Providing statistical 'evidence' of the effects of 'class' does not tell us whether class itself places limits on educational achievement. The issue should involve rigorous analysis of the nature, dynamics and causal properties of class. This is why the atheoretical nature of statistics readily lends itself to neo-liberal appropriation. Whilst Goldstein and Woodhouse and others explicitly discuss class, statistical methods cannot adequately incorporate it and thus any statistical findings should only be used as a tentative starting-point.

The managerial co-option of Alexander and others

Finally, I want briefly to discuss Galton and Alexander, for, whilst not specifically within the school effectiveness camp, their critiques of progressivism complement the managerialist project. Professor Robin Alexander is well known for his co-authorship of the DES discussion paper, *Curriculum Organisation and Classroom Practice in Primary Schools* (Alexander *et al.*1992). The remaining co-authors were Chris Woodhead (former Head of OFSTED) and J. Rose. Equally influential is Maurice Galton. Silcock notes that, whilst warning against a return to wholly didactic teaching, Galton 'promotes "factory models" of learning (designing techniques which guarantee outcomes, such as "direct instruction") as well as, rather more cautiously, recommending the learner-centred, negotiated curricular models...' (1996: 199). Logically, Galton cannot have it both ways. The very use of the factory analogy enjoins a non-negotiated curriculum. There is an obvious congruence between the OFSTED model of linear causality and Galton's proposal: factors that may (and often do) intervene to prevent 'direct instruction' are not countenanced. As I have argued, the managerialist ontology secretes a factory model. Thus Galton is treading a thin line between unleashing a constraining, as opposed to a competitive, contradiction. Galton would firmly deny that he is erasing children *qua* children from the learning process. However, his factory approach is quintessentially concerned with the product – like the egg hatched by the factory chicken – and not the process. Indeed, the straightforward, linear causal process of instruction → outcome implicitly denies the varied cognitive capacities and needs of children. Like the school effectiveness researchers, I submit that Galton and Alexander are also culpable of 'ideological commitment', for their proposals are ultimately managerialist rather than educational.

Galton's ORACLE studies (Galton *et al.* 1980) bolstered Alexander's influential attack on child-centred rhetoric (Alexander 1992; Alexander *et al.* 1992) and Alexander's own promotion of pragmatism. Both critiques give public credibility to the death of Plowden progressivism, justifying scapegoating speeches made by politicians (e.g., Kenneth Clarke 1991; John Major 1991). The generic emphasis now is on pragmatism, which, tied to a social constructivism, is close to social determinism. As Silcock puts it:

> If classroom problems are only resolved 'in situ' (pragmatism), and children learn, in any case, what cultures prepare them to learn (social constructivism), then successful education will follow from a firm control by teachers over what pupils do, and an associated firm control, by governments, over what teachers do.
>
> (1996: 201)

Alexander's pragmatism resonates well with OFSTED's school-level emphasis, which disavows the importance of extra-school factors. At its strongest, social constructivist theory views rational thought as impossible outside structures internalised from social intercourse (e.g. Hamlyn 1978). In its slightly weaker form (Vygotskian), it maintains that non-social cognitive elements are either displaced or transformed by the social so that little long-term account need be taken of them. The Vygotskian view that the mind is structured by the social rather than vice versa neatly complements the managerialist restructuring of education. For in playing down the role of children in their own cognitive development, teachers *qua* technicians can get on with the business of instructing. Such instruction is largely unimpeded, enabling swift improvement in standards. It should be recalled that Vygotsky is not denying the child's innate capacity for reflective cognitive development. However far he attenuates the extent of children's innate reflective capacities, nevertheless he maintains that children's development occurs inside the child, but only after social intercourse: 'Every function in the child's cultural development appears twice...first between people (interpsychological) and then inside the child (intrapsychological)' (Vygotsky 1978: 57).

This is in contradistinction to the Piagetian approach, which convincingly demonstrates that non-social cognition gained through interaction with objects provides a structural ground for social perspective-taking, rather than vice versa. Our first grasp on reality is derived from what Piaget calls 'reflexive abstraction'; whereby infants become 'operative'; that is, they 'reflect' upon the objects they handle in order to develop sense-motor skills. Thus, to Silcock,

> The reflexivity of practical thinking is unlike reflection on internalised symbols in that the latter, being reliant on social perspective-taking, introduces shared meanings into consciousness and is creative of 'mind' as the arena for constructivism. It is, of course, an immensely important development. Until individuals identify other social objects as individuals, they cannot recognise themselves as individuals, or know their own humanness...The actions of an infant reaching for an object are structured by a combination of learned control and spatio-temporal parameters – no one has to 'tell' a child how to reach, or suggest it might be a good thing to do so (though such suggestions are not precluded – the point is that the learning proceeds on individual not social volition)...
>
> (1996: 206)

Indeed, as Silcock rightly points out, it is simply not credible that we gain the rich quality of tacit meanings underwriting our grasp of the physical world simply through linguistically mediated social influence. Galton's critique of child-centred philosophy and practice draws upon Simon's advice that diverse curricula, as related to individual needs, are too difficult to manage. Simon draws upon the findings of the ORACLE project, arguing that '...primary classroom practice, based loosely on Plowden, creates an "excessively complex" classroom management situation which presents, overall, an almost impossible task to the teacher. Exaggerated individualism as I argued earlier, presents the main problem' (Simon 1994: 154). It goes without saying, of course, that even a residual form of individualism would be anathema to the dehumanising thrust of the new managerialism. Here we reach the main problem with the academics' critique of child-centred practice. For, whilst young children of mixed ability cannot realistically be taught en masse, at the same time a high degree of curricular differentiation is unavoidable. As Silcock argues, the question is not whether there should be differentiation, but how the inevitable diversity should be managed. An approach that attends to individuals' needs undermines Galton's 'factory model'.

Furthermore, Alexander's pragmatism is simply about how to manage the National Curriculum: again, the focus is managerial rather than educational. Instead of questioning the increasing numbers of children per class, the validity and reliability of SATs and the generic de-professionalisation of teachers, we are told about the need to combine didactic or whole-class teaching with an individualised approach plus high-level questioning by teachers. Alexander's disparaging reference to primary discourse as 'Primaryspeak' resonates well with the managerialist critique. For here the emphasis is on know-how, whereas managerialism necessitates neat, tidy packages of codified prescriptions for practice.

> The dilemma here is that though a vivid account of a particular, live classroom experience is much more arresting to an audience than abstract analytical framework, to extract general principles from such an account for teachers and children working in different contexts is a considerably more difficult enterprise. That leaves ideological language…so much so that we might term it 'Primaryspeak'. Primaryspeak is about assertion rather than argument…It is peppered with…slogans and buzzwords: flexibility, freedom, spontaneity, start with the child…
>
> (Alexander 1990: 71)

The one-hundred year difficulty of articulating the conceptual framework of know-how practices was revealed in Chapter 2. That teachers rely almost exclusively on practical classroom experience as the main source of their professional knowledge is hardly grounds for disparaging censure. Whatever the reasons underlying Alexander's critique of 'Primaryspeak', the demand for generalised abstract principles lends itself to appropriation by OFSTED and school effectiveness research. For (a) know-that procedures are the only valid forms of knowledge within the new managerialism, since they provide the technicist basis for 'teaching'; and (b) Alexander's emphasis on generalisable procedures equally neglects contextual factors. Such 'Primaryspeak' shibboleths as 'start with the child' are not slogans but transcendental states of affairs that are prior to teaching.

Finally, Alexander has replied that the 'Three Wise Men' discussion paper was not an unprincipled invitation to pragmatism. Instead, '…good practice…can never be singular, fixed or absolute, a specification handed down or imposed from above…Good practice is plural, provisional and dynamic: there are thus as many versions of good practice as there are good teachers striving to attain it' (Alexander 1996: 71). Yet 'good practice' for child-centred teachers is grounded in the nature of children *qua* children: what is 'fixed' is the nature of children and their psychological development. Different practices and activities simply reflect the different needs and socio-cultural backgrounds of children. If 'good practice' can never be fixed, one wonders what Alexander is identifying by the term! However, the assertion that there are as many versions of good practice as there are teachers hardly provides a watertight case against the 'anything goes' of pragmatism!

Background to 'Southside' and 'Westside'

The above provides the backdrop to my year-long period of participant observation in two primary schools, i.e. the proximate interface between where the structural and cultural contradictions shape everyday situations and how agents cope with them on the ground. Southside is situated in the southern region of a prosperous city in the south of England. Its children come primarily from socio-economically deprived backgrounds. As will be discussed in Chapter 6, its catchment area has mainly local authority housing and high levels of economic deprivation. It is a Church of England (CofE) primary school, with the local vicar being chair of the governing body. Historically, the school has never performed well in terms of achieving high levels of literacy and numeracy. The retiring head pointed this out during interview. However, this was deemed unacceptable by an OFSTED team of inspectors in 1996, which concluded that the school was not providing 'value for money'. On the whole, facilities are good. There is a full complement of staff and an additional special-needs teacher was employed at the time of my research. However, a recurring problem at Southside was the high turnover of staff. Two newly qualified teachers joined the staff; both left within two years.

'Westside', in contrast, is located in the western region of the city. This region is rather prosperous. The majority of children here come from relatively wealthy socio-economic backgrounds. Historically, the school is well known for its academic success. In particular, teachers and parents (both past and present) underscore its 'strong', traditional Catholic education for children. It is a voluntary-aided Roman Catholic primary school, and the local priest is chair of the governing body. Unlike Southside, however, the school was housed in what used to be a nunnery and consequently pupils had to climb many stairs to get to their classrooms. This was deemed to be particularly unacceptable for the infants by OFSTED (1996b). Furthermore, because of severe financial constraints, there was no caretaker and only part-time secretarial assistance. The level of cleanliness was relatively poor. Children had to provide their own stationery; art material was in short supply; and parents had to pay insurance costs each time the children left the premises to attend mass, visit the local sports centre for swimming and engage in outdoor activities. Unlike Southside, the playground was smaller and inadequate for the number of children on the roll. However, Westside did not receive a poor OFSTED report.

6 Southside

New Managerialism to the rescue

The 'failing' school: background and research methodology

The OFSTED inspection at Southside was carried out in July 1996 over a period of five days. At the time the school had 206 boys and girls on roll aged 7–11. As the OFSTED report mentioned, the catchment area has mainly local authority housing and 'high levels of economic and social deprivation: 54.4 per cent of pupils receive free school meals and 18 per cent live in overcrowded conditions, nearly twice the national average' (OFSTED 1996: 6). The 'key indicators' in the report focused on results at Key Stage 2, and then looked at levels of attendance, number of exclusions and 'teaching quality'. Southside came bottom of the league table in its area, with 38 per cent of children achieving level 4 or above in English, 14 per cent achieving level 4 or above in mathematics and 44 per cent achieving level 4 or above in science. The main findings of the report are as follows:

> Most aspects of the management of the school are sound, although there are some weaknesses…The management responsibilities of staff are not always appropriate and in some cases do not match their expertise. Staff development lacks rigour and some staff feel they lack support. There is insufficient monitoring of both teaching and the progress of individual pupils, other than those with SEN [special educational needs]…Pupils enter the school with low levels of attainment and generally make progress in acquiring basic skills. However, there is a high proportion of unsatisfactory teaching and more able pupils do not progress to the higher levels of attainment. When these facts are linked to the generous level of funding, *the school gives unsatisfactory value for money*.
>
> (OFSTED 1996: 4–5, emphasis added)

Following this report, an Action Plan was drawn up under the supervision of an LEA advisory team and was evaluated by the team in June 1997. I spent three weeks in Southside almost immediately after the LEA advisors had conducted their OFSTED-style evaluation of the implementation of the Action Plan (see Willmott 1999b). This LEA evaluation was initially flagged up as an informal affair, but in the event was OFSTED in style and content, much to the disbelief of the staff.

However, the three weeks spent in June were an experiential prelude to a whole term of participant observation, which was completed in the autumn term of 1997. The head announced his intention to take early retirement and informed staff that a temporary replacement would be found. Towards the end of the three-week period, a senior member of staff became aware of the identity of the temporary head (a position which became permanent half-way through the term) and spent much time informing a small clique of staff about the 'trouble-shooting' status of the incoming head, a woman who, it was alleged, 'got rid of six staff' within the first term of arriving at a similar 'failing' school. The hearsay talk about the temporary appointment palpably unnerved all staff, many of whom were, according to a senior member of staff, used to 'doing their own thing'. As one senior teacher remarked, '[the head] never came in to see what we were doing...that was the problem!'. The outgoing head commented during interview that one of the LEA advisors recommended that he treat his staff 'like children':

> ...one of the advisors she said to me teachers are like children...You've got to treat them like children. Well, I'm afraid I just can't...You see, there's no way that I'm going to change to be like that. So that's one of the reasons I took the decision I did [i.e., to take early retirement]...

Indeed, for the outgoing head the new managerialist programme was anathema. For the incoming head, however, such a programme was enthusiastically endorsed and undertaken with a strongly personalised imprint. Pseudonyms are used throughout and analysis draws upon interview transcripts and fieldnotes of observations and discussions with staff.

The new head arrives: 'We're not social workers!'

During the short time I spent at Southside in the summer term, all staff were aware that the school faced the real threat of closure because of the relatively poor SATs results and below average OFSTED report. (However, the threat of closure was not made public.) In essence, the LEA brief to the incoming head was to respond to the weaknesses outlined in the OFSTED report, but, more crucially, to improve the SATs results. Undoubtedly some of the weaknesses identified in the OFSTED report were reasonable and accepted by staff. The pressing problem of pupil behaviour and lack of direction provided by the outgoing head were issues that each teacher accepted as requiring urgent attention. Indeed, the considerable improvement in behaviour that quickly followed the appointment of the 'trouble-shooting' head was welcomed. However, the analytical concern here is whether such improvement was enacted for educational or managerial reasons. The managerialisation of education enjoins well-behaved pupils who 'learn' what is delivered to them at the chalkface in order to perform well in SATs. Yet, on the other hand, child-centred practice enjoins that we respect the fact that children are not empty vessels, have needs that are shaped by such factors as socio-economic background, and behave well in order to maintain and enhance collective well being. As Abbott rightly notes, OFSTED and government publications ignore the complexity of classroom interaction: 'teaching and learning are not part of a simple input–output model. This is to take the "empty vessel" view of children's learning, seeing pupils as passive receivers of knowledge, poured into them by the teacher' (1996: 117). However, it is my contention that the 'empty vessel' approach is an unavoidable practical (S-C level) secretion of managerialism rather than an ontological presupposition. In other words, at the CS level managerialism dehumanises children, yet transcendentally cannot avoid some recognition of the human element (however that human element is conceived). Thus, as I argued in Chapter 2, we are dealing with a constraining, rather than a competitive, contradiction. I also argued that some form of 'practical syncretism' is unavoidable, as we shall see in a moment. The head was openly in favour of managerialist 'solutions' to improving SATs. Thus we have here a fundamental contradiction between the child-centred (humanist) concern for behaviour and self-esteem and the strategic manipulation of managerialism, which denies the very humanistic path that facilitates (potentially) success in SATs.

Yet some of the changes introduced by the head were grounded in child-centred philosophy and practice, but contradictorily used by the head for explicitly managerial aims. From day one, the managerialist restructuring of the school was explicitly made top priority by the head. In the first morning of term, an INSET session was provided for both teaching and non-teaching staffs in which the staffs were asked to talk about what they wanted from children. One of the key issues emphasised by the head at the start was that 'we are not social workers'. This was a *leitmotif* throughout my time at Southside, and sat rather uncomfortably with the relatively high number of children on the 'at-risk' register: every weekly staff meeting and every morning briefing dealt with the issue of 'children requiring positive praise' for reasons stemming from home problems.[51] What the head meant by 'social workers' was never spelled out from my observations, and from my informal conversations with staff it was clear that they never asked for clarification. Here, of course, we can discern a consistent managerialist response: dealing with 'social work' (caring) issues is an encumbrance.

Pugh (1998) has documented the conflict between care and the curriculum in the context of a residential school for EBD (Emotionally and Behaviourally Disturbed) pupils aged 11–16. Like the new head at Southside, Pugh also took on the (temporary) role of 'trouble-shooter' for this school in December 1993. He concedes that to fail an EBD school was generally held unfair because many of the pupils were too emotionally disturbed (the pupils required therapy and understanding rather than a daily diet of the National Curriculum) and because EBD schools are places that only manage to operate through a careful balancing act, and are thus too complex to be understood via the OFSTED 'snapshot' approach. As with the new head at Southside, Pugh began by developing a vision of what the school should look like. Such a vision had to embody a full National Curriculum. Yet given the 'difficult' nature of the pupils, many of the teachers were contracted to perform additional duties. These duties involved working alongside the full-time residential care assistants. It was hardly surprising, then, that staff had little time for lesson preparation, let alone developing new schemes of work. Pugh candidly writes that,

...[b]y late February, about three months since I had assumed the acting head-ship, I began to lose my nerve. I felt that I had achieved nothing beyond a few room changes and an arbitrary extension to teaching time which had done no more than enrage pupils and further tire staff. I had an overwhelming sense that I was failing both staff and pupils and daily adding another nail to the coffin of what was once quite a promising career.

(Pugh 1998: 109–10)

Pugh oversaw the establishment of a scheme of work for every subject and, as with Southside, each pupil was tested for reading ability, and clear schemes were developed for marking, recording and assessment. 'Vandalism remained a significant problem...[and] aggression between pupils was unacceptably high and the school still projected an atmosphere of unpredictability and tension' (Pugh 1998: 111). Pugh was aware that, whilst the staff were never openly hostile, a number felt that the curriculum-based approach to working with emotionally and behaviourally disturbed pupils was wrong. This was evident during my time at Southside. In my conversations with most teachers, fundamental concerns were aired about the changes that were being imposed by the head, but these were not aired at either staff meetings or privately with the head. It was not always possible to elicit the reasons for the lack of such opposition. However, the threat of closure, combined with deep-seated resentments among some staff, precluded the possibility of a united front. This is not to suggest that staff could have remained wedded to previous practices. Like the head at Southside, Pugh established weekly briefings and refined the good behaviour system.

Moreover, Pugh, on the one hand, is aware of the seriously disrupted educational histories of the pupils yet, on the other hand, does not rule out success as a possibility. Here we reach the flaw of the OFSTED model and, indeed, of past Conservative and present 'New' Labour policy – namely the fallacy that *all* schools, given the correct dose of management and concomitant 'cultural change', should 'succeed'. Instructively, Pugh concludes:

I am sure that many would argue that reference to a conflict between care and curriculum is an unnecessary polarization; that it is more appropriate to assert that EBD pupils cannot live on the bread of education alone, and emotional needs which cannot be reached through the curriculum must also be nourished. While I would not take issue with the sentiment, the compromise position is ultimately unsustainable because the resources to do both are not available. The conflict is not about caring or not caring, or educating or not educating, but where the line is drawn in deciding when as much as possible has been done within existing resources. *The staff at Brookside accepted the view that educational objectives are more attainable, more measurable and, most immediately, more inspectable.* I would not say that this acceptance means that they have ceased to offer a caring environment to pupils. The object of caring has become the need to ensure that every individual is able to take advantage of the education offered. *In this sense, the school has defined itself firmly within an educational context rather than as an auxiliary branch of social services or the Health Authority...*The purpose of the school is to educate, and without that clear direction and purpose, *caring too easily becomes an object in itself and then a law unto itself.*

(Pugh 1998: 115–16, emphasis added)

The point here is that there *is* a contradiction between care and the *managerialist* nature of the National Curriculum and attendant testing arrangements. Children are not growing human beings but targets, numbers that can be tabulated in competitive league tables. Moreover, socio-economic factors are erased at a stroke. Indeed, I have quoted Pugh at length here because it underscores (a) the dehumanising thrust of the new managerialism; and (b) the fact that schools do not operate in a vacuum but are necessarily responsive to factors determined elsewhere. It also provides a neat example of how agents live syncretically with contradiction. In other words, here Pugh is attempting an A (managerialism) ← B (caring) manoeuvre. He is arguing that one can (somehow) 'over-emphasise' caring, but at the same time cannot eschew it: the force of the constraining contradiction involves the playing-down of caring and its simultaneous unavoidability. Thus, to Troman and Woods:

'Too much caring, not enough learning…' was an early slogan of the new era. Teachers thus have to be purged of these feelings if they are to be reincorporated into their new roles. There is a new brand of professionalism here, which involves being part of a hierarchical management structure, less democratic participation, less autonomy, more prescription.

(Troman and Woods 2001: 75)

The head at Southside emphasised on numerous occasions during staff meetings and briefings that 'we are not social workers' and, like Pugh, would have maintained that the school was not an auxiliary branch of social services. However, the familial and socio-economic backgrounds of many of the children meant that staff *had* to be a quasi-auxiliary branch of local social services. One particularly poignant example will suffice. A Year 6 pupil attempted suicide because of familial problems. Considerable time was taken up in one meeting, during which we were told what to do in the event of the boy's father turning up at school (essentially, not to confront the father and to contact the police). The point here is that such 'social work' (or 'caring') issues are fundamentally anathema to managerialism – put simply, they get in the way of pupils becoming 'independent learners' in order to perform well in their SATs. Indeed, Pugh traces through the managerialist logic when he notes that the care of his pupils is acceptable *in the end* given that it facilitates successful implementation of the National Curriculum. The contradiction is palpable: on the one hand, *as educators* the staff at Brookside view caring as integral to their daily work with pupils, yet, on the other hand, caring is (oddly) elevated into an object that becomes a law unto itself. Such mental contortions are the result of the constraining contradiction – children *because they are children* must be cared for, yet the (New) Managerialism erases children *qua* human beings. Hence the playing down of caring and the simultaneous recognition on Pugh's part of the need to care. This is the force of the constraining contradiction – for managerialism denies the reality of children *qua* human beings yet in theory and in practice cannot avoid some (basic) propositions about children *qua* children in order for SATs to be taken, successfully or otherwise.

Pugh talks of the acceptance of the view that educational objectives are more attainable, more measurable and more inspectable. It would be interesting to know whether such acceptance was more apparent than real. The majority of staff at Southside nodded in agreement during staff meetings, but their actions and conversations with me belied this. However, it is not educational objectives that are more attainable, but managerial ones. To suggest that something is more measurable is specious – either something is intrinsically tractable to measurement or it is not. As we have already seen, proxies are used by OFSTED as part and parcel of the managerialist drive towards 'educational efficiency' (value for money). Jeffrey and Woods (1999) have documented the dehumanisation engendered by the managerialist nature of the inspection process. The teachers in their study 'could not accept the OFSTED definition of knowledge...the managerialist approach to assessment, the distancing of themselves from colleagues and pupils and the culture of blame and failure' (1999: 83). Jeffrey and Woods' research paints a picture of teachers as being very much on the defensive:

> Their time and space have been colonized, their sense of reality disturbed, and they have experienced feelings of deprofessionalization. But...teachers are very resilient. In previous studies we have remarked on their powers of adaptation and resistance...To some extent, this reaction has been facilitated by the 'implementation gap'...Part of the rationale in establishing OFSTED was to decrease this gap...and to close down resistance. This is a comparatively new kind of constraint on teachers...We found teacher responses here to be complex, and in some respects contradictory...On the one hand teachers *distanced* themselves from the OFSTED process in order to maintain their selves and professional identity. At the same time, they *engaged* extensively with the process in order to satisfy the corporate pressures...
>
> (1999: 141)

I would take issue with their contention that teacher responses are contradictory. Instead, there is a contradiction at the structural and cultural levels; namely, between the previous role requirements and the new form of government imposition and between child-centred philosophy and the secreted anti-humanism of managerialism. The simultaneous distancing and engagement referred to by Jeffrey and Woods is an agential response to contradiction rather than a contradictory response. As the authors rightly emphasise, the OFSTED regime constitutes an additional constraint for child-centred teachers, with which they are stringently conditioned to contend. Indeed, teachers are resilient, but such resilience does not eradicate the 'corporate pressures' of the OFSTED regime, as they put it. Whitty *et al.* (1998: 59) refer to Raab *et al.*'s (1997) study in which variation in head-teachers' responses depended on the degree of LEA decentralisation and marketisation. In the areas where schools remained relatively protected from the latter, there was less conflict between educational values and new managerialist practices. Whitty *et al.* thus suggest that the strategies adopted by head-teachers are to some extent determined by local context rather than personally held values. Furthermore, the research by Gewirtz *et al.* (1995) suggests that 'if schools are particularly "buoyant" in the market, head-teachers may be able to retain elements of "professional" management. However, head-teachers with fragile market positions [such as Southside] *have little choice but to engage with the business ethics of new managerialism*' (Whitty *et al.* 1998: 59, emphasis added).

I would not dispute the need for heads of schools with fragile market positions to engage with the business ethics of the new managerialism. (Recognition of this was one of the key reasons that led the previous head to take early retirement.) However, my research at Southside provides an example of a head who positively welcomed reorienting the school along new managerialist lines. For her, teachers are now 'managers' and pupils are 'customers'. In interview, she described Southside as '...obviously dysfunctional; otherwise I wouldn't have been brought in here'. In order to get the 'dysfunctional' organisational back on track, she talked of the need for 'strong leadership' and for changing the system 'that people did well out of'.[52] In brief, then, we need to distinguish between anterior socio-cultural conditioning at the macro, school and individual levels. In other words, the head entered a complex set of anterior cycles in September 1997 – notably the school history mediated by local socio-economic context and the (macro) OFSTED regime. That *any* new head had to improve SATs at Southside is indisputable. Whitty *et al.* are right to emphasise the stringent nature of the OFSTED regime and assessment procedures that confront schools in relatively poor socio-economic areas. Indeed, the 'creaming off' of ten or so pupils to a rival school evidenced the precarious market position of Southside.[53] However, the new head not only recognised the harsh reality of the need to improve SATs but that the only solution was managerialist, as we shall see. We are not dealing here with a reluctant head, whose deeply held educational values are at variance with the new managerialism. On the contrary, her unrelenting drive towards improving SATs was firmly grounded in the school effectiveness literature and the new managerialist nostrums for achieving 'success'.

School effectiveness, organisational culture and autocratic management

The afternoon INSET session for teaching staff focused on how to improve the school, with specific reference to SATs scores. During this session staff were asked to write on a flip chart what they expected of her, and what they believed 'enthuses children'. The head made explicit that 'there were going to be some battles', that some 'I'll lose and staff will lose some'. More important, however, is the extensive use she made of the school effectiveness research. She issued each member of staff with a handout documenting the key findings of the effectiveness research. She listed the key determinants of successful schools as follows:

- Professional leadership
- Shared vision and goals
- A learning environment

- Concentration on teaching and learning
- Purposeful teaching
- High expectations
- Positive reinforcement
- Monitoring progress
- Pupil rights and responsibilities
- Home–school partnership
- A learning organisation

The reference for this list was Sammons *et al.* (1995), *Key Characteristics of Effective Schools*, which has been criticised in the Preface to Part III of this book. The factors listed above provided the springboard for restructuring what the head referred to as the 'organisational culture' of the school throughout the term. One of the documents draws upon Fullan (1990), in which assumptions about change *vis-à-vis* school improvement were listed, with the final bullet point emphasising that 'the real agenda is changing institutional culture'. The issue of organisational culture *qua* managerialist tool was addressed in Chapter 5. The 'cultural' issue of shared vision and goals (one of OFSTED's so-called Eleven Factors) is crucial for the success of any managerialist regime. (The bullet point 'Shared vision and goals' was also part of a further list, referred to as 'Cultural Norms which Underpin School Improvement'.) As was argued in Chapter 5, corporate culture's key feature is to promote employee (i.e., teacher) 'commitment' to a monolithic structure of feeling and thought in the name of empowerment or 'expanded autonomy'. It was pointed out that programmes of corporate culturism seem to promote a corporate ethos that demands loyalty from employees as it excludes, silences or punishes those who question its creed. Indeed, the so-called 'strength' of culture is tied to the extent to which contradictory or 'rival' values are absent (at the S-C level). In other words, S-C unification is sought. Finally, it was mentioned that, in so far as employees are drawn to the allure of 'technocratic informalism', employees come to discipline themselves with feelings of anxiety, shame and guilt that are aroused when they sense or judge themselves to fall short of the shared values of the organisation.

The substantive focus of this part of the book is on how teachers mediate the (necessary) contradiction between child-centred philosophy (and practice) and the new managerialism. More specifically, we are interested in the extent of S-C uniformity and the reasons behind it. At Southside it was very much a case of S-C *imposition* of the OFSTED-cum-School-Effectiveness framework. The key factor that facilitated the successful use of power was of course the somewhat precarious position of the school. However, because schools, like all organisations, are operative in an open system, the managerialist style of the head and the generic lack of resistance could not have been predicted. What we *can* say, however, is that even if the 'trouble-shooting' head had been child-centred, stringent costs would have attached to a half-hearted adoption of the OFSTED framework. The fact that the head was determined to exercise autocratic control certainly aided 'improvement', as we shall see in a moment, but counterfactuals are not the issue here. The issue is to explicate why things were so and not otherwise. In this school, the threat of closure, internal schisms exacerbated by personality differences, and so on, buttressed the *de jure* power of the new head. Again, however,

> [whilst] the discourse [CS level] of quality management anticipates and cele-
> brates a radical process of attitudinal and behavioural restructuring...*it has to
> confront [at the S-C level] the everyday realities of shop-floor and office politics that sculpt the
> 'contested terrains' on which control struggles are fought and decided.* Self-subordination to
> the ideological and operational demands of quality management regimes is
> likely to be extremely imperfect, and to be mediated through the power strug-
> gles which actually shape organizational outcomes. *Thus, in practice, the
> organizational reality of TQM will fall far short of the totalizing and universalizing ideals to
> which it aspires.*
>
> (Reed 1995: 53–4, emphasis added)

Indeed, it was precisely because the new head was employed initially on an acting basis that she adopted a more 'softly, softly' approach at the beginning. During a conversation in the staff room one morning, the head said that for the time being she was constrained to take a 'softly, polite approach' to two senior members of staff. In essence, she felt she could be more 'assertive' if she got the headship (which, in the event, she did). The head used the analogy of handing 'these people as much rope as they like – the trick is to yank it in at the right moment' and candidly stated that she was 'biding her time'. However, this was a strategic reading of the situation, whose objective potentialities have to be trans-acted: at the end of the day the head was objectively more powerful, given the precarious position of the school, but raw bargaining power has to be converted into negotiating strength. Negotiating strength is by definition relational and its outcome has no exact price that can be read off the head-teachers' equivalent of an OFSTED shopping list. Whilst throughout the term staff generally undertook the tasks set by the head (often referred to pejoratively as 'directives' by staff), other changes were subject to negotiation and compromise. Ultimately, of course, compro-mise entailed facing the reality of the pupil intake itself. This is what I mean by 'practical syncretism', whereby the reality of children places limits on the A (managerialisation) ← B (child-centredness) manoeuvre. However, as one staff member commented in interview:

> LYNNE: I'm slightly worried about some aspects of it [programme for 'inde-
> pendent learning'], but well I think it's a wait-and-see. In terms of umm,
> obviously I'm preoccupied with standards of reading, but she seems to have
> made a compromise with that because this isn't a school where children can
> write poetry all day, everyday and be artistically creative at all the language arts
> and all of the rest of it.

Lynne then went on to comment:

> She might say that is a prejudiced statement, *but I'd never dare make it in front of
> her.* But they need a balance of the two really (emphasis added).

Before analysing in more depth the 'improvement' programme introduced by the head, I want to focus on autocratic management. In fact, in many ways this head personified, with amazing consistency, the central organisational tenets of the new managerialism, namely the focus on output, entrepreneurship and the 'right to manage'. As we have seen, the new managerialism enjoins a 'shared' culture. The very notion of a shared culture, whilst empirically refutable, implies a sense of arrived-at agreement. Managerialism, however, is quintessentially concerned with the imposition of values. It is not so much that there is no time for agreement. The whole point of the (contradictory) nature of managerialism is that because human agency is denied, critical reflection simply does not figure in the equation (despite the fact that cultural ideas and their attempted imposition presuppose reflective human beings). Although child-centred philosophy never reached the mythical heights of generic S-C uniformity often depicted during the 1960s, disagreements were none the less permitted and divergent practices prevailed. In respect of Reed's point that the totalising – or totalitarian (according to Hugh Willmott) – nature of the new managerialism will fall far short, research here overwhelmingly confirms the opposite.

As Ball (1998) rightly notes, managerialism objectifies humans – they are simply to be managed. More importantly, he points to what he calls the 'discourse of right' that attempts to legitimate the exercise of power, which we discussed in Chapter 2.

> Its primary instrument is a hierarchy of continuous and functional surveillance. Effectiveness research can be seen to have played a crucial role in laying the groundwork for the reconceptualization of the school within which management discourse operates and has played its part in providing a technology of organizational measurement and surveillance.
>
> (Ball 1998: 74)

The importance accorded to organisational measurement was discussed in Chapter 5 and will be discussed later in the present chapter. The 'discourse of right' was one to which the head subscribed. Her approach was autocratic and often confrontational. This is not to suggest that she operated in an untrammelled fashion. Even after securing the post on a permanent basis, she had to work with and support the deputy head, as well as supporting some staff with whom she privately disagreed (although on many occasions the deputy head talked about her rudeness and subsequent apologies). The head would ring the deputy almost every evening to assess the staff's response to the ever-increasing array of effectiveness initiatives that she introduced. Fergusson (1994) points out that it is by no means unusual that managers generally exploit their special accountability for budgetary matters in order to justify autocratic behaviour. Information is almost invariably kept secret on the grounds that sole possession of expert knowledge yields advantage. 'By these means managers often by-pass or truncate normal processes of consultation, or take executive action against advice or without resolving conflicting views, or allowing financial considerations to prevail over educational...' (Fergusson 1994: 101). Whilst this is in the context of school financial management, it is applicable to the overall management of Southside. We can now return to the comment quoted above in which the member of staff conceded that she would never engage in a potentially conflict-ridden situation. Her comment that she would not dare contradict or question the head's requests evinces the anxiety that a full-blown endorsement of new managerialist nostrums engenders. Of course, as Reed rightly notes, such anxiety is not a foregone conclusion and is, *inter alia*, explicable in terms of personal psychology.

The same member of staff went on to comment:

> LYNNE: I think I am in a fortunate position that I'm not resistant to this particular load of change. If I was, I would be very, very scared because she is not going to let go. She is going to have what she wants. And umm she's going to play mean. I don't think she'd play dirty, but she'd play mean. I mean, she's put me down a few times in front of the class.

A few sentences later, Lynne commented:

> She's cleverly autocratic. You don't mess with her. She tells you what she wants on that list and you put up your hand and say it…so, she's an autocrat, but she's a clever one, you can't have her on it…

Another senior member of staff remarked:

> LOUISE: I think she is more a figure of authority, I think, and I do think she has a sense of direction and she has a vision of the school.

The senior dinner assistant mentioned that every time she questioned the changes introduced (such as seating arrangements, putting out knives and forks before children sat down to eat their lunches…) 'she tells you what to do but if not clear or you wish to challenge, she keeps throwing up in your face "have you got a problem with that?"' A good example of 'clever autocracy' centred on the use of teachers' desks in the classroom. Briefly, during one weekly staff meeting, the head requested that all staff look at 'Managing and organising the classroom to enable and empower'. She said that 'there should be no queue' – instead 'there should be swathes of children finding out for themselves and finding out from each other'. She said that cupboard doors need to be removed and, more controversially, that teachers' desks should be removed. One staff member replied:

> HILARY: I need a base where children can dump down whatever they need me to see later

Whereupon the head retorted:

> they [desks] take up so much space and get smothered…Trays for completed maths and locker units…

The deputy head commented that she did not have a desk and used a bright coloured box. The head immediately added that 'desks make a wonderful display area!' Hilary then posed the problem of where staff can work without desks. Louise replied that she used hers for marking. The head then replied:

> I hear what you say. But I personally don't think they waste space. There are other means of putting things away…tables somewhere else for teachers…I do think that if you get behind a desk you get stuck there – children start coming out…It's all about you looking in your room and saying, Right! Get the skip in!…The time is to do it *now* – not during the holidays. If you're more organised, they're [i.e., the children] better at their learning. We'll get lovely coloured containers…pencils go into at the end of the day…

What was 'clever' about the head's autocratic approach is that she allowed staff critically to contribute to weekly staff meetings yet would not brook any *real* opposition to the direction in which she *alone* wanted the school to go. Staff meetings and early morning briefings were contrived – indeed, in this instance the dialogue between the head and her deputy had been prearranged in the head's office. Whilst this underscores the 'cleverly' autocratic approach, equally it underscores her dependence upon the deputy. Essentially, the democratic approach to meetings was more apparent than real. At the end of September the head announced a set of ground rules for staff meetings as follows:

1   Keep to the point
2   Don't interrupt
3   Start/end – keep to time
4   No side-tracking
5   Put no. 4 on separate agenda
6   'Thinking time' before meeting
7   Listen to each other
8   No moaning
9   Problem-solving attitude
10   One meeting in progress

After announcing these rules, she said 'All in agreement?' and immediately requested that there be 'no grizzling if from time to time I have to remind staff of the rules'. These rules were imposed without consultation. Part of the Improvement Plan for Southside involved the production of a mission statement and a logo. The head often invoked 'working together for the best' when she issued 'directives'. At the start of one November morning briefing, for example, she said 'Today we have to work together for the best…block capitals underlined 24 million times!' This was said in the context of the absence of the teacher in charge of the unit and the comment was intended to deflect any possible 'grizzling' about the need for staff to take on extra children.[54] The meeting was interrupted by a learning support assistant (LSA) who informed the head of a woman waiting outside wishing to speak to her about two new children, whereupon Hilary said: 'If year 5 then we're stuffed!' The head retorted: 'Well, if year 5, then year 5…£1000 per child. Would we all like to keep our jobs?' Here the morphogenetic approach underscores the analytical utility of distinguishing between degrees of freedom versus stringency of constraint. Whilst on the one hand children had left to go to a more 'successful' junior school because of the extant 'failing' status of Southside, on the other hand an over-subscribed year 5 meant that stringent costs would necessarily attach to a decision to accept the two new pupils. Instead of concurring with the pressures evident in Hilary's comment, the head consistently embodied the (new) managerialism in attempting to stifle any agential reflection and/or distress. During interview, the head openly remarked that

> ...there is definitely a feeling of Yes we want change, but then people, by and large, don't like change or they resist it...people do well in the existing system, they're the ones who don't like change. I think it comes as a shock to some people as to what you actually have to do in order for those things to be able to work. *Some people don't like it because they're now instructed...* (emphasis added)[55]

I suggested that she was adopting an autocratic style of leadership:

> ROBERT (the author): ...in a way you have to tell people this is how it's got to be

> JILL (the head): Oh yes

In talking about the following term, she stated:

> ...and if there's a common agenda...and I see everybody first half of next term and we talk about what that means...The definitions of statements that were made – both parties [lower and upper school] need to be clear about what they need *and I need to let them know my interpretation* (emphasis added).

Furthermore, she talked about her 'openness' towards staff:

> Now, openness has an upside and a downside, doesn't it? You can't ask for openness, get it and not like what you hear, can you? It's like I got question-naires and then not like the answers. You've got to talk about the answers so that you are quite clear...

Such 'openness', however, was solely in relation to a questionnaire she had given staff halfway through December about her management skills and style. The questionnaire was developed by Belbin Associates © and asks assessors (in this case staff) to tick the words from List A that are descriptive of the person being assessed. Assessors are also asked to tick the words from List B that are at least *partly applicable*. In brief, the head was annoyed that some of the staff had ticked 'erratic' (she would not divulge anymore information about what else – critical or otherwise – had been ticked). *Vis-à-vis* the questionnaire, she remarked:

Chances are that...that their definition and their understanding of the words to delegate are not mine so therefore...so the only way you can find out if things are different is by having a piece of paper...which...maybe you weren't clear, I mean I know what my agenda is and its...people will often put things down but actually haven't thought about what they are writing down. Like the one from that course I went on about [which provided the Belbin question-naire]...the management course commented about...like erratic or I'm forgetful

ROBERT: Are you erratic?

JILL: I don't know...What I have to do is respond to situations. Yesterday morning I was erratic and bad-tempered because I had 'erraticism' – if there is such a word – and 'bad temperedness' forced upon me by staff who haven't got good organisational practice, so we were buzzing in the office like three bees...

Clearly, here we witness one of the contradictions of the new managerialism. On the one hand its nature is to deny, or rather to stifle, conflict, yet it cannot be avoided – hence the management course and the differing approaches to 'conflict management' the head was taught. Her reaction *vis-à-vis* staff criticism neatly high-lights the contradiction: permit criticism (whose agenda was imposed by the head), yet deny its validity. Here we are dealing with two complementary (congruent) levels: the secreted quasi-totalitarian nature of the new managerialism and the psychological characteristics of the head herself. Such autocratic management char-acterised the 'improvement programme'. This is an apposite juncture at which to discuss the adoption of the 'improvement programme', geared towards substantially increasing SATs scores. The programme drew explicitly from the school effective-ness findings and policy prescriptions.

Contra child-centredness: the tyranny of measurement

Central to the 'improvement programme' at Southside was the pressing problem of low self-esteem for many of the children. Now, the contradiction here is between the child-centred underpinning of any esteem-building programme and the new managerialist ends. Thus, to return to the issue of the removal or repositioning of teacher desks, the arguments for the latter were compelling and congruent with a child-centred approach. In fact, one member of staff took 'sick leave' at the head's request, during which her classroom was completely reorganised. Notwithstanding the head's worries about the legality of her emptying this teacher's cupboards and so on, such changes as the location of the desk and the placing of names, rather than numbers, on children's work trays made a palpable difference to the ways in which children related to each other and to the stand-in teacher.[56] Essentially, there was a substantial reduction in the level of aggressiveness, and children remained on task and generally evinced contentment (from my observations). Yet the sole reasoning behind the head's insistence stemmed from the need for children to improve in SATs. SATs are managerialist and negate the child-centred reasons for reordering a classroom in order to provide a caring environment conducive to learning. Staff meetings centred on fostering independent learning, which all staff concurred was a crucial goal of primary education. But, again, the very rationale behind SATs is to make teachers (externally) accountable. Hence the focus on the products of independent learning and not the processes, which of course are implicitly disavowed.

The self-esteem programme included, *inter alia*, the use of stickers, 'special days' and extended circle time. There was a considerable improvement in behaviour throughout the school. For example, one recently appointed teacher highlighted lining up at lunchtime.

> NICKY: That's a change and that's a lot more strict; it's very well monitored – all the classes lining up and the playground procedure for blowing the whistle. At playtime as well as lunchtime, with children 'freezing' and then lining up. It's very orderly. The atmosphere in the school has changed, with quiet in the corridors and that's being policed by all staff, but [the head] is at the head of it – policing corridors and checking for quiet.

During interview, the deputy head mentioned that, in order for children to reach their full potential, they have to be happy. But she also pointed (implicitly) to the contradiction embodied in the new managerialism:

> First of all you can't get good SATs results without the children being happy...because without being happy they won't work to their full potential. So, the first thing, I think, when [the head] came here, particularly the staff meetings...were based on building up self-esteem...so we did all that so we've got all that in place and then it's 'Right, how are we going to meet targets?' So we're looking from year 3 right through to year 6 at targets to raise their standards. We're doing that for the children but we're also doing that for public image. And to make sure that the school stays open because we're getting good SATs results and the children want to come to this school.

Most primary teachers would not dispute the need for happy children and an orderly – or better still caring – atmosphere. But how far are we away here from 'social work' concerns? The contradiction derives from the managerialist instrumentalism: raise the esteem of the children in order to raise 'standards'. The point is that self-esteem is a separate matter from whether targets can (and should) be met. The head repeatedly exhorted that 'we're not social workers' yet spent £200 on stickers as part of the self-esteem programme. A 'Positive Praise List' dominated almost every early morning briefing. Children have transcendental needs to be happy (and how they then perform in any form of assessment is a separate matter), but the managerialist nature of SATs, league tables and targets negates this. In other words, let them be happy as long as they perform well in tests.

It is worth quoting one senior staff member:

LYNNE: What she's interested in...she's got a very clear idea of the end result...What she's got is fairly dictatorial views of the how that should be attained and I think, you know, she is well trained and well educated and has been an advisor. I think she's right and *she sees SATs as something you have to do. And you do them in a fairly cynical way, you train the children* (emphasis added).[57]

We have already touched upon the autocratic style of the head.[58] 'You train the children' is crucial here. The 'factory' approach evident in the above is ineluctable, and, of course, contradicts the recognition that children have the quintessentially *human* capacity for self-worth, which in this school needed building up and reinforcing. The point is that 'training the children' does not sit comfortably with developing independent learning. On the contrary, it can only undermine it. In talking about the comprehension work required by SATs, Lynne commented:

...there's these ridiculous things when you get these passages and then you get these answers in the same order as the passage, you haven't got to understand anything: all you've got to understand was, you know, you read the first question and then you find the key words in the first sentence and copy them out. Well, that's a technique...I've got nothing against teaching children the technique to do something that we need to do. You know, there's no escaping it.

The part-time special needs teacher echoed this:

I mean things that they're doing, you know they're doing, because they have to do a comprehension test in SATs and they'll spend, you know, year 6 children and all other school children will spend a lot of time doing quite boring comprehension, which really isn't reading for meaning.

I also suggested that the catchment area further problematises the move away from child-centred practice. She replied:

...cos these children need lots of practical experience which they don't get now. These children find it difficult, you know, as soon as you say right, pencil-and-paper tasks, I mean that's the trouble in the class [teacher who was 'advised' to stay off work for health reasons by the head]. The children that can't write, what do they do? When you say right, you are going to write a story, you're going to write a comprehension test, they can't do it...

At the end of the term, I engaged in a lengthy conversation with the Unit LSA (who declined the offer of a taped interview). She mentioned that a few years ago cookery, for example, played a prominent role: 'We call it "Basic Life Skills" and sometimes children would come back in the following day and ask for the recipe for mum.' She talked at length about the urgency accorded to SATs by the head.

Thing here is that being told to prepare for SATs from Year 3 – ticking forms with children...yet children haven't been taught properly and don't understand what they're ticking…SATs and the National Curriculum just don't take into account differences between children…For example, Richard [a pupil] would come in grumpy and moody because dad at work and because Richard has to get some children dressed. Dad came in and agreed…then we received a letter from mother the following day saying things like 'My husband agrees with you that I'm a bad mother – it's none of your fucking business!'

She went on to question an approach that likens children to cars in a factory. Clearly, raising the self-esteem of Richard (along with many other children in Southside) is time-consuming and fundamentally hard work: increasing the school's SATs scores necessarily negates any such lengthy process. However, the resonance with Pugh's predicament is palpable. As we saw, the context of a residential school for EBD pupils underscored the wholesale inappropriateness of the OFSTED regime. Indeed, in such schools as Southside, the generic low levels of attainment means that core subjects of the National Curriculum ultimately receive little, if any, attention. As Jane commented:

…you know, a lot of interesting work that you might want to do you can no longer do. It's gone…classroom teaching. It's what parents want, it's what schools want, it's what everyone wants really – isn't it? To see schools at the top of the league tables. I think you are forced down that road unless you're very, very strong and say 'we're not doing that', which some schools I think have resisted, but have now had to succumb. What do you do?

This encapsulates the stringent constraints that schools like Southside come up against. It also highlights one of the morphogenetic approach's key propositions – namely that stringency of constraints does not entail determinism. As Jane points out, strength of resolve can (and does) lead some to say, 'we're not doing that' (c.f. the head in this school) but, on the other hand, because of the especially stringent nature of the constraints at Southside, many have had to succumb. This I would not dispute. What has occurred at Southside is manifestly in contradistinction to 'we're not doing that'. Indeed, at the beginning of the interview, the head maintained that '…we can be in the top 5 per cent of schools…'. Clearly, then, the drive towards reaching that goal was bound to engender almost impossible work requirements on the part of both staff and pupils alike. As we saw in Chapter 2, just as in much modern business, where targets are set beyond the unreachable, so they are increasingly set in education (by those who do not have to reach them). It was hardly surprising that the head herself was absent for sometimes three successive days in the weeks towards the latter half of the term. (The deputy head told me that she suffered from 'burn-out'.) Other staff was absent due to stress-related illness and I witnessed deterioration in the health of the deputy during the last few weeks of the autumn term. Without digressing into a futile speculative account about the exact causes of the overall rise in the incidence of ill health among staff, instructively the head gave me a copy of a substantial document she prepared on managing stress at her previous school (where she was also employed on a 'trouble-shooting' basis). Thus one can infer that the head was aware of the likely impact of managerialist restructuring – namely the (oft-reported) increase in 'burn-out'.[59]

As the OFSTED report mentioned, many children enter the school with low levels of reading attainment. Thus, what exacerbates matters in a school such as Southside in particular is that low levels of attainment are by no means remedied by managerialist nostrums. But the head at Southside took up the managerialist gauntlet. As she said during interview, 'What I'm doing is just getting the pickaxe and just starting to pick away at the concrete.' Whilst this was said in the context of staff management, it is equally applicable to the children: the pickaxe used was that of measurement, and the concrete, children. During the second week of the term, the head announced that she had met with County officials, who told her that she had to be proactive in measuring 'added value':

> We've got to have targets and measures. [Southside] is to produce figures…We need to make some prognosis about the children so that parents can see we're making professional judgements…We need some data now!

And data she got! Over the subsequent two weeks SAT-style tests for year 6 were carried out, and for the rest of the school. Now, this in itself increased the teachers' workload. However, concurrently they were requested to devise ways of how they could plan children's work in order to assess outcomes; devise ways of monitoring outcomes and how to improve monitoring processes; devise strategies to engage children in reading; complete annotation slips for children to enable them to monitor their own progress[60] and so on. The results were tabulated quickly and a subsequent staff meeting was geared to an analysis of them. The framework for analysis was anchored in the effectiveness research and also the Investors in People (IiP) quality improvement programme.

In brief, IiP concentrates on training and development. Brown and Taylor (1994) claim that schools are the fastest growing sector of the take-up of IiP. Roberts (1996) argues that its philosophy is congruent with the central purpose of education:

> …there is a tangible pay-off as it can assist a school *to meet the requirements of OFSTED inspections*…[IiP] clearly can be linked to change management as well as quality; it has the potential to address *the problem of persistent resistance to change*…The IiP exercise in quality assurance provides a model for the client-centred culture demanded by quality management.
>
> (1996: 6, emphasis added)

Roberts points out that IiP promotes reassessment and fine-tuning of *business* plans and objectives to create an operational framework for *continuous* professional development. Of course, one would question Roberts's assertion that IiP is congruent with the central purpose of education! However, the cards are firmly on the table: IiP is a neat accompaniment to the OFSTED regime and addresses the 'problem' of resistance. At the end of September the head chose a goal in IiP terms – namely a confident and competent reader. A session was devoted to this and staff was required to specify the main indicators. Such indicators were held to underpin 'quality characteristics'. All teachers were asked to draw up reading strategies in terms of the IiP framework. The following week the meeting addressed such strategies and the OFSTED 'Strategic Diamond'.

The head argued that outcomes must be delineated first, i.e. before any discussion of provision. In turn, 'we will get better at identifying indicators the more you do it'. She suggested targeting the top two English sets – 'we can measure on the way throughout'. She informed staff that IiP 'always talks in terms of one hundred per cent'. She also suggested that staff have the strategic diamond at hand whilst plotting indicators of performance. The confident and competent reader example was referred to as an 'operational target'. The sheets for such goals were sectioned and included such headings as 'Plotting Indicators of Performance', 'Identifying actual Indicators using the Strategic Diamond'; 'Setting Indicators' and lastly 'Targets'. Now, designing strategies for improving reading on its own is an educational aim and many of the ideas proffered by staff and the head were varied and useful (e.g., collaborative reading). The head often emphasised the need for children at Southside to become independent learners (the same was the case at Westside). She talked about the need to foster independence of thought. But fostering independence of thought in the context of Southside was not something that could be done overnight. The head said that once the children became independent they would 'not have the time to be naughty'. Yet children are, to varying degrees, naughty – but particularly so at Southside. The managerialist regime demands success here and now. Hence the impatience that characterised many a staff meeting and events where naughtiness prevailed. Indeed, not only do the children not have time to be naughty, they do not have time to be children! This is part and parcel of the A ← B imposition that characterised managerialisation in Southside. However, it must be remembered that the head's 'improvement' strategies were more managerial than educational, designed specifically with SATs in mind (meeting the operational target). Let us take the reading tests carried out during 'Test Week'. They were seen by many as not measuring what they purported to measure. Indeed, the type of test bought by the head was done so for reasons of temporal expediency. The issue of quality thus becomes marked, but was not openly criticised by staff. During interview, however, Jane commented:

> But if you're just churning out stuff for SATs I think it's very poor quality as well. You don't get anything...

The deputy gave an example of a boy in her class who, whilst she felt he would never reach level 3, was nevertheless talented artistically. But because of the priority accorded to improving SATs scores, she was unable to provide work outside Maths, English and Science. The head at the outset told staff that for the time being she was permitting them to concentrate on the latter foundation subjects. The deputy maintained that if I conducted the same interview in five years' time 'this wouldn't be happening'. Whilst this is a contingent possibility, the point is that, educationally (and morally), is the continuous quality programme warranted? And even if the school reached the coveted top 5 per cent – at what cost? Specifically, does not a school like Southside pay most, since, whilst schools such as Westside contend with the OFSTED regime, their catchment area permits more time for child-centred and religious (Catholic) education. Sarah pointed out during interview that less time is devoted simply to play (the bane of anti-child centred approaches), which she felt was wrong because children in the Southside area did not have the same opportunities for play. Indeed, Christine also mentioned that she spent more of her lunchtime painting with children because the SATs-driven timetables precluded such activities. Sarah admitted that some of the changes engendered by the 1988 Education Act were useful – providing direction in particular – yet, at the same time:

> You've got to always be climbing; you've always got to be being the best. I don't… there's nothing wrong with having high expectations with yourself and high aims for yourself, but people are happy with different, with different things in life…We don't all have to have the same aim.

There are two points to be made here. First, not only does the mountain never end (Jack's beanstalk, if you like), nor do all schools start at ground level and with the same climbing equipment. Second, climbers do not climb in exactly the same way. In other words, the 1988 Act enjoins unfair competition (which entails winners and losers) while at the same time erasing local needs and differences. Thus, to Troman and Woods:

> 'Improvement' might occur at a technicist level, as indicated by measurable tests, but at a cost to other aspects of what teachers regarded as a full education, such as creativity, education of the whole child, caring and sharing, multicultural education.

> (2001: 33–34)

However, the following week, the head launched the weekly staff meeting with 'Targets – going to have to meet them! It's as simple as that! Standards funding (renamed)…got to meet the targets or no money!' She referred to the Local Authority Directors' meeting that she attended: 'The way now moving forward is absolutely the way we are moving forward. The Authority has to insist that we do that! Some Heads mumbled…but we've already started it!' Fundamentally, the head's overriding concern was to provide written evidence of improvement. Thus upper/lower school meetings were to be documented in formal minutes, creating yet more work for staff. Levels of truancy and graffiti, for example, were discussed. I brought up the latter issue one morning whilst photocopying in the staff room. I asked her whether she felt the improvement in behaviour was attributable to her stronger personality (*vis-à-vis* the former head) or the increasingly religious accent that she placed on assemblies and class circle time. Her response was: 'It isn't important', whereupon she retracted her statement and affirmed that I had asked an important question. I do not wish to delineate the remainder of the conversation. Simply, her comment that it was not important is consistent with managerialism. Her reasons for her retraction need not detain us. The salient point here is that even if Southside were able to show a 100 per cent decrease in the level of truancy, why is this important? That pupils turn up to school does not tell us whether they are happy, learning or alienated. Again, *why*-questions are consistently eschewed. As White sums up: 'We are left in ignorance of how effective schools are in bringing about outcomes of a non-measurable sort...This is a central difficulty with the SER [school effectiveness] programme and cannot be emphasised too much' (1997: 51).

Following the parents' evening in mid-November, the head asked to know the percentage of parental turn out. There was approximately a 60 per cent turn out. The figure was discussed at the staff meeting. The head commented thus:

> Parents whom we haven't seen are the ones with the biggest problems. Do a trawl. See what that brings and then go back to the drawing board...So, if no response from the trawl – the next stage...Say, letters go out tomorrow – could they? First letter – then what? Give them a week.

The crucial question here is in what sense are such parents a 'problem'? I would suggest they were problematic largely in terms of the managerialist project. Taken at face value, one would certainly want to see all parents (or as many as possible). However, context is crucial here, since the overriding concern for the head was to produce figures that show improvement in parental interest. In other words, parents were a problem from a managerialist framework: if they did not show interest, then this would be problematic in terms of performance indicators. Following the discussion of the parents' evening, the head responded to staff concerns about their workload:

> Can't do everything at once – Right. But next term – year 3 – weekly table tests against the clock...whole school – marked in the same way. Literally parrot-fashion...need to see more 'word banks' on the walls...need to keep seeing them...

This hardly sits with the need for staff to ensure that children develop into 'independent learners'. In fact, during the same meeting she brought up the issue about the need for pupils not to use rubbers: 'If they [the children] didn't keep rubbing out, output would increase immeasurably!'[61] Here we are back in the managerialist input–output mentality. The head paid for all staff (including myself) to attend a session on understanding and using Bloom's Taxonomy, which was followed by a staff meeting. The example used at both sessions was the topic of the Tudors. In essence, the school effectiveness movement and OFSTED value Bloom's taxonomy for demonstrating that 'learning can be managed' (Shipman 1990: 102, cited in Butterfield 1995). As Butterfield (1995: 163) points out, particular educational practices (such as Bloom's) are preferred because they are overtly managerial and not because they represent best educational practice. In other words, such books as Shipman's *The Management of Learning* overlook 'very influential constructivist and interactionist theories of learning, and [choose] rather to support its case by examples from psychologists who more readily fit the technical view of management'

(1995: 163). In relation to the GCSE, Bloom's taxonomy is used for the selection of items rather than for evaluation of the quality of the response (see Chapter 5 for the critical discussion of the TGAT model). This applied equally to the ways in which staff used the taxonomy in relation to the Tudors topic.

Finally...the contradiction

The contradiction between child-centred philosophy and the new managerialism embodied in SATs, teaching strategies and leadership directed the taped interview with the head. All teachers concurred that the contradiction was real and, more-over, found it constraining. (The degree of stringency depended on the extent to which the changes diverged from their understanding of child-centred philosophy.) During the interview, I asked the part-time special needs teacher whether she thought that, given the specific catchment area, her work is even more problematic in view of the move away from the child. She replied:

> Yes, cos these children really need lots of practical experience which they don't get now. These children find it difficult, you know, as soon as you say, right, pencil and paper tasks, I mean, that's the trouble in that class. The children that can't write, what do they do? When you say right, you are going to write a story, you're going to write a comprehension test – they can't do it.

Instructively, she commented about the literacy hour as follows:

> Like I said about the literacy hour, it is very restrictive because when I did my training, I mean, you would, you know, if children were really engrossed in what they were doing and they would, you know, learning something prac-tical, you wouldn't say 'right, stop now!' You know, you would let them carry on.

For Nicky, child-centred practice is about a mixture of teaching styles:

> So, sometimes if you're doing an investigate lesson, it will work very well. The children are, yes, this is for you, you need to find this out, let them, you know, develop their own experiment or something like that, learning by touching and feeling. Occasionally it's appropriate, but sometimes it's not. So, really, a mixture of all the different teaching styles.

This is interesting, given Nicky's newly qualified status, since, as argued in Chapter 4, child-centred philosophy (and practice) has been subject to vociferous critique by the philosophers of education and, of course, by New Labour's modernisation project.

In terms of the SATs' negation of child-centredness, Sarah commented thus:

> ...SATs is saying by level to get to level 4 they have got to know this, this and this, which would be good if every child left knowing all of those things and

maybe more to get to level 5 or 6. But there are some children who will never get to there and we seem to be teaching at a higher level because they know that the children need to know this whereas they have not actually looked at what do the children know already…

Rose, a year 6 teacher, confirms this:

ROBERT: Were you at any point in your career committed to child-centred learning?

ROSE: Child-centred learning is the dodgiest thing, I think! It depends on the way you define it. Child-centred learning could be – are you ready for this?

ROBERT: Go on then

ROSE: It could be umm start with where the child is at

ROBERT: Right

ROSE: Now, if that is the case then yes, then there is this massive sort of airy fairy bit…that says, you know, the child should discover…meditate or let them talk about it and they'll discover how to deal with multiplication. You know, and maybe it would, but then again, there is the old saying of umm, you know, what is it about monkeys and Shakespeare? Given them long enough, but they haven't got long enough. You know, give them the strategy to start with.

[…]

ROBERT: Would you say that SATs has altered this at all in any way, shape or form?

ROSE: Yes. They no longer have time to stimulate knowledge; they no longer have the chance to return to something. When I was on, when I was training, you could go into a classroom on your teaching practice and you could teach something and you would go all round the houses and you would explain it forty different ways and the child would look at you blank. You come back to it a week later and it would have sunk in to the extent that they knew what you were on about. And they knew, oh, that's it then. *Now, there's no opportunity to do that anymore. Particularly in year 6 because you have to cover the whole curriculum again* (emphasis added).

However, the head's comments are more interesting, given her specific role in the school and the ways in which she personalised it. Already we have seen how her style was autocratic. I put the question to the head:

ROBERT: Would you say...is there a contradiction between child-centred learning and SATs?

JILL: Well, it's like...there is a contradiction between child-centred learning and the national curriculum, you know, it's a continuation of that argument. It depends on how you see, whether you see coming to school as an education person...is a broad, holistic, complete person, aren't they?

ROBERT: Yes

JILL: Or whether you see it as coming in to produce robots for technology, say, I see it as the more rounded and there is room for all of that. So there doesn't have to be all...you can't get through the national curriculum anyway so why try, that's my general view. Is that what you were asking about the tension between

ROBERT: Uh, SATs, sorry, is there a contradiction between child-centred learning and SATs? It's very

JILL: You see...You...There needn't be. Teachers make it a contradiction because they have SATs in their head rather than children becoming competent and confident learners. Now, if you are about children becoming and having all the skills that make them independent about being able to learn and social ability and those things then there is no problem with SATs because what you are doing is you just say sort of...what do you mean by child-centred learning?

ROBERT: I don't know

JILL: If you mean all that claptrap about children playing until they feel the readiness to learn, then, yes, but I never did see...like that anyway. That's where

ROBERT: OK. Thanks.

JILL: It all started to go pear-shaped...in the 60s you've got to learn through play. Of course children learn through their fingertips, we all learn through our fingertips, but for a lot of primary teachers it was to throw everything else out they began to play all day and discover by themselves and wait for...readiness to drop out of the sky. You know, you've got to make children ready. What it did, or should have done, is to release you to be able to put children in problem-solving situations. Because I was doing problem solving in 1960, you know. Children were in the sandpit and they had tasks to do.

The above provides a fascinating insight into how one particular cultural agent lives with, and makes sense of, objective contradiction. In particular, equivocation and tension (S-C matters) characterise the head's response. That there 'needn't be a contradiction' is (ontologically) independent of whether there is. Teachers may indeed perceive contradiction or be manipulated into misperception, but this is analytically distinct from, and irreducible to, the objective existence of contradiction (at the CS level). The head commented that teachers make the contradiction – 'they have SATs in their head'. Yet this is hardly surprising! The difficulty for any researcher is whether to intervene to point out inconsistencies. However, the rest of the sentence indicates that the head was unsure about her argument. She talked about children becoming independent and having skills that facilitate that independence, yet the point at which she asked, 'what do you mean by child-centred learning?' suggests recognition that SATs negates this. Reasonable inference aside, however, her caricature of child-centred practices during the 1960s as 'claptrap' did not engage with the psychological and developmental theories discussed briefly in Chapter 5. Her comment that she 'did not see it like that anyway' evinces at best impatience with the notion of readiness. The notion of readiness was discussed in Part II. Unfortunately I did not ask if she rejected the notion altogether. But she accepted that children learn through their fingers yet immediately maintained that you've got to *make* children ready. One of the key precepts of child-centred philosophy is that you cannot enforce readiness. As we saw in Part II, the notion that children played all day is a media-fuelled myth.

The final sentence is crucial. The head stated that 'children were in the sandpit and they had tasks to do'. This resonates well with the managerialist education regime, for quite simply cognitive stages of development are temporally conflated with the emergent capacity for problem-solving. Whilst the head was right in stating that 'readiness' does not drop out of the sky, nevertheless it cannot be enforced. Indeed, what makes 'enforcement' especially problematic at Southside is that many children needed to engage in cookery *before* they could even begin literacy and numeracy skills because of specific familial and other contingent factors. During interview with one of the year 3 teachers following the LEA 'inspection' during the preceding summer term, I asked the following:

ROBERT: Umm. Did you feel that they asked you yourself any umm relevant questions or was it just a question of, you know, I'm coming in to look at you.

LOUISE: They didn't ask umm one of them asked what levels I think the children were at and he did comment it was a science lesson and there was the first lesson they'd done on floating and sinking so they...were two children...you can imagine which two! I was just letting them play with a bowl of water and he said what level are those children, how are you extending them? You know...and what is the purpose of that activity. He obviously didn't like it at all and I said well, my view is that before children can actually carry out the science experiments they have to be allowed to see through play...about the properties of water. I said I think that's a very valuable thing because, you know, he had his hand up like that and was just watching the water go like that and then he was keeping his hands together and seeing if it would come through...

The point is that we get back to the constraining contradiction at the practical level: managerialism erases its human subjects yet requires them so that they can be 'managed'. Thus, if we take the above example of children learning about the properties of water through play, this presupposes fundamental cognitive processes, yet the SAT denies them but cannot do without them. Hence the rush for success – since the time taken for children to develop cognitively is implicitly denied. Crucially, it is being argued here that the constraining contradiction generates practical problems that do not simply encompass the thrust and counter-thrust of ideational debate in academic books and journals. Those who engage in some form of (new) managerialist restructuring are conditioned to engage in some form of practical syncretism, since the reality of flesh-and-blood children enjoins that they be taken into account.

To conclude, the arrival of the head highlighted the contradictions immanent in the OFSTED regime. Of particular interest was how the objective contradiction shaped agential activity. It was argued in Chapter 2 that the contradiction between child-centred philosophy and SATs is constraining rather than competitive. Without wishing untenably to impute mental processes, the above discussion exemplifies the mental contortions engendered by the constraining contradiction. This was not explicitly stated to the head. But her thinking evinces mental anguish and uncertainty. The causal powers that inhere between CS logical properties are only operative through agency and thus, even if I had been more explicit, it does not follow that the head would have engaged in a near-linear process of corrective repair. Indeed, all data showed how at the S-C level agents do not operate in robot-like fashion, pinpointing objective contradictions and complementarities and acting in strict accordance with their actionable logic. However, Southside is clearly a case of A ← B correction (where, to recapitulate, A = New Managerialism; B = child-centredness). Indeed, the head bought the whole New Managerialist package (A) and thus endeavoured to mould children (B) to fit the packet (e.g., her 'smiley' badges and stickers, and the 'affirmation' sessions at Assembly for children who played ball with her). In other words, she did not just treat children as commodities, but their *commodification* is a very active process. That she could not make such commodification 'stick' derives from the 'school mix', which means that some children just are not amenable to being processed into SATs fodder. Furthermore, it underscores the constraining nature of the contradiction, since children *qua* reflective young human beings cannot be expunged. The extent of any commodification depends upon a variety of factors that cannot be determined *a priori*. In short, then, syncretism generically took the form of A ← B correction, as evidenced empirically (her dealings with staff, tick-boxing, data-collection, IiP) and in interview with the head.

7 Westside:

'You can run, but you can't hide!'

The OFSTED inspection at Westside was carried out at the beginning of 1996 over a period of five days. At the time the school had 364 boys and girls on roll, aged 5–11. Westside is a Roman Catholic voluntary-aided primary school serving four Roman Catholic parishes. Approximately 18 per cent of the pupils came from non-Catholic homes. The report noted that:

> Forty-three pupils [12 per cent] are on the school's register of special educational needs. The pupils are predominantly from white, ethnic backgrounds. Ten per cent of pupils are from dual heritage homes. The pupils come from a wide range of social backgrounds. Thirty-eight [10 per cent] are eligible for free school meals. The school occupies two sites, two and a half miles apart. The main site is in a relatively prosperous area in the [city] centre…and the annex is in a residential suburb [equally relatively prosperous]…The deputy head is based on the main site and there is a teacher-in-charge at the annex. The school's mission statement emphasises the purpose of Catholic education. The school aims to provide an education for children by which their whole lives may be inspired by the spirit of Christ and which develops the pupils' knowledge of God, the world and themselves.
>
> (OFSTED 1996: 5)

At Key Stage 1, the percentage of pupils achieving level 2 or above in 1995 was greater than the national average in reading and writing. Based on teacher assessments and tests, the percentage of pupils attaining level 2 or above was 'broadly in line with national expectations'. In science, on the basis of teacher assessment only, the percentage again was 'broadly in line with national expectations'. In assessments at Key Stage 2, the percentage of pupils reaching level 4 (the level to be expected for pupils of this age) or above, on the basis of teacher assessments and tests, was 'well above the national average' in English and mathematics. In science, on the basis of teacher assessment and tests, it was 'broadly in line with national expectations'. The report went on to comment that pupils under five 'are attaining good standards in reading and writing' but '*attainment through structured play is underdeveloped in both classes*' (1996: 9, emphasis added). The report noted further:

...the information technology curriculum is not fully developed. In music, pupils attain satisfactory standards overall but the standard of singing in both key stages is unsatisfactory. In physical education, attainment is in line with national expectations in Key Stage 1 and at Key Stage 2 it is good; there is variation between the two sites and this is due to resources and provision. Pupils with special educational needs meet the targets set for them and are working to their potential.

(1996: 9)

As expected, there are sections on attitudes, behaviour and personal development and attendance, but, unlike the report on Southside, use was made of a parental questionnaire. The report commented thus:

Attitudes are satisfactory overall and those of older pupils are good... Behaviour in and around the school is generally good. Pupils are courteous, trustworthy and show respect for property. However, individual lapses in good behaviour do occur from time to time. Occasionally, self-discipline lapses part way through a lesson and time is lost while the teacher re-establishes a working atmosphere...Attendance is satisfactory overall, reaching above the 90 per cent benchmark. However, the 92.3 per cent for 1995–6 is lower than the rate which is achieved in the majority of primary schools. The number of unauthorised absences last year was 1.6 per cent. This is higher than rates achieved in the majority of primary schools. The punctuality of the majority of pupils is good. However, a number of pupils are late and this affects standards. Pupils who travel on the bus provided through local authority contract frequently arrive late, and because of the bus schedules, habitually need to leave school early. The bus timetables are unsatisfactory.

(1996: 10)

The 'quality of teaching' was found to be 'satisfactory or better' in 77 per cent of lessons, was 'good or better' in 38 per cent of lessons and was 'very good or better' in 5 per cent of lessons. The quality of teaching was 'unsatisfactory or worse' in 23 per cent of lessons and 'poor or worse' in 5 per cent of lessons. One hundred and eight lessons in whole or part were observed during the inspection and form the basis of the latter. However, it was maintained that, whilst there is a systematic, whole-school approach to planning for teaching and learning, 'learning outcomes are not always clearly identified. *This means that teachers do not always have a clear basis for evaluating their own effectiveness and efficiency*' (1996: 11, emphasis added). In terms of behaviour management, it was stated that a 'unified, whole-school classroom behaviour management strategy is needed which must be clear and straightforward so that it can be readily understood by pupils and *so that teachers can implement it efficiently*' (1996: 12, emphasis added).

As at Southside, animosities existed (the inconsistent and hearsay reasons for which need not detain us). Such animosities are important in so far as they impinged upon, and shaped the response to, the OFSTED report. However, unlike

Southside, both the extent and degree of animosity was somewhat attenuated. (Whether such attenuation was in part due to the more 'manageable' intake is a matter for conjecture.) The head at Westside, like the outgoing head at Southside, was not in favour of the majority of changes engendered by the education reforms; in particular, of the devolution of budgetary control and the tying of the budget to 'market forces' (that is, to pupil intake). At the beginning of my term spent at Westside, the head announced that she was to take early retirement. The reasons for this decision will become evident. Her response to the OFSTED report and LMS evince the importance of the need to distinguish between agency and the personal beliefs of the actor. Her *personal* response was in diametric opposition to that of the trouble-shooting head delineated in Chapter 6. Yet this is not to underplay the fact that both heads had to contend with structural and cultural changes that were not of their making, which conditioned their responses. We saw at Southside that such changes were congruent with the head's personal beliefs. For the head at Westside, however, such changes were incongruent with her deeply held beliefs and convictions, which were underpinned by her Catholic faith. Thus we must not lose sight of the fact that objective socio-cultural properties may or may not gel with agency, and even if they do not gel, their stringent nature may nevertheless enjoin (varying degrees of) compliance.

Back to the tyranny of measurement: assessment, causal linearity and the disavowal of contingency

The OFSTED inspection process occurs over a five-day period, at the end of which comments are made, in particular, about teaching quality and value for money. Neither are spelled out for teachers and both are quintessentially contestable. We saw in Chapter 5 that the OFSTED framework is underpinned by 'procedural objectivity', which is designed to eliminate the scope for personal judgement. Yet the Registered Inspector, a female academic, designed and distributed a parental questionnaire. This is inconsistent with the homogenising rationale of the inspection process. Moreover, the limitations of the questionnaire were not discussed. In fact, both the methodology and rationale were not spelled out. The 'parental survey' was attached at the end of the report, under the heading of 'Data and Indicators'. The percentage return rate was 27.47 per cent. At best, a warning as to the unreliability of the data should have been included. More appropriate would have been its omission from the report.

However, the report does not proffer any discussion of the validity of the use of questionnaire and its design. The teachers were not involved in the process of questionnaire design nor were they permitted to comment upon its findings. This is not at all surprising, since the effectiveness literature not only evades why-questions but also is inextricably bound up with accountability. To reiterate, such accountability is external; that is, it is not concerned with pupils – a teacher's work is judged in relation to his or her peers. In terms of the report's comments on attainment in science, we are not told what are 'national expectations' and, moreover, why they are such. As we shall see, targets imposed by the LEA (via the DfEE) are not accompanied by an *educational* rationale. The Inspectors did not (and legally cannot) tell staff what 'satisfactory teaching' entails. Unlike Southside, reference here is made to the 90 per cent national benchmark for attendance. Again, why 90 per cent and not, say, 65 per cent? Whether such a figure is TQM-cum-IiP driven is not the issue. What is the issue is (a) why attendance is accorded such prominence, and (b) why should schools in particular areas be penalised for failing to achieve such benchmark(s)? Most teachers would welcome a full complement of pupils and therefore the (complex) question of why this is not the case for all schools necessarily arises. But precisely because the OFSTED model is decontextualist (an intra-school affair), such questions would be deemed inappropriate at the outset.

In relation to attendance, it was pointed out that the 92.3 per cent for 1995–6 is lower than the rate that is achieved by the majority of primary schools. This is instructive, (a) for its implicit disavowal of the reality of contingency, and (b) for its elevation of a facet of primary school life that is secondary. Instead of assessing the likely impact of socio-economic background on attendance figures and the more pressing issue of whether schools are organised in ways that take this into account, OFSTED erases this at a stroke, reproving those schools that do not achieve the shifting numerical sands of national benchmarking. The disavowal of the reality of contingency at all levels (classroom, school, systemic, local...) is clear from Westside's OFSTED report. Such disavowal is an unavoidable concomitant of the managerialist underpinning of the OFSTED framework. This is because, whilst children are erased *qua* children, ineluctably they resurface to disrupt teaching. It was noted that 'individual lapses in good behaviour do occur from time to time. Occasionally, self-discipline lapses...and time is lost while the teacher re-establishes a working relationship'. Given that the OFSTED report is designed with improvement in mind, it can be reasonably inferred that this state of affairs is meant to be ameliorated (hence the recommendation for a school-wide policy on discipline).

Yet, without chaining pupils to desks and/or gagging them, this state of affairs cannot be erased. The very nature of young children *qua* reflexive beings validates this transcendental axiom. Certainly, attempts can be made to attenuate the frequency and severity of misbehaviour, but again children *qua* children, socio-economic and familial background and the teacher combine to make things unhelpfully complex (or 'messy') for OFSTED. Even interruptions by the head are regular events in primary schools. More crucially, even if all pupils behave all of the time, it cannot be assumed, *contra* OFSTED, that what is taught will be understood. At the level of observable events, an orderly classroom, populated by 'courteous and trustworthy pupils', does not mean that learning and understanding will concurrently occur. That children behave well is efficient in terms of cost and indeed may be effective in terms of examination results. Yet are we talking about educational effectiveness? The argument throughout this book is in the negative. SATs are not concerned with understanding but with accountability: rendering teachers accountable for the inadequate level of money paid to them via examinations that test effective knowledge imposition rather than understanding and application. The issue of bussing and lateness – again seen as indicators of inefficiency and ineffectiveness – are (contingent) factors that are beyond the control of the school. They are contingent in two senses: structurally the school does not require pupils at specific start/end times for it to be a school; and whilst the school could contract with any bus firm, the local authority provided the cheapest deal.

In recommending that a classroom behaviour management strategy be 'clear and straightforward' so that pupils can readily understand it, there is no acknowledgement that it does not follow that pupils will understand it or accept it. The various strategies employed by the head at Southside were readily understandable, but extraneous factors often intervened to preclude success. Hence her frustration at pupil misbehaviour inside and outside the classroom. 'Difficult' children cannot be rendered 'well behaved' overnight (or possibly never). Moreover, all strategies for behaviour modification are not immune from ethical considerations. Yet such ethical considerations are not discussed by OFSTED. The focus on identification and measurement of learning outcomes exemplifies the denial of contingency. For, as we saw in Chapter 5, the model of causality is linear, whereby a straightforward cause leads to a straightforward effect. OFSTED assumes that learning outcomes can be linked directly and unambiguously to inputs (viz. teaching). Indeed, it was argued that the tacit OFSTED assumption is that causal factors are independent, universal and additive; that is, they do not interfere with each other and are uninfluenced by their contexts. Hence the frustration with even minor pupil misdemeanours that impede the flow of teaching → identifiable learning outcomes. But even the best teaching cannot guarantee success. Moreover, learning outcomes are (now) proxies, which, as we have seen, distort reality since they cannot measure what they purport, or try, to measure. If we recall the discussion with Louise in Chapter 6 about children playing with water, this was a learning situation which, at that particular point in time, can never be considered in terms of an identifiable learning outcome. The whole point of the Piagetian approach is that specific processes have to be undergone *before* we can establish any assesment situation that may or may not be tractable to some form of measurement.

Again, there is no proper consideration here that we are dealing with children, which in turn enjoins that we place a huge question mark over an assessment process that is accountability, rather than educationally, driven. During interview the head referred to the OFSTED report's criticism of assessment procedures.

> PAT: The other thing that they [OFSTED team] complained about is our assessment procedures, which I thought, I mean, there is no perfect way to get round assessment. And to be honest, I think that the teachers are doing their own spot assessment. They are making judgements on the children, which they file away without necessarily writing it down and you go in and ask any teacher about a child and they will be able to help you.

> ROBERT: Did they want to see lots of paperwork?

> PAT: They wanted lots of paperwork, and I kept saying to them, we don't have time. I said I defy you to go into any primary school and find the primary teachers with the time. And you must give them time, I said... I wanted her

[the key Registered Inspector] to tell me how I was going to provide release time when I didn't have the money, when I didn't have the time.

ROBERT: What did she say?

PAT: I didn't get an answer to that…'That's up to you to decide Mrs […]'

The local authority drive towards improving SATs was discussed in relation to Southside, as evidenced by one particular staff meeting in which the head referred to the local authority directors' meeting *vis-à-vis* target setting. Westside's overall response to this will be discussed later. However, the head referred to the increasingly proactive role played by the local authority:[62]

…So you see, it has now become a game, really and that's why, as from this year, the children in this school will be doing assessment tests. Year 2, uh year 1, sorry, year 2 at the end of Key Stage 1, that's mandatory, in years 3, 4 and 5 it is optional, but we are doing them…and in year 6. *By the time they get to year 6, doing tests will become second nature.* (emphasis added)

Doing tests until they become second nature is certainly a familiar phenomenon for those preparing for 16-plus examinations. Notwithstanding their demerits, should children as young as 5 be 'doing tests until they become second nature'? This is not to suggest that teachers should never assess their children from a young age. Indeed, the whole argument at the primary level is that teachers are assessing all the time: what matters is the *process* and *context* of assessment. The report noted:

Pupil profiles are maintained within the school and they provide a good guide to pupils' progress…Statutory assessment is undertaken as appropriate. Baseline assessment is undertaken when pupils enter the school…However, there is no overarching system throughout the school for assessing and recording pupils' progress and attainment, which can be used systematically to inform future planning for learning.

(OFSTED 1996: 13)

One of the Key Stage 1 teachers proffered the following about assessment and OFSTED:

PENNY: Well, they are obsessed at the moment with assessing children. We're supposed to assess children all the way through. Each piece of work they do you are supposed to assess. You're supposed to assess this, you're supposed to assess that. You're supposed to keep records.

ROBERT: You were doing that when I came…

PENNY: Yes, that was actually for SATs

ROBERT: Oh, right.

PENNY: But four years ago we used to have to produce our assessments of the children...I used to keep cupboards full of it. Nobody does that now. When it came to my doing my teacher assessment for the children for SATs, I knew what my children could do...Well, I, one of those cupboards there used to be full of all the things I kept for the children to show what, so that if an auditor came in...

ROBERT: Yes

PENNY: They could look at it. Nobody ever does and that's it. And so nowadays I spend my time teaching. I'm preparing the things for the children, and when it comes to, um, an audit I'll take some of their ordinary work and I will then say 'Right, OK. Well, I think this child is at a Level 2' and I'll then take a piece of their work and then prove that it is a Level 2. But I don't waste hours and hours of my time doing...

ROBERT: Yes.

PENNY: I mean, I give my children homework every week. They each get different homework. I go, I sit down and I spend a whole morning on Saturday going through the books and going through what they have done thinking about what they need to do next. *But I don't do it based on endless pieces of paper...I used to keep mountains of it – it was stupid.* (emphasis added)

At Southside the head ordered proof of 'improvement' in the form of vastly increased amounts of paperwork. Such proof ranged from annotation sheets to minutes of all meetings. But all the paperwork in the world is not an indicator of *educational* improvement. Penny's point, as echoed by the majority of primary teachers, is not only that such assessment is educationally flawed, but also most assessment is continuous and resides in the teacher's head. Furthermore, as was argued in Chapter 5, much knowledge of children's ability and extent of understanding is quasi-propositional; teachers have an intuitive 'feel' for a child's understanding. That such knowledge cannot lend itself to speedy formal codification and measurement is problematic for the (new) managerialism. This accounts for the impatience that characterised the advisors' approach to children playing with water. Of course, both teachers and children are under pressure from an early age. As Sally put it:

And they [children] are under pressure from the moment they start school. They are tested on entry at school. They are tested at 7 and 11 and we make judgements about those children based on those tests as well as our own continual observations...

Indeed, the infants' teacher at the main school commented:

HELEN: When they come into school we have baseline assessment. They've got certain tasks that we have to test them on. Um, can they take a message, can they remember instructions, you know, do they recognise any letter of the alphabet, things like that. So I think there is pressure on them from the first day they come into school.

ROBERT: Do you think that is good?

HELEN: No. I can honestly say that I don't think it serves much purpose because we always had our own baseline assessment here in that we always devised something: do they know three colours; can they recognise their name; can they sit and listen to a story. All the things that *we* thought were important....What the baseline assessment has done...is we go through various stages, it's quite intense and it lasts through the whole half term – it's got be completed within the first half term. But you usually find that brighter children who come into school hold back because they think they can't do it. They know, or when you try to do it in a play situation, they know that there is something different and they have clicked on to the fact that you are actually questioning them. So therefore, for example, if you say to them 'Can you say a nursery rhyme?' the brighter ones will go 'No!' because they don't know why you want them to do a nursery rhyme, or shy ones will say 'No' because they don't know me very well at that point. The ones who maybe aren't so bright can't see anything beyond it and say 'Well, OK. Yes.' And away they go. And if you ask them to letter, for example, one of the tasks is that they have to see if they can write letters, write messages and what have you. Basically, it's to see whether they hold a pencil properly and they can write something down. The brighter ones will say 'No. I can't. I can't write'. The not-so-bright ones will say 'Oh, write. OK. Yeah'. So actually, the bright ones are scoring quite badly.

ROBERT: Yes.

HELEN: And the not-so-bright ones are actually scoring really well.

ROBERT: So, it doesn't help you at all really?

HELEN: I mean, I know that I am meant to look at these baseline assessment results all through the year, but I actually, they have no bearing on my teaching whatsoever.

In echoing Penny's point about unnecessary paperwork and work overload, Helen commented thus:

The National Curriculum I think personally was a complete and utter waste of time. It wasn't thought out. We were presented with ten folders, we were expected to take up and do it. To go, it was just, we didn't have the any time to get to know the children – it was just this race to tick off boxes. All the paper work that came with it and nobody would actually listen to us that it was wrong. Now they have agreed it's wrong [hence the Dearing Review discussed in Chapter 5]. And all the little folders and files have gone (laughter) *So it has cost the taxpayer a lot of money.* (emphasis added)

The irony is palpable. Part of OFSTED's *raison d'être* is to establish whether schools provide 'value for money'. Basically, this translates into more (SATs results) for less (cash) via technicist-cum-managerialist measures. Yet the unfeasibility of the (initial) National Curriculum folder onslaught and attendant box ticking was costly. The money could have been spent on adequate funding for all primary schools. Indeed, it was pointed out in Chapter 5 that establishing and maintaining quasi-market mechanisms in education has been (and remains) equally costly. Whilst Westside has undertaken to eschew the timely, costly and educationally unsound practice of box ticking and generic form filling, Southside undertook the opposite. However, the reasons for the agential eschewal of such time-consuming practices are largely attributable to the high league table position, which itself may be attributed to the 'middle-class' intake. In other words, such teachers could be confident that such eschewal would not lead to a damning OFSTED report in view of the success in SATs, among other things. And the reason for success at SATs may be attributed to the particular socio-economic intake. In this case, Thrupp's (1999) focus on 'school mix' is crucial, since it underscores the fact that (a) schools have to work with whatever intake they are given, and that (b) such intake may either facilitate, expedite or vastly inhibit examination success.

It is interesting to note that Westside's OFSTED report did not engage nearly to the same degree as Southside's *vis-à-vis* socio-economic intake. We are told that the main site is in a relatively prosperous area in the city centre and that pupils 'come from a wide range of social backgrounds'. This indicates the lack of consistency between different OFSTED teams and thus throws a question mark over the putative 'procedural objectivity' that is held to underpin the inspection process. However, whether intentional or not, the report is not explicit in detailing the socio-economic background of pupils. The number of children receiving free school meals is provided. In comparison with Southside, the figure is considerably lower: one in every ten compared to one in every two pupils at Southside. Despite the obvious sociological problems attaching to the use of eligibility for free school meals as a proxy for 'social class', the obvious difference should not be played down. In fact, the Westside report does not indicate the considerable extent to which the majority of pupils were from particularly affluent backgrounds. The Southside report, in contrast, did convey the generic relatively poor background of the majority of pupils.

That the OFSTED team played down the relatively prosperous nature of Westside's intake is to be expected given OFSTED's focus on the school level alone. Yet the prosperous background of the pupils is a facilitating factor *vis-à-vis* 'effectiveness'. Of course, it cannot be assumed *a priori* that relative prosperity equates to parental interest in, and concern for, the welfare and educational success of their children. However, the sheer visibility of parental interest was striking at Westside. Many of the complaints that dominated lunchtime staff discussions were not about the pupils but about the 'interference' of *parents* (c.f. Southside). The one or two 'troublemaker' pupils at Westside would have been regarded as relatively well behaved at Southside, as I remarked to staff (and such remarks were met with unqualified agreement). In both schools, I spent time reading with all pupils, noting the number of pages read and the quality of the reading in a pocket reading note-book. At Westside, all the infants' parents read at least five nights per week, with many parents taking the time to write educationally informative notes for the infant teacher.[63] The key impedimenta to 'effectiveness' at Westside were not pupil oriented but market- and, to a lesser degree, parent-based.

Beyond macro conditioning: Catholicism and the importance of (local) context

> PAT: But you see, my personal feeling, Robert, is that we are fast approaching the stage in this country where we can no longer be described as a Christian country. I really do feel that…I find it very sad and I think it's an uphill struggle at times to keep those Christian beliefs…

Despite the explicit Christian (Church of England) ethos of Southside's educational rationale, Christian beliefs and practices did not play any significant role. At Westside, in contrast, Catholic beliefs and practices permeated throughout. Formal class prayers are conducted both at the beginning and at the end of the school day. Parents are invited to class and whole-school mass, both of which are attended by the majority of parents. Religious – specifically Catholic – education is accorded a prominent role in the curriculum. The majority of parents are practising Catholics and the school admits a minority of pupils whose parents are non-believers. Here, we need to emphasise (a) the importance of local mediation, and (b) the over-determining role of the Catholic faith as one of the non-quantifiable factors that account for success in SATs. First, then, as I have already mentioned, macro factors do not operate in hydraulic fashion but are mediated locally. In the case of Southside, anterior morpho-genetic cycles and socio-cultural factors at a number of levels and sites (i.e., both intra- and extra-school) conditioned the response to the quasi-marketisation of educa-tion. Two of the key conditioning factors at Southside were, of course, the poor examination success and 'school mix'. The involvement of the (clerical) chair of the governing body was, in contrast to Westside, low-key. The priest – who was chair of the Westside governing body – was often seen in the school.

Whilst the head's deep sense of frustration and anger engendered by LMS and the publication of league tables does not enjoin Catholic (ideational) underpinning, commitment to Catholicism can only exacerbate such feelings. For now we come to my second point about the over-determining nature of the Catholic (Westside) context. In Chapter 1, I discussed how the structural 'upper hand' of the teacher may be reinforced or counteracted by the familial structure, whereby the mediation of the parental request to behave well in class buttresses the power of the teacher. This is conceptualised as over-determining the position of the teacher because of its reinforcing effects. This also applies to the response of the head and her staff to the parents and pupils. Again, whilst parental concern and encouragement do not ideationally imply a specifically Catholic rationale, the practising Catholics that are the majority of parents at Westside over-determined the chances of success, since Catholic beliefs celebrate education and its role in the wider community. No exact measure can be placed on the relative efficacy of such factors and processes. However, Westside has a long history of educational success – specifically 'traditional' teaching methods – and Catholic values and practices that marked it out from its local counterparts. Its known success ensured a steady supply of largely Catholic pupils.

The stringency of constraints: LMS, market values and lived contradiction

As Pring (1993) rightly argues, the philosophy of the education reforms is incompatible with the Catholic idea of the nature and purpose of schools. The primacy accorded to 'the market' and individual self-interest contradicts Catholic educational values that emphasise the importance of community and concern for the common good. Thus, to Pring, the market model 'leads not to an improvement of the general good but only to an improvement of the positional good of some *vis-à-vis* other competitors and also to a deterioration of the overall situation' (1993: 8). However, as Grace remarks, prior to the 1988 Education Reform Act, Catholic schools were insulated to a large extent from market forces by state and diocesan funding, 'by the historical loyalty of large Catholic communities, and by large pupil enrolments resulting from large Catholic families...' (Grace 1995: 174). Such autonomy enabled Catholic school leaders to articulate a distinctive mission and set of Catholic values independently of market nostrums. Grace's research found that a minority of head-teachers took the view that the spiritual and moral resources of Catholic schooling were strong enough to resist possible corruption by market values. At the same time, he notes, with irony, such moral resources were being recontextualised as potent market assets in the competitive appeal for parental choice of schools in a wider constituency. But such assets do not depend upon market values for their efficacy. The point now is that they must be vigorously marketed and manipulated for purposes antithetical to Catholic educational values.

Whilst at Southside the flow of cash was relatively generous because of the socio-economic status of the majority of its pupils (see OFSTED 1996), Westside had to contend with a steadily declining role and debilitating financial contingencies. Spiritual and moral resources simply exacerbated the painful process of how to deal with an impending financial crisis at Westside. It is worth tracing through some of the discussion among staff about the impending crisis and the painful propositions that were proffered by committed Catholic teachers. Prior to this discussion, during mid-February 1998 the issues of finance and the impending budgetary deficit were raised at the statutory Governors' Meeting with Parents. The previous year witnessed a surplus of £19,504. One of the PTA (Parents–Teachers' Association) asked why they were being implored to fund-raise in view of this surplus. The head replied as follows:

Formula funding...Definite decision made by the Governors that would not spend full amount. However, every child would not go without...Therefore managed to save...Under the law, we can save 5 per cent of the budget and we amassed quite a sum a few years' ago...Classrooms at the Annexe with this money...But it [the surplus] has been spent. Supply cover: £2,760 actually rose to £7,897; £8,300 repairs *back* to [local council] – 'a retrospective adjustment'; £1,300 on chairs; £2,000 on stationery, but at the moment that figure is now £4,500; secretarial and GA [General Assistant] time: £1,000. So, £19,000 been spent or will be spent.

The Vice-Chair of the Governors, the recently appointed parish priest, added:

The reality is that schools spend more than allocated...would mean cutting of a teacher to carry over money...

Whereupon one governor, himself a secondary school teacher, talked about formula funding and what he called 'business practices' in his secondary school where a £60,000 contingency was recommended. He described this a 'good business practice, which cushions fluctuations'. A parent remarked that it would have been prudent to set aside £2,000 for supply cover, whereupon the head interjected with the point that it would be unlawful to set a deficit budget. In contrast to Southside, where the unremitting pressures were largely attributable to the managerialist drive to improve SATs, here such pressures stemmed from inadequate funding (that could not be attributed to mismanagement) and the threat of redundancy. Pupils had to provide stationery during my time at Westside and each parent had to provide 11 pence each time her child left the premises (for swimming, or to visit the nearby Church for mass) to cover insurance. This was raised at the meeting by one of the parents. The head could only reiterate that the school did not have the funds. Extra responsibilities that statutorily attracted additional money were offered to staff but not matched by any increment. One year 6 teacher admitted to taking on the role of information technology coordinator in order to enhance her curriculum vitae, knowing that she would not receive an additional increment. Staff complained about the head's hostility to them when off sick, but accepted that this was due to the expense incurred. Furthermore, the school secretary had her hours reduced to thirty per week, which meant that every afternoon an electronic answer phone became her replacement. Finally, there was no caretaker.

Ironically, what is particularly interesting about Westside *vis-à-vis* Southside is that the particular 'school mix' (generically well behaved and bright) at Westside enabled a far more child-centred approach and thus did not pose any significant impediment for the majority of staff. As we shall see, the Senior Management Team was paid lip service by staff. However, the inevitable could not be postponed for much longer and a staff meeting was convened in mid-March to discuss the school's precarious financial position. As with Southside, all notes of staff meetings are verbatim. The following underscores the fact that stringent structural constraints are mediated processually: agents thus stringently confronted do not react in robot-like manner but critically reflect upon their conditions of action, strategically making the best of an inauspicious situation. In this instance, the LMS aspect, rather than specifically SATs, undermined the capacity of staff to provide a child-centred environment.

> PAT: A lot to get through...Umm can we get started, please as a lot to get through? [Prayer] Thank you Philippa and Claire for coming. I want to start with the budget. Provisional formula allocation is £480,000. Final allocation when get it – I expect only addition to be inflation contingency; and that money based on a school (September) roll of 356...I estimate 363 – allowing for people returning and going. Out of £480,000, about 80 per cent taken up to pay staffing salaries. I've done a provisional budget...obviously you're going to be bombarded with figures. Can be summed up in one sentence: not good! Supply [teaching] budget put at £1,000. Equivalent of 10 days supply cover for the whole school! Supply cover budget for last year was £2,760 and at the end of March (this month) will be in excess of £10,000. For things like stationery, books, I have budgeted £2,000. There is a shortfall. Added to all this is 'clawback' – estimate of £8,300 because of number of children lost last year. So, all in all things do not look very good. There are things that can't be cut – for instance, cleaning time can no longer be reduced; admin time, too. So, the Governors have to sit and make decisions to make savings – April 1998 to April 1999 – and remain solvent: impossibility. Literally means that they are going to have to look at everything. Our budget has been cut like everybody elses...usually a surplus each year....Governors don't have a choice – got to make savings. Sorry to be the bearer of bad tidings...Isn't a shortfall *yet*. Last year's surplus of £19,500 – virtually gone. Will have spent up to £1,800 on the appointment of the new head...

> CLAIRE: A teacher's salary?

> PAT: I don't know, Claire.

> DIANA: At St Helen's [Westside feeder for this Catholic secondary school] each parent pays £5.

> PENNY: But can't have a crisis situation every year!

> PAT: Well, I've set a provisional budget that actually balances – but totally, completely unrealistic; can't set a deficit budget – it's illegal...will literally be 'austerity rules!' for everyone...I feel really badly about it.

> CLAIRE: Swimming: do we have to do it?

> ...

(At this point a member of staff asked why this had been asked, whereupon Claire remarked that would make savings. However, it was pointed out that swimming is part of the National Curriculum.)

KATIE: Would more pupils make a difference?

PAT: Yes, but not a lot.

CLAIRE: How much is each child worth?

PAT: Between £1,100 for an infant to £900 for a junior.

CLAIRE: Hiring out premises?

PAT: But might need a caretaker – either we have a caretaker or a cleaning contractor.

(At this point the head discussed her contact with the manager of the adjacent sports centre. She mentioned that he wished to discuss the feasibility of using the playground as a spillover car park, from which the school could earn £100 per week. The head mentioned that a while ago the Governors turned down the offer without discussion. She referred to the problem of oil on the playground and who would be responsible. She also mentioned that a meeting was scheduled for after Easter.)

CLAIRE: Used to be aerobics in the school hall...

LIZ: But the caretaker used to close...

PAULA: Parents would massively object [to car park proposal]...it's a pity...

PAT: Well, I shall know more after this man has been to see me. I don't think there's a choice.

PENNY: Parents will take their children away.

ANDY: But so many schools do it.

CLAIRE: We ought to go to the Governors...advertise fact. We need to act quickly, don't we?

[Silence]

PAT: Does anybody want to ask me anything else?

SALLY: We need marketing!

PAT: Governors got to do something…Can't do nothing…

PAULA: Tell them we're prepared to bite the bullet – have the car park.

ANDY: Do you know when the Governors are going to discuss this?

PAT: 25th March…but I may be mistaken…Dinner ladies cost us £13,500.

ANDY: Get rid of dinner ladies. We can have 'glorified' break time duty on a rota basis.

SUE: Can I say? I have a friend [at another school] and each class teacher has dinner in the classroom [with her pupils].

ANDY: Yes. Rota system – each teacher does lunchtime duty. Only one of us each lunch time.

PAT: Depends on everybody.

ANDY: Of course it does!

PAT: Well, can I just ask: anybody who does not want to do dinner duty?

I am not aware of the outcome of the Governors' subsequent deliberations. However, the above attests to the morphogenetic proposition that structural properties do not force in hydraulic fashion. Certainly such constraints may be (and are) experienced as such by agency. Yet whilst subjective *manque de choix* feelings are, of course, no guarantor of objective room for manoeuvre, the crucial theoretical point here, *contra* Giddens, is that there was no possibility 'to do otherwise'. Clearly, there were such possibilities as letting the playground to the local sports centre or making the dinner ladies redundant. But this was *in response to* an objective situation that (a) was not of the staff's making and, moreover, (b) could not be agentially willed away. In other words, all the collective praying, sense of dismay, lengthy discussion and analysis could not eradicate the fiscal predicament that was due to contingencies not covered by LMS, but which could not be ignored (for much longer). The very structurationist proposition of 'can do otherwise' erases such temporally prior (stringent) conditioning at a stroke. Giddens would reply that letting the playground or sacking the dinner ladies is 'doing otherwise'. This is undeniable. However, he would have serious problems if such possibilities did not exist. Moreover, sacking the dinner ladies would have simply resulted in further unwelcome constraints for staff. The fiscal crisis constitutes a new cycle, whose mediated conditioning effects are temporally posterior. Thus, at any given point in time, agents contend with a number of conditioning cycles at various levels (DfEE, school…). Such cyclical conditioning may complement, contradict or cancel out the influence of other cycles. Thus, to take an example, the cycle engendered by the SMT may, unintentionally, contradict the conditioning cycle engendered by a *de jure* working party on the role of the literacy hour. Whether any such objective contradictions are recognised and/or exploited is a matter for empirical investigation.

However, how can Westside now provide 'value for money' when such money does not exist? When one shops in Tesco Stores for own-brand tinned foods, one receives 'value for money' because of the quality of the goods in relation to the relatively higher price tag placed on similar quality goods at, say, Sainsbury's. But 'value for money' provided by Tesco *presupposes* a sustainable degree of *profit*. The OFSTED report pointed to the poor quality of toilet facilities and the unsafe nature of the stairs leading to the infant classrooms, yet commented that the school provides 'satisfactory value for money'. But what is the OFSTED team 'buying' in order to make comments about 'value for money'? Not children's safety, it seems. Of course, this would be denied, yet the fact remains that the value for money was nevertheless satisfactory. Devolving blame for such matters as infants' safety to the Governors is not only unfair but immoral. The irony of the fiscal crisis is that blame could neither be attributed to mismanagement or to poor teaching. Here, then, is a fundamental flaw in the quasi-market rationale of the education reforms. For failing schools are such because of either poor teaching and/or mismanagement and, as such, should be penalised via market rationality. But how can Westside remain successful if unable to avert a severe fiscal crisis that could lead to closure? Essentially, it cannot. The case of Westside evinces the wholly inadequate levels of (educational) funding, whose unequal distribution is exacerbated by expensive, contradictory quasi-market mechanisms.

Back to managerialism: the senior management team and targets

On the one hand, the quasi-marketisation of the education system constitutes recognition of its open nature, since competition necessarily presupposes varying degrees of uncertainty (depending on starting position). On the other hand, OFSTED's secreted social ontology disavows not only that educational reality is structured but also that it is operative within an open system. Thus the implicit assumption is that successful schools will remain so until such a time that *intra*-school factors may disrupt such success. But this does not fit well with the assumption that the intrinsic condition for closure is also presupposed by OFSTED research methodology. It is therefore not surprising that the OFSTED report was content with Westside's School Development Plan that covered four years. It was noted that:

> Financial planning is satisfactory in that the budget allocation is broadly related to the school's needs...The school development plan would benefit from further development to facilitate its use to support financial planning and evaluation of its effectiveness. At the moment it covers four years. The plan does not have any introductory statement setting out the school's objectives for the year ahead and its vision for the future...The school is operating within budget. Income and expenditure per pupil are close to the national average. Budget reserves are rather more than five percent of annual expenditure *but provide a sensible level of contingency in view of the need to implement the forthcoming action plan.*
>
> (OFSTED 1996: 17, emphasis added)

Here, an OFSTED team recognises the propriety of reserving money. Yet what happens when contingencies lead to crisis point? To what extent do crisis-level contingencies (that are not due to mismanagement) become the responsibility of the local authority or central government? This we are not told. Finally, to what extent can one plan for the unforeseen? Quite simply, OFSTED-imposed planning within an open system that is grossly underfunded is a recipe for stress, overwork and the attenuation of educational priorities. Prior to 1988, local authority planning meant that schools could get on with teaching. Now, the degree of systemic openness engendered by the quasi-market reforms means that uncertainty becomes not just the property of individual schools but is exacerbated. Hitherto local authority funding would have cushioned unexpected drops in pupil intake. As we have seen, the unforeseen expenditure created serious exigencies for staff at Westside. At the same time, the government's unremitting pressure resulted in a series of targets that schools have to meet by 2002. This created further exigencies. However, before delineating the response, briefly I wish to discuss the SMT in order to show not only how agency responded both before and after the OFSTED report but also how the degrees of freedom afforded by Westside's market position facilitated an (initially) apathetic approach.

The report commented that

> [the] senior management team has a restricted influence. The role of the deputy head is unsatisfactory both as part of the senior management team and in the daily running of the school. This role should be more clearly defined to enable the senior management team to share much of the responsibility, which is presently carried by the head alone…The involvement of the senior management team in the educational and financial planning process [re the school development plan] is not clear and there is no defined route for its recommendations to influence long-term development planning.
>
> (OFSTED 1996: 16)

Essentially, the 'restricted influence' of the team was deliberate. In stark contrast to Southside, the head consciously avoided managerialist practices wherever possible. The disdain she had for the notion of a senior management team (and, indeed, for such programmes as Investors in People) was evident from our numerous discussions about LMS and the education reforms. In response to my question about whether the head's style of management had changed following LMS and SATs, the special needs coordinator commented thus:

> PAULA: I've got say yes to that. Umm, the reason I have got to say yes is that I think, I think she is very tired. I think it has all been thrust on her teachers, particularly LMS, which I think has made very, very difficult demands on teachers…Particularly head-teachers because they were trained quite a while ago. And I think that they are being asked to be money managers, which is not what they set out to do at all…And I think that poor Pat, it has been, she's jolly good at it I have to say, she is an excellent manager in terms of the money side of things…You know, it's not what people set out to be teachers for, is it? To

manage money? They come because they are interested in children and they don't want to be dealing with, you know, all these problems of finance...

Most staff remarked that the head no longer had the time to help out in class-rooms. The head herself complained bitterly about LMS and how, in particular, it greatly lessened her time to spend with the infants. She told me during interview that it took her three weeks to prepare the finance report for the OFSTED team:

And one evening, I was at home, it was a Sunday evening and I had been working on it virtually all weekend and if I didn't have the double-glazing it would have gone through the window...

This encapsulates the head's sentiments about the OFSTED regime. Such senti-ments account for the half-hearted commitment to the senior management team. When a team vacancy needed to be filled during the term, she had to bargain with a year 6 teacher in order to persuade her to become a member. Unlike at Southside, staff meetings in general occurred once or twice a month. However, a minority of staff complained about the SMT's lack of teeth. One year 5 teacher complained that no decisions were ever made. This was echoed by the special needs coordinator. What exacerbated the apathy of the team was the animosity between the head and her deputy. In the event, such animosity simply facilitated the head's decision not to take the SMT to the same corporate extent as her counterpart at Southside. Furthermore, such agential freedom is due in large part to the SATs success. However, given that the SMT was a focal concern of the report, it is interesting to note how personal factors precluded action. The role of the deputy was not clari-fied during my term at Westside. This did not perturb the head nor the staff in general.

Nevertheless, some days were less half hearted than others. Stringent constraints have a habit of catching up or suddenly rearing their head at awkward moments. The imposed targets constitute one such moment. This was the only occasion on which the senior management team met to deliberate and make school-level deci-sions. The meeting was convened in March 1998 to discuss the government's new National Literacy Strategy and to amend the School Development Plan accord-ingly. It was only during this particular meeting that I experienced the sense of urgency that existed at *every* meeting at Southside. The local authority target was that 86 per cent of all 11-year-olds should achieve level 4 or above in 2002. In 1997 69 per cent of all 11-years-olds achieved this; the national average was 63 per cent. The local authority was given a target band of 84–89 per cent: about a 4 per cent per annum increase to reach the national target of 80 per cent by 2000. The authority was also allocated £155,765 out of the government's 'Standards Fund'. A month before the SMT meeting, a staff meeting was convened to discuss this. The English coordinator reported back on a National Literacy Strategy meeting, which was attended by the authority's advisor.

LIZ: OK. Thanks. Main bit [of the meeting] is in there [the Hall]...National Literacy Strategy a couple of weeks' ago – [the head] went with me. Still doesn't tell you what to do – at what time during the day – that's what people want to know! We do know it's going to be very prescriptive…One or two sheets I think you need to have (I'll photocopy them tomorrow).

PAT: Can I just say something? It's not the government's intention to impose structure rigidly, yet [the advisor] told us otherwise on Monday…our 83 per cent level 4 – we're expected to improve upon that.

LIZ: Won't get it!

PAULA: How can they?

The last comment by the special needs coordinator is crucial, for it underscores the fact that children's varying innate cognitive capacities cannot be moulded in Durkheimian fashion in order to achieve ever-increasing government targets. This point permeated discussion during the SMT meeting, as we shall see in a moment. However, the head pointed out that girls did better in general at Key Stage 2, adding that this was part of the national trend. The teacher-in-charge at the Annexe replied that boys were bottom in her group in reading and described them as 'so immature'. Liz asserted that 'boys haven't got the staying power' and the deputy likened his boys to 'little lion cubs'. The point here is that we are not dealing with robots that equally digest inputs and then regurgitate them with the same degree of success. In other words, in this instance the salient factor of sex difference attests to the untenability of the (new) managerialist target-setting agenda, since sex differences cannot be erased, along with other factors (be they biologically and/or ideologically based).

The English coordinator pointed out that the new teaching requirements were already in the school's Scheme of Work. The head informed staff that the £1000 is to be given to each school irrespective of size, to which the English coordinator commented: 'It will take away a great deal of creativity out of the children.'

Sally nodded in agreement. However, the head immediately added that the local authority has to agree to targets and develop a strategy with schools or it will not receive any funding. The deputy head argued that standards at Westside would 'plummet', whereupon Liz commented: 'We have no choice.' One of the Annexe teachers complained that children 'should not be seen as commodities'. Finally, the English coordinator remarked:

LIZ: The government has reinvented the wheel – back to class-based teaching. Almost payment by results…Victorian times!

Up to this point the school, largely because of its specific 'mix' (i.e., its high socio-economic background), was able to provide a child-centred environment. Now, however, increased targets and the incoming Literacy and Numeracy hours represent new *antithetical* conditioning cycles. As we have seen, the development and nurturing of creativity is quintessential to child-centred philosophy and practice. What facilitated (minor) accommodation to SATs at Westside was undoubtedly the intake of the pupils, the help afforded by their parents and the commitment of the staff. It was precisely because of Westside's 'school mix' that child-centred activities and practices could be sustained. One of the few staff meetings during the term focused on the practical ways in which to foster independence in year 3 children. This would not have been possible in such schools as Southside because of the specific 'school mix'. At the same time, about half of the staff recognised that parents saw them as providing a 'traditional education' and saw themselves as providing such an education. Yet staff proffered child-centred reasons for their teaching approaches, maintaining the need for structure and class-based teaching. Indeed, memories of Tyndale were clear in the head's mind (as well as those of older staff members) and each equated child-centred philosophy with these (and subsequent) events. However, I will return to this in the final section of this chapter.

As Gunter notes, education management is

> ...very seductive, and the promise of reprofessionalism through managerial competences is very tempting within a climate where private sector practices are valued. Certainly teachers are legally required to conform to managerial strategies, whether it is in formulating an OFSTED Action Plan or administering SATs. *What is fascinating is the extent to which teachers subvert, fudge and resist these developments as being contrary to the teaching and learning process.*
>
> (1997: ix, emphasis added)

We have seen that for almost two years managerialisation was subverted (that is, competitive marketing; the invocation of 'right to manage' discourse in providing strong leadership...). Such subversion was school-wide and reflected the Catholic and child-centred values adopted at Westside. It included the reduction in paper-work and lip service paid to the senior management team. It also included a decision not to opt out of local authority control. Grace (1995: 171) remarks that the official discourse of the Catholic hierarchy has made it clear that it has great reservations about the autonomous advantages of grant-maintained (GM) schools and perceived serious moral dilemmas arising from conflicts between Catholic community values and the values of the GMS option. He notes further that the Catholic community is as divided on these issues as the non-Catholic constituency. What is interesting in the context of Westside is that, despite the fiscal crisis, the Governors voted (10:2) against GM status. Of course, for how long Westside can retain this moral stance remains to be seen. Indeed, such subversion started to break down as a result of both the fiscal crisis and the new literacy and numeracy targets set by the government and local authority. Despite the complaints by a minority of staff that the SMT had no teeth, such teachers were not prepared to become members of it. The year 6 teacher who was cajoled by the head to join admitted that the staff were not interested. However, the target issue provided a structural kick-start to the SMT and led to a forceful sprouting of teeth.

> PAT: What we have to do is specify targets by summer 1999. We will aim to achieve an increase of ...in Level 4 Key Stage 2.

ANDY: SATs

PAT: Yes, SATs. [At this point the head handed out the local authority's *Primary Performance Tables 1997 Key Stage Two Results*.] Can we be specific? I've brought little target sheets. One of the things that came up last week was one child at Key Stage 2 who achieved Level 4 in English and yet she got a 5…

PAULA: But Pat are we going to teach to Level 6?

PAT: But we've got to provide for the more able. I'm not saying we should teach to level 6, but should this have not been better?

ANDY: But at 11 a very high standard…level 6 paper – last year many were floored by it…

PAULA: I don't think we're going to have to teach it…

ANDY: I agree with Paula. Main concern is to get as many people as possible to a good level 4.

PAT: Right. Are you going to make that a target?

ANDY: As many children get a good level 4 as possible…me and Liz were talking about how it's going to be difficult to get a good set of level 4s (this current year 5 we're talking about now).

PAULA: Concentrate on maths…

ANDY: But this damn literacy hour – got to concentrate on English.

PAULA: But if you compare us with other schools [in the area].

ANDY: Can't go through any Scheme page by page. Some schools I know use SPMG as a main resource – there are other Schemes.

PAT: …which is what we're supposed to be doing…

ANDY: Well we *are* Pat.

PAT: But we have to say what we're going to aim for as a percentage increase. Aiming for at least 75 per cent…whole point going to be reasonable.

ANDY: I see no reason why that shouldn't be bettered following year…working their socks off, you know [i.e. current year 5] Some children really can't retain…Retention, this is the thing…20–25 per cent will be pleased if get a good level 3.

PAT: So, 75 per cent then is realistic? This is what we want, something realistic...pull the others up.

[...]

PAT: No choice: English ought to aim for 85 per cent Level 4.

ANDY: Trouble. Difficult if...

PAULA: Yes. When we know year not as bright...can't set same target...I don't think we'll get 85 per cent with the year 5 we've got.

PAT: But can't we focus on improving knowledge of words...I think we have to try.

PAULA: If they haven't got it you can't put it there...One boy got a 3 when should have got a 5!

PAT: Yes, but Paula you're talking about four terms away.

PAULA: I think a lot of others will get a Level 3...Lot more to teach to the papers

MEG: Yet in September can give more time to it, as we don't have National Curriculum subjects. So, in fact we could give more time.

PAULA: So, flog English and maths and hope they get to a Level 4!

ANDY: Aim for the sky!

PAT: I think you have to aim for it.

(At this point the head asked what the target ought to be for Key Stage 2 Science. She read out the figures for 1996 and 1997 (63 per cent and 76 per cent respectively). The deputy suggested an extra one percentage point.)

PAT: Why do you say 77?

ANDY: I'm very aware...it's being fair on what they can attain.

I referred to this meeting during my tape-recorded interview with the head. It is interesting to note her reply.

PAT: The targets will have to be altered, you see, because the targets...I know that Paula and Andy kept on about targets, the children...I think right, they can have their whinge and their moan and think that's it. But the targets will be raised, because I think if you're going to be complacent, then you are on a slippery slope and those targets will have to go up, to certainly by 2 per cent at least up to 85 per cent. Purely and simply because if we don't do that then it could be interpreted or construed as not having high enough expectations.

ROBERT: But then…

PAT: If you've got children who aren't performing as well as the previous year it's as…it's a challenge.

I would suggest that the head's reluctance to spell this out during the meeting itself stemmed from her conviction that the meeting should be democratically run. The head at Southside would not have brooked such lengthy discussion and reiterated Pat's point about charges of low expectations. Such reiteration would have been foregrounded by an autocratic demand that targets be met. The problem with Pat's final point is that challenges cannot always be met. The nature of children, *inter alia*, means that the government's targets will not be met. Yet even if they are, at what price? The price tag, already being paid for at Southside, was suggested during the SMT meeting, namely a focus on maths and English at the expense of the rest of the National Curriculum. Yet this is a primary school that, prior to the target mania, was relatively successful. So, notwithstanding the contingent fiscal crisis, 'successful' primary schools are undergoing a further managerialist onslaught in the form of national targets. This is contrary not only to child-centred philosophy but also to Catholic values.

The head's unwillingness to adopt an autocratic approach was not an aberration. She permitted a continuum of child-centred teaching strategies, whereas the head at Southside enforced a process of standardisation whereby each teacher had to adopt a specific classroom layout; classroom layouts at Westside were distinctly different. Education management did not prove seductive. Before entering the staff room, the head would invariably knock at the door. I found this intriguing and asked her why she knocked prior to entering. She explained that this was because of her respect for her staff and that she saw the staff room as a haven for them alone. (Of course, the new managerialism would deem such respect to be at best sentimental.) Nevertheless, the head's comment that the target challenge had to be met underscores the stringency of constraints embodied in the National Literacy Strategy. One would expect Westside to be more cushioned than its lower socio-economic counterpart. Yet, because of the differing year intake, such drastic measures as the truncation of the National Curriculum were mooted. In other words, it seems reasonable to maintain that, just as Westside feels the bite of the new conditioning cycle engendered by the target setting, Southside is dealt a further blow.

And finally…the contradiction

The fiscal crisis and, in particular, the Government-cum-LEA targets signalled a (tentative) end to the relatively generous degrees of freedom that staff were afforded *vis-à-vis* child-centred teaching practices. The fact that Westside was constrained to deal with a fiscal crisis which was not due to mismanagement but contingencies disavowed by the quasi-market reforms is not ironic: it further underscores the flawed rationale of the quasi-market reforms. Southside, as we have seen, was given extra money because of its relatively poor 'school mix' (which OFSTED maintained should have resulted in higher 'standards'). It is a pity that I was unable to spend a year or so documenting the response to the targets and the extent to which prior child-centred and religious practices were sustained, undermined or abandoned. However, apart from the deputy head at Westside, during conversations with me all teachers viewed themselves as child-centred; my observations and participation in classrooms did not on the whole belie this. Compared with Southside, the extent of independence that pupils exhibited in their approach to class work was astounding. This meant that considerable time was available for child-centred activities. Year 6 teachers spent approximately 6 weeks 'cramming' their pupils. In fact, I noticed that tables were re-arranged in a style more akin to the late nineteenth century. I pointed this out to Sally, who replied that it was the most time-efficient, rather than educational, way of ensuring success in SATs. This was lamented by both year 6 teachers, but was, as they agreed, a (necessary) strategic move in order to maintain high SATs scores.

Except the deputy head, all staff when asked about the contradiction between SATs and child-centred philosophy, accepted its objective reality but maintained that prior to the 1988 Act some form of structure was needed. The English coordinator was not against tests *per se*.

> LIZ: I think basically I don't see anything wrong with tests. I don't see anything wrong at all because it does sort of, you know, tell you where children are at a given time.
>
> ROBERT: Sure.
>
> LIZ: But I think they can take on too much importance.
>
> ROBERT: Yes.
>
> LIZ: You know, where everybody is actually sort of teaching what's on test papers...and that's all wrong. That's ridiculous because that is not developing the whole child anymore. It's just making them sort of numerate, literate but...
>
> ROBERT: Yes.
>
> LIZ: Not original.

I asked her whether on balance she felt that the reforms (LMS, etc.) have had positive or negative effects on the majority of children.

> LIZ: Umm, that's a difficult one. Not sure about that one really. In some respects it's good, you know, I mean you have to test children as I said.

ROBERT: But do you think there is a tension then between how perhaps you used to teach prior to SATs?

LIZ: I think you are aware of it the whole time, we don't talk about it, but it's always there. You think, ah now I must do this really in depth because I know it comes up in SATs.

What Liz is getting at here is the need for both summative and formative assessment that is educational, as opposed to managerial, in nature. Despite the strain SATs place on prior teaching practices, she pointed out that as a team, the staff shared basic values about the priority of the individual and her spiritual, cultural and emotional needs. But one of the infant teachers felt that the school was not child-centred enough. There is some validity to her claims. I would suggest that the move away was due to the pressures from both the recently imposed targets and from parents. Indeed, parental involvement at this level was most prominent *vis-à-vis* other years. Chloe often talked about the need to project the 'right' image for parents.

CHLOE: I'm more interested in what the children are learning than what to produce at the end of the day for the parents to look at really.

ROBERT: Yes.

CHLOE: I mean, but there again there is pressure on you to get that right as well. And it is very difficult, I think the children learn more to work in groups than in pairs and so on. But that's not looked upon well here because you need to have a very quiet classroom, you need to have wonderful outcomes. You do have to make a lot of compromises really. And also there'd be so much work to do because they'd [infants] come into my classroom not being used to working in groups...

ROBERT: Sure.

CHLOE: There would be a lot of work if we were going to do that and there is no point unless it is backed up through the school...and you don't know what anyone else is doing.

That Chloe did not know what 'anyone else is doing' not only warns one as to the general validity of her comments but also shows the contrast between the two schools. At Southside, such a state of affairs did not exist, for the head not only standardised classroom layouts but also regularly inspected teaching in each classroom. Indeed, weekly staff meetings, regular SMT meetings and early morning briefings provide the stark contrast. However, I witnessed group work in the majority of classes as well as independent learning situations, particularly in years 3, 5 and 6. Certainly children were quieter and more orderly than their Southside counterparts. Such orderliness was the goal of all staff at Southside and it would be unfair to accuse Chloe's infant colleagues as anti-child-centred because of the extent of orderliness that prevailed. When I asked her about child-centred philosophy, traditional Catholic teaching and the negation of the former immanent in SATs, she commented thus:

> CHLOE: Because if you start with the child when he comes to school, if you have two children coming through the door, one as I said who can just about do handstands and wonderful things and the other who really can't do anything, umm, you can start with both of those children and work with them individually to bring them up, you know, to let them work at their own pace but, (1) very few head-teachers accept that because they want results at the end of the day, and (2) even fewer parents accept that it doesn't matter whether a parent has given four years of endless time to their child so that their child can do wonderful things, is very confident, you know, can mix with others or that the parent has done very little with their child...

> ROBERT: Yes.

> CHLOE: Both of those parents will expect the moment he or she comes to school that they are (a) going to have a reading book, (b) be reading fluently, (c) do wonderful things.

> ROBERT: Yes.

> CHLOE: So, you start with the child but you do have to put pressure on, and even more so now that we are working towards SATs because, umm, there was a time that I would allow the children endless time in the sand tray with water, with paint...

Thus parental pressure militated against child-centred practices, which in large part was due to the 'traditional' Catholic reputation that dates back to the early 1970s. Yet Chloe felt she had to qualify her comments about children playing in the sand tray and with water:

> CHLOE: Now, I'm not saying it's doing nothing playing with sand and water, it's all discovering and they need it and it's very important but there does have to be an element of formal education in that. They have to learn to alphabet, they have to learn certain words, they have to learn to count to do maths, to do addition. All those things somehow in that reception year have got to be covered. *But I still hold on to the fact that they are children and that they all need to move at their own level, they are small children and they need sand, water and paint to play. So I have stuck fast and held on.* (emphasis added)

It is precisely this balance that is being destroyed by SATs, LMS and national target setting. The Piagetian approach is not antithetical to the 'formal' teaching methods outlined by Chloe. The point is that the discovery learning that is playing in the sand tray and with water necessarily precedes them. The problem for child-centred primary teachers is that the 1960s popularised a false dichotomy between child-centred = play and informality and non-child-centred = formality, and denial of spontaneity within structure means that we encounter primary teachers who feel compelled to qualify or defend the need for children to play in the sand tray. It is interesting that the Westside OFSTED report maintained that structured play is underdeveloped. However, this was belied by my observations and therefore undermines the validity of the five-day inspection process.

Of all staff, the deputy head was openly anti-progressive in his teaching approach. What was particularly frustrating here is that both before and after our tape-recorded interview, contradiction permeated his analysis of SATs, child-centred philosophy and the new managerialism. The problem for me specifically as a researcher is how far to point out objective contradictions, since one does not wish to be viewed as arrogant or patronising. As with the special needs coordinator at Southside, I tended to veer on the side of caution. For the deputy, as with the head and the special needs coordinator at Southside, there 'did not have to be a contradiction between child-centred philosophy and SATs'. To suggest that there does not have to be a contradiction is to recognise that one exists objectively. Ironically the deputy head commented that SATs has made his teaching slightly more pupil focused!

> ROBERT: Do you feel that your teaching has changed quite a bit since SATs?
>
> ANDY: I find that my teaching has changed anyway. I think it would have changed with SATs, I guess I got into a rut. I have tried to be a little more questioning. How could I do it with this, in a different way, rather than 'just turn to page 10'?
>   Umm, in a funny sort of way the last, since SATs, the last few years I have been far more keen on saying 'Right, you know you have got to learn to work on this by yourself. You've got to go in and try to find out how to do yourself rather than this constant how do I do this'. Now whether that is child-centred learning I'm not sure...

He referred to progressivism as a 'mish-mash of the seventies' and said that he adopted a 'more rigid formal approach' during and since then. He said that SATs means that he is no longer 'one hundred per cent formal'.

It is rather difficult to take at face value what the deputy said. From my own observations of his teaching, it was clear that lessons were, on the whole, overly structured and directed and that a 'turn-to-page-10' style predominated. It would be futile to guess at the reasons for his (often) contradictory comments (both ideational and practical). Interestingly, in relation to the targets, he commented:

> ANDY: Note the government's targets have got to be 80 per cent. Well, that just underlines that totally doesn't it? It's like being on the production line. I want 55 more Sierras this week...

Whilst this analysis fits well with the deputy's own approach to primary teaching (despite contradictory self-analysis), it encapsulates the government's managerialist approach. However, when I asked the head during interview whether she had ever been committed to child-centred learning, she replied that she did not know what I meant by it. Before elaborating, she referred to the Plowden report.

> PAT: What I would take as child-centred learning was the...going back to the days of the Plowden Report of 1967...*which really I think was chaos. And that's where things started to go wrong.* (emphasis added)

This could have been said by one of the Black Paper authors. However, equivocality characterised the head's remarks about child-centred practice, and I would proffer that because of her internalisation of the derogatory connotations attaching to child-centred practice during the late 1960s and 1970s, she was overly cautious. In fact, she played up the need for teacher direction and accepted that this did not negate child-centred philosophy and practice. Her comments in relation to the OFSTED report and the National Curriculum dispelled any anti-child-centred beliefs that may be inferred from the initial part of the interview.

> PAT: I think that what you are talking about, and correct me if I'm wrong, but I think that what you might be getting at is are we, all right, we are giving the children the basic skills but we are also giving them those other skills to take themselves forward as independent learners, that's what you're after isn't it?

(This highlights one of the researcher's key dilemmas: viz. how far to direct an interview!)

> ROBERT: Yes.

> PAT: You see, I would define that [child-centred teaching] as making provision or to, if you like, empower the children to direct, well not direct, to channel their own learning, *because I think their learning should still be directed by the teacher.* (emphasis added)

(It would have been useful to have paused at this juncture to ask whether the head thought that child-centred philosophy presupposed limited, if any, teacher direction. For I sensed both before and during the interview that she (wrongly) equated child-centred philosophy with lack of structure; hence the 'chaos' she referred to as being characteristic of the Plowden era.)

> ROBERT: Yes, I wouldn't want to deny that. I just wonder, do you think...and you may think SATs fits in very well with that...

> PAT: No, I don't. No I don't. I used to teach 11-plus classes.

> ROBERT: Did you?

PAT: Yes. But everything was geared towards the 11-plus and I think that, now, everything is geared towards SATs because of the publication of league tables, which don't really tell you about a school....I think that SATs and the National Curriculum, I think that what they have really done, *they have taken the joy out of teaching because the whole thing now has become so prescribed,* particularly when you first started to do the National Curriculum...SATs, which in their first couple of years, were absolutely horrendous...and the amount of time teachers had to spend collecting evidence of assessment, and you had to keep that evidence, so that if somebody said well I want you to show me why you assessed that child...Yes, we've cupboards full of it...it's a fire hazard. But that, there was no time at all, any more for a child bringing I've brought this back. Now you say very nice, but we have to get on. Whereas you could stop, all right, dear, let's talk about it. *Spontaneity went, and the joy went.* (emphasis added)

Spontaneity and joy are the hallmarks of child-centred teaching. They also occur within a structured context. The differentiation of children and appropriately structured situations are part and parcel of child-centred primary practice. That teachers attempt to retain an element of joy in their teaching does not eradicate the (structurally imposed) necessary contradiction between SATs rationale and child-centred philosophy. At Southside, staff confused how they adapt (at the S-C level) with the objective contradiction itself. Hence the views (also espoused by the deputy at Westside) that there 'does not have to be a contradiction'. This is a practical (S-C) syncretic response to an objective necessary contradiction (CS level). Like her Southside counterpart, the Westside head associated child-centred teaching with the rhetorical (unfounded) anti-progressivism of the late 1960s and 1970s. Both heads referred to Plowden and Tyndale without prompting on my part. The fundamental difference between the two, of course, centred on a qualified acceptance of child-centred philosophy versus its qualified rejection.

However, unlike the generic $A \leftarrow B$ form of syncretism that characterised Southside, practical 'syncretism' here took the form of $A \rightleftarrows B$. Certainly at the commencement of my research staff toyed with $A \rightarrow B$. Basically, they wanted to retain their notion of an independent child (B) and continually asked themselves how far can A, viz. the managerialist package, be reduced, propitiated, accommodated to B, which they wanted to uphold. Perhaps without the fiscal crisis and the imposition of national targets they could have pursued $A \rightarrow B$ much further. However, this would require good parental pre-preparation and, as I argue in the concluding chapter, a continual supply of 'bright' children.

Part IV

Concluding remarks

8 What about the children?

Some concluding remarks

Introduction: maintaining the need for analytical dualism

Gewirtz *et al.* (1995: 87) argue that, in order to begin to conceptualise the operation and effect of quasi-marketisation, a multi-level analysis is needed. From the morphogenetic approach such levels are not heuristic (that is, they are not observational ordering devices) but are *sui generis* real. The analysis of the interplay of structure, culture and agency is possible because socio-cultural properties pre-date the agency that transforms or reproduces them. The realist methodological device of analytical dualism employed here is due to the fact that any socio-cultural change is the outcome of a temporal sequence, whereby such change post-dates the action(s) that led to it. Such action itself was conditioned by an anterior context. The realist (morphogenetic) approach to theorising about the interplay of structure, culture and agency was elaborated and defended (in contradistinction to Giddens' structuration theory) in Part I, applied historically in Part II, and contemporaneously in Part III. One of the key problems of structuration theory is its

> ...tight binding of structure and agency to avoid structural reification [that] does not allow a judgement to be made about particular structures working on human beings in particular ways, i.e. some are more binding than others, and some act in a more coercive way and to different degrees. Indeed, depending on circumstances and context, they may not coerce at all. Conversely, the degree of enablement in structural properties can only be determined by empirical investigation of particular activities embedded in particular contexts.
> (Scott 2000: 30–1)

Here Scott is underscoring (a) the fact that (fallible) knowledge of generative socio-cultural properties is generated through qualitative investigation; (b) socio-cultural emergent properties do not constrain or enable in abstract isolation; and (c) the extent of constraint or enablement again enjoins empirical investigation at the interface between the CS and S-C interaction, which itself is rooted in the structural domain. Equally, the current ascendancy of positivism in education disclaims the explanatory utility of analytical dualism because of its secreted erasure of relatively enduring emergent properties. Hence the use of mathematical modelling techniques – as opposed to qualitative ones – by many school effectiveness researchers. Thus, Scott rightly argues that the research strategies of school effectiveness 'are implicitly positioned within a model of schooling, which denies the existence of real structural properties' (2000: 67). This complements my transcendental argument for the charge of ideological commitment levelled against school effectiveness researchers, whereby the implicit denial of enduring socio-cultural emergent properties degenerates into voluntarism (Willmott 1999c). In turn, this explains the unremitting pressures placed on heads and their staffs, particularly in low socio-economic catchment areas.

Analytical dualism enables the practical researcher to examine the independent causal properties of structure and culture in order to examine the degrees of freedom or stringency of constraints they afford agency. As I have already argued, those who wish to misconstrue the morphogenetic approach as 'objectivist' tend to focus on the first part of the morphogenetic cycle, namely the identification of socio-cultural properties without reference to agency. To reiterate, the whole point of this is to examine how the socio-cultural context is shaped for actors in order to gain explanatory insight upon what they subsequently do in it or what they can do about it. In Chapter 2 I outlined the objective nature of the 'constraining contradiction' between child-centred philosophy and the new managerialism as embodied in SATs, the publication of national league tables and nationally imposed targets, which exists independently of agential cognisance. It has been argued that the contradiction is a *necessary* one, which in turn directs agency to repair it if, and only if, agency wishes to uphold it non-dogmatically or is forced into recognition of its logical necessity whilst being upheld. However, this necessary contradiction is one that has been imposed on all primary teachers, irrespective of (a) their desire to defend the new managerialism, and/or (b) their recognition of its constraining nature. In other words, those who do not wish to uphold the new managerialist philosophy underpinning assessment, whilst not constrained to engage in ideational repair work, nevertheless have to reorient their teaching in order to accommodate SATs (A ← B). The extent of such accommodation cannot be predicted or inferred from abstract socio-cultural properties but must be established empirically.

The ideational constraint experienced by child-centred primary teachers of the new managerialism is conceptualised as a 'third-order' emergent property because its incongruence is exacerbated by incongruent structural properties (LMS, league tables and national targets). The extent to which incongruent second- and third-order emergent properties can be deflected depends on local factors. My research shows how the extent of accommodation is conditioned by local context, namely prior history and the nature of 'school mix'. Such prior history consists of a number of conditioning cycles and factors, which range from religious underpinning to deep-seated personal animosities.

Stringent conditioning and the tendency towards isomorphism

Whilst such accommodation is contextually mediated, as Gewirtz *et al.* rightly point out, we must not lose sight of the macro (systemic) conditioning cycles unleashed by the 1988 and 1993 Education Acts in particular. Prior to the 1993 Act and the Dearing Review, Bonnett argued that:

> …the National Curriculum is not inherently hostile to the relationship-centred principle…but that the cumulative requirements of planning, teaching, monitoring, and reporting such an extensive and detailed set of objectives as comprise the National Curriculum will pre-occupy teachers to such an extent that there is a real danger of the concerns of children simply disappearing from view.
>
> (1991: 291)

Bonnett is correct not to isolate the National Curriculum from the rest of the Education Reform Act. It should be recalled that the National Curriculum and the 1988 Education Act were contradictorily underpinned by educational and managerial concerns. One of the central arguments of this book has been that the new managerialism enjoins erasure of children. Transcendentally, it cannot erase them, which in turn accounts for the constraining nature of the contradiction. However, following the Dearing Report, Woods and Jeffrey, writing only five years ago, argued that Dearing constituted a 'distinct swing in the direction of process and away from objectives and technical rationality', to the extent that…

> Coherence, holism and process could well come back into favour, it would seem, and be less matters of strategic adaptation for teachers. On the other hand, Galton (1995) argues that Dearing neglected certain key issues, namely 'entitlement'; the issue of 'broad and balanced' against excellence or depth…The recommendation by Dearing that there should be no more change for five years is seen by Golby…'as surely a triumph of hope over experience'. The National Curriculum has clearly moved into a second phase, more favourable to our teachers than the first, but we are still some way from a settled state…
>
> (Woods and Jeffrey 1996: 143)

The second phase here constitutes the fourth phase of compromise for Scott (1994, 2000), which followed the reassertion of control in 1990 by Kenneth Clarke. Clarke wanted to reassert the power of the central authority and thus to limit and circumscribe the power of the teaching profession. However, it should be recalled that Dearing argued that there was still a need to collect and publish summative data about pupils and schools. The ten-level system remained intact and the revised assessment model remained within a standards and accountability framework. As we saw in Chapter 5, this framework is a decontextualised one that prioritises external accountability.

Subsequent events have borne out Bonnett's assessment. Of course, Woods and Jeffrey could not have anticipated that the Labour victory in 1997 would involve a consolidation of the neo-liberal restructuring of education. Even if the head at Southside has been less in favour of managerialist 'solutions' to the relative lack of SATs success, a narrowing of curricular focus was ineluctable (unless the school as a whole was prepared to pay the ultimate structural price, namely closure). At Westside, staff reoriented their teaching strategies to accommodate SATs at the earliest possible moment. Yet the relative success in SATs meant that staff had more room for manoeuvre, in turn permitting a continuation of child-centred practice. But during my time there, New Labour's managerialist drive continued unabated and the imposition of national targets began to attenuate Westside's room for manoeuvre and thus matters were becoming less to do with 'strategic adaptation'. As we saw, Westside's staff rejected the new managerialism. Despite some of the staff's self-professed claims to be 'traditional', their teaching practices and proffered reasons for the latter were child-centred. This underscores the usefulness of the morphogenetic sequences delineates in Part II, since the impact of the anti-child-centred rhetoric of the late 1960s and 1970s is evident from my research. Equally, at Southside the majority of teachers were openly child-centred. The difference here is that such staff did not qualify their endorsement of child-centred teaching. In a nutshell, the structural upper hand lay firmly with the head, whose vision of the school's future success was openly managerialist.

Now, whilst one would not wish to generalise on the basis of what may be two special cases and despite the inherent problems that necessarily attach to generalisation (see Sayer 1992), recent research confirms the trend towards isomorphism. Gewirtz *et al.* write:

> We have evidence of a decisive shift in the values informing and reflected in management decision-making, as educational considerations are increasingly accommodated to image and budget-driven ones...We are also seeing school management and organization increasingly geared towards realizing instrumental, narrowly-focused academic ends as schools respond to the national curriculum, OFSTED inspections and league tables. Some schools are also employing techniques like total quality management (TQM) and quality assurance (QA) to formalize, disseminate and inculcate the messages of performance evaluation, feedback, measurement and comparison.
>
> (Gewirtz *et al.* 1995: 97)

This analysis is depressingly familiar. I do not need to recapitulate the overly narrow managerialist restructuring of activities at Southside. In short, what must now be added to the list is the imposition of national numeracy and literacy targets, which now forces open the back door in *every* (state) school to technicist practices. For, whilst possible (and likely) fluctuations in SATs attainment at Westside would enjoin some, albeit limited, narrowing of the curriculum, the added imposition of targets means that Westside must now narrow the curriculum, especially when the school's year 5 is not as collectively 'bright' as its predecessor. This was precisely the deputy head's point, which accounts for his target of an additional one percentage point. But the head later admitted during interview that the deputy's suggested target would invite charges of low expectations. However, it is not simply a case of a verbal reprimand but rather a reduction in funding if schools do not meet such targets. Indeed, whilst any back door can be closed, both targets and the fiscal vicissitudes engendered by quasi-marketisation mean that this door cannot be shut. Rather, a weather eye must be kept on how much is being let in. In other words, a 'brighter' year would signal attenuation in any technicist-cum-narrow approach to the curriculum, but this would be a matter of degree.

What about the children?

It is reasonable to argue that only those schools that not only attract a homogeneous and strong 'school mix' but also remain financially solvent will (potentially) remain immune from any serious technicisation and narrowing of the school curriculum. The league tables and targets, along with literacy and numeracy hours, perforce will affect teaching practices; whether such practices are wholly managerialist remains a matter for empirical investigation. Either way, the (new) managerialist onslaught is gaining strength (via government legitimation and funding). Indeed, a paragraph of the government's 1997 White Paper maintained that

> ...we shall put in place policies which seek to avoid failure. But where failure occurs, we shall tackle it head on. Schools which have been found to be failing will have to improve, make a fresh start, or close. *The principle of zero tolerance will also apply to local education authorities...we intend to create an education service in which every school is either excellent, or improving, or both.*
>
> (DfEE 1997: 12, emphasis added)

Ozga emphasises the overall tone of the White Paper as *dirigiste* and managerialist:

> Things *will* happen, there will be, we will have, standards will rise. It is a tone that is very instructive in terms of understanding how the new Labour administration understands policy making...it is a valuable source of information on the model of governance that lies behind policy. It is a highly centralist and managerialist model...
>
> (Ozga 2000: 105, original emphasis)

Where does this leave *the educational needs of children?* The answer is simple: they do not matter. As Gewirtz *et al.* succinctly point out, the question now facing schools as they vie with one another for competitive advantage is not what schools can do for children but what children *as commodities* can do for schools. This state of affairs is the logical outcome of an ontology that attempts to efface children, admits only observable events and measurable end products. One should not be surprised that commentators such as Rose rightly maintain thus:

> If we determine success primarily in terms of test scores, then we ignore the social, moral and aesthetic dimensions of teaching and learning – and, as well, we'll miss those considerable intellectual achievements which aren't easily quantifiable.
>
> (Rose 1995: 3)

Indeed, the very notion that schools somehow provide 'value for money' indicates the sheer extent of the commodification of teachers and pupils. This strikes at the very heart of child-centred philosophy, since no price can be put on the social, spiritual and psychological needs of an individual child. I have argued in this book that the lip-service paid by OFSTED and school effectiveness researchers to the spiritual, moral and emotional aspects of child development is a necessary concomitant of the new managerialism. Furthermore, that such dimensions of the human condition cannot be ignored at the S-C level is attributable to the constraining contradiction that is the new managerialism, since, transcendentally, humanity cannot be expunged, and thus resurfaces at various contradictory moments at the S-C level.

I concur with Morley and Rassool (1999) that the primacy accorded to measurable output and target setting is resulting in organisational isomorphism. Furthermore, they rightly point out that, whilst New Labour has reinserted the concept of disadvantage via the creation of Education Action Zones, the implicit assumption remains that such schools can perform independently of school constraints. This is consistent, of course, with the atomised social ontology of OFSTED and school effectiveness research and the neo-liberal inflection of the Education Acts. Morley and Rassool comment:

> School effectiveness has become a vast industry, legitimised through public policy, finance and educational research...it currently frames the language of school practice and management. We have attempted to fracture the discourse by uncovering its epistemological bases. We have aimed to open up some discursive space, as a counterpart to the closure and certainty embedded in school effectiveness. It has been an objective to uncover submerged structures and ideologies...We have endeavoured to interrogate what is hidden, contradictory, silenced and distorted and avoided in the common sense rhetoric...
>
> (1999: 129)

This book has provided a transcendental realist argument that is, namely, the *ontological* propositions secreted by OFSTED that (*qua* CS denizens) exist independently of agential awareness. Whether the constraining contradiction that is the New Managerialism is recognised is an epistemological contingency. In other words, Morley and Rassool are confusing the logical and the causal. Whilst as academics they have (correctly) delineated the contradictions (at both CS and practical S-C levels), this book has shown that the overall problem for the primary teaching profession as a corporate body is its lack of exploitation of the CS fault-line, prior and subsequent to the Conservative onslaught. In fact, it has been argued that child-centred practice has never achieved S-C predominance. More contemporaneously, my research in both primary schools bears witness to the S-C confusion surrounding child-centred philosophy and the lack of full discursive penetration of the constraining contradiction. Thus, coupled with the New Labour primacy accorded to OFSTED, nationally imposed targets, literacy and numeracy hours and the continuing role played by school effectiveness academics, the future quite simply remains bleak for children in England and Wales.

Notes

Chapter 1

1   Hence the use of natural analogies by social realists to explain emergence and stratification (Sayer 1992). Many critics rightly point out that social reality is unlike natural reality since (a) it does not exist independently of us, and (b) it can never be likened, for instance, to a magnetic field precisely because it is quintessentially peopled (Manicas 1997). However, it will be argued that the dissimilarities are unhelpfully emphasised at the expense of the similarities between natural and social reality.

2   The notion of structure (or culture) as possessing *sui generis* properties has been wrongly assumed to entail reification; viz. that such properties are either disconnected suprahuman 'substances' or beyond agential grasp. But the phrase '*sui generis*' means nothing more than 'of its own kind'. As Archer notes,

> The confusion arises etymologically because the same word *genus* (of which *generis* is the genitive) means 'birth', deriving from the older Sanskrit verb 'jan', meaning 'to be begat'. Hence the source of the Holistic error that (reified) society begets or generates its own (equally reified) properties. However, when referring to things, such as 'society', it denotes merely 'sort' or 'kind'.

(Archer 1995: 48–9)

3   Any research methodology presupposes a social ontology. This cannot be avoided. However, school effectiveness research, for example, refuses to examine its ontological presuppositions and conducts its defence purely at the methodological level. (See the Preface to Part III of this book, and Willmott 1999c, for a critique of their positivist methodology and how its ontological presuppositions provide the necessary, though insufficient, conditions for the charge of ideological commitment.)

4   As Layder (1990: 120) argues, methodological individualism presupposes a flat ontology of social reality and insists that facts about social phenomena can be explained solely in terms of facts about individuals. The principal reason for the emphasis upon the individual stems from its empiricist underpinning, and hence any reference to unobservable social relations is taken to entail reification or the positing of a dubious social 'substance'. (See the useful collection of essays in O'Neill (ed.) *Modes of Individualism and Collectivism* (1973), in which empiricist propositions preclude a full-blown endorsement of ontological emergence.) Indeed, the empiricist ghost has yet to be fully exorcised. In their discussion of Lukes' (1974) three dimensions of power, Deem *et al.* write that, 'because three-dimensional power is not directly observable, we can only speculate about its existence' (1995: 135). The foregoing should be sufficient to dispel any need to speculate about the existence of powers that may remain unexercised or are exercised but unperceived.

5 Furthermore, the parental request that their children behave well in class is reinforced by the existence of truancy officers, education social workers, formal legal responsibilities and so on.

6 Generally, however, most people are aware of their vested interests and undertake the requisite social action to promote and defend them. What is more interesting theoretically is the extent of what Giddens calls 'discursive penetration' of social reality. Even when full discursive penetration is attainable, it does not follow that such knowledge and any concurrent use of power will codetermine successful action.

7 Following Archer, a state educational system is held to be

> …a *nation-wide and differentiated collection of institutions devoted to formal education, whose overall control and supervision is at least partly governmental, and whose component parts and processes are related to one another.* It should be noted that this definition stresses both the political and the systemic aspects, and insists that they should be present *together* before education can be considered to constitute a state system.

> (Archer 1979: 54, original emphasis)

8 Centralised educational systems are intrinsically less 'bumpy' than their decentralised counterparts. But this does not negate the *open* nature of both systems. In other words, the reasons for successful steering in centralised systems certainly derive from its centralised configuration *but other factors co-determine this outcome.* Conceivably, newly elected governments intent upon radical reform, whilst constrained by the nature of centralised systems, may nevertheless make inroads and confront enablements generated at the same time (e.g. teaching unions' backing). As Archer (1979) points out, the nature of centralised systems means that the locus of potential for change rests with political manipulation, rather than with what she calls 'internal initiation'.

9 As Hacker notes:

> The thought that a human being is a composite creature consisting of body and soul (or mind, or spirit) is an ancient one…This conception…was articulated in the religious and philosophical thought of antiquity and the Middle Ages. It was given its most powerful philosophical expression in our era by Descartes. According to Descartes, a human being is composed of two distinct substances, the mind and the body. A person's innermost self, that in which his (*sic*) essential identity consists, and that to which he refers when he uses the first-person pronoun 'I', is his mind or soul, the *res cogitans.* The essence of the mind is thought, the essence of the body extension. A person is an embodied anima, for while the body is destructible, the mind or soul is not.

> (Hacker 1997: 14)

It is thus not difficult to understand why those theorists who openly adopt a 'dualist' approach to social reality are often held to be culpable of reifying society, since society (or structure) is taken to be like Descartes' human body, disconnected from agency and unnecessary for its existence.

10 Ronald King's (1983) fear of reification leads him to conceptualise structure in terms of 'repetitive encounters'. Structure's explanatory status is thereby erased at a stroke. Thus, to King, 'the *social structure of a school* consists of the patterns of social relationships occurring between those defined as members of 'the school'…In social terms they are not 'inside' the structure of the school; what they repetitively do is the structure of the school' (1983: 13). Here, King is conflating structure and agency (in an 'upwards' direction). Social realism posits the notion of *sui generis* structure precisely in order to *explain* such repetitive or routine behaviour. Without a notion of the school *qua* irreducible relational entity, we cannot explain why different cohorts of individuals behave in similar

(structured) ways. Indeed, we posit the concept of the school in order to denote (a) its relational nature, and (b) how its structured activities are qualitatively different from, say, those of a civil service department.

11 However, Giddens writes of Durkheim that:

> The point here [Durkheim's] is that 'social facts' have properties that confront each single individual as 'objective' features which limit that individual's scope of action. They are not just external but also externally defined... There is surely something correct about this claim, but Durkheim was prevented from spelling it out satisfactorily because of ambiguities about the notion of externality...In linking externality and constraint...he wanted to reinforce a naturalistic conception of social science. In other words, he wanted to find support for the idea that there are discernible aspects of social life governed by forces akin to those operative in the material world. Of course, 'society' is manifestly not external to individual actors in exactly the same sense as the surrounding environment is external to them...

> (Giddens 1984: 172)

Again, the knee-jerk reaction to naturalistic comparisons leads Giddens to wrap objective and society with scare quotes. Giddens rightly counteracts Durkheim's over-emphasis upon structural constraint, but side-steps the issue of externality, preferring instead to wrap it, too, with scare quotes. In fact, I will argue that he conceptualises structure in such a way that constraint deriving from the latter is rendered impossible. The school *qua* organisation can be conceptualised as external because of its causal irreducibility. To take a different example, would-be benefit claimants confront an external Benefits Agency in the sense that (a) truistically the individuals who work within it are not dependent upon the claimant for their existence; but more fundamentally, (b) the Agency is *sui generis*, for the would-be claimant confronts not individuals but role-incumbents, who possess irreducible powers to disallow any benefit claim.

12 Archer (1982) has discerned an oscillation between determinism and voluntarism in structuration, whereby all rules are held to be inherently transformable at any given time, yet instantiation of structure is also held to embroil agency in the entire structural matrix. The notion of inherent transformability resonates well with Watkins's methodological individualist maxim that 'no social tendency exists which could not be altered *if* the individuals concerned both wanted to alter it and possessed the appropriate information' (1973: 168–9). This cannot be squared with the untenable agential invocation of the entire matrix. Moreover, by maintaining that agents invoke the entire matrix, he is unable to specify which parts of it are analytically more important.

13 Porpora (1989) argues that structure *qua* rules and resources confuses structure with culture, since it disavows any notion of social *relations*. Porpora rightly maintains that culture shapes our behaviour, which must be complemented by an adequate (i.e. relational) concept of structure. Chapter 2 will show how culture can be theorised in the same way as structure, possessing irreducible relations among its component parts that predispose agency towards specific courses of action.

14 To Giddens, the systemic level is only action at a distance by big groups; that is, nothing organisational.

15 Morphostasis '[r]efers to those processes in complex system–environment exchanges that tend to preserve or maintain a system's given form, organization or state. Morphogenesis will refer to those processes which tend to elaborate or change a system's given form, structure or state' (Buckley 1967: 58).

16 The *Next Steps* initiative followed Sir Robin Ibbs' report *Improving Management in Government: Next Steps* and was a result of the persistent demands for 'value for money'. *Next Steps* laid the foundation for the creation of agencies that were to be accorded greater self-determination and the right to seek and achieve trading fund status. It was highly critical of the civil service 'culture' that disavowed risk-taking.

17 The morphogenetic approach identifies four institutional configurations and their situational logics. Such 'logics' entail different forms of strategic action by predisposing different sections of the population (or organisation) to maintain their vested interests by *defensive, concessionary* or *opportunist* modes of social interaction. The example in this chapter addresses the situational logic of concession.

Chapter 2

18 The fact that race ideas are causally influential *vis-à-vis* structure should not lead us to conceptualise them as a *necessary* feature of concrete entities, such as the police force. Therefore, when using such concepts as 'institutional racism', one must be careful not to forget that any police force does not require that its incumbents be of a specific skin colour or ethnic background. In other words, the notion of 'institutional racism' is an elision, since cultural and structural properties are compacted together. The task of the social researcher is to theorise about the relative interplay between race ideas, structural conditioning and agential mediation.

19 To reiterate, it is untrue theoretically to assume that all concrete phenomena within any organisation are necessary for the organisation *qua* organisation. Meek maintains unconvincingly that

> [a] university, for example, would not be a university without the ritual and symbols that surround such events as graduation ceremonies and inaugural lectures. The ritual is as old as the idea of the university itself. At graduation, academics and graduands clothe themselves in medieval garb and speak in foreign languages – Latin....most members of the university...all know that these artifacts symbolize the university, and they share a feeling of belonging to an academic community whenever the artifacts are displayed and the ritual performed.

> (Meek 1988: 468–9)

The issue of whether people feel a sense of 'belonging' is an empirical matter and cannot be decided *a priori*. However, does a university cease to be a university if (successful) students are posted their degree certificates in the absence of any form of degree ceremony? And does its signposting require symbolic representation? In sum, those who maintain that an organisation *is* culture *inter alia* conflate the distinction between necessity and contingency. Whilst it is contingent that any organisational configuration exists, it is composed of internal necessary relations (generically those between employer–employee); issues surrounding who fills the roles and the actuality of symbolisation are contingent matters for investigation.

20 See Sayer (2000) for an excellent critique of 'strong' social constructionism.

21 As Layder (1997: 128) notes, 'objective' here is not meant to express a claim about truth or falsity, but is instead a claim about the relation between knowledge and the human beings that produce it. Furthermore, 'objective' should not be taken to imply that such knowledge (CS) is unchanging and beyond the grasp of human intervention.

22 Even those who possess 'photographic memories' would not have the time to digest and retain an ever-expanding CS. Moreover, a photographic memory does not endow one with the capacity to pinpoint every conceivable logical contradiction and/or complementarity among its components, whose logical relations may bear upon an infinite number of situations.

23 Propositional knowledge is that which instantiates truth (or falsity). Truth is thus metaphysical, not epistemological.

24 It may be argued that sexist ideology, beliefs, etc. are not so neatly lodged in the Library or the CS, for there exists no equivalent of a mathematics manual or literary

journal. Whilst there is no 'sexist manual' *per se* (although historically one can easily dig up numerous pamphlets regarding women's 'natural' role in the home and so on), *propositions can be passed on orally*. As Popper argues, as far as objective knowledge is concerned, 'it may be said to be the world of libraries, of books and journals, but also of oral reports and traditions' (1994: 32). That such propositions are passed on establishes their irreducibility to human minds (or 'World Two' thought-processes).

25 As Geoff Esland puts it:

> Of all the areas of social policy subjected to the New Right's 'cultural revolution', the reform of education has arguably been the most central to its moral and political project...like those in other parts of the public sector, educational institutions have been compelled to incorporate elements of the 'new public management' designed to eliminate 'waste' and 'inefficiency' and to induce a greater responsiveness to the new 'customer culture'.
>
> (Esland 1996: 26)

26 As Hatcher (1994: 55) notes, it is the market that is intended to provide not just a source of new material powers for management but also a new legitimising discourse, 'which has been fostered by the government under the key concepts of "choice", "accountability" and "quality"...The struggle to create this new school culture takes place on the terrain of ideologies of teachers' professionalism'. In creating a 'new culture', Hatcher is not suggesting that child-centred, ethically-based approaches to management and so on are somehow expunged from the CS, which is an ontological impossibility. Instead, the aim is to *impose* such ideas in legitimating new structured working arrangements. The fact that he talks of struggle (i.e, competition between ideas at the S-C level) means that success is by no means a simple, untrammelled process of top-down implementation. As he rightly points out, it would be wrong to take management rhetoric at face value:

> The creation of a permanent common ideological discourse encompassing management and workers is an unattainable goal. Coercion is always present and necessary too. While it is true that the ideological element in the new management offensive is crucial (in education as in the private sector), its success does not depend on ideologically convincing teachers...It depends on ensuring their compliance in practice, in other words on installing a set of management practices that prevent teachers carrying out a different agenda. There is a danger in adopting an over-ideological approach...
>
> (Hatcher 1994: 55)

In other words, given the specific structural conjunction that gave the Tory Government the 'upper hand', *inter alia*, quasi-marketisation did not require its ideological legitimation, even though this was part and parcel of the process of the imposition of the various Education Reform Acts. However, I do not wish to suggest that such processes of ideological legitimation are mere structural window-dressing. As I will go on to elucidate, championing ideas conditions its upholders to follow specific courses of action by virtue of the situational logic in which they embroil themselves.

27 The morphogenetic approach identifies four cultural configurations and their situational logics. Such situational logics entail different forms of action by predisposing different sections of the population or organisation towards *correction, protection, elimination or opportunism*. The examples in this chapter address the situational logics of constraining and competitive contradictions respectively (for a discussion of the remaining two, see Archer 1995: 229–45).

28 The capital–labour internal relation is one of one-sided domination, which accounts for the fact that much pro-labour legislation was hard-won. However, this does nullify the

situational logic of compromise/concession: it remains in the capitalist's vested interests to 'soften' the inherently exploitative nature of the contradiction in order to sustain it. As Sayer points out, the causal powers of capitalist ownership are not absolute: '...sometimes they are limited by state regulation (e.g. regarding employment legislation); sometimes they are rendered worthless, as in the ownership of obsolete means of production; and sometimes they can be overridden by other forces, such as powerful occupational groupings or organized labour' (1995: 49).

29 The use of A/B relations should not be taken to imply that we are dealing with 'stand-alone' propositions. As Davis (1998) rightly argues, many propositions are part of connected clusters. For example, the proposition 'that Faraday discovered the dynamo' is 'not a "stand-alone" entity. Its essential nature is inextricably bound up with other propositions...[It] cannot be separated from other propositions about dynamos, electricity, coils, magnetic fields...' (1998: 53–5). In the context of educational assessment, Davis's critique of extant arrangements centres on the oft-neglected problem of assuming that pupils are aware of the connections between propositions and, moreover, that they *under-stand* them. Unwittingly, Davis underscores the tenability of differentiating between the emergent relations of propositions (CS) and what people do with them (S-C), since pupils do not necessarily have an adequate understanding, despite performing well in assessment situations. This applies equally to the Staff Meetings I observed in the first school, for example, and thus constitutes a methodological problem for any substantive research. In other words, when staffs express agreement with the proposition 'that pupils learn best when...', are they (a) agreeing upon the same thing and (b) is such public agreement contrived? The problem in this instance is that it was not practicable at the end of each weekly staff meeting to enquire as to what individual staff meant by the use of specific educational terms and, if aware of any objective CS contradictions, why they did not point them out, accentuate them, deny their salience, etc.

30 See Willmott (2000a) for an example of a 'constraining contradiction' in the scientific field of sex hormones.

31 It might be reasonably countered that the head is not responding to the determinate effects of a constraining contradiction even though she engages in corrective repair, since the philosophy of the SATs simply implies a (competitive) contradiction between child-centred approaches and their antitheses. Certainly the antithesis of child-centred approaches acknowledges that they cannot avoid the cognitive processes by which children learn; yet even here they often deny such processes. However, the recently re-enacted quasi-payment-by-results system of examining *evades* its cognitive import. The implicit philosophical position is left for others to tease out. The reason why the head engaged in such corrective repair work stems from her avowed acceptance of managerialist approaches to primary education, as will be discussed in Part III of the book. Julie Fisher rightly points out that '[i]t is a lack of understanding of young children's learning processes and the impact these have on their educational development which characterises current policy decisions' (1996: 39). However, two pages later she maintains that:

> While I do believe that there are serious tensions between the National Curriculum and a developmentally appropriate early years curriculum...I also believe that there are ways of looking at the apparent dichotomies which may make the application of one not wholly incompatible with the constraints of the other. I believe that the answer to the tension lies within a better definition of the major stages of curriculum planning.

> (Fisher 1996: 41)

Here, the morphogenetic approach would maintain that (a) systemic contradictions and complementarities exist independently of knowing subjects and (b) focus on what cultural actors make of them. In this instance, Fisher is trying to live with the objective contradiction between the National Curriculum and child-centred philosophy and practice. She is attempting to reconcile the irreconcilable and this attests to the fact that, at the S-C level, actors do not operate in rational, Mr Spock-like fashion.

32 In fact, Butterfield (1995: 200) notes that the initial evaluation of SATs and teacher assessment was later sabotaged by managerial considerations; that is, classroom convenience has been of greater importance than considerations of validity of results, etc. Indeed, Clegg and Billington note that it is the basis of the prevalent school management studies to consider

> ...means rather than ends: hence the emphasis upon the senior management team and staffing structures, school development planning, action planning and the constant need to be able to demonstrate and illustrate the apparent efficiency of the organization...As we have said, accountability has been reduced to a crude set of limited figures which relate only to those aspects...amenable to measurement, and the corollary of this has meant that if it cannot be measured it is not important.
>
> (Clegg and Billington 1997: 17)

33 Yet 'the cheapest possible cost' in reality means ever below the level that is required for minimal resource requirements for those schools that have greater need. In brief, Local Management of Schools is a centrally imposed means of enforcing schools – not all – to manage inadequate levels of funding. I say not all schools since, when introduced, more affluent schools, often based in equally affluent areas, had the advantage and subsequently were able to maintain their advantageous position. The nature of quasi-marketisation means that necessarily there will be winners and losers. Inexorably, this will increase the pressure on socially deprived areas to adopt more technicist ways of improving test scores. But because the system is competitive – that is, schools compete for a slice of the inadequately funded cake – the pressure is unremitting. The existence of league tables will almost invariably direct resourceful and strategically minded parents to those at the top: in other words, we are dealing with a perpetual vicious circle.

Chapter 3

34 However, Hodgson (1999) argues that these are abuses of the word 'capital', which is properly confined to the notion of the money value of an owned stock of assets that exists in, or is readily convertible into, a monetary form.

35 See also Lowe (1997).

36 The influence of Peters *et al.* is discernible in Barrow and Woods' *An Introduction to Philosophy of Education*. This was first published in 1975. The second edition appeared in 1982 and subsequently has been reprinted seven times. A 38-page chapter is devoted to a critique of the child-centred approach, specifically the interrelated notions of needs, interests and experience. Barrow and Woods charge child-centred theorists with vacuity and ambiguity. Yet the nature of the constraining contradiction enjoins that they cannot disavow child-centred philosophy in its entirety. Thus, contradictorily, the authors write that 'Our conclusion must be that although much of what passes for child-centred education may be extremely valuable and although there may be points of importance embedded in various child-centred theories, the term "child-centred" itself is too obscure to be of much practical benefit...' (1997: 135–6). Yet I would argue that the focus on practicality is a mere ruse that disguises the verificationist hue of their book. Like Ayer, they want 'conceptual precision' and deny the tenability of such metaphysical talk as 'children's needs' largely on the basis of subsequent S-C disagreement. But S-C disagreement is not the issue. The issue is *what* people (teachers, parents, etc.) are disagreeing about. The fact of S-C disagreement does not negate its (unavoidable) metaphysical underpinning.

Chapter 4

37 As Lowe notes, after the collapse of the Bretton Woods agreement in 1971, Britain suffered as much 'and probably more than any of the developed countries from the effects of the rise in world oil prices which began in 1973 and from the downturn in world trade which resulted' (1997: 24).

38 At this stage – indeed, up to the few years prior to promulgation of the 1988 Act – Taylorist curriculum structures were not on the agenda. That control was to be wrested from the teachers did not entail strictly managerialist approaches to the curriculum and tests.

39 As Sealey (1994) rightly notes, complexity does not have populist appeal and is difficult to condense into newspaper headlines. Although ahead of our time, Sealey writes of the LINC (Language in the National Curriculum) controversy during the early 1990s in the following terms: 'The LINC controversy is only one example of the compression of complex educational issues into binary opposite slogans: real books versus phonics; abstract theory versus practical training; trendy experiments versus the traditional basics' (1994: 133).

40 In a 1989 BBC interview, Rhodes Boyson referred to Tyndale as evidence of the supremacy of progressive education. 'Colleges of education…were turning people about with a sort of liberation, the equivalent in religion to a theology…Suddenly ILEA [the Inner London Education Authority] did not like it, and it was a turning point' (cited in Riley 1998: 53). Yet the supremacy of progressive practice was mythical and, as we saw in Chapter 3, colleges of education confronted the antithesis of progressivism in the form of the education philosophers' S-C ascendancy. That Tyndale was a turning point is correct, for reasons to be discussed later in the book.

41 Similarly, Lowe, in discussing the Black Paper attack on progressivism and the impact of comprehensivisation, argues that the greatest significance of the Black Papers lay in the fact that they began to articulate a Conservative philosophy in an area hitherto monopolised by socialist and social democratic writers. Moreover, he accentuates the insularity of the Left: 'Trapped in the conviction of their own intellectual superiority, the supporters of comprehensivisation grossly underestimated the extent to which these authors preyed on the fears of the new middle classes…' (1997: 153).

Chapter 5

42 Scott (1994), for example, uses a phase (or cyclical) approach to the evolution of National Curriculum assessment arrangements. He posits four phases over a five-year period: mixed messages, adjustments by central authority, reassertion of control, and compromise. Each new phase differently conditions agential activity. (Again, the four phases delineated by Scott are linked to his substantive concerns.)

43 However, because of Thatcher's predilection for relying on her ministers for advice she reduced the size of the Policy Unit, which in turn reduced its role in policy formation. As Chitty notes, it was her experience of working with a cautious set of ministers – the oft-dubbed 'wets' – that led her to revise her earlier judgement.

44 As I have already argued (Willmott 1999c), as with the epithet 'Thatcherism' considerable caution needs to be exercised. The employment of 'right wing' is a portmanteau. Its components do not comprise a neatly woven (CS) web of logical complementarities. The contradictions within 'Thatcherism' are not variations along a Conservative theme, since *inter alia* some of its components do not adopt an individualist social ontology; that is, an ontology of the social world as flat, undifferentiated and unstructured. The generic basis for education policy during the 1980s drew upon individualism, however inconsistently enacted in practice.

45 The idea here is that money available for publicly provided education would be given directly to parents in the form of a voucher, which could be cashed in for a place at any school that had available space. The voucher could also be used as a contribution to the

fees of a private school. But such a system would be bureaucratically unwieldy and involve a substantial increase in the subsidisation of private education. This is simply the logical end result of the neo-liberal ideology. The fact that the voucher scheme requires bureaucratic regulation is (conveniently) by-passed by the Hillgate Group and, indeed, by Keith Joseph himself.

46 As we see in the Preface to Part III, the School Effectiveness Movement has been success-fully co-opted by past Conservative and present Labour Governments because of its congruence with neo-liberalism. At the same time, key educationists such as Professor Robin Alexander (co-author of the so-called 'Three Wise Men' Report) were also co-opted because of their focus on classroom management rather than learning *per se*.

47 As Broadfoot argues, it is important not to lose sight of the fact that, in both decen-tralised and centralised education systems, assessment procedures have a different, but equally central, role to play – they act as one of the greatest constraints on classroom practice.

> In this sense, much of the variation between systems in terms of their dominant patterns of control can best be understood in terms of the particular *form* that control by assessment takes in each case. Such differences in control cannot be reduced simply to differences between centralized and decentralized systems...This does not mean that the importance of assessment factors makes the centralization issue *per se* irrelevant to the study of control. Indeed, a central-ized, government-controlled, external assessment apparatus possesses great power to enforce the pursuit of a centrally determined curriculum...It is...important to distinguish between the *degree* of assessment control on the one hand (strong or weak) and the *source* of that control (central or local) on the other. This distinction is crucial, for the tendency to conflate *strong* control with *central* control...has led to an over-preoccupation with administrative variables in the study of differences between educational systems...

> (Broadfoot 1996: 119)

48 As Gunter puts it, 'Education management has grown rapidly in the last ten years to the extent that it is an industry driven by the market with ever-changing products in the form of books, courses and contract work' (1997: vii). She goes on to note that current ortho-doxy in management text and training 'is the human resource management model, which has its origins in the excellence and quality models of US business writings' (1997: 1).

49 Gewirtz *et al.* (1995) reveal how schools are increasingly spending money on marketing strategies. The authors calculate that if every school spent £1000 on marketing each year, the total annual marketing bill for the UK as a whole would be around £28 million! In terms of resource efficiency – a term beloved by the New Right – this state of affairs is untenable.

50 It is, as Butterfield emphasises, important to consider some of the problems not identified by the Secretary of State for review. The Attainment Targets and Schemes of Work are pragmatically derived; essentially they are functionalist. Yet there were no workplace studies carried out. The pragmatic approach breaks down because it has included more than can be reasonably done altogether.

> The objectives are not operating within any overall statement about educational purpose. The National Curriculum has no overarching statement of its educational aims, nor is there any statement of the educational contribution each subject area is intended to make...[and again there is] the overall arbitrariness of the 10-level framework.

> (Butterfield 1995: 67)

Chapter 6

51 Following Hargreaves (1994), Bottery (2000) argues that there is evidence to suggest that collaboration between teachers is a 'contrived collegiality' in the context of school improvement, which does not acknowledge and work from the needs of teachers but from the needs of management.

> Thus, meetings may be scheduled to fit in with school needs rather than those of teachers themselves. Hargreaves argues that most meetings are best when convened if they are needed, and this can be occasionally or every day, depending on the problem. This, however, is a decision to be made by those involved, and not by managers scheduling meetings for (say) once every week, for this fails to catch the momentum of the problem.
>
> (Bottery 2000: 153)

Each weekly staff meeting's agenda was pre-arranged by the head and not open to democratic consultation.

52 OFSTED makes it quite clear that failing schools are to be remedied by a managerialist definition of leadership, for they assert that a common characteristic of improving schools is that they have made sure that 'strong leadership is provided. Many schools subject to special measures have appointed a new headteacher just before or soon after the inspection of the school' (OFSTED 1997: 6). The specific task for such leaders is 'to put into place performance management arrangements to help raise schools' performance, including systematic assessment of teacher performance to a suitable level of reward' (DfEE 1999: 6). Thus, as Bottery (2000: 75) sums up, such leaders are being cast as scientific experts, directing and monitoring their staffs in the use of managerial techniques.

53 One of the pupils returned to Southside because, according to his mother, he missed his friends and was unhappy. The school that accepted the extra pupils was in turn oversubscribed, causing problems for staff there. Whilst the school obtained more money, the extra cash was insufficient to deal with the problem of over-subscription. Bringing back or stemming the exodus was a key concern for the head. This is the reality of the education 'market place' and clearly any exodus from 'failing' schools runs the serious risk of entering the vicious cycle and ultimately resulting in closure.

54 The head never explored the issue of *whose* best. I would argue that the invocation of 'working for the best' here is merely ideological rhetoric. 'Working for the best' was working according to the managerialist dictates of the head.

55 Troman and Woods similarly researched a 'failing' primary school. The newly-appointed head at Gladstone Street primary school also embodied the new managerialism. In talking about Sean, one of the school's teachers whom the new head 'changed', he commented as follows:

> He [Sean] would actually fight against the process of producing better academic standards which was necessary to get out of special measures. His personal philosophy wouldn't allow for it. So I approached it from two issues really. One is I came in with a mandate of we're going to move forward with the academic standards like it or not, and you either come with me or we'll have to go into whatever procedures are needed to make you come over. *But it is going to happen.* So I set my stall up very early on…Now if he didn't like his job he needs to go and find another one. Now I had no problem with that. What I had a problem with was his not doing the job which he was being paid to do.
>
> (Troman and Woods 2001: 52, emphasis added)

This was Jill's position, which is wholly congruent with the managerialist and *dirigiste* nature of New Labour education policy-making.

56 At Westside, one year 6 teacher had her desk positioned next to the wall and used it as a work-base for herself and the children.

57 What's interesting to note here is that this teacher is against the SATs philosophy and concomitant teaching practice, yet ends up contradicting herself in agreeing that children should be 'cynically trained'. I did not proceed to point out the contradiction, since it may be that she feared disagreeing on tape with the head. Of course, it may be that once such cynical training had finished, child-centred teaching could take place. However, the latter was not likely given the poor SATs results and the overall managerialist approach of the head. During interview, I asked her whether there is a contradiction between SATs and child-centred philosophy, to which she replied:

> LYNNE: Well, she [the head] calls it independent learning.
>
> ROBERT: Right, independent learning...
>
> LYNNE: That's probably a better term than child-centred...

A few minutes later on:

> ROBERT: Yes (laughs) so, I was just saying, you know, has SATs altered this commitment to child-centred learning?
>
> LYNNE: Yes, but you'd better change child-centred.
>
> ROBERT: To independent.
>
> LYNNE: It's umm it would be called Independent Skills Based, it's the emphasis on the skills.

I would suggest that Lynne is embroiling herself in the throes of a constraining contradiction. Such re-definitional manoeuvres are the (logical) outcome – and reflected the head's approach – but were surprising, since Lynne is committed to child-centred philosophy and practice. One can only speculate as to why she engaged in corrective repair-work (unlike the head, whose reply to my question about the contradiction is discussed later in the chapter). The change from child-centred to independent skills was aired by the head, who was openly managerialist and against child-centred philosophy. It would have been useful to tease out more of what Lynne meant by independent skills based (and indeed why she felt the need to redefine child-centred learning): are the two antithetical, for example? During the hour-long interview, I felt that Lynne was trying to adopt the mind-set of the head.

58 It is further instructive to note that, upon being formally appointed, the head informed staff that, in relation to her vision for 2001, 'If this is not your view we need to talk about it'.

59 As Troman and Woods (2001) note, there is now a considerable international body of work that links teacher stress with the wholesale restructuring of national education systems, which began in the 1980s. Comparing 1989 and 1998, 3,800 more teachers took premature retirement in 1998 – an increase of 43 per cent.

60 The annotation sheets were issued to staff and were designed with pupil completion in mind; namely, how they would improve their work, if necessary. For example, year 3 work on the human body – specifically knowing the bones of the body – resulted in differing degrees of success. I helped an LSA attached to this year to complete the anno-

tation sheets with pupils. In a nutshell, most of the children had problems not only in understanding why they were filling in the form but also in writing upon it! The teacher suggested that both the LSA and I tell pupils with particular writing difficulties what to write. In fact, I wrote down comments for one child. Here the managerialist programme is reaching into the very hearts and minds of the children. Whilst on the one hand there is nothing anti-educational about children reflecting upon their work, the 'need' for quantifiable evidence overrode the needs of the children – in this case the ability to write! When discussing the use of such slogans as 'I am a good ambassador', one newly qualified member of staff commented thus:

> All those slogans – 'I'm a good ambassador for [Southside] United' or whatever. Yet it's all to make the children feel part of the school. They've got something to be part of for them to realise that the discipline, that it should be a self-discipline that they know that the only person who can do something about the way they are behaving is themselves. They are in charge of their doings...

In the context of a school where self-esteem was problematic, imposing a system whereby such pupils should become aware of the need to exert self-discipline is not only unfair but also unrealistic. At Westside, self-discipline and independent learning went hand-in-hand for children in years 5 and 6. (The reasons for this are discussed in Chapter 7.) Again, we encounter the vexing issue of whether such discipline is deemed necessary for educational or managerial reasons or both. Eight weeks into the term, the head held an assembly where she asked all the children why they were in school. She told them that they should know more than they did at nine o'clock and know more at three o'clock. She asked whose job it is to ensure that work gets done, to which one boy commented: 'Us!' The head then emphasised that children need to specify targets and try to meet them: when filling in their 'Golden Goal' books, 'You need to think about goals more and whether they are being met'.

61 This 'directive' was ignored by three-quarters of the staff, some of whom kept a rubber to erase children's work while others permitted children to use them on their own initiative.

Chapter 7

62 As we have seen, such proactivity is unavoidable if local authorities do not wish to face extinction.

63 In fact, one parent wrote two pages of notes suggesting a specific reading strategy for her son! This would not be regarded as abnormal at Westside.

References

Abbott, D. (1996) 'Teachers and Pupils: Expectations and Judgements', in P. Croll (ed.) *Teachers, Pupils and Primary Schooling: Continuity and Change*, London: Cassell.

Abraham, J. (1994) 'Positivism, structurationism and the differentiation–polarisation theory: a reconsideration of Shilling's novelty and primacy thesis', *British Journal of Sociology of Education*, 15: 231–41.

Ackroyd, S. and Bolton, S. (1999) 'It is not Taylorism: Mechanisms of Work Intensification in the Provision of Gynaecological Services in a NHS Hospital', *Work, Employment and Society*, 13, 2: 369–87.

Ahier, J. (1991) 'Explaining Economic Decline and Teaching Children About Industry: some unintended continuities?', in R. Moore and J. Ozga (eds) *Curriculum Policy*, Oxford: Pergamon Press.

Alexander, R. (1990) 'Core Subjects and Autumn Leaves: The National Curriculum and the Languages of Primary Education', in B. Moon (ed.) *New Curriculum – National Curriculum*, Milton Keynes: Hodder & Stoughton.

—— (1992) *Policy and Practice in Primary Education*, London: Routledge.

—— (1996) 'In search of good primary practice', in P. Woods (ed.) *Contemporary issues in teaching and learning*, London: Routledge.

Alexander, R., Rose, J. and Woodhead, C. (1992) *Curriculum Organisation and Classroom Practice in Primary Schools: A Discussion Paper*, London: DES.

Alvesson, M. (1993) *Cultural Perspectives on Organizations*, Cambridge: Cambridge University Press.

Angus, L. (1993) 'The sociology of school effectiveness', *British Journal of Sociology of Education*, 15, 1: 79–91.

Anthony, P. (1994) *Managing Culture*, Buckingham: Open University Press.

Archer, M. S. (1979) *Social Origins of Educational Systems*, London and Beverly Hills: Sage.

—— (1982) 'Morphogenesis versus Structuration: on combining structure and action', *British Journal of Sociology*, 33, 2: 455–83.

—— (1988) *Culture and Agency*, Cambridge: Cambridge University Press.

—— (1995) *Realist social theory: the morphogenetic approach*, Cambridge: Cambridge University Press.

—— (1996) 'Social integration and system integration', *Sociology*, 30, 4: 679–99.

—— (1998) 'Foreword', in W. Buckley *Society: A Complex Adaptive System. Essays in Social Theory*, Amsterdam: Gordon and Breach Publishers.

Athey, C. (1990) *Extending Thought in Young Children*, London: Paul Chapman Publishing.

Audit Commission for Local Authorities and the National Health Service in England and Wales (1993) *Adding up the Sums: Schools' Management of their Finances*, London: HMSO.

Ayer, A. J. (1936) *Language, Truth and Logic*, London: Gollancz.

Ball, S. J. (1990) *Politics and Policy Making in Education*, London: Routledge.

—— (1994) *Education Reform. A Critical and Post-Structural Approach*, Buckingham: Open University Press.

—— (1995) 'Intellectuals or technicians? The urgent role of theory in educational studies', *British Journal of Educational Studies*, 43, 2: 255–71.

240   *References*

—— (1998) 'Educational Studies, Policy Entrepreneurship and Social Theory', in R. Slee
and G. Weiner with S. Tomlinson (eds) *School Effectiveness for Whom? Challenges to the School
Effectiveness and School Improvement Movements*, London: Falmer.
Barber, M. and White, J. (1997) 'Introduction', in J. White and M. Barber (eds) *Perspectives on
School Effectiveness and School Improvement*, London: Institute of Education.
Barber, M. (1996) *The National Curriculum: A Study in Policy*, Keele: Keele University Press.
Barrow, R. and Woods, R. (1997) *An Introduction to Philosophy of Education*, 3rd Edition,
London: Routledge.
Bate, P. (1994) *Strategies for Cultural Change*, Oxford: Butterworth-Heinemann.
Bates, I. (1984) 'From Vocational Guidance to Life Skills: Historical Perspectives on Careers
Education', in I. Bates *et al.* (eds) *Schooling for the Dole? The New Vocationalism*, London:
Macmillan.
Beck, J. (1983) 'Accountability, industry and education', in J. Ahier and M. Flude (eds) *Contem-
porary Education Policy*, Beckenham: Croom Helm.
Bhaskar, R. (1975) *A Realist Theory of Science*, London: Verso.
—— (1989a) *The Possibility of Naturalism*, Hemel Hempstead: Harvester Wheatsheaf.
—— (1989b) *Reclaiming Reality*, London: Verso.
—— (1993) *Dialectic: the pulse of freedom*, London: Verso.
—— (1994) *Plato Etc. The Problems of Philosophy and their Resolution*, London: Verso.
Blau, P. M. (1964) *Exchange and Power in Social Life*, New York: Wiley.
Blenkin, G. M., Edwards, G. and Kelly, A. V. (1997) 'Perspectives on educational change', in
A. Harris, N. Bennett and M. Preedy (eds) *Organizational Effectiveness and Improvement in
Education*, Buckingham: Open University Press.
Bloor, D. (1997) *Wittgenstein, Rules and Institutions*, London: Routledge.
Blyton, P. and Morris, J. (1992) 'HRM and the Limits of Flexibility', in P. Blyton and P.
Turnbull (eds) *Reassessing Human Resource Management*, London: Sage.
Blyton, P. and Turnbull, P. (1992) 'Afterword', in P. Blyton and P. Turnbull (eds) *Reassessing
Human Resource Management*, London: Sage.
Boden, D. (1994) *The Business of Talk*, Oxford: Polity Press.
Bonnett, M. (1991) 'Developing children's thinking…and the national curriculum', *Cambridge
Journal of Education*, 21: 277–92.
Bottery, M. (2000) *Education, Policy and Ethics*, London: Continuum.
Bowe, R., Ball, S. and Gold, A. (1992) *Reforming Education and Changing Schools*, London: Rout-
ledge.
Broadfoot, P. M. (1996) *Education, Assessment and Society*, Buckingham: Open University Press.
Brooks, I. and Bate, P. (1994) 'The Problems of Effecting Change within the British Civil
Service: A Cultural Perspective', *British Journal of Management*, 5: 177–90.
Brown, A. (1995) *Organisational Culture*, London: Pitman.
Brown, M. and Taylor, J. (1994) 'Achieving School Improvement through INVESTORS IN
PEOPLE: a Case Study of Six Staffordshire Primary Schools', BEMAS Conference
Paper.
Bruce, T. (1997) *Early Childhood Education*, Oxford: Hodder & Stoughton.
Bryant, C. G. A. (1995) *Practical Sociology: Post-empiricism and the Reconstruction of Theory and
Application*, Oxford: Polity.
Buckley, W. (1967) *Sociology and Modern Systems Theory*, Englewood Cliffs, NJ: Prentice Hall.
—— (1998) *Society – A Complex Adaptive System. Essays in Social Theory*, Netherlands: Gordon
and Breach Publishers.
Butcher, T. (1995) *Delivering Welfare: The Governance of the Social Services in the 1990s*, Buck-
ingham: Open University Press.
Butterfield, S. (1995) *Educational Objectives and National Assessment*, Buckingham: Open Univer-
sity Press.
CACE (Central Advisory Council for Education) (1967) *Children and their Primary Schools* (the
Plowden Report), London: HMSO.
Callinicos, A. (1985) 'Anthony Giddens: A Contemporary Critique', *Theory and Society*, 14, 1:
133–66.
Campbell, R. J. and St J. Neill, S. R. (1994) *Primary Teachers at Work*, London: Routledge.
Chitty, C. (1990) 'Central Control of the School Curriculum, 1944–1987', in B. Moon (ed.)
New Curriculum – National Curriculum, Milton Keynes: Hodder & Stoughton.
—— (1994) 'Consensus to conflict: the structure of educational decision-making trans-
formed', in D. Scott (ed.) *Accountability and Control in Educational Settings*, London: Cassell.

—— (1997) 'The school effectiveness movement: origins, shortcomings and future possibilities', *The Curriculum Journal*, 8, 1: 45–62,

Clarke, J. and Newman, J. (1997) *The Managerial State*, London: Sage.

Clarke, J., Gewirtz, S. and McLaughlin, E. (eds) (2000) *New Managerialism, New Welfare?* London: Sage.

Clegg, D. and Billington, S. (1997) *Leading Primary Schools: The Pleasure, Pain and Principles of being a Primary Headteacher*, Buckingham: Open University Press.

Clegg, S. and Dunkerley, D. (1980) *Organization, Class and Control*, London: Routledge & Kegan Paul.

Coe, R. and FitzGibbon, C. T. (1998) 'School effectiveness research: criticisms and recommendations', *Oxford Review of Education*, 24, 4: 421–38.

Collier, A. (1994) *Critical Realism: An Introduction to Roy Bhaskar's Philosophy*, London: Verso.

Collins, D. (1998) *Organizational Change: Sociological Perspectives*, London: Routledge.

Consultative Committee, Board of Education (1931) *The Primary School* (the Hadow Report), London: HMSO.

Cox, C. B. and Boyson, R. (eds) (1975) *The Fight for Education: Black Paper 1975*, London: Dent.

—— (1977) *Black Paper 1977*, London: Maurice Temple Smith.

Cutler, T. and Waine, B. (1994) *Managing the Welfare State: The Politics of Public Sector Management*, Oxford: Berg Publishers.

Dahlström, E. (1982) 'Kan sociologin förtöja kulturanalysen?' ('Can Sociology anchor cultural analysis?'), quote taken from: M. Alvesson (1993) *Cultural Perspectives on Organizations*, Cambridge: Cambridge University Press.

Dale, R. (1989) *The State and Education Policy*, Buckingham: Open University Press.

Darling, J. (1994) *Child-centred Education and its Critics*, London: Paul Chapman Publishing.

Davis, A. (1998) *The Limits of Educational Assessment*, Oxford: Blackwell.

Dearden, R. F. (1968) *The Philosophy of Primary Education*, London: Routledge and Kegan Paul.

—— (1969) 'The Aims of Primary Education', in R. S. Peters (ed) *Perspectives on Plowden*, London: Routledge and Kegan Paul.

—— (1976) *Problems in Primary Education*, London: Routledge and Kegan Paul.

Dearden, R. F., Hirst, P. H. and Peters, R. S. (eds) (1975) *A Critique of Current Educational Aims*, London: Routledge and Kegan Paul.

Dearing, R. (1993) *The National Curriculum and its Assessment: Final Report*, London: SCAA.

Deem, R., Brehony, K. and Heath, S. (1995) *Active Citizenship and the Governing of Schools*, Buckingham and Philadelphia: Open University Press.

Dewey, J. (1897/1974) 'My Pedagogic Creed', in R. D. Archambault (ed.) *John Dewey on Education*, Chicago: University of Chicago Press.

—— (1900) *The School and Society*, Chicago: University of Chicago Press.

DfEE (1997) *Excellence in Schools*, London: The Stationery Office.

—— (1999) *Teachers: Meeting the Challenge of Change*, London: Department for Education and Employment.

Dunleavy, P. and Hood, C. (1994) 'From old public administration to new public management', *Public Money and Management*, 14, 3: 9–16.

Eisner, E. W. (1991) *The Enlightened Eye*, New York: Macmillan.

Elliott, J. (1996) 'School effectiveness research and its critics: alternative visions of schooling', *Cambridge Journal of Schooling*, 26: 199–224.

—— (1998) *The Curriculum Experiment: Meeting the Challenge of Social Change*, Buckingham: Open University Press.

Esland, G. (1996) 'Knowledge and Nationhood: The New Right, Education and the Global Market', in J. Avis *et al.* (eds) *Knowledge and Nationhood: Education, Politics and Work*, London: Cassell.

Exworthy, M. and Halford, S. (1999) 'Professionals and managers in a changing public sector: conflict, compromise and collaboration?' in M. Exworthy and S. Halford (eds) *Professionals and the New Managerialism in the Public Sector*, Buckingham: Open University Press.

Fergusson, R. (1994) 'Managerialism in Education', in J. Clarke, A. Cochrane, and E. McLaughlin (eds) *Managing Social Policy*, London: Sage.

—— (2000) 'Modernizing Managerialism in Education', in J. Clarke, S. Gewirtz and E. McLaughlin (eds) *New Managerialism, New Welfare?* London: Sage.

Ferlie, E., Ashburner, L., Fitzgerald, L. and Pettigrew, A. (1996) *The New Public Management in Action*, Oxford: Oxford University Press.

Fisher, J. (1996) *Starting from the Child?* Buckingham: Open University Press.

Fitz, J., Halpin, D. and Power, S. (1994) 'Implementation Research and Education Policy – Practice and Prospects', *British Journal of Educational Studies*, 42, 1: 53–69.

Flynn, R. (1999) 'Managerialism, professionalism and quasi-markets', in M. Exworthy and S. Halford (eds) *Professionals and the New Managerialism in the Public Sector*, Buckingham: Open University Press.

Fritzell, C. (1987) 'On the concept of relative autonomy in educational theory', *British Journal of Sociology of Education*, 8, 1: 23–35.

Fullan, M. (1990). 'Staff Development, Innovation, and Institutional Development', in B. Joyce (ed.) *Changing School Culture Through Staff Development. The 1990 ASCD Yearbook*, Alexandria, VA: Association for Supervision and Curriculum Development.

—— (1991) *The New Meaning of Educational Change*, London: Cassell.

Galton, M., Simon, B. and Croll, P. (1980) *Inside the Primary Classroom*, London: Routledge and Kegan Paul.

Gamble, A. (1988) *The Free Economy and the Strong State. The Politics of Thatcherism*, London: Macmillan.

Gewirtz, S., Ball, S. J. and Bowe, R. (1995) *Markets, Choice and Equity in Education*, Buckingham: Open University Press.

Giddens, A. (1979) *Central Problems in Social Theory: Action, Structure and Contradiction in Social Analysis*, London: Macmillan.

—— (1984) *The Constitution of Society: outline of a theory of structuration*, Berkeley: University of California Press.

—— (1989) 'A reply to my critics', in D. Held and J. B. Thompson (eds) *Social Theory of Modern Societies*, Cambridge: Cambridge University Press.

—— (1990) 'Structuration Theory and Sociological Analysis', in J. Clark, C. Modgil and S. Modgil (eds) *Anthony Giddens: Consensus and Controversy*, London: The Falmer Press.

Glaser, R. (1963) 'Instructional technology and the measurement of learning outcomes: some questions', *American Psychologist*, 18: 519–21.

Goldstein, H. and Woodhouse, G. (2000) 'School Effectiveness Research and Educational Policy', *Oxford Review of Education*, 26, 3/4: 353–63.

Goldstein, L. J. (1973) 'The Inadequacy of the Principle of Methodological Individualism', in J. O'Neill (ed.) *Modes of Individualism and Collectivism*, New York: St Martin's Press.

Gordon, L. (1989) 'Beyond relative autonomy theories of the state in Britain', *British Journal of Sociology of Education*, 10: 435–47.

Grace, G. (1995) *School Leadership: Beyond Education Management. An Essay in Policy Scholarship*, London: Falmer Press.

Guest, D. (1987) 'Human Resource Management and Industrial Relations', *Journal of Management Studies*, 24: 503–21.

Gunter, H. (1997) *Rethinking Education. The Consequences of Jurassic Management*, London: Cassell.

Hacker, P. M. S. (1997) *Wittgenstein*, London: Phoenix.

Hambleton, R. K., Swaminathan, H., Algina, J. and Coulson, D. B. (1978) 'Criterion-referenced testing and measurement: a review of technical issues and developments', *Review of Educational Research*, 48, 1: 1–47.

Hamilton, D. (1998) 'The Idols of the Market Place', in R. Slee, G. Weiner with S. Tomlinson (eds) *School Effectiveness for Whom? Challenges to the School Effectiveness and School Improvement Movements*, London: Falmer.

Hamlyn, D. W. (1978) *Experience and the Growth of Understanding*, London: Routledge and Kegan Paul.

Hampden-Turner, C. (1990) *Corporate Culture: From Vicious to Virtuous Circles*, London: Hutchinson.

Hargreaves, A. (1978) 'The significance of classroom coping strategies', in L. Barton and R. Meighan (eds) *Sociological Interpretations of Schooling and Classrooms*, Driffield: Nafferton.

—— (1994) *Changing Teachers, Changing Times*, London: Cassell.

Harré, R. (1970) *The Principles of Scientific Thinking*, London: Macmillan.

Harré, R. and Madden, E. (1975) *Causal Powers*, London: Macmillan.

Harvey, D. (1989) *The Postmodern Condition*, Oxford: Blackwell.

Hatcher, R. (1994) 'Market Relationships and the Management of Teachers', *British Journal of Sociology of Education*, 15, 1: 41–61.

Hays, S. (1994) 'Structure and agency and the sticky problem of culture', *Sociological Theory*, 12, 1: 57–72.

Hirst, P. H. (1974) *Knowledge and the Curriculum*, London: Routledge and Kegan Paul.
Hirst, P. H. and Peters, R. S. (1970) *The Logic of Education*, London: Routledge and Kegan Paul.
Hodgson, G. M. (1999) *Economics and Utopia. Why the learning economy is not the end of history*, London: Routledge.
Holloway, J. (1995) 'From Scream of Refusal to Scream of Power: The Centrality of Work', in W. Bonefield *et al.* (eds) *Open Marxism Volume III – Emancipating Marx*, London: Pluto Press.
Holloway, J. and Picciottio, S. (1977) 'Capital, crisis and the state', *Capital and Class*, 2.
Hood, C. (1991) 'A public management for all seasons?' *Public Administration*, 69, 1: 3–19.
Hopkins, D. (1996) 'Towards a theory for school improvement', in J. Gray *et al.* (eds) *Merging Traditions: The Future of Research on School Effectiveness and School Improvement*, London: Cassell.
Jang, S. and Chung, M.-H. (1997) 'Discursive Contradiction of Tradition and Modernity in Korean Management Practices: A Case Study of Samsung's New Management', in S. A. Sackmann (ed.) *Cultural Complexity in Organizations: Inherent Contrasts and Contradictions*, London: Sage.
Jeffrey, B. and Woods, P. (1999) *Testing Teachers: The Effect of School Inspections on Primary Teachers*, London: Falmer Press.
Johnson, T., Dandeker, C. and Ashworth, C. (1984) *The Structure of Social Theory: Strategies, Dilemmas and Projects*, New York: St Martin's Press.
Jonathan, R. (1997) *Illusory Freedoms. Liberalism, Education and the Market*, Oxford: Blackwell.
Jones, K. (1991) 'Conservative Modernization', in R. Moore and J. Ozga (eds) *Curriculum Policy*, Oxford: Pergamon Press.
Kilpatrick, W. H. (1916) *Froebel's Kindergarten Principles Critically Examined*, London: Macmillan.
—— (1918) 'The Project Method', *Teachers College Record*, 19: 319–35.
King, R. (1983) *The Sociology of School Organization*, London and New York: Methuen.
Knights, D. (1997) 'Organization theory in the age of deconstruction: Dualism, gender and postmodernism revisited', *Organization Studies*, 18, 1: 1–19.
Kogan, M. (1971) *The Government of Education*, London: Hutchinson.
—— (1986) *Educational Accountability: An Analytical Overview*, London: Hutchinson.
Layder, D. (1990) *The Realist Image in Social Science*, London: Macmillan.
—— (1997) *Modern Social Theory. Key debates and new directions*, London: UCL Press.
Legge, K. (1989) 'HRM: A Critical Analysis', in J. Storey (ed.) *New Perspectives on Human Resource Management*, London: Routledge.
—— (1995) *Human Resource Management: Rhetorics and Realities*, London: Macmillan.
Lockwood, D. (1964) 'Social integration and system integration', in G. K. Zollschan and W. Hirsch (eds) *Explorations in Social Change*, Boston: Houghton Mifflin.
Lowe, R. (1997) *Schooling and Social Change 1964–1990*, London: Routledge.
Lukes, S. (1974) *Power: A Radical View*, London: Macmillan.
Manicas, P. T. (1997) 'Explanation, understanding and typical action', *Journal for the Theory of Social Behaviour*, 27, 2: 193–212.
Mann, P. (1996) 'Improving quality in a primary school', in B. Fidler (ed.) *Strategic Planning for School Improvement*, London: Pitman.
Martin, J. (1992) *Cultures in Organizations*, Oxford: Oxford University Press.
Mathieson, M. and Bernbaum, G. (1988) 'The British disease: a British tradition?', *British Journal of Educational Studies*, 26, 2: 126–74.
McFadden, M. (1995) 'Resistance to schooling and educational outcomes: questions of structure and agency', *British Journal of Sociology of Education*, 16: 293–308.
Meek, V. L. (1988) 'Organizational culture: origins and weaknesses', *Organization Studies*, 9: 453–573.
Menter, I., Muschamp, Y., Nicholls, P., Ozga, J. and Pollard, A. (1997) *Work and Identity in the Primary School*, Buckingham: Open University Press.
Meyerson, D. and Martin, J. (1987) 'Cultural Change: An Integration of Three Different Views', *Journal of Management Studies*, 24: 623–47.
Mills, A. J. and Murgatroyd, S. J. (1991) *Organizational Rules: a framework for understanding organizational action*, Buckingham: Open University Press.
Morley, L. and Rassool, N. (1999) *School Effectiveness: Fracturing the Discourse*, London: Falmer Press.
Mortimore, P. and Sammons, P. (1997) 'Endpiece: a welcome and a riposte to critics', in J. White and M. Barber (eds) *Perspectives on School Effectiveness and School Improvement*, London: Institute of Education.

Nedelsky, L. (1954) 'Absolute grading standards for objective tests', *Educational and Psychological Measurement*, 14: 3–19.

Nellhaus, T. (1998) 'Signs, Social Ontology and Critical Realism', *Journal for the Theory of Social Behaviour*, 28, 1: 1–24.

Norris, C. (1996) *Reclaiming Truth: Contribution to a critique of cultural relativism*, London: Lawrence and Wishart.

Office for Standards in Education (OFSTED) (1996) Report of an inspection carried out under Section 9 of the Education Reform Act 1992.

—— (1997) *From Failure to Success*, London: HMSO.

Ollman, B. (1990) *Marxism: An Uncommon Introduction*, India: Gopsons Papers.

O'Neill, J. (1973) *Modes of Individualism and Collectivism*, London: Heinemann.

Ozga, J. (2000) *Policy Research in Educational Settings*, Buckingham: Open University Press.

Perkmann, M. (1998) 'Social Integration and System Integration', *Sociology*, 32: 491–507.

Pestallozi, J. (1894) *How Gertrude Teaches her Children*, Translated by L. Holland and F. C. Turner, London: Swan Sonnenschein.

Peters, R. S. (1958) *The Concept of Motivation*, London: Routledge and Kegan Paul.

—— (1963) 'Education as Initiation', in R. S. Archambault (ed.) *Philosophical Analysis and Education*, London: Routledge and Kegan Paul.

—— (1964) 'The Place of Philosophy in the Training of Teachers', in R. S. Peters (ed.) *Education and the Education of Teachers*, London: Routledge Kegan and Paul.

—— (ed.) (1967) *The Concept of Education*, London: Routledge Kegan and Paul.

—— (1969) 'A Recognisable Philosophy of Education: A Constructive Critique', in R. S. Peters (ed.) *Perspectives on Plowden*, London: Routledge and Kegan Paul.

Pietrasik, R. (1987) 'The Teachers' Action 1984–86', in M. Lawn and G. Grace (eds) *Teachers: The Culture and Politics of Work*, Lewes: Falmer Press.

Pollard, A. (1982) 'A model of classroom coping strategies', *British Journal of Sociology of Education*, 3, 1: 19–37.

Pollard, A., Croll, P., Broadfoot, P., Osborne, M. and Abbott, D. (1994) *Changing English Primary Schools?*, London: Cassell.

Pollitt, C. (1990) *Managerialism and the Public Services*, Oxford: Blackwell.

Popper, K. R. (1979) *Objective Knowledge: An Evolutionary Approach*, Oxford: Oxford University Press.

—— (1994) *Knowledge and the Body–Mind Problem*, London: Routledge.

Porpora, D. (1989) 'Four concepts of social structure', *Journal for the Theory of Social Behaviour*, 19: 195–211.

Pring, R. (1993) 'Markets, Education and Catholic schools', paper presented at the conference 'Contemporary Catholic School and Common Good', University of Cambridge.

Pugh, S. (1998) 'Failing the Failures: The Conflict Between Care and the Curriculum', in L. Stoll and K. Myers (eds) *No Quick Fixes: Perspectives on Schools in Difficulty*, London: Falmer Press.

Punch, M. (1973) *Dartington Hall School*, PhD Thesis, University of Essex, taken from J. Darling (1994) *Child-centred Education and its critics*, London: Paul Chapman Publishing.

Raab, C. D., Munn, P., McAvoy, L., Bailey, L., Arnott, M. and Adler, M. (1997) 'Devolving the management of schools in Britain', *Educational Administration Quarterly* 33, 2: 140–57.

Reed, M. I. (1992) *The Sociology of Organizations*, Guildford: Harvester Wheatsheaf.

—— (1995) 'Managing quality and organizational politics: TQM as a governmental technology', in I. Kirkpatrick and M. M. Lucio (eds) *The Politics of Quality in the Public Sector*, London: Routledge.

—— (1997) 'In Praise of Duality and Dualism: Rethinking Agency and Structure in Organizational Analysis', *Organization Studies*, 18, 1: 21–42.

Rikowski, G. (1996) 'Left alone? End time for Marxist educational theory?', *British Journal of Sociology of Education*, 17: 415–51.

—— (1997) 'Scorched earth: prelude to rebuilding Marxist educational theory', *British Journal of Sociology of Education*, 18: 551–74.

Riley, K. A. (1998) *Whose School Is it Anyway?* London: Falmer Press.

Roberts, J. (1996) 'ISO9000 and Investors In People in Education: A Discussion', *Working Papers in Education: Educational Research Unit*, Walsall: University of Wolverhampton.

Rose, M. (1995) *Possible Lives – The Promise of Public Education in America*, New York: Penguin Books.

Rousseau, J.-J. (1911) *Emile*, London: Dent.

Sammons, P., Hillman, J. and Mortimore, P. (1995) *Key Characteristics of Effective Schools: A Review of School Effectiveness Research*, London: Institute of Education.

Sayer, A. (1992) *Method in Social Science: A Realist Approach*, London: Routledge.

—— (1995) *Radical Political Economy: A Critique*, Oxford: Blackwell.

—— (2000) *Realism and Social Science*, London: Sage.

Schein, E. H. (1992a) 'Coming to a New Awareness of Organizational Culture', in G. Salaman (ed.) *Human Resource Strategies*, London: Sage.

—— (1992b) *Organizational Culture and Leadership*, 2nd Edition, San Francisco, CA: Jossey-Bass.

—— (1996) 'Culture: The Missing Concept in Organizational Studies', *Administrative Science Quarterly*, 41: 229–40.

Scott, D. (1994) 'Making schools accountable: assessment policy and the Education Reform Act', in D. Scott (ed.) *Accountability and Control in Educational Settings*, London: Cassell.

—— (2000) *Realism and Educational Research: New Perspectives and Possibilities*, London: Routledge.

Sealey, A. (1994) 'Language and educational control: the construction of the LINC controversy', in D. Scott (ed.) *Accountability and Control in Educational Settings*, London: Cassell.

Secretary of State for Education and Science (1977) *Education in Schools: A Consultative Document*, London: HMSO.

Selleck, R. J. W. (1972) *English Primary Education and the Progressives 1914–1939*, London: Routledge.

Sharp, R. and Green, A. with Lewis, J. (1975) *Education and Social Control: A study in Progressive Primary Education*, London: Routledge and Kegan Paul.

Sharp, R. (ed.) (1986) *Capitalist Schooling: Comparative Studies in the Politics of Education*, South Melbourne: Macmillan.

Shilling, C. (1992) 'Reconceptualising structure and agency in the sociology of education: structuration theory and schooling, *British Journal of Sociology of Education*, 13, 1: 69–87.

—— (1997) 'The Undersocialised Conception of the (Embodied) Agent in Modern Sociology', *Sociology*, 31, 4: 737–54.

Shipman, M. (1990) *In Search of Learning: A New Approach to School Management*, Oxford: Basil Blackwell.

Silcock, P. (1996) 'Three Principles For A New Progressivism', *Oxford Review of Education*, 22: 199–216.

Silver, H. (1994) *Good Schools, Effective Schools: Judgements and their histories*, London: Cassell.

Simon, B. (1994) *The State and Educational Change. Essays in the History of Education and Pedagogy*, London: Lawrence and Wishart.

Sinclair, J., Seifert, R. and Ironside, M. (1995) 'Market-driven reforms in education: Performance, quality and industrial relations in schools', in I. Kirkpatrick and M. Lucio (eds) *The Politics of Quality in the Public Sector*, London: Routledge.

Slavin, R. E. (1987) 'Mastery learning reconsidered', *Review of Educational Research*, 57: 175–213.

Smith, R. (1995) *Successful School Management*, London: Cassell.

Stewart, W. A. C. (1968) *The Educational Innovators*, London.

Stoll, L. and Fink, D. (1996) *Changing our Schools*, Buckingham: Open University Press.

Sutherland, P. (1992) *Cognitive Development Today. Piaget and his Critics*, London: Paul Chapman Publishing.

Taylor, F. W. (1911) *Principles of Scientific Management*, London: Harper and Row.

Teddlie, C., Reynolds, D. and Sammons, P. (2000) 'The methodology and scientific properties of school effectiveness research', in C. Teddlie and D. Reynolds (eds) *International Handbook of School Effectiveness Research*, London: Falmer.

Thompson, J. B. (1989) 'The theory of structuration', in D. Held and J. B. Thompson (eds) *Social Theory of Modern Societies: Anthony Giddens and his Critics*, Cambridge: Cambridge University Press.

Thrupp, M. (1999) *Schools Making a Difference. Let's be Realistic!*, Buckingham: Open University Press.

—— (2000) 'Sociological and Political Concerns about School Effectiveness Research: Time for a New Research Agenda', paper presented at AERA Annual Meeting, New Orleans, April 24–28.

—— (forthcoming) 'Recent School Effectiveness Counter-Critiques: Problems and Possibilities', *British Educational Research Journal*.

Tomlinson, J. (1993) *The Control of Education*, London: Cassell.

Troman, G. and Woods, P. (2001) *Primary Teachers' Stress*, London: Routledge.

Turner, J. H. (1986) 'A Theory of Structuration', *American Journal of Sociology*, 4: 969–77.
Volpe, R. (1981) 'Knowledge from theory and practice', *Oxford Review of Education*, 7, 1: 41–57.
Vygotsky, L. S. (1978) *Mind in Society*, London: Harvard University Press.
Warnock, M. (1989) *A Common Policy for Education*, Oxford: Oxford University Press.
Watkins, J. W. N. (1973) 'Historical Explanation in the Social Sciences', in J. O'Neill (ed.) *Modes of Individualism and Collectivism*, London: Heinemann.
Weick, K. (1988) 'Educational organizations as loosely coupled systems', in A. Westoby (ed.) *Culture and Power in Educational Organizations*, Milton Keynes: Open University Press.
White, J. (1997) 'Philosophical perspectives on school effectiveness and school improvement', in J. White and M. Barber (eds) *Perspectives on School Effectiveness and School Improvement*, London: Institute of Education.
Whitty, G. (1985) *Sociology and School Knowledge: Curriculum theory, research and politics*, London: Methuen.
—— (1991) 'The New Right and the National Curriculum: state control or market forces?', in R. Moore and J. Ozga (eds) *Curriculum Policy*, Oxford: Pergamon Press.
Whitty, G., Power, S. and Halpin, D. (1998) *Devolution and Choice in Education. The School, the State and the Market*, Buckingham: Open University Press.
Willmott, H. (1993) 'Strength is ignorance; slavery is freedom: managing culture in modern organisations', *Journal of Management Studies*, 30: 515–52.
Willmott, R. (1999a) 'Structure, Agency and the Sociology of Education: rescuing analytical dualism', *British Journal of Sociology of Education*, 20, 1: 5–21
—— (1999b) 'Structure, Agency and School Effectiveness: researching a "failing" school', *Educational Studies*, 25, 1: 5–18.
—— (1999c) 'School Effectiveness Research: an Ideological Commitment?', *Journal of Philosophy of Education*, 33, 2: 253–68.
—— (2000a) 'The Place of Culture in Organization Theory: Introducing the Morphogenetic Approach', *Organization*, 7, 1: 93–126.
—— (2000b) 'Structure, Culture and Agency: Rejecting the Current Orthodoxy of Organisation Theory', in S. Ackroyd and S. Fleetwood (eds) *Realist Perspectives on Management and Organisations*, London: Routledge.
Woods, P. and Jeffrey, B. (1996) *Teachable Moments. The art of teaching in primary schools*, Buckingham: Oxford University Press.
Woods, P., Jeffrey, B., Troman, G. and Boyle, M. (1997) *Restructuring Schools, Reconstructing Teachers*, Buckingham: Open University Press.

Index

Abbott, D. 165
Abraham, J. 12
abstract concepts 43
accountability 70, 112, 113, 116, 117, 118, 133, 134, 139–40, 141, 223; and Westside 192, 193, 194
Ackroyd, S. 142
actualism (Bhaskar) 9
Adam Smith Institute 125
agency 9; Cartesian legacy 17–19; concession and compromise 36, 56; cultural morphogenesis 44–62, 75; and culture 38, 40–4; emergent stratum of social reality 11–17; failure to exercise 93, 104, 110–17; morphogenetic approach 31, 36–7, 38, 63, 221, 222; responses to new managerialism in education 65–6, 169, 189, 206, 207; and stratified social ontology 20–1; and stringent constraints 85–6, 201–4, 222; structuration theory 21–30; theory of structure and 2, 7–39, 81, 155, 221, 222
Ahier, J. 114–15
Alexander, R. 3, 49, 146, 159–62
Althusser, Louis 81
analytical dualism 2, 17, 30, 34, 35, 39, 42, 43, 75, 221–2
Angus, L. 150
Anthony, P. 52
anthropology 53
Archer, M.S. 1, 24, 31, 37–8, 46, 48, 57, 58, 61, 62, 79, 81, 82, 84, 92, 227n2, 228nn7,8, 229n12
arm's length contracting 128
Arnold, Matthew 69

assessment 3, 83, 134, 135–7, 223; managerialist usurpation of 121, 137–41, 142, 170; Westside 194–7, 214, 218
Athey, C. 46–8
attainment targets 134, 136, 139, 235n9
Audit Commission 143
Auld Inquiry (1975–6) 106, 108–9, 110
authoritarian management 71; Southside 143, 170–7, 212, 214
autonomy 3, 29–30, 61, 90, 120; Catholic schools 200; of education system 80–90; expanded 171; see also teachers, autonomy
Ayer, A.J. 96, 97

Baker, Kenneth 113, 122, 123, 132, 133, 135, 136, 145
Ball, S.J. 16, 17, 60, 66, 69, 70, 103, 123, 125, 134, 135, 149, 150, 173
Barber, Michael 14, 69–70, 134, 150
Barrow, R. 98, 233n3
Bate, P. 35, 36
Bates, I. 116–17
BBC 'Panorama' programme 115–16
Beck, J. 114
Belbin Associates © 176
beliefs see values and beliefs
Bennett, Neville 115
Bernstein, B. 26
Better Schools (White Paper 1985)134
Bhaskar, R. 8–10, 19, 156
Billington, S. 55, 63, 233n15
Black Papers 80, 96, 104, 106, 107, 109, 110, 111, 113, 116, 118, 124, 125, 217
Blau, P.M. 16, 37